DOING TIME:

25 YEARS OF PRISON WRITING

DOING TIME:
25 YEARS OF PRISON WRITING

A PEN American Center
Prize Anthology

Edited by
Bell Gale Chevigny

Foreword by
Sister Helen Prejean

Arcade Publishing • New York

FIRST EDITION

Library of Congress Cataloging-in-Publication Data

Doing time: 25 years of prison writing—A PEN American Center Prize
Anthology / edited by Bell Gale Chevigny ; with foreword by Helen
Prejean. —1st ed.
     p.   cm.
  ISBN 1-55970-478-0
    1. Prisoners' writings, American. 2. Prisoners—United States—
Literary collections. 3. Prisons—United States—Literary
collections. 4. American literature—20 century.   I. Chevigny,
Bell Gale.
PS508.P7D65   1999
810.8'09206927—dc21   98-51940

Published in the United States by Arcade Publishing, Inc., New York
Distributed by Time Warner Trade Publishing

10 9 8 7 6 5 4 3 2 1

BP

Designed by API

PRINTED IN THE UNITED STATES OF AMERICA

To the memory of
Charles Caldwell (1941–1973)
and
to all the other men and women
who find their voice in prison

CONTENTS

Foreword

When I read anything I'm always hoping the writer will take me into realms of experience I wouldn't otherwise have, experiences that push the edges of human life and our ways of doing things, put me up against myself and make me ask: What would I do in this situation, who would I become? Adventure stories are like that. Prison writings are like that. "Come with me," these convict writers say, "I'll take you into my world. Hang on. It's quite a ride."

Quite a ride indeed. I am not unacquainted with prison life. I've visited prisoners for fourteen years, accompanied four men to execution, know a lot about death row, wrote a book, *Dead Man Walking*. But I know I'm an outsider. I've never heard the clang of bars behind me as I said good-bye to freedom. Never had all the eyes in the room turn to me, "fresh meat," coming in. At the end of each visit I get to walk out. And every time I find myself taking deep gulps of freedom.

Here are fifty-one writers who take us into a world we hope we never do more than visit. A world where you never touch a doorknob, where you have no control over your environment. A world without privacy, a world of frequent strip-searches, a world where the "shake-down crew" swoops down upon you and throws all your stuff out of your "box" into a heap, laughing, pointing at your photos, walking across your baby's smile. A world where many of the people have serious personality disorders, and you can't get away from them. A razor-wired world where you never sit under a tree because the yard is stripped bare for security reasons, where security governs everything.

We incarcerate a whole lot of people in this country: 1.8 million, more than any other country in the world. We are building a small country of these throwaway people. How can you expect literature from the refuse pile of humanity? Who would look for eloquence from convicts? Or insight or depth of thought or honesty or the intimacy of self-revelation? Watch for the self-serving subtext. When your heart is moved, can you trust it? When you feel for the writers of these words, are you being had? Cynicism about convicts is in our bones.

Test this doubt by sampling these pages. The words in them have made their way into our hands against great odds. Several of these writers have done long stretches of time in the hole for their writing. Why, at such cost, do they write? Read their reasons in the back of this book. To bear witness, to stay sane, to keep their heart pumping, to not be eaten up by rage or despair, to figure out how they got there, or to discover what truly matters — these are just some of them.

And then they hone their craft — if they're lucky, in workshops, more often in the horrific din of the cellblock — learning to get past the words other people say to that voice of their own they almost doubt they have. Somehow they hear of the PEN prison writing contest, hear that at the very least someone will read what they wrote and write back. They decide to take a chance.

I think this book is a significant piece of literature. What do you think? The writers are locked away from you, but you've already opened a door to their world. Step inside. You'll never be the same.

Sister Helen Prejean
March 1999

Introduction: Doing Time at Century's End

I write because I can't fly.
— Jackie Ruzas, Shawangunk Correctional Facility,
Wallkill, New York

Writing is my way of sledge-hammering these walls.
— Alejo Dao'ud Rodriguez, Sing Sing Correctional Facility,
Ossining, New York

The writing coming out of U.S. prisons has never been as strong, rich, diverse, and provocative as in the final quarter of the twentieth century. Each year during this period the writers' association PEN has sponsored a contest for American writers behind bars nationwide. *Doing Time* presents the best work of the winners. By bearing witness to the secret world that has isolated and would silence them, these writers offer an incisive anatomy of the contemporary prison and an intimate view of men and women struggling to keep their humanity alive.

The quarter century covered in this anthology has been marked by an extraordinary shift in American attitudes toward prisoners and a growth in incarceration never before seen in this or any other industrial democracy. The period opened with wide acceptance of the value of rehabilitative programs, a growing prisoners' rights movement, and an unprecedented interest in prisoners' writing. It is ending with punitive policies that have swelled the prison population to six times its size in 1972, created a prison-construction boom that promises to continue well into the twenty-first century, and eviscerated prisoners' constitutional rights.

The social turmoil of the sixties and early seventies profoundly shaped public attitudes toward prisoners and prisoners' experience. The civil rights and student movements, and opposition to the Vietnam war created a climate critical of established authority. In rapid succession, blacks, Puerto Ricans, Chicanos, Native Americans, women, and gays developed self-awareness and political consciousness and demanded recognition. In response American culture grew more receptive to their voices and needs. And for a while the War on Poverty was committed to building a more participatory democracy by offering opportunity to the poor and marginalized.

Prisoners, especially African-American male prisoners, played a strong role in these explosive times. *The Autobiography of Malcolm X* awakened readers to the powerful claims of this dispossessed group, and showed how a man could find himself and his voice behind bars. Within five years, Eldridge Cleaver and George Jackson had added their challenging social analyses and influenced the rhetoric of many political activists, black and white. And when movement activists were jailed in the sixties and seventies, they helped politicize prison culture. Inmates began to compare incarceration with slavery, to call themselves *political prisoners,* and to protest conditions rather than attacking one another.

A prisoners' movement began to grow outside as well. In 1967, David Rothenberg had produced *Fortune and Men's Eyes* in New York, a play by Canadian ex-prisoner John Herbert that brought to life the devastating effects of incarceration on one young man. When, in a dialogue after the performance, a member of the audience challenged the play's authenticity, another, an ex-convict, rose to defend it. More ex-cons streamed to the theater and when they made public their past for the first time, the postcurtain debate became as absorbing as the play. Rothenberg's theater office became the first headquarters of the Fortune Society, an organization that provides a therapeutic community for ex-prisoners and advocates criminal-justice reform.

Dramatizing the social upheaval of the time were the inner-city riots that became more destructive each summer in the sixties and helped spark riots behind the razor wire. Like slave revolts and revolutions, prison riots tend to come in clusters. Forty-eight were reported from 1968 through early 1971, growing in intensity, racial or political ideology, and organization. In New York in 1970 riots rocked Manhattan's Tombs and upstate Auburn Prison. In July 1971, a "Liberation Faction" of prisoners in Attica Prison presented the corrections commissioner with demands to change "brutal, dehumanized" conditions. In California, on August 21, 1971, George Jackson, a revolutionary hero to many prisoners for his book *Soledad Brother,* was shot by guards in an apparent escape attempt from San Quentin. The next day, Attica prisoners protested with a mass hunger strike. On September 9, they seized the prison, killing one guard and three inmates. The uncompromising state response four days later was a police assault that wounded 128 and took 39 lives, 10 of them hostages.

The assault was necessary because hostages were having their throats slashed — or so state officials told the media. But the next day, autopsies revealed that all had died of state-inflicted bullet wounds. Public outrage over this and the guards' brutal beatings of the retaken prisoners created a generation of prison activists and a storm of litigation. Court orders reformed prison conditions across the country, while new statutes and regulations expanded prisoners' constitutional rights. As a class, prisoners could challenge "cruel and unusual" conditions of confinement, and, as individuals, won rights to due process, to receive literature, and to practice the religion of their choice.

"A prison renaissance," as prison poet William Aberg characterizes it, flourished nationwide in the seventies. Prisoners organized to form unions, to fight for humane treatment, and to bring educational, cultural, and religious programs inside the walls. The fruit of their efforts and outside pressures, prison college programs and other rehabilitative programs sprang up everywhere.

But in the same decade, forces were mounting that would make penal policy swing back from treatment to custody, from a rehabilitative to a retributive approach. Penologists Andrew von Hirsch (1976) and Robert Martinson (1974) assailed the rehabilitative ideal. When Martinson later tried to modify his argument that "nothing works" to reduce recidivism, he was ignored; the phrase provided a sound-bite to politicians who began to find "get tough" rhetoric indispensable to their success. Indeterminate sentencing practices which permitted prisoners to shorten their sentences by good behavior came under attack. New York's governor Nelson Rockefeller scrapped a whole system of drug treatment, replacing it with the most punitive drug laws in the United States.

In the eighties much of the country followed New York's lead on drug laws, and Ronald Reagan's war on drugs generated mandatory, and longer, sentences. The prisons were increasingly flooded, especially as more and more of the poor were lured into the drug trade. Laws have targeted crack cocaine primarily used in inner cities (rather than powder cocaine preferred by middle-class white users). People of color have been disproportionately incarcerated for all drug crimes. Moreover, the harsh sentencing of women for minor drug offenses (like being a courier or "mule") has made the incarceration rate of women rise at two times that of men, and the percentage of women of color is again disproportionately high. To many the war on drugs seems a war on men and women of color, now numerically predominant behind bars. It has also made prison construction a major growth industry. As former warden of Oklahoma State Reformatory Jack Cowley put it, "The war on drugs is a miserable failure because it has not stopped drug use in this country. It's a great success [for prisons] because it's the best economic boom we've ever seen."

The effect of these changes on prison culture is staggering. Political life has evaporated; in the place of political leaders are the rash youth delivered by the war on drugs. In New Mexico State Penitentiary at Santa Fe, overcrowding, understaffing, and fiscal austerity generated a system that rewarded snitching. In 1980 a riot erupted in which there were no demands, no political consciousness, no agenda, and the prison was retaken without a shot fired — but only after inmates had tortured and killed thirty-three of their own, many of them informers. If the Attica riot represented political organization and prisoner restraint, its successor in New Mexico epitomized the new regime where prisoners have more to fear from one another than from their keepers.

Life Without Parole: Living in Prison Today (1996) by Victor Hassine details the transformation in the 1980s of Graterford State Prison, warehouse for Pennsylvania's most violent felons. A typical 1930s Big House (holding fifteen hundred or more, all sharing common facilities), Graterford kept military-style order when Hassine arrived in 1981. By mid-decade, the influx of homeless, mentally ill, juvenile offenders, seasoned gang members, drug addicts, and dealers had changed everything. According to Hassine, the population explosion made Graterford "a predatory institution where nothing worked right and everything was for sale." Bathroom-size cells designed for one inmate had to accommodate two; rape became a common occurrence. As in New Mexico, overworked guards' dependence on informants divided inmates, raised the level of violence, and facilitated the entry of drugs. "Old heads" recall bygone days of honor, quiet solitude, and routine, Hassine writes, when "the outside world was kept outside, when inmates' natural enemies were the guards." Now other inmates pose the greatest threat, especially "young bucks" for whom robbery and assault have become addictive. Instead of trying to control gangs, the administration plays one against the other. "Anger and hatred are a prison's cash crop," another lifer explains; they produce "more money, more guards, more overtime."

Although less is known about the still relatively small female population behind bars (about 7 percent of the total), it is safe to say that there is dramatically less violence between inmates than in men's prisons. (Their detractors compare male inmates to animals, women to children.) Drugs circulate less freely, and though gangs are emerging, they are fewer and smaller. But physical violence by staff and guards against women prisoners is rising, according to Ellen Barry, who draws on her twenty years of experience with women prisoners as Director of Legal Services for Prisoners with Families. She suggests that public contempt for poor female prisoners of color, apparently legitimized by their more severe sentences, sanctions, in the minds of their keepers, more brutal treatment. The incidence of sexual violence and molestation by corrections officers has also increased, drawing human rights protests. Prison writer Barbara Saunders adds that "Being a woman in prison is like being in a domestic violence relationship. You never know when the rules will change and you will get 'beaten' again — psychologically or emotionally — by anyone who has power over you."

The cascades of reform flowing from the sixties have by the nineties all run into the sand. While the international trend has been to abolish the death penalty, in the U.S., after a brief suspension, it has returned to thirty-eight states. Our rate of executions is on par with the rate in Iraq, Iran, and Saudi Arabia. Chain gangs have returned to three states. With the ascendancy of the victims' rights movement, political energies have turned to increasing the misery of imprisonment. Not since the fifties have the courts so restricted prisoners' rights, and Congress has limited prisoners' access to courts. Government grants enabling prisoners to pursue higher education have been wiped out, despite evidence that education dramatically reduces recidivism.

As we enter the twenty-first century, incarceration rates continue to soar despite falling crime rates in recent years. At 1.8 million, the jail and prison population is roughly equal to that of Houston, the nation's fourth largest city. Only Russia now rivals the U.S. for the highest incarceration rate on the planet. While some politicians privately admit that unmitigated retribution and longer sentences for more people are not productive solutions, most believe that to oppose ever tougher policies is political suicide. The prison-building boom, the growing privatization of prisons, and private industry's use of prison labor have so transformed the nation's economy that it seems harder than ever to reverse the trend. With the cold war gone, many see the prison-industrial complex as destined to replace the military-industrial complex in the economy; as communist demons once did, criminals, especially criminals of color, now satisfy the nation's psychic need for scapegoats.

Yet, as Elliott Currie points out, the U.S. approach to violent crime is "almost schizophrenic" in the division between understanding and action. Politicians ignore the findings of experts that harsh treatment has negligible effects on crime control while crime-prevention strategies have scarcely been tapped. In keeping with what Currie calls the "new social Darwinism," the prison is absorbing people abandoned by social programs that used to help them survive, and in the process decimating and demoralizing whole communities.

Signs of change are emerging, however, on political, legislative, and academic fronts. A gathering in September 1988 of several thousand grass-roots activists at a Berkeley, California, conference on critical resistance to the prison-industrial complex reflects growing opposition. Legislative and philanthropic efforts to bring back post-secondary education are proliferating. Along with grass-roots movements in harm prevention and restorative justice, they seek to create better ways of rehabilitating and reintegrating errants into the community, effectively reducing the likelihood that prisoners will offend again, and to build alternatives to incarceration. Many know, as Dostoyevsky told us long ago, that you can measure the level of a civilization by entering its prisons. Prisons are so tightly woven into our social fabric that who we are is implicated in our definitions of crime and punishment. Finally, academics are seeking ways to integrate prison issues into American studies. Many are again prizing prison writing as the supreme expression of America's underclass and an important field of American literature with its own complex traditions.

Prisoners, too, know that they dwell "behind the mirror's face" (in Paul St. John's telling phrase; see **Reading and Writing**), that prison reflects the state of society. This book aspires to dissolve the silver and leave us face to face. Our future is one. The complex humanity of prisoners and the very real aptitude for growth evidenced in *Doing Time* should affect our design of the future.

*　　*　　*

My life was one of perpetual conflict. I held an apocalyptic view. I have spent most of my existence on this earth inside one prison or another, so my mindset toward the world was one of complete antipathy and alienation . . . I was reluctant to submit my story to

the PEN contest. I at no point thought I had a chance of winning. When I won the award, it gave me an overwhelming sense of acceptance. I now felt that I had something to offer humanity.
— Anthony Ross, Death Row, San Quentin Prison, California

Public reception of prison writing over the past twenty-five years parallels the plunging and rearing trajectory of attitudes toward prisoners we have seen: enthusiasm and broad-based support in the seventies, doubt growing in the eighties, cynicism dominating the nineties, and beginning to give way at century's end. To some degree PEN's engagement has followed these vicissitudes, but with an important distinction: Every year PEN has provided an outlet for these forgotten voices.

PEN's involvement in this unique creative movement began in a curious way. Born in 1921, PEN (Poets, Playwrights, Essayists, Editors, and Novelists) is dedicated to consolidating world peace through a global association of writers. Since 1960 a Freedom-to-Write Committee within PEN's American Center has defended the rights of writers in other countries who have been jailed for their beliefs. But concern for saints of free expression abroad did not translate into concern for ordinary domestic sinners. In fact, this committee's chair in the late sixties, historian Tom Fleming, had taken a dim view of convicts (his father was a New Jersey sheriff and prison warden). But one day, he appeared on a talk show with an impressive ex-prisoner — a Fortune Society spokesman — who remarked that some of the best people he knew were behind bars. "I never forgot it," Fleming said.

As PEN president in 1971, Fleming encouraged colleague Lucy Kavaler to investigate freedom to write in U.S. prisons. Her report spurred Fleming into intensive lobbying with corrections officials, resulting in reduced censorship, improved access to typewriters, courses, and better prison libraries. Then the revelations of Attica made a prison writing program (PWP) seem a moral imperative to some PEN members. Convinced that writing is inherently rehabilitative, they persuaded other writers to read, teach, and mentor behind bars and publishers to send materials. "To be able to say what you mean, to put in words what you perceive as truth, to impose form on the formless — this is a way to reconstruct a life, to restore one's sense of meaning, of responsibility to oneself and to others," PWP chair Kathrin Perutz wrote. "But the others — at least some others — must be listening."

And so in 1973 PEN launched its first annual literary competition for prisoners in federal institutions and extended it to state prisoners in 1974, soon engaging some fifteen hundred prisoners annually. Winning works of fiction, poetry, and nonfiction (drama was added later) were read at annual celebrations, and *Fortune News* (the Fortune Society's paper for prisoners) and other journals published them. The contest reinforced the seventies' prison renaissance nationwide. As college programs grew behind the walls, so did creative writing workshops, some funded by the National Endowment for the Arts. Journals devoted to inmate writing — with names like *"Joint" Conference* and *Sentences* — sprang up overnight. Some academics embraced this literature of the American dispossessed as part of their project of challenging, or enlarging, the canon. The bibliography of H. Bruce Franklin's 1989 edition of *Prison Literature in America: The Victim As Criminal and Artist* lists 320 books by prisoners published from 1971 through 1981. Then everything changed.

The year 1981 saw the publication of *In the Belly of the Beast,* a volume of Jack Henry Abbott's prison letters to Norman Mailer, describing the rage he cultivated through his lifelong institutionalization. Readers were more excited by the writing than mindful of its warning; the book went through five printings and Abbott was released with fanfare. David Rothenberg recently described Abbott on his second day at liberty, sweating through an appearance on *Good Morning, America,* in which Mailer answered Abbott's questions for him. Rothenberg invited Abbott to drop by the Fortune Society for help with the deinstitutionalization process. Abbott was not interested. Within a month, he had killed a man in a fight. The romance between writers and convicts had run its course, and prisoners went out of fashion in the eighties.

Support for prison writing plummeted as well. Under Reagan, the NEA severely cut financial aid to fledgling magazines, and by 1984, every journal devoted to prison writing had gone under. Prison newspapers, a vital branch of this literature, began to lose support in this era. Now, with the notable exceptions of the distinguished *Angolite* in Louisiana and *Prison Legal Notes* in Washington State, most have been suppressed.

The PWP persisted, though many members, always volunteers, fell away, and PEN's executives took little interest. By the late 1980s, most committee work had fallen to overburdened receptionists, and the PWP nearly expired. It is to the credit of a few dedicated members that, even so, there was a never a year without a PEN prison writing contest. In 1990 PEN president Larry McMurtry appointed Fielding Dawson, who in 1987 had edited a special issue on prison writing for *Witness* and had taught in prison, to head a reinvigorated PWP committee, strengthened further by his successors Bibi Wein and Hettie Jones. PWP director Jackson Taylor has restored a rich mentor program, and at a stirring twenty-fifth-anniversary ceremony in 1998, Sister Helen Prejean, author of *Dead Man Walking,* offered the keynote address.

In twenty-five years, PEN has accumulated a rare archive of testimony, a mine of information about linguistic and literary culture as well as social culture behind bars. Prisoners have their own evolving lexicon, well known in their home neighborhoods. Inventive language travels from the street to the "joint" and back, ripening with each journey. Much penitentiary argot is decades old: "joint," "slammer" for prison; "hack," "screw," "canine," "roller," "C.O." for a guard or corrections officer; "fish" for a new prisoner, "rap partner" for crime partner, "road dog" for friend, "cellie" for cellmate. "Homeboy," "homey," or "homes," shedding its origin in *hometown,* is simply buddy. Solitary confinement (Administrative Segregation, Special Housing Unit, Control Unit, in bureaucratic lingo) is for convicts simply the "hole" or the "box." An arrest and conviction is a "fall"; "down" is serving time; a sentence is a "bit" or "bid"; near the end of it, one is "short." The crafted repartee in *Doing Time* owes much to the "dozens" — stylized verbal battles perfected by young African-American men.

Poetry coming out of the seventies was often stamped with Black Arts movement stylistics (including spelling: "Amerikkka") and marked by revolutionary fervor. It was a heady period for African-American prisoners. (Students in my Westchester County Penitentiary class admired George Jackson's stoical self-discipline in *Soledad Brother.* After Jackson's death, Charles Caldwell wrote, in "A Poem with George Jackson": "my dying just / as yours will be / a whip to sorrow / 'cause tears won't build / a body / & you are on the lips / the angry skin of life / that calls tomorrow.") Vera Montgomery's indignant poem (see **Players, Games**) about her sisters' failure to seize their common cause sits squarely in this tradition. Matching the proud attention to cultural specificity fostered by the black consciousness movement was that of Latinos — Puerto Rican Young Lords in the Northeast and Chicago, Chicanos in the Southwest and California — represented here by Raymond Ringo Fernandez and Jimmy Santiago Baca.

Some early PEN prison poetry reflected the "toast," an older African-American narrative in ballad form that my penitentiary students had introduced to me. Passed from performer to performer in jails, toasts glorify the "life" (of con games, pimping, and other hustles). The toast's flamboyant hyperbole persists in the "lies" and tall tales that enliven yard culture, and its rhythmic insistence is one of the sources of rap music and hiphop.

Established white poets are also woven into the literary culture of our lockups; dead white men (and a few women, notably Emily Dickinson and Sylvia Plath) are revitalized by writers who draw on their energy to their own emergencies. Chuck Culhane says he read Whitman and Ginsberg in that spirit, and it shows in the voices of "After Almost Twenty Years" (see **Time and Its Terms**). I thought I recognized Dylan Thomas's compound words in Jon Schillaci's "For Sam Manzie"(see **The World**), and Wallace Stevens's juggling of lush illusions in M. A. Jones's "To Those Still Waiting" (see **Getting Out**), and the authors owned up to their devotion. Vladimir Mayakovsky's line breaks, rhythms, and direct address are revived in Judith Clark's homage to him (see **Family**), as are — more surprisingly — Robert Browning's dramatic monologues in Henry Johnson's "First Day on the Job" (see **Race, Chance, Change**). Regionalism is strongly valued, and folk traditions — of the backwoods, the Deep South, and the inner city — are kept alive.

Existentialism, surrealism, and the absurd leave their mark on PEN fiction, most explicitly in stories like J. R. Grindlay's "Myths of Darkness" (**Time**). But, because lockup life itself is so often surreal or absurd, these features also shape realistic stories like Judee Norton's "Norton #59900" (**Family**) and Richard Stratton's "Skyline Turkey" (**Work**). Robert Rutan's resonant simplicity also harks back to Hemingway (**Getting Out**), Ralph Ellison's mordant wordplay resounds in Anthony Ross's story (**Death Row**), and Joseph Sissler (**Players, Games**) evokes Thomas Pynchon's layered realities.

In style and substance, prison nonfiction covers a wide gamut: from personal memoir, like Jimmy Santiago Baca's (**Reading and Writing**), to naturalist essay, like Kenneth Lamberton's Thoreauvian observations of the habits of barn swallows and bugs in the yards of Arizona lockups.* (Many fine pieces by PEN prison writers cannot be included, but, unwilling to sacrifice insights gathered, I refer to these pieces — signaling them by an * — here and throughout.) Some of our best nonfiction writers have met the proliferating crises of prison life — like riots, rape, gangs, AIDS, and psychotropic drugs —

by documenting them in the manner of testimonial writers writing under duress everywhere; some use interviews in their exposés. Many describe constructive programs in literacy, for example, or propose detailed reforms. Some write polemics about the death penalty or clemency; others about college education and parole (Jon Marc Taylor in **Reading and Writing** and Diane Hamill Metzger and Larry Bratt in **Time and Its Terms**). The urgencies of life behind bars drive some to do research in the library.

Others turn to the outside world and offer topical (and often perishable) bulletins from dangerous fronts and sordid undergrounds few of us know. An escaped prisoner hiding among the homeless in New York's Penn Station, John Springs III, seized the opportunity to study their habits and became their advocate.* Some have told subversive truths about our wars, Vietnam and its counterpart and successor, the war on drugs; see Robert Moriarty's dispatch on drug pilots in **The World.** Others have followed the course of the drug culture as it shaped their experiences. Though they present divergent realities, we have come to rely on many prison nonfiction writers to bear witness without flinching.

The anthology is divided into thematic sections, largely dictated by the concerns of our best writers over the years. These experiential categories evoke the many aspects of doing time and cover the lifespan of imprisonment, from its multiple beginnings to its several ends. They are: entry; coming to terms with expanded and emptied time; deadening routines and ways they are ruptured; work; education, from literacy to creative writing; games (con games, hustles, sports) and their players; race relations; interactions, past and present, with family; the recall and evocation of the outside world; ways of getting out; and death row. While perhaps a third of manuscripts received treat experiences outside prison (represented here in **Family** and **The World**), this anthology reflects the findings of contest jurors: that some of the most powerful work reveals what no other writers can offer — the unknown life of this nation hidden in our midst.

*   *   *

Writing forces me to remain conscious of the suffering around me and to resist getting numb to it. I write to keep my heart open, to keep pumping fresh red blood.
      — Susan Rosenberg, Federal Correctional Institution Danbury
      Danbury, Connecticut

Many prisoners write as if their lives depend on it. Quite often they do. Reading this material makes one reflect on the rich affinities between *doing time* and *doing writing. Do time or be done by it:* This is the overt text of some of the pieces, the subtext of all. The act of writing gives us all the feeling of doing, not being done, but writers behind bars find the obstacles greater and the stakes higher. *Do your own time,* convicts say. Meaning, *Mind your own business,* but also signifying *Don't make anyone else do it* and *Or someone will make you do theirs.* Doing time can mean enduring with dignity, respect for others, and some measure of independence; at best it means growth and transcendence. Doing writing exponentially heightens one's power to pursue these goals. The collection illuminates two routes to transcendence — rising above and going through. Yet all routes lead the writer to intolerable choices, or double-binds.

Long-termers with an enduring commitment to writing some-times figuratively break out of penal institutions by rising above, by positioning themselves outside as analysts and critics. Some, like Victor Hassine and Easy Waters, become time-professionals — chron-iclers. Incarcerated since he was sixteen, Waters has become a profi-cient and incisive historian, writing essays on the links between slavery and incarceration and the unfolding of the prison-industrial complex. In verse Waters traces the voyage of convicts up the Hudson in 1825 to build Sing Sing (**Work**). Others, as we have seen, diagnose the current crisis. In the process, some gain the strength to withstand the almost inevitable ensuing punishment. After publishing in the *Washington Post,* Larry Bratt, for example, began to research a piece on Maryland's first execution in thirty-three years. For canvassing guards, many of whom opposed the death penalty, the administration segregated him, but in court he won the right to continue research. Many writers with convictions, drawn into muckraking and thrown into the hole, find themselves in First Amendment battles, sinners become First Amendment saints. *To save one's integrity is to risk one's hide:* This is the chronicler's double-bind.

While jailhouse chroniclers risk censure to map the outer reality of prison, other writers face subtler dangers to chart the inner expe-rience. Rather than transcend their environment by anatomizing it, they sound its depth to gain some measure of control, keep body and mind intact, and even nurture the soul. Their work enacts and describes these ventures and also leads to hazardous choices.

The climate of pervasive menace makes physical survival the first burden of doing time. With a series of minute adjustments the psyche perfects its equivalent of the body's animal vigilance, producing a cool, latently aggressive stance. This stance is *attitude* — the immemorial resource of the slave, of anyone whose dignity is threatened by wanton power. If nothing else, attitude confers some measure of independence and self-respect. It is Nietzsche, highly prized behind the wall, who gives these survival artists their ambiguous shibboleth: "What doesn't kill us makes us stronger." Plots of countless prison stories take form around the ambiguity; in some the toughening disciplines preserve, in others, they kill. Although violence between women is rarer, they, too, adopt defiant postures, often at high psychic cost, as Judee Norton shows in "Norton #59900" (**Family**). As rigid as a shield, attitude flattens feeling. *Bodily survival jeopardizes the psychological.*

Another burden of doing time then is mental survival — preserving sanity. Convict authors scrounge for sanity under maddening circumstances. Humor, nature, work — resources that pull the desperate back from the edge — are compromised behind bars. Prison writers attest to a lot of shallow joking — about violence, for example — to block the terror of taking seriously their vulnerability. Laughter can also be restorative, a straw for drowning reason. The range of the best prison humor is narrow, from absurd to savagely ironic to gallows (see Michael Saucier's "Black Flag to the Rescue" [**Reading and Writing**], William Orlando's story [**Initiations**], and Jarvis Masters's poem [**Death Row**]).

Nature is the more valued for its scarcity. Contraband cats are cherished; in one story a kitten killed by a malicious guard is brutally avenged. Tributes to birds nesting in penitentiary beams or swooping into yards testify both to human hunger for transcendence and its cruel starvation (see "After Almost Twenty Years" in **Time** and Daniel Roseboom's piece in **Routines and Ruptures**). Work, the sovereign remedy for the faltering mind, helps many to develop competencies that serve other inmates. Far too often, however, it is debased and fraught with danger, as in Saucier's "Cut Partner" and "Gun Guard" (**Work**).

Taking note of other people snatches many from despair. Prison writing presents such a wealth of idiosyncratic characters that the cultivation of personality comes to seem a fundamental survival skill. Despised and scorned by the world and their keepers, prison personalities are registered, celebrated, and preserved by self-made griots, their literary cellies and work partners. These scribes in turn take heart from their models.

Camaraderie arises in the most unlikely situations, even between kept and keeper (who, some note, do time as well). In Scott A.

Antworth's understated story "The Tower Pig" (**Routines**), a prisoner and a despised officer effect a subtle rapprochement. Relationships between convicts and guards — who often share class and ethnic background with prisoners — are by no means predictable.

The richest stay against madness — genuine friendship — is also the most perilous. The universal riddle of intimacy is magnified in prison: *Letting down one's guard to trust is risking betrayal, grief, rage, more madness.* As Diane Hamill Metzger puts it, "Staff and prisoners play a lot of phony games with one another, when in reality neither trusts the other." Prisoners' alliances are undermined by contention for scarce rewards: "We must compete for our very lives." Yet up and down the tiers, friendship flickers like the mirrors, called "eyes," held periscopically outside bars to enable sight down the tier. Some relationships, as in William Aberg's "Siempre" (**Initiations**) flower though voice contact only.

In several stories, the most vulnerable console one another, the mad relieve the mad ("Myths of Darkness" in **Time**, "Skyline Turkey" in **Work**). In Robert Kelsey's story, "Suicide!" (**Work**), the protagonist Kerry, tormented by guilt for his drunk-driving homicide, works as a suicide-watch. By drawing out Kerry's humor and his compassion, his real value in the world, the damaged restore his balance.

It is the concern of a young black in particular that steadies Kerry, a white man. In prison accounts of friendship, a surprising number cross racial lines. African-Americans now make up 51 percent of the prison population. This skewed demographic picture, coupled with the explosive growth of racial gangs, intensifies the race hatred of many inmates. Firmly in the majority, blacks can exercise a reign of terror — and whites can hone their hatred. Or these and other groups can make common cause, as prison prose shows they sometimes do — in daily life and in riot situations (see "Eleven Days Under Siege" in **Race**). Moral survival is thus a third burden of doing time. All prisoners face ceaseless moral pressure that is unknown — or duckable — on the outside. This ranges from routine decisions — like whom to play ball with — to whether or not to ignore a monstrous wrong. In this context, stories of interracial friendships are especially poignant. (See stories by Charles Norman, Susan Rosenberg, and Michael Wayne Hunter in **Race**.)

Cultivating such prison relationships reflects and can further moral growth. Other writers do time by working through outside relationships, real or fictionalized — with family members and others (offensive or offended) in the past. By taking responsibility for repairing family ties or addressing the painful past, they write their way toward emotional survival and self-rehabilitation. No easy task, and prison lore warns against it: *Clinging to the past is risking failure to survive in the present.* Family ties can provoke crippling guilt, grief, anxiety, or jealousy. Many cannot drop the defensive mask when relatives visit and find it less wrenching to sever ties. Men write of turning their women loose rather than face the painful erosion of bonds.

But other men and many women take on the risk of engaging past abuse and of seeking family reconciliation. Three-quarters of women in prison are mothers and usually the primary care-givers. As a group particularly committed to the family structure, they suffer acutely from separation from those who depend on them, especially children; some write of their families "doing hard time." At Bedford Hills Correctional Facility, the existence of a nursery and a children's center signals the administration's belief that strong ties to family help rehabilitate women and that learning to parent a child helps a woman care for herself. Coupled with opportunities to explore feelings and intentions, such programs help prisoners grow emotionally. This aim animates the writing workshop at Bedford Hills, as participants describe it in "Tetrina" and "Sestina" (**Reading and Writing**). Emboldened in the workshop to face and untangle her past, and strengthened by her ongoing relationship with her daughter, Judith Clark traces in "To Vladimir Mayakovsky" (**Family**) her progress toward complex reconciliation.

Recreating the outside world, many writers seek other forms of reconciliation. For example, J. C. Amberchele's powerful pair of stories of a fictional victim (**The World**) symbolically attempt to make reparations. And reconciliation, albeit sad, with the self shaped by crime and punishment, is at the heart of Robert Rutan's tour-de-force (**Getting Out**).

Men and women sitting on death row confront the myriad violence — physical, mental, emotional, and moral — endured by ordinary prisoners. But they also have a uniquely precise foreknowledge of death; such knowledge earned its owner the famous Louisiana salute, "Dead Man Walking!" *Doing Time*'s final section shows how brilliantly some face this ultimate imaginative challenge of transcending their conditions.

Editor's Note

The selection process for this anthology has depended first on the prisoners, for all texts were written by contest winners. The contest is announced in prison journals, and in the late nineties, PEN receives annually about seventeen hundred stories, poems, plays, and non-fiction pieces. Most are by men. As we have seen, women represent only around 7 percent of the prison population. Those who write seem to send their work out more reluctantly than men unless they have political backgrounds (as is the case with many women here). To compensate for this imbalance, I have sought out additional work by prizewinning women for this collection.

Painstakingly handwritten manuscripts, sometimes illustrated, arrive alongside computer-generated text. Some send novels and treatises, others a few words, as if thrust into a bottle and tossed into the sea. The texts range from barely literate to highly polished. The strengths are those of the once-fortunate, or passionate, or reflective, or self-educated few; the weaknesses are those of any poorly educated group. Themes reappear obsessively — mother, shame, loss, salvation, the treacherous woman, the perfect crime, and the criminal-justice system. Some writers turn to desperate conventions — in verse, the Hallmark greeting; in narrative and drama, sci-fi, Dungeons and Dragons Gothic, the violent thriller, stand-up routines, and TV sit-com. Rich material and fresh language are often trapped in bankrupt literary formulas; simple morals are tacked onto undigested trouble. Those who have had the benefit of writing workshops offer more finished pieces, but some who toil alone take our breath away. Most contestants have become writers in prison, many are natural writers. Few professional writers compete.

Contest entries are divided into genres and distributed by the heap to members of generic subcommittees. Winnowing each haystack of manuscript for the irresistible needle is a daunting task. Subcommittees share their best manuscripts and deliberate for hours over winners.

Not all winning manuscripts could be found. *Fortune News* had published some winners from 1978 on; obliging collectors lent old issues. Materials from early years, stored in Princeton University archives, proved spotty, yet offered clues to some missing work. All honorable mentions had been mysteriously preserved, among them gems like Roger Jaco's "Killing Time" (**Time**) and Jimmy Santiago Baca's "Letters Come to Prison" (**Routines**).

After making a raw selection, I decided reluctantly to exclude drama. (Though powerful playwrights have won awards, drama is our smallest category; space limitations force us to omit examples.) Then authors' permissions had to be secured. For most recent winners still incarcerated, this posed little difficulty. Several, however, had been subjected to punitive transfer from prison to prison, in the process often losing their friends, scant possessions, a painstakingly constructed life — and their mail.

One day sleuth, the next posse, I pursued many writers from one prison or parole board to another, often across state lines. Teachers of prison workshops helped me find some ex-prisoners who, in turn, led me to others. (I discovered an American penal archipelago; prisoners' nightmare of transfer — some call it "diesel therapy" or "plane therapy" — results in many comradely networks.) Otherwise I was dependent on the goodwill of parole officers. "I can't help you" is the bureaucrat's "hello." I learned to explain my mission fast and to keep talking. Sometimes they amplified thus: "Even if I could help you, you don't have the right information." I learned that without the ex-prisoner's birthdate or proper identification number, an unusual effort was being demanded. Everything hung on who picked up the phone.

"Is this Michael E. Saucier a black man or a white man?" a Louisiana parole board employee asked. "I don't know! Have you really one of each?" "Yes!" she replied crisply, but she let me leave a message for the parole officer of one of them. That gentleman laughingly doubted that his client was a writer, but agreed to give him my number. And two weeks later, Saucier phoned.

Roger Jaco maxed out of parole in Newport News more than a decade ago. No Virginia Jacos knew him, but one referred me to a Jaco-genealogist in McMinnville, Tennessee; he held Jaco reunions, but knew no writing Jacos. But by then I had the information that Roger had a bunch of brothers whose names all began with R. "Ah!" said the genealogist. "*Those* Jacos! There were nine of them, and both their parents were killed in an automobile accident when they were little children." He sent me to one brother who referred me to Roger's adoring sister, Gladys, in Kentucky.

Vera Montgomery's case was particularly intractable. She had also been paroled too long ago, central records said. I contacted her final parole board, then, desperate, the next-to-last. There a woman heard me out. "I wish someone would give *me* some money for *my* wonderful poetry!" "Are you a poet?" She was, and she gave me Montgomery's birthdate, alias, her parents' names, and the information that she'd left the system in Newark. The Newark phone book listed none of these Montgomerys. I phoned one with her mother Elsie's initial, though I knew Vera herself was born in 1936. "No Elsie lives here," a man assured me. "Have you ever heard of a Vera

Montgomery?" "She was my favorite aunt," was the thrilling reply. Albert Montgomery recalled how Vera had died in a senior citizen facility, how she'd always spoken of writing and her desire to write a book. No one in the family had any of her writing — would I please send him some?

Final selection for the anthology was a complex balancing act, governed by commitments to honoring literary excellence and to encouraging some beginning writers. (The contest has always honored both.) I also looked for fine examples from each decade, and work representative of different subgenres, expressive of regional, racial, and gender diversity, and of prison experiences our writers have taught us they find crucial. While endeavoring to present as many writers as possible, this collection sometimes offers for depth more than one piece by a single author. Out of respect for the integrity of a work, excerpts are avoided.

Note on the Text

Some work has been lightly edited, with the author's consent. Each text is followed by the name of the institution where (and in two cases, about which) it was written, and, to my best knowledge, the year it was submitted to the contest.

An asterisk in editorial introductions marks texts described or cited for their useful insights, but regretfully excluded from the anthology for space reasons.

As **About the Authors** was shaped in collaboration with all living authors, an unforeseen range of striking histories emerged in sharply individual voices. Each was asked to write something about his or her literary development, education, and background, including — only if the author cared to do so — mention of crime, conviction, or sentence. We do not condone crime, but we agree with Sister Helen Prejean that a person is more than the worst thing he has ever done. Focusing on the self-rehabilitative work of writing, the committee rarely knows anything of criminal backgrounds. For this reason, though many claim innocence or are appealing their sentences, this data does not appear in the biographical section. Our emphasis rather is on the illuminating stories of how they became writers and what writing has meant to this extraordinary group of practitioners, how it has enabled them to do time.

Bell Gale Chevigny
February 1999

Acknowledgments

I am grateful to the Center on Crime, Communities and Culture of the Open Society Institute for awarding me a Soros Senior Justice Fellowship to pursue this project. I thank especially director Nancy Mahon, Katherine Diaz, Miriam Porter, Mary Cotter, and Soros Justice Fellows Joycelyn Pollock, Ellen Barry, and Angela Brown.

My greatest debt is to all members of the PEN Prison Writing Program committee over the years who cared enough to read through the formidable mass of manuscript and to write something constructive to each contestant. And especially to our invaluable Prison Writing Program director, Jackson Taylor, and the current members of the committee who entrusted me with this task and pointed me in the direction of interesting work: Susan Braudy, Beth Dembitzer, Bob Hamburger, Starry Krueger, Claudia Menza, Janine Pommy Vega, Marie Ponsot, Rochelle Ratner, Sue Rosen, Joan Silber, Layle Silbert, and Chuck Wachtel. Members Fielding Dawson, Hettie Jones, Bibi Wein, and Jackson Taylor offered very useful reactions to my first raw selection. Anthologists Fielding, Janine, and Hettie also helped locate texts and ex-prisoners, Chuck and Marie offered poetic counsel, and Bibi editorial experience. Current chair Hettie was a ready ear and wise adviser every step of the way.

For searching files and memories to recreate the story of PEN's origins, I am grateful to Thomas Fleming, Lucy Kavaler, Vicki Lindner, Ann McGovern, Kathrin Perutz, and especially John Morrone, who for several years helped place prison writings in magazines. At PEN in the late eighties, Gara LaMarche helped rescue the PWP from near-death and later supported it materially from his position at the Open Society Institute. From the PEN staff, special thanks to PWP Coordinator Agustin Maes for swift provision of vital PWP materials. I appreciate the consistent backing of PEN American Center's former and current executive directors, Karen Kennerly and Michael Roberts, and especially President Michael Scammel.

From Fortune Society, Harvey Isaacs, Sheila Maroney, and Sylvia McKeane helped me locate past winners' texts; so did Harry Smith, of the *Smith,* and Martin Tucker, of *Confrontation.* Anthologists and prison teachers Joe Bruchac, Janet Lembke, and Richard Shelton aided in locating authors. For generously sharing their myriad expertise, I thank Claudia Angelous, Jennie Brown, Raymond A.

Brown, Scott Christianson, Lois Morris, H. Bruce Franklin, Jim Knipfel, Mark Mauer, Dorothy Potter, and Richard Stratton. I am indebted to John and Sue Leonard and the *Nation* for publishing my article on PEN prison writing.

I thank Elizabeth Kronzek for archival research at Princeton, Brennan Grayson, Lesley Scammell, and Chloe Wheatley for research assistance, and Sara Lorimer, Bob deBarge, Grazyna Drabik, and Laura Schiller for typing the manuscript. I am blessed with friends who are passionately opinionated readers — Janet Brof, Bill DeMoss, Marilyn Katz, Danny Kaiser, Lee McClain, Antonia Meltzoff, Howard Waskow, Grey Wolfe, and Paul Chevigny.

A writer could not ask for a more energetic agent than my friend Sydelle Kramer at the Frances Goldin Literary Agency nor a more sympathetic editor than Coates Bateman at Arcade Publishing.

"Hands like yours help cup the flame," William Orlando wrote in thanking PEN. The authors' eloquent reminders of how much this work matters to them and others behind bars has made the work most gratifying. For generous research assistance, I thank especially William Aberg, Marilyn Buck, Chuck Culhane, Victor Hassine, Diane Hamill Metzger, Paul Mulryan, Charles Norman, Barbara Saunders, Joe Sissler, William Waters, and members of the writing workshop at Bedford Hills. And finally, I am forever indebted to those who got me started — my parolee students in the Queens SEEK Program in 1967–68 and my class at Westchester County Penitentiary, 1969–71, especially Charles Caldwell, whose example of self-transformation through reading and writing has stayed with me over the decades.

DOING TIME:

25 YEARS OF PRISON WRITING

Initiations

. . . I have been classified, collated and rated
fingerprinted photoed and filed
I am an examined, inspected cut of meat
dressed in khaki and set in concrete.

The ritual dehumanization of entry is a powerful theme for prison writers. In the excerpt from "Fair Hill Prison"* above, 1987 prize-winner Nolan Gelman resisted the process by naming it. Fundamental disorientation may strip one of words as well as of civilized garb. M. A. Jones's "Prison Letter" here captures the problem of wordlessness — another name for fear — at the most private level.

To become a prisoner is to enter an alien universe. One's most trusted resources fail to help interpret the new setting, and the simplest social interaction may be fraught with peril. Sometimes seasoned inmates help newcomers begin to do time. In William Aberg's "Siempre," set in an unusual Arizona jail that housed both men and women, a veteran talks a novice through fear of the penitentiary (the *pinta,* in Mexican argot) to which she is being sent.

More often it is a "cellie" who helps a "fish" to learn the ropes. In Clay Downing's 1974 story "The Jailin' Man,"* the title figure teaches the narrator how to heat water for coffee in the glass part of a lightbulb and in the process to feel less sorry for himself. Ingenious ways to prepare food are also shared with newcomers. Jarvis Masters describes learning how to make powerful wine in "Recipe for Prison Pruno" (**Death Row**). Advice on how to avoid danger abounds: "Drink plenty of water and walk real slow" is a typical admonition.

"Symbiosis" between inmates is possible, according to the avuncular mentor in David Wood's story by that name (1996),* if you learn how to carry yourself like a true convict: "Look every man square in the eye and let him know you'll fight back. You don't have to win a fight, just hurt the other guy bad enough so he won't want to scrap with you again." This swift cultivation of *attitude,* a particularly male response, is not restricted to men. Thus in Denise Hicks's 1996 entry "Where's My Mother?"* the neophyte reports: "I was learning the none-of-your-business stare; the no-you-don't-know-me stance; and the why-I'm-here-could-not-possibly-be-of-any-concern-to-you pivot."

Old hands school new prisoners in the cons' rules, as crucial to survival as institutional regulations. Each prison has its underground economy and its informal government, with leadership ranging from fluid to stable. Prison mentors elucidate the "code" of the "stand-up" convict, a signal feature of prison subculture for generations, particularly among men. Akin to "honor among thieves," it has tenets like "Be loyal to cons," "Don't let anyone disrespect you," and "Never snitch." This ideal is still nurtured by old-timers who nostalgically lament the bygone days when convicts, they say, ran penitentiaries. In "Ring on a Wire" (1996),* a story by George Hughes, the narrator's "cellie" celebrates a mythicized golden age when they could "take your freedom, take your property and everything else away from you, but not your word." For such as he, only a "convict" was a "real man."

But beginning in the 1980s, new throngs of rash and fearless teenagers doing time made a much more menacing experience. The "code" began to degenerate into little more than vengeance against snitches or, as Victor Hassine puts it, "Darwin's code: survival of the fittest." In his poem "Convict Code" (1988),* Alex Friedman describes "walking on by" scenes of weapon-making and gang rape, and then being stabbed twenty-eight times by a stranger — "and everybody walked on by."

In "How I Became a Convict" (extracted from his book *Life Without Parole*), Victor Hassine describes his adaptation to Pennsylvania's prison for the most violent criminals. His first impulse was to retreat and build himself a cocoon. His ultimate decision to engage the life around him typifies that of most effective prison writers.

For many, survival begins with mastery of prison lingo. (See "I See Your Work" in **Players, Games**). Some novices feel compelled to create lexicons of their new argot. Often harsh and minimal, this patois is sometimes rich in nuance. For the transferred prisoners facing reorientation on a new turf in William Orlando's "Dog Star Desperado" (the first chapter of a novel-in-progress), battles of rhetoric are all they can afford. Like the "dozens" played on ghetto streets and the rough banter of the armed services, this patois allows its performers to position themselves against one another while strutting their stuff. It also offers them a kind of collective armor as they size up their new surroundings and their new keepers, who are also pulled into the force field of prison language.

On another level, Orlando's story enacts the galvanizing of the spirit to meet the shock of dehumanization. In their own way, women, too, cultivate such resources. In "Arrival" here, for example, Judee Norton calls up the inviolable inner liberty of the Stoics and converts her shackles into jewelry. Her summoning of her innermost self marks her starting point as she begins to do time.

Prison Letter

M. A. Jones

You ask what it's like here
but there are no words for it.
I answer difficult, painful, that men
die hearing their own voices. That answer
isn't right though and I tell you now
that prison is a room
where a man waits with his nerves
drawn tight as barbed wire, an afternoon
that continues for months, that rises
around his legs like water
until the man is insane
and thinks the afternoon is a lake:
blue water, whitecaps, an island
where he lies under pale sunlight, one
red gardenia growing from his hand —

But that's not right either. There are no
flowers in these cells, no water
and I hold nothing in my hands
but fear, what lives
in the absence of light, emptying
from my body to fill the large darkness
rising like water up my legs:

It rises and there are no words for it
though I look for them, and turn
on light and watch it
fall like an open yellow shirt
over black water, the light holding
against the dark for just
an instant: against what trembles
in my throat, a particular fear
a word I have no words for.

1982, Arizona State Prison–Perryville
Buckeye, Arizona

Siempre

William Aberg

She tells me through the vent
from the cell below
that they're taking her
on the morning train to the *pinta*,
that the guards have already packed
everything but her sheets, blue jumpsuit, and towel.

Through the floor,
with my heart as with an eye,
I can see her as she sits
on the bunk, face
cupped in her hands,
elbows propped on her thighs,
cheeks smudged by fingermarks
and tears, her dark
hair eclipsing her knees.

I try to reassure her
with wisdom I do not have,
and hope I try to fake,
that the hammer
and anvil of coming days
will forge us into
something stronger.

By the time they unlock
my cell at breakfast,
she has already gone. But later
as I walk back in my boxers
from the shower, an older guard,
the kind one, slips a note
into my hand, whispers,
She sent her love. Back in my cell

I unfold a note that says,
Te amo, siempre in crude letters
formed by a finger and menstrual blood.

1994, Pima County Jail
Tucson, Arizona

Dog Star Desperado

William Orlando

It had been a journey.

We were bussed from USP Leavenworth during one of those polar Novembers in Kansas. It was a day cold and white and hushed, a solitary morning of the snows.

Our prison transport showed its age. It looked as knackered as some of the convicts it had aboard — men in bad flesh who'd let themselves go, turning gray with the years and bitter for it. The bus smelled funny. The odor of cigarette butts and rusted apple cores, the odor of stale, brooding sweat. A prisoner smell. We sat in our chains and stared holes through the bus windows. We had little rap for one another, anyway. Most of us were just faces — a surly face that grunted at you over a morning bowl of grits. We were content to look hard and forbidding. Desperadoes all.

Those that did talk, talked shop. Who was hot and snitchin'. Who got stabbed and good for the motherfucker. Who bugged out. Who busted loose one fine morning in Kool-Aid lipstick, cue-chalk blue eye shadow, and bikini briefs over buns of steel. Gossip and lore. Amazing, I thought, that so little could be so absorbing. Still, absent any stone tablets, this was how they passed on the tribal Decalogue — defining value and boundary. This was how they staked out their claims as regulars, as men, as convicts. Real ones. Very few of us left, they would have you know. Rats and queers taking over.

"Yo, baby!" a six-plus-footer dubbed Wonder Woman called out to me from the back of the bus. "Yeah — you, cutie. You can break me down like a shotgun, and ride! Just two hundred cash."

All heads turned. I grinned, embarrassed.

"Two hundred?" I replied at last. "You bump your head, bitch? For that much you can fuck me." The bus rocked. Laughing just to laugh. Prisoner laughter, and afterward gravity.

It grew, the distance between us and the prison and the distance between each other. Who could acknowledge the thoughts, let alone share them? We rode quietly out of Kansas and through Oklahoma, passing here a frosted wood and there a stubbled field, a ragged scarecrow under leaden skies; rode across Texas, New Mexico, and

Arizona, across miles and memory and heartbreak in a country song; rode, finally, the last leg westward to California and the sea, so by the time the bus reached Lompoc's gate we could've lifted our heads and howled — Lompoc looking, to transfixed eyes, as welcome as hoofprints in the snow to winter wolves.

It had been a journey.

The guard riding shotgun stood up and unlimbered his weapon from its overhead mount. Then he stepped heavily off the bus, plucking free the imbedded seat of his pants. This correctional officer wore the dark blue blazer, dress shirt with tie, and gray slacks — new image, new name.

The driver, likewise uniformed, followed after his lumbering partner, but returned in minutes to key open the bus security grill — a steel mesh partition between their inviolate space and ours.

"Let's move it out, happy campers."

"But, officer!" fretted someone. "There's criminals in there!"

The driver shifted a wad of chaw in his mouth. "Hot grub, too."

Our response was Pavlovian. Hands cuffed, feet shackled, and chained at the waist in twelve-man coffles, we rattled off and away from the bus — shuffling like coolies. The bright Lompoc afternoon was typical for this part of the central California coast. The sun batted our eyes into a squint, and the aggressive breeze nipped at our prison khakis.

"The more the merrier," needled one of the escort guards. "I like seeing all these inmates!"

"Job security," quipped another behind his M-16.

These guards all matched: boots, mirrored sunglasses, guns. They were many, and they deployed themselves around us. Such overkill made you feel at once hopeless and proud at being considered so fierce a beast. For the nonce you weren't some tame and humble inmate. Hell, no. You were a barbarian being whipped to the imperial gates, straining at your bonds and snarling defiance at your captors.

By now we'd passed through the main entrance sally port. Ahead loomed the administration building; straight to the door, the long strip of pavement ran a flowered gauntlet between annuals gay and nimble in the breeze. A ribbon on a pig.

"Hey, you! Take a right." I turned left — busily straining at my bonds, absently leading the coffle. I'd been daydreaming since my youth and was getting better at it.

"Your other right, Twinkle Toes."

I stopped in my tracks to make up for my blunder, and caused a bigger one. The chain reaction was literal. The coffle bunched into folds, like a caterpillar at the end of a leaf.

"What kind of a Polish fire drill . . . C'mon, shake the fuckin' lead!" came the same loud and abrasive voice.

"Aww — shake these hairy nuts, cop!" This voice belonged to the Georgia boy right behind me. They called him June Bug. Nicknames came in two ways: The con dug deep and flattered himself with one, or the world slapped a handle on him. June Bug. It stuck. It rubbed salt. He had griped the loudest about the joys of being in transit with no property — "nary a toothbrush or a stamp." He had stayed in the Man's face, selling death from behind the safety of the security screen. The transport guards just rolled their eyes. Who took seriously a balding, short little fat guy? He got too mouthy you raised your hand at him and that was enough.

"Chill out, June Bug," advised the third man on the chain, a black convict. "Dude's a fool. I knows that Hoosier from Terre Haute."

"Indiana?"

"Yessir. Him and the gooners rushed my cell — I was in the hole — and jive tossed me up."

"Is that right? Well, he don't move me none." June Bug bunched his pudgy fists. "Just let me get my hands on him. Two minutes!"

"Easy, killer," I pitched in, thinking he was out of place in the catchall of prison.

The black threw back his smooth-shaven head and laughed. "Hey, y'all seen his wife? Big ol' tits. She's got some kind of secretary job — warden's office or some shit, and they say she's fuckin'."

"Now I likes me a gal with round heels," said June Bug.

"Ain't no question!" agreed the shiny-pated one. "I'd like to dick her down and him watching — the dirty Klansman."

"I wouldn't fuck a pig's wife," I said, playing to the gallery. "Might squeal."

June Bug added his chortle to Cranium's and then said, "Right about now I'd fuck a snake? Just hold the head."

"I hear ya," said Cranium. "Ain't no shame in your game."

"None in the fed's, either," I told them both. "We need a law like the one passed in California."

"What law?" asked June Bug.

"He means SP42. It's one of them . . . uh . . . radioactive laws. They lettin' all kinds of motherfuckers go."

June Bug hissed through chipped teeth. "We ain't going nowhere for a while. Fuck with Uncle and get retired."

"Yeah. And stuck with fools like that one over there," complained Cranium. "He's some shit."

The correctional officer in question sported a lieutenant's gold badge. He posted himself just ahead of us, on the wide expanse of lawn edging the walkway.

"How you be, Lieutenant Griggs?" I heard an escort C.O. ask him in passing. "Where's your jacket?"

"Don't need one in California." The C.O. did a double take. Lieutenant Griggs was not kidding. The El-Tee stood with arms akimbo above the trestle of his legs, raking humorless eyes over the length of the prisoner chain. A big, unlit cigar jutted from his mouth.

"Why, Rufus!" came the loud voice as we shuffled before him. "Last time I seen you we was dancing." The black con surrendered a tepid smile.

"Ain't gonna have no trouble out of you here — are we?"

"Nossir. Got my mind right, boss." Rufus had introduced himself on the bus. "Money is my game, Well-to-Do is my name."

"Well-to-Do?" challenged his homeboy from Miami. "My nigga . . . every since I done knowed you, you been doin' dirtball bad. Well-to-do!" he snorted. "Nigga, y'name needs to be Food Stamp." Merciless, the guffaws.

"My name ain't Rufus, it's Well-to-Do," he huffed as we descended the basement ramp into Receiving and Discharge.

Once inside, we were unchained, strip-searched yet again, handed towel rolls, and, the first twelve of us, sent naked to the next holding cage to dress. There we opened our rolls, and got a surprise.

"What the fuck?"

"Kiss my black ass!"

"*!Que la chingada!*"

The problem was comic; the problem was grave. Each of us stared at the drawers we'd been issued. These were not the loose-fitting boxers of custom. These were jockey shorts. Dainty shorts — shrunken and the brown all faded. They were, in effect, pink panties.

"Ain't no fun when the rabbit's got the gun," mused one convict aloud.

We wrapped towels around our waists and started wailing for the Man.

"C.O."

"C.O.!"

"Hey, you deaf? C.O.!"

Footsteps approached, and a gravelly voice grew louder. "Hold on, hold on. Damn! I ain't got but two hands and two feet . . . and half a dick." The officer, reaching the screen-fronted cage, grinned. "But I got a split tongue!"

"Dig this," started Rufus, "These here —"

"Do I know you?" The C.O. had scanned our faces, pointing to the ugliest one. June Bug. "Hey, you think I'm good-looking?" His own round and homely face creased into another grin. "It ain't easy being fat and greasy — huh?"

It had sounded suspicious to me when my mother first said: "You can be ugly and your personality can make you charming." She sat in her slip before the dresser mirror, painting her face. "Just be nice to her."

"But I don't want to be nice. She smells, too."

"You love me?"

"Yes."

"Then do it for your mama, Handsome."

She always used that on me. It was just me and her, and so I went up to the front house where the landlady lived. We were behind on the rent.

Moms was right, of course. Take this grizzled C.O. He exuded a crude charm — just the thing for inmates. You could tell he knew people, liked people. His job was a paycheck, not a calling. This was obvious in the shit he talked. But for timing, we would have laughed at his next remark.

"All right, little darlings, you got me down here. Who tore their panties now?"

We howled. Our clamor brought another officer on the run, keys jangling. "What's wrong?" the second asked the first.

"This hee-uh is what's wrong!" June Bug held up the offending briefs between thumb and index finger.

The blond and burr-headed second officer shrugged. "So?"

"So look at these — how can I — I can't — just get me some more, Mister Police."

"That's a negative. Laundry only gave us a set amount."

"Well, you gots to do somethin'." June Bug gestured at his rotundity. "How you figure me getting these on?"

"Try one leg at a time."

"Try these nuts, you —"

"Calm down," cut in the wearied veteran, waving a placatory hand. "Main thing's don't fuckin' panic. Come laundry tomorrow, you prima donnas will get squared away."

A big white con — all muscles and inky tattoos — got up from one of the backless benches bolted to the wall. The dragons, the demons, the damsels of heroic fantasy muraled his upper body. "Fuck that," he said. "Call the laundry now."

"Laundry's closed," informed Blond Burr.

"Well, send somebody . . ."

"That's right," broke in Rufus. "Earn some of them taxpayer dollars."

". . . somebody over there and get us some decent drawers. Some bonaroos. Come on, pops. Do the right thing!"

"Anything else?" came the veteran's arch reply. "How 'bout a reach-around, too? Now I've got to get you guys processed and —"

"Fuck you then, you old fart."

"Fuck me and you'll never go back to a woman." I pondered the exchange. C.O.'s sounded like convicts — even unto sex-talking each other, and they had women. Environment rubbed off.

Rubbing a sleek head — one kept shaven in fear and concealment of balding age — Rufus stalked over to the cage door. "Man, we got our rights. Constitutionally amendated. I'll call my lawyer, and take y'all to court on one of them there, uh . . . a writ of hocus pocus! You can't be doggin' us like this. I ain't going for it."

"Me neither," chimed in June Bug. "I'm tired of suckin' hind tit. Don't make me come out and whip somebody now!"

The younger C.O. ran a hand over his fair, burr-cut head. He could bite it back no longer. "Uh, gentlemen — this is not the Holiday Inn. You don't like the treatment, you shouldn't have come to prison. Your fault for breaking the law."

He spoke from on high. His prissy manner riled the natives all over again.

June Bug grabbed his crotch and sallied forth with his all-purpose response: "Break — these — nuts!"

Blond Burr smiled thinly. "You write your own material?"

June Bug was stumped, but not the others. They counted coup.

"Bring us a fuckin' lieutenant!"

"Guard, guard! My dick is hard!"

"Get the nurse; it's gettin' worse!"

"Get the president!"

"Hell, yeah!"

"We buckin'!"

Leave it to a group. Who was impressing who?

"Fellas," warned the old-timer, "don't make it harder on yourselves. You know where you are. Use your heads for a change."

June Bug was consistent in his trademark reply.

Shaking their heads, the two guards trudged away from the impasse. A cocky June Bug took a parting shot at their backs. "For heaven sakes, look at those cakes! Hey, blondie! Let's do a sixty-nine, and I'll owe you one."

The two C.O.'s let us stew a while. Then they came back to order us over to the next processing station. We refused. "You can't win," they said matter-of-factly.

Fuck winning, fuck prison, fuck you. Men eat bear. We got our chance. A lieutenant showed up soon afterward. He did not come alone. Clomping in formation behind him was the goon squad — the special operations response team. Goofy menace.

They were eight strong, and not a corn-fed one of them was under six feet or two hundred pounds. They were military — real paratroopers in jumpsuits and jump boots. They were riot-garbed and ax-handle armed. They were dressed to dance.

1998, United States Penitentiary Marion
Marion, Illinois

How I Became a Convict

Victor Hassine

I have heard Graterford called the Farm, the Camp, the Fort, and Dodge City, but I have never heard it called safe. When I was in the county jail awaiting trial, I saw grown men cry because their counselors told them they were being transferred to Graterford.

Graterford State Prison, Pennsylvania's largest, was built in the early 1930s to hold the state's most violent prisoners. On June 14, 1981, while it could not contain all eight thousand of the state's most wanted, it certainly had enough room to hold me. Its steel-reinforced concrete wall measures four feet thick by thirty-two feet tall and encloses over sixty-five acres of land. The five cellblocks are huge, each containing four hundred cells. Each cellblock is a three-story rectangular structure, measuring about forty-five feet by eight hundred twenty feet, over twice the length of a football field.

I knew none of this as I sat handcuffed and shackled in the backseat of the sheriff's car, waiting to be taken inside to begin serving my life-without-parole sentence. All I could see was a blur of dirty, grainy whiteness from the giant wall that dominated the landscape before me. It made me feel small and insignificant, and very frightened.

A giant steel gate rose up to allow the sheriff's car to drive into Graterford's cavernous sally port area. Once the gate fell shut, I was immediately hustled out of the car by some very large, serious-looking corrections officers. I knew I would have to submit to a cavity search, but it wasn't the strip-search that would dominate my memory of this event. It was the *noise*.

Since concrete and steel do not absorb sound, the clamor and voices from within just bounced around, crashing into each other to create a hollow, booming echo that never ended. It sounded as if someone had put a microphone inside a crowded locker room with the volume pumped up to broadcast the noise. It was this deafening background noise that would lull me to sleep at night and greet me in the morning for the next five years. Though I have been out of Graterford for many years now, its constant din still echoes in my ears.

The prison guards finished their search and escorted me up

Graterford's main corridor, a dim, gloomy, fifteen-hundred-foot-long stretch. The lack of natural light and the damp, dungeonlike air was oppressive. As I took one tentative step after another, I became so disoriented that I lost track of how far I had been walking. I promised myself never to take bright and sunny places for granted again.

Things changed with sudden permanence once I reached the central corridor gate that separated the administrative section from the prison proper. I saw, for the first time, the faces, shapes, and shadows of the men who would become my friends, enemies, and neighbors. They stared at me and I stared back, as scared as I had ever been in my life.

Once inside, I was walked through a gauntlet of desperate men. Their hot smell in the muggy corridor was as foul as their appearance. Most were wearing their "Graterford tan," an ashen gray pallor. The discoloration of these distorted human forms reflected the prison landscape. At Graterford you work, eat, sleep, and idle indoors. You never have to go out unless you want to risk the sometimes deadly yard. Many inmates served their time like cave dwellers, never leaving Graterford's concrete-and-steel shelter.

My first impression was that most of these men brandished their scars and deformities like badges of honor. None seemed to have a full set of front teeth. Many displayed tattoos of skulls or demons. They all seemed either too tall or too small, but none seemed right. Eyes were buggy, beady, squinted, or staring. Heads were too big, too small, pointed, swollen, or oblong, some with jutting foreheads, twisted noses, massive jaws. None seemed human.

One could argue whether it was the look of these men that led them to prison or whether it was the prison that gave them their look. What tales of suffering their bodies told seemed to be of no concern to them. They were content to wear their scars openly like a warning, the way farmers use scarecrows to keep menacing birds away. Today I feel pity and compassion for those who have had to suffer so much pain and tragedy. But on that hot June day, all I wanted was to get away from these ugly creatures as quickly as possible.

Now when I watch a new arrival walking "the gauntlet of desperate men," I can always sense his hopelessness. I know my stare is as horrifying to him as the stares were for me on my first day, and I know what I must look like to him.

Getting Classified

Toward the end of the main corridor I was shepherded into yet another corridor that led to the Clothing Room, a cold, damp place equipped with a tile-walled shower, and endless rows of mothballed clothes hung on racks like mismatched goods in a thrift shop.

I was still wearing my nice suit and tie from the courthouse. My escort guard ordered me to "get naked" and surrender my personal effects to an inmate dressed in brown prison garb. As I stripped down, I handed the silent inmate the last vestiges of my social identity. He tossed them impatiently into an old cardboard box. The guard conducted another "bend-over-and-stretch-'em" search; I was given delousing shampoo and ordered to shower. Afterward, as I stood naked and shivering, I was assigned two pairs of navy-blue pants, two blue shirts, three T-shirts, three pairs of boxer shorts, three pairs of socks, a blue winter coat, a blue summer jacket, two towels, and a pair of brown shoes. Everything but the shoes and socks had AM4737 boldly stamped in black. This number was my new, permanent identity.

Once I had dressed, I was fingerprinted and photographed, then escorted to E Block, officially known as the Eastern Diagnostic and Classification Center (EDCC). E Block was treated as a separate facility, which inmates and staff called "Quarantine." Because all new receptions to Quarantine were issued blue prison uniforms, they were labeled "Blues." General population inmates, who wore brown uniforms, were referred to as "Browns."

Soon I found myself before the E Block sergeant, who walked me to a room full of bedding. There another inmate in brown dropped a rolled-up mattress on my shoulder. Inside it were stuffed a blanket, pillow, metal cup, plastic knife, fork, and spoon, a pack of rolling tobacco, soap, toothbrush, and a disposable razor.

Awkwardly balancing the mattress roll on my shoulder with one arm and carrying my prison-issued clothes with the other, I followed the sergeant down a flight of stairs to my cell. The moment I twisted my body and cargo sideways into the dark, narrow cell, the sergeant slid the door shut and disappeared from sight.

I spent the next two days in the prison's infirmary for shots and a complete medical examination. While it was a doctor who examined me, it was an inmate who drew my blood and wrote down my medical history. A guard followed me and the other Blues everywhere we went. I wondered about this constant surveillance. Why were we so heavily guarded? One reason, I later learned, was that although the infirmary was also used by Browns, contact between Blues and Browns was strictly forbidden. Nonetheless, because they had more liberties than the new arrivals, Browns often tried to barter privileges with Blues. For example, a pack of cigarettes could buy extra phone time or a library pass; for a pack a day, you could rent a TV or a radio. Also, some Browns were homosexuals and would exploit weaker Blues. Many were point men for prison gangs, who reported back on the new prospects for possible gang membership or future victimization.

Two weeks of idleness followed the medical examination process. Finally I was taken to an examination room for a series of psychological and literacy tests. From the inmate point of view, the testing was an utter sham. For one thing, the written tests were given to everyone without even determining who could read or write. I was tested in an unsupervised room with about thirty other men, most of whom just picked answers at random or copied them from someone else.

Because the tests were given so irrelevantly, inmates tended to see their results only as a tool of manipulation. Under this assumption, many men had developed theories on how to answer the test questions. Some felt it was best to copy from the brightest men in order to improve their chances at getting a clerk's job over kitchen or laundry duty. Others felt they should give lunatic answers so they could be medically released from work altogether. Still others gave no answers at all and faked illiteracy, reasoning that they could enroll in school and appear to do extremely well, thereby fooling the parole board into believing they had worked hard to make a positive change in their lives. All these connivances were based on the inmates' understanding that they were being conned as much as they were doing the conning. They believed that the tests were used by the administrators just to maintain the semblance of educational purpose at best and at worst to harvest information from them that would some day be used against them (for example in job placement or for parole eligibility).

Two more months of idleness followed as I waited to be interviewed by my counselor. To occupy time, people played cards and worked out. During these early idle days, long-standing friendships and alliances were made. I also noticed that every time the four hundred members of E block were let out into the yard, a fight would break out. It is my experience that when convicts are let loose after being locked up for long periods of time, aggressive behavior is an immediate and natural consequence.

This was also a time when inmates distinguished the weak from the strong, predators from victims. The first impressions I made on others during classification have followed me through prison ever since. Since I was not a career criminal, I was initially viewed as a "square john": a middle-class outsider with no experience of the social world of inmates. To both my advantage and disadvantage, I was seeing everything through the eyes of a foreigner, making many foolish mistakes yet gaining just as many unique insights.

When I was finally called in for my interview, the counselor examined my test results and asked me a few questions about my conviction and sentence. The interview took only ten or fifteen minutes.

Two weeks later, I was summoned to appear before the Classification Committee. Sitting before a counselor, the block sergeant, and a major of the guards, I was informed that I had been classified to Graterford. Just before I left, the major added in a pleasant voice, "You'll be working for me." At the time I didn't consider the significance of my job assignment — a fortuitous clerical job. I was too relieved to know that the tortuous classification ordeal was finally over.

The introduction of the classification process was originally a major prison reform but for me and most of the others, as I later discovered, classification was a total waste of time. While different prisons in Pennsylvania purportedly provided different types of rehabilitation programs meant to serve the needs of various kinds of offenders, in reality it seemed that only three considerations were used to determine a convict's ultimate destination: (1) race, (2) hometown, and (3) availability of cell space. At the time, most of the minority inmates in the state were classified to Graterford or Western Penitentiary. The other seven prisons consisted of mostly white inmates under an all-white civilian staff.

Getting Dug In

Once I was classified to Graterford, I traded in my blues for browns and moved off Quarantine to B Block. This was a working block, reserved for those inmates who had been assigned a job. Though it mirrored the design of E Block, B Block was considerably less crowded and noisy. Most of the men on B Block were much older than those on the classification block. These were the "Old Heads" of the prison, inmates who had done a long stretch.

When I arrived at my new home, I quickly signed in at the block sergeant's desk and requested cleaning supplies. Then I spent the morning scrubbing down every inch of my cell. By noon count I was able to lie down on my bed, smoke a cigarette, and consider my surroundings. My cell measured about six feet by twelve with a ten-foot-high ceiling, from which dangled a single light bulb with a pull chain. For furniture, I had a flat, hard steel bed and a steel desk and chair which had been assembled as one unit. The mandatory toilet afforded a sink directly above it with a steel medicine cabinet above that. High over the toilet was a rusty radiator, my only source of heat in the winter. Finally, I had a flimsy wooden footlocker with a hasp that could be locked with a commissary-bought combination lock. My entrance was a solid steel sliding door with a fixed glass window on the top quarter. On the opposite wall was a window that could be manually opened and closed, just a little. The concrete walls were painted a dingy off-white and adorned with graffiti and cigarette stains.

This was my home. I was due to report to work the next morning and I could feel myself getting dug in. In prison it doesn't take much to make a man happy: food, some quiet, a good book, a job, and enough heat in the winter. That day I was happy just to be able to lie on that hard bed with a seventy-watt light bulb glaring in my face. I felt the worst was over. I could now begin to serve my time.

Escape from Reality

Like most first-time arrivals to Graterford, I was preoccupied with survival and how to avoid becoming the victim of violence. When there was general movement in the prison, for example, the main corridor would fill with hundreds of inmates in transit. This made the corridor an extremely dangerous place to be. I was more likely to see a stabbing than a guard on duty.

The cellblocks were just as insecure. A guard at one end of a cellblock could not identify anyone at the other end; the distance of seven hundred feet was just too great. Because of their fear of being assaulted where no one could see them, many block guards never patrolled the inner perimeter and spent most of their time avoiding conflicts at all cost, even turning the other way. In fact, inmates serving long sentences preferred to lock at Graterford because, even though it was violent, it afforded them the most personal liberty. The more violent a prison is, the more reluctant guards are to enforce petty rules for fear of being assaulted.

If I made eye contact with a stranger, I would feel threatened. An unexpected smile could mean trouble. A man in uniform was not a friend. Being kind was a weakness. Viciousness and recklessness were to be respected and admired. I could feel my habits, my personality, and even my values change. I came to view the world as a place of unrelenting fear. Oddly enough, these changes were in some way comforting. In the struggle to survive, it was easier to distrust everyone than to believe in their inherent goodness.

By the time I had settled in, however, I found myself feeling safe enough to think beyond the moment, something I had not been able to do since my arrest. Unfortunately, this new sense of security brought with it the "sleeping phase." I began to sleep twelve to fourteen hours a day. My whole life consisted of eating, working, and sleeping. I never dreamed. I only tried to stay unconscious for as long as I possibly could. Though I had no way of knowing it at the time, I had entered a very common prison-adjustment phase, one so common, in fact, that walking in on a newcomer while he sleeps is the most practiced technique of cell thieves and rapists. In Graterford, a man who spends too much time in bed sends the same signal as that of a bleeding fish in shark-infested waters.

"You can't be sleeping all the time," cautioned my chess partner one day, waking me to play a game. "You can't sleep away your sentence. You have to stay awake to stay alive in here."

I resolved to keep myself busy. I took up reading and painting. I was allowed to buy almost as many books, magazines, and newspapers as I wanted, as well as canvases, brushes, and paints. Self-help was encouraged so long as you could pay for it.

Soon I was reading everything I could get my hands on and painting well into the wee hours of the morning. My cell became crowded with books, magazines, canvases, newspapers, even an easel. I went so far as to rig up extra lighting, hang pictures, and buy throw rugs for the cement floor. I had successfully transformed my cell into a cluttered boardinghouse room.

"You have to spend more time out of that cell, Victor," insisted my chess mate and only friend at that time. "It's not healthy to do a 'bit' [time] like that. Look at your cell, you have junk everywhere. You even have lights that look like they belong in a room somewhere else."

"I'm just getting dug in," I replied in defense, annoyed that my efforts at avoiding reality had been detected.

"This isn't getting dug in, this is foolishness. You're in a penitentiary — a tough one. You should never try to forget that. Never try to make yourself believe you're somewhere else. Do you know what a lit match could do to this cell?"

His words struck an unnerving chord. Only a few months earlier, I had watched a man whose cell across the way had been deliberately set on fire. He had screamed and banged helplessly on his locked door, flames dancing around him, biting at his flesh. Through his cell window, I could see billowing black smoke envelope his pleading, twisted, horrified face until he disappeared. It had taken some time before guards responded to his screams.

The very next day I gave away my books, magazines, newspapers, art supplies. I knew I had to fight as hard for my safety as I did for my sanity.

1995, State Correctional Institution Rockview
Bellefonte, Pennsylvania

Arrival

Judee Norton

bright shiny bracelets
    jangling on my arm
wide leather belt
    snug about my waist
chains dangling seductively
        between my legs.
I am captured
    but not subdued
THEY
    think they have me
but
    my mind
      wheels and soars and spins and shouts
no prisoner
I am free
    to look to see
all that I ever have been
all that I ever may be

I hold the small and sacred part of me close
    like a royal flush
      my poker face
      must not betray
THEY
    cannot touch it
      not even in their dreams
I
   am light and air and fire
I
   slip through their clutching fingers
      like the night
even as they grasp my puny wrist
    of simple bone
    and blood
    and flesh

body here
spirit there
I
      am still
       free.

1990, Arizona State Prison Complex–Perryville
Goodyear, Arizona

Time and Its Terms

It is so peaceful on the bank of the river,
one can almost forget youth tick tick ticking
its way into memory.

Coming to terms with time is a solitary, existential experience, forever the province of poets. Poets know time's brevity, its repeats and deceits, and also how rhythm mimics time, how imagination cheats it. Loss of physical freedom compounds and intensifies these universal experiences, as Henry Johnson knows, viewing the Hudson from Sing Sing in "Sailboats"* excerpted above.

The state reduces the stuff of time, as it does the captured human, to number. It makes time the prisoner's only possession, while emptying it. The state's appropriation of human time and domination of its meaning is epitomized in the harshness of the "count," for which prisoners must at regular intervals be locked in their cells. In "Counting Time" by M. D. Goldenberg (1985),* "The officers count / the prisoners / The prisoners count / the days / The days count / for nothing." Doing time is also doing space, for the temporal distortion is paralleled by tyrannical control of space, as William Aberg's poem "Reductions" here discloses.

Like a sorry mathematician, Derrick Corley worries the impossible calculus of space and time, punishment and crime. In "Cell" (1996),* he notes that his is getting smaller: "I wonder how / they do that / taking a little more / each day." Asked name in "Arrest,"* Corley says "Methuselah"; asked age, "a thousand." They "thought me mad / when I was just so very — weary / to find myself yet again / made old by my actions." Others recover human time and space in fragments of dream (like Jackie Ruzas in "Where or When") or in a scrap of music or of fantasy (like M. A. Jones in two poems here). Some try to do time on their own terms. They triumph over the state's possession of their years with irony, bravado, or a moment of pure rapture. Chuck Culhane does all three in "After Almost Twenty

Years"; his darker poem "There Isn't Enough Bread" registers the collapse of such resources. Roger Jaco's "Killing Time" pits the recall of the world's rich calendar against the flattened time of prison.

The possibility of doing "good time" to reduce one's sentence and win parole sometimes enables the state to manipulate prisoners by appropriating their future. ("Lee's Time" in **Race, Chance, Change** dramatizes the moral crises such control can generate.) Here Diane Hamill Metzger illuminates the tortuous effects on prisoners of a system that teases prisoners' expectations through indeterminate sentences, the hope of clemency, or the phantom of parole. In the face of the growing movement to eliminate parole, however, Larry Bratt offers a sharply differing point of view from Metzger's.

Exactly how J. R. Grindlay's "Toledo Madman" expected the sparrows to help him escape remains a tantalizing mystery, and the author is dead. But the Madman finds "ultimate freedom" by electing insanity and becoming master of his own time.

Reductions

William Aberg

Afternoons, in this plague
of flies and white, Sonoran heat, we rarely sing —
to be honest, not at
all. The porter unrolls the hose
and waters the dirt to keep it from blowing
up in our faces when the southern winds
hit. Crouched on the walk
outside our cells, we keep busy
lying about what we would do
if a woman appeared
to us, her lips a coarse violet
wanting each one of us

right now. Or how easily
we could distract the guard
from his perch on the guntower —
one fake fight
and we would make it
over the fence before the count
officer found us missing. I remember
one cynic, locked up
twelve years, spat tobacco
in a paper cup, pushed up the brim
of his cap, and told us

the jagged range
of mountains outside the prison
fence marked the edge
of the world, and the sky
was simply a revolving backdrop
someone painted with clouds
and stars. We laughed
but for him, it was the truth:
there could be no other world.

1982, Arizona State Prison–Santa Rita
Tucson, Arizona

Where or When

Jackie Ruzas

Huddled under a tent with strangers,
my woolen clothes soaking wet.
Sharks swim undisturbed over cars, grass,
and concrete dividers.

Hiding in a tree I watch Mom argue with
the seltzer man. He enters my yard. I climb
down from the tree into — a prison yard
where Frankie "Bones" and Georgie Bates
are playing gin with comic size Alice in Wonderland
cards. Their bodies petrified, clay like
resembling Homo Antiquitus in the Hamburg Museum.
I pass them by.

The yard becomes a winding road, desolate.
I walk and walk as seasons fall behind me and
voices fill the night.

> 1985, Sing Sing Correctional Facility
> Ossining, New York

An Overture

M. A. Jones

Something in the darkness
has given birth to a sky
spinning with a fierce impossible light. Here
night and day have different sounds,
the seasons varying textures. We could say
it's *October*. On a sidewalk
that goes somewhere blue plaid sweaters

float above the hands of lovers
dampening the crisp air. They sweep
past walls privileged with windows,
transparence lit with small faces, a hush
a hand opening. This story begins

and ends in separate places, with interruptions
where sun-veiled women step out
of themselves, fall
then lift *andante,* continuing . . . in this story
there's always the possibility of morning,
      a chance
that the screams which drip down at midnight
are not really threatening
but wishing us well,
wishing us a life
    in another story.

    1979, Arizona State Prison–Florence
    Florence, Arizona

Vivaldi on the Far Side of the Bars

M. A. Jones

for William Aberg

Maybe nothing can save us tonight,
not love or religion
or the needle that comes to us
in sleep and flowers in our veins.
Maybe none of those things:
lawyers, guns, the blonde
we imagine waiting

beyond the gates, her hair lifting
the wilted air, the heat of her body
or the perfume that still sleeps
in our sleep. Maybe not even
her hand on our leg, the single word
we thought would once stop our hearts
or start them again, that we were certain
would change us. Maybe nothing changes

and maybe not even blood
splashed across this concrete
would make a difference, would buy
our way back. Maybe there's no currency
they'll take, no promise
they'll believe. Maybe not even
death can get us out this time,
and maybe it's finally too late

for us, brother, maybe what remains
is just a little static on your radio,
a music that plays on the far side
of these bars, something we confuse
for church bells, a child singing,
a shadow that steps to meet us in the dark.

1982, Arizona State Prison–Perryville
Buckeye, Arizona

Killing Time

Roger Jaco

Memorial Day

This dusty May
I sit in yesterday's kitchen
watching the rain pound
against windows that reflect poverty.
Pa says the corn will grow

higher than a Georgia pine
and Ma sighs with relief
carefully placing her knife
on a mound of potato peelings.
Strange how I long for those days
when I was free
from luxury.

*After Independence
Day*

Revolving doors:
Feeling
alone again and
as empty as my bare cell.
Longing
for the hatred to return
and justify my wrongs.
Knowing
that revenge never works.
Trapped in the game
waiting
for my turn.
Ad infinitum.

Labor Day

I sit in silence
listening to the katydids
of a good ol' September.
Somewhere in the sweaty night
a whippoorwill
disturbs the noises of nostalgia and
Kathy's freckled face returns
haunting my cell,
whispering softly,
"Please don't rob again.
We can make it."
I crush my cigarette,
stretch out on my bunk,
and bleed to sleep.

After Thanksgiving

Monday in prison,
I live
steel thoughts
and the concrete reality of time.
Keys jangle

and I rise.
Standing barefoot in my cell
I watch
Jimmy come shuffling by,
shaved head,
escorted by guards,
followed by priest,
making his way
toward eternity's chair.
Briefly our eyes meet
and exchange a thousand
        screaming words:
Life is too short to burn.

Easter

With captured friends
beneath the dull coolness
of a concrete sky
I sit and sweat
inwardly.
Drenched in bitterness,
smelling of remorse,
we tug and strain
under laden backpacks
of unwanted time.
God, if only,
damn it if only
we could give it to the dead
we could all be
resurrected.

1979, Rustburg Correctional Unit 9
Rustburg, Virginia

After Almost Twenty Years

Chuck Culhane

for Judge Rose Bird*

This is getting difficult.

Perhaps there's another formula
    for happiness and contentment
    I haven't explored or exhausted yet.

But I talk to birds.
I have to put in my partial plates tho
w/tip of index finger fanning wet lips

      do it!

    the sound near-identical
      which amazes me.

Recently the birds woke me up
    with their clamorous love
      wings beating around the bars and glass
        in animated flight
jailbirds in the rush of lusty spring.

I was barely awake, grumbling at my broken sleep
then somehow drawn out
    into the quiet light
    sitting on the side of my bed.

And there they were
    two of em
      beaking it up!
Oh! I could've fallen into curled glee

---

* Chief Judge of the California Supreme Court, voted out of office in 1986 after frequently reversing death sentences.

wound with the spring's redemption.
And the nest already built
   under the highest beam in the block.

   1988, Sing Sing Correctional Facility
   Ossining, New York

There Isn't Enough Bread

Chuck Culhane

With the small birds
the sparrows and the grackles
there seemed enough bread
to stave off the fighting and death.

Then the gulls came
hollow desperate and shrieking
replacing the peaceful feeding rituals
with survival's bare wings
beating at the windows.

   1981, Attica Correctional Facility
   Attica, New York

The Manipulation Game

Doing Life in Pennsylvania

Diane Hamill Metzger

If you are serving a life sentence in Pennsylvania's prison system, you should be well acquainted with the game I'm about to describe. If not, it's not hard to learn. The only rules are to have enough hope in happy endings to be gullible and to want something so badly that you'll grasp at any straw. The game is called the Manipulation Game, and this is how it goes.

You're arrested for the crime of murder in the first or second degree. It really doesn't matter if you did it or not, or what your degree of involvement was, because when you go to court, chances are good that you'll be convicted. Let's face it: Any self-respecting jury member *knows* that if the cops *say* you did it, you *did* it. So, the verdict comes in and, with it, a sentence of life in prison, mandatory in Pennsylvania. (Either that or death — are the two different?) And now, my friend, you are a *statistic*. You can never have work-release. You can never have a furlough, not even at Christmas, even though your buddy with ten to twenty for third-degree murder ("plea-bargain murder") just won one. You are the best player on the prison softball team, but don't expect to go to any away games (though those not doing life are going). You have earned your college degree, but don't expect to go to graduation (although the baby-killer with ten to twenty went to hers). Your mate may be doing time in another prison, but don't ever expect visits. Your whole family may die, but don't expect to go to the funerals. *But,* if you've got to go to court to get more time, they'll sure let you off of the prison grounds for that! Or if you're breaking your back at eighteen cents an hour on the prison farm crew, that's *different!* After all, you are a LIFER! That label makes you more "dangerous," more of a risk than any other kind of prisoner — no matter what the others are here for, or plea-bargained their sentences down to. None of the good you've ever done, are doing, or will do will change that. If you are innocent of the crime, in the eyes of the state and society you are guilty. If you are guilty, the remorse you may feel, the desire to change your life around — they don't matter, either. You owe time to the state. An infinite time. In Pennsylvania, that time amounts to an average of twenty-three years, usually more. The average is going up, and the slogan "Life means life" is becoming a chilling reality. As a Pennsylvania lifer, you are now four times more likely to die in prison than to ever be released. After all, by taking your life and turning it into a living death, the state and society will give meaning to the life of your alleged victim: an eye for an eye, a tragedy for a tragedy . . . right? You begin to consider taking drastic measures — maybe suicide, maybe escape, maybe a descent into madness . . .

But wait! They tell you that you have hope. Your lawyer can put in an appeal with the Pennsylvania Superior Court. So you wait . . .

You've been in prison seven years now. Your appeal has been denied. But wait! They tell you that your appeal can go to the Pennsylvania Supreme Court, and you can win a new trial. So you wait . . . You really want to do the right thing. You have patience.

You've been in prison for nine years now. They say the wheels of justice grind slowly. You heard from your lawyer today: Your appeal was denied. It's time to look at alternatives, drastic alternatives. But wait! They tell you not to be a fool. You have nine years in, nine "good" years. File a P.C.R.A [Post Conviction Relief Act]! Get back into court. So you do; you have a hearing and you wait . . .

You've been in prison for twelve years now. Oh yeah, your P.C.R.A. was denied some time back. Thoughts of *taking* your future back enter your mind . . . but wait! They tell you to file for commutation of sentence with the Pennsylvania Board of Pardons. So you begin the long, soul-killing process of applying for clemency.

Your case was heard by the Board of Pardons for the second time. You were denied, again. You look back on the fourteen years you've wasted, years you can never get back . . . But wait! Don't be a fool, they tell you. You've put in fourteen years now, and it would be crazy to throw them all away. You're always turned down for commutation the first couple of times. Try again in another couple of years. So you wait . . .

You've been in prison eighteen years now. You've been denied by the Board of Pardons for the third and fourth times. This has gone far enough; it's time to do things *your* way now. But wait. They ask you how you could even consider throwing away eighteen years. Try commutation again in a couple of years. When you have twenty years in, you'll have a *real* good shot. So you wait . . .

You've been in prison twenty years now. The Board of Pardons denied you again. They want more time out of you. After all, you're asking for *mercy.* When you first came to prison, the average time done on a life sentence was between eleven and fifteen years; it's almost double that now. You've done all that was expected of you, and more, but they've kept changing the rules on you. Maybe you're too tired to think of alternatives now . . . but *no,* damn it, you've had *enough.* But wait! *Twenty years!* You're almost there, they tell you. Don't throw it all away! So you wait . . .

How long *do* you wait? When should the waiting end? At seven years, fifteen years, twenty years? Your children are grown now. Your parents have passed away. Everything out there has changed, and you're just too damned tired and empty to start all over again, and maybe too old . . .

The manipulation game is an insidious game. Its perpetrators are those in power, maybe even your own family and friends play their parts, and the object of the game is to dangle the carrot, that hope of freedom, endlessly, until with each passing year it seems more and more foolish to risk blowing the time you have accumulated, the time you have *wasted* . . .

Hope is a beautiful thing, *if* you are one of the very few lucky ones in this game of political roulette and you make it out. But if hope turns out to be fruitless, then it becomes destructive — a tool used by the vicious to control the helpless.

Tell me, where do you draw the line?

1994, State Correctional Institute Muncy
Muncy, Pennsylvania

Giving Me a Second Chance

Larry Bratt

The jury deliberated for fifty minutes before delivering their guilty verdict against me. With their decision thirteen years ago, I was convicted of murder and sentenced to spend the rest of my life behind bars.

Since then, I have witnessed the ugliest side of what prison life can be about: the fear and mistrust, the violence and chaos, the isolation and emptiness, the hollowness of spirit that at one point brought me to contemplate suicide. But in these last few months, a setback of the worst kind has gripped me. Maryland governor Parris Glendening has said that, except in extraordinary circumstances, he will not consider parole for violent offenders who have received life sentences. He may not realize it, but in the eight months since he rendered that decision, the governor has drained the state's prison culture of a crucial, if intangible, element: its sense of hope.

This may seem insignificant to those on the outside, but in the steel-and-concrete world of the Maryland penitentiary system, it is everything. The tension and fears that have been set off since Glendening's decision are almost palpable, not just among those of us serving life sentences, but even among other prisoners who, strange as it may sound, have come to look upon us lifers as role models.

From the perspective of those inside the prison, it seems like there's a new breed of mean-spiritedness among politicians, and more of a concern with public opinion polls than rehabilitating criminals. The problem is that, if the governor's goal is really to reduce crime and target those most apt to commit it, Glendening wouldn't be going after lifers. Why? Because, perhaps surprisingly, we're not the most dangerous felons behind these walls.

Indeed, according to research conducted by the Maryland Department of Corrections, young felons go through a natural maturation process. By the time they reach their late thirties to early forties, these once-radical youngsters tend to drift away from criminal behavior. For those who committed a violent act when they were young and have been in prison a long time, there is often a realization that bucking the system is futile.

I see this in my own life, and the statistics bear it out. Recidivism rates are much lower for felons who serve ten or more years at one time than they are for those repeat offenders who do life on the installment plan — serving numerous shorter sentences over a long stretch of time. In fact, from 1978 to 1987, seventy lifers were paroled in Maryland; only five returned to prison, according to the correction department's *Parole Release Rates for Life Sentenced Inmates.* According to the state's Department of Public Safety, this compares with a recidivism rate of 47 percent for the prison population as a whole.

So why isn't this kind of data reflected in the policies that emerge from the governor's mansion? It's hard to find any plausible answer except politics: The public wants to feel safe, and politicians offer up simple solutions.

I know from my own experience that most lifers who have spent twelve or more years behind bars are no longer even thinking about crime. Most of us have taken the initiative and are motivated, despite our tribulations past and present, to transform ourselves into mature, productive human beings. We've been told that if we worked hard, and followed the rules, that the system would work fairly for us, as it does equally for law-abiding citizens outside these walls. We had to earn parole, they told us. But it was possible, something to work for.

Now that's changed. Since Glendening's new policy was announced last fall, none of the 110 lifers living here at the Maryland Correctional Institution in Hagerstown have won parole. And though there is less hope, we haven't reacted with anger and rage at being betrayed by the system. There is still the possibility of parole under special circumstances, for the very old or terminally ill, for example, but the chance of any of us winning parole is greatly diminished, since the parole commission can release anyone serving a limited sentence, but any parole of a felon serving life must be approved by the governor.

In my case, I was convicted of a double homicide in 1983 and am scheduled to have my first parole hearing in 2006. Although I maintain my innocence, I readily confess that my life on the streets was undisciplined, unfocused, and out of control. And I accept that I am in prison for being a threat to society, and to myself. But having been incarcerated now for fourteen years, I can say unequivocally that I want to change my life. I have remorse not only for the wasted years of my youth (I'm now fifty-four) but for the deaths of the two people I was convicted of killing. And as a result of these feelings, I have made a commitment to never again repeat a malicious act.

And so, when the time comes, I think I should be considered for parole, and so, apparently, did the judge who sentenced me or he wouldn't have allowed for the possibility. In 2006, when I will have the opportunity though by no means the certainty of parole, I will be sixty-four years old and will have served twenty-three years in prison. And for every year I've been in, I've been sustained by the hope that I might one day earn my release — until now.

Like many others, I'm simply trying to show I'm worth a second chance. Even when the rules were changed midstream, most of us have continued to work on our rehabilitation, through education, vocational training, psychological counseling, whatever we can find. In effect, our faith and perseverance demonstrates our iron will to change our lives. It is perhaps this strength of character among lifers that has turned us into positive role models and mentors to those inside the Wall. People on the outside don't realize this, and clearly the governor doesn't, but it's true.

The lifers I live with in Hagerstown are involved in all kinds of projects to better themselves and the community. Obviously, they have made terrible mistakes in their lives and some have been convicted of heinous crimes. It's also true that not every lifer is sincerely committed to getting back on track. But by and large, my experience shows, a lot are. Douglas Scott Arey singlehandedly puts out the prison newsletter that serves as the center of information for our community. He's also the only prisoner in the state who earned a master's degree while in prison. Jeffrey Kersey, another lifer, acts as our in-house social activist by working with members of a prisoner self-help organization — Lifestyles — and by writing letters on behalf of lifers to politicians and community groups throughout the state. Another man, David Belton, has written a book about his conversion to Christianity and continues to serve as a guiding force in the institution's drug and alcohol abuse programs. I, myself, have chosen a more spiritual path of resistance. Through yoga and meditation I have discovered that kindness is a virtue respected by others and not a weakness.

By doing all this, lifers have effectively challenged younger prisoners to become the kind of men who command rather than demand respect. We help the younger men pursue their education, resist negative peer pressure, and gain self-awareness and understanding.

I, for one, plan to continue on with my struggle. What I worry about is whether other lifers, who for two or more decades have worked to rehabilitate themselves, will simply surrender to the loss of hope. With the reality of no parole for lifers and the possibility of no parole for violent crime offenders, what could life inside the prison be like?

One lifer here, who goes by the initials M.C., received his first parole hearing for a homicide three years ago, but now sees little chance of ever getting out. It has affected his spirit: "As long as a man has hope, the authorities have control. They destroyed hope. Unfortunately in time they may learn a man with no hope becomes a desperate soul," he told me.

Michael Tully, serving a life sentence for homicide, has had an even worse time. Since Glendening's announcement, Tully has lost his family support group. His wife has asked for a divorce, and he has lost all contact with his family. If not for the support of his friends in prison, who've encouraged him not to lose hope, as he says, "I would have flipped out and resorted to ancient self-destructive habits."

That is something all of us should pray never happens. If it does, our state's prisons are going to become pits of despair that make conditions today look mild: rampant drug use, assaults, even murders will become commonplace. Both prisoners and officers will live in jeopardy. We shouldn't forget that the majority of the prisoners I live with, maybe not the lifers but the others, will someday be released. And we should think carefully about what we want to teach them before that day arrives.

1996, Maryland Correctional Institution–Hagerstown
Hagerstown, Maryland

Myths of Darkness: The Toledo Madman and the Ultimate Freedom

J. R. Grindlay

Before the darkness fell, I used to sit on the edge of my bed looking out at the starless sky pondering meaningless abstractions, sipping halfheartedly at my instant coffee and reading the prophecies in *The Book of Doom*. I've always been moody — it seemed a proper state of mind for an artist. Except when I was being Dylan Thomas or Norman Mailer — then there were always parties and shouting and loud music. It's difficult to carry on when you have to view each action through the eyes of a future biographer. Have to keep it interesting, yes, you owe that to generations of future readers. There's nothing worse than reading those dead, dry biographies of men whose bodies crumbled to dust and ash long before they ever died. Now that the darkness has come, it's all a lot easier: Nobody can read in the darkness, ergo, I am free.

So strange, to stumble across freedom in the darkness — the way you'd trip over the coffee table in the room while fumbling for the light switch . . . Actually, it wasn't that simple — for me, anyway. I've always been a little slow at such reasoning. The Toledo Madman explained it all to me, one day sitting out on the yard, throwing pebbles at the fence. The Toledo Madman isn't really a madman, that's just the disguise he wears to help him serve his time. But since he's serving two consecutive life sentences, it's a role he has a lot of time to perfect. Sometime, not so long ago, he had another name, and once in a while a new hack in the cellblock will try to call him that. But he never answers to it. The rest of us just call him Toledo or Madman. Most of us have forgotten his old name anyway. What's the use of saving up scraps of dead information?

We used to go out on the yard to exercise and run the track, just to keep in shape. After that, we'd sit around on the grass, talking and throwing pebbles at the fence. Everyone throws pebbles at the fence. They've got little mercury switches on the fence that set off an alarm in the towers when something jiggles it. When you hit it just right with a pebble, the tower hacks slide back their windows and pop their heads out, looking up and down the wire, suspiciously eying the sparrows perched on it, as if wondering, maybe, if the sparrows and robins are working with us in some great conspiracy.

The Toledo Madman actually did have a plot worked out for an escape, using the sparrows. He took bread out on the yard every other day for six months, once, feeding the sparrows, coaxing them. We tried to tell him, but you can't tell the Madman anything, once he's got an idea in his head. He just kept feeding them and coaxing them. And they kept taking his bread and looking serious, then laughing at him behind his back — little groups of them would gather over on the fence after he'd gone back inside, you could see them talking it over and laughing. He got the idea from the Polack. The Polack caught a bumblebee in between his window and screen. When it had finally exhausted itself, trying to batter down the window, he slipped a loop of thread around it. If you've never seen a bumblebee on a ten-foot thread leash, you won't really appreciate the commotion it caused when he walked into the dayroom with it. The Polack loved commotion, anyway. He used to fashion fake turds out of wet toilet paper, using dirt to dye them brown, and leave them on the hacks' chairs or in the chow hall or next to the TV in the dayroom. The Toledo Madman fed the sparrows for six months, getting ready to try his plan. Finally the day came and he made his try. It had a limited, partial success. The sparrows all escaped okay. The hacks took the Toledo Madman off to the hole for six months. Now he throws pebbles at the fence and at the sparrows. They sit on the fence, mostly out of range, and laugh at him. But he told me that he's been practicing in secret, in his cell at night, getting his arm in shape for longer throws. The sparrows' days, he assures me, are numbered.

The Toledo Madman used to hang with Burnout — they were road-dogs for years, like flawed carbons of the same copy. Except that Burnout had a habit of looking like a demented Chinaman. He had a silk robe with a huge dragon flying across the back, imprinted over a yin-yang, its tail curled like a spiked whip. You'd walk by his cell and he'd be sitting in the dark, reading by the light reflected off his shaved head. He used to shave his eyebrows, too. Not completely, just at each end, tapering them to points. And his Fu Manchu mustache and scraggly gook beard. He took a secret delight in sitting there, where the darkness hid him, in a full lotus, looking for all the world like some inscrutable, insane old Buddhist monk.

You'd see the two of them walking off to chow, heads together — the shaven inscrutable head nodding to meet the nodding flurry of the

Madman's head. And the piercing cackle of their laughs, like two old cannibals reminiscing over the succulent child-flesh of their past. An unnerving pair, wild eyes hidden behind dark glasses. Like brothers of a different flesh.

Then, one spring, you could see a new wildness in Burnout's eyes — like an eagle that's caught sight of a mouse in an open field. He began to circle. It was plain to all of us, and most painfully to the Toledo Madman, just what sights were lurking behind those wild eyes and stares. There was a new earnestness and depth to the way the two of them talked. You could see the madman goading Burnout into strange laughs and wary answers. In the back of the library, they argued at loud length about unheard subjects. Finally, in desperation, the Toledo Madman smuggled his pet mouse, in his kite-can cage, down to Burnout's cell. As time went by, I'd get up in the middle of the night and walk to the front of my cell to take a leak. And across the way, there was a strange aurora of light and color in Burnout's cell, emanating from those mad eyes. And I could feel and hear Toledo standing there, in the cell next to mine, helplessly watching for hours on end.

After they pulled Burnout off the fence the first time, they sent him out to lunch — put him on Thorazine, those huge doses they forcefeed you like a turkey before Thanksgiving. The zombies are everywhere, the smile, the blank-eyed stare, you go out to lunch and wake up in some distant someday when you're ready for release.

But Burnout wasn't just another zombie, he was a crafty old Chinaman trapped in a strange body. He managed to vomit up a dose, one day. And went to the Toledo Madman for help. Toledo agonized, but zombies don't have road-dogs in their hazy dreamworlds. So to help was better than letting them trash Burnout's mind.

Every day for a week, Burnout was there with a smile when they came to pump him full of his Thorazine. And an hour later, the Toledo Madman would appear at Burnout's cell with a handful of Dexedrine. You could see the mad glint in those eyes again, fiery and confident, floating like a song of love in the summer air, as he paced his cell for hours. The air was as thick and electric as the hour before a thunderstorm, that week, while Burnout kindled a fire in his mind and a rage in his body, beyond knowing.

They never had to pull him off the fence, that second time. His body leaped and danced up off of it and landed like a lost rag doll a few feet away. And he crawled over and grasped the wire in both hands, trying to pull himself up, while the hack fired at him and people were scattering like ducks and I stood there next to the Toledo Madman, watching his shoulder bunch up and tremble under the strain of standing there like it was all happening in a movie a thousand miles away, beyond the reach of any arms to help and hold. When the jeeps pulled up outside the fence and the tower hacks stopped shooting, he turned and looked at me across all the many miles, with his eyes shining behind the dark glasses, as if all the world was plain to see and nothing he could say would add a lick to it. Then he walked off, back to his cell, stopping on the way to retrieve Hercules, his mouse, from Burnout's cell.

I stayed in my cell most of the next week, as if food and death were hard to swallow at the same time. And the idea of going back on the yard right away seemed obscene, like fondling your best friend's mother. The Toledo Madman, on the other hand, was the same as ever. He even was on the crew that raked and sifted the dirt where Burnout got wasted, to get rid of the bloodstains. Me, I sat in my cell, tasting the horror and trying to fit it into poems.

Eventually, you hit the gearshift and find it all remains the same. It wasn't anything when I came up out of hiding, just the same old shit. None of the James Cagney anger seeping through the place, building up to a cry for vengeance. Just card games and working out and walking the yard.

It was somewhere around there that I was sitting on the yard, rapping with the Toledo Madman, throwing pebbles at the fence, and he told me about freedom. Not the usual jabber about hitting the street to be free, because a man can be more free inside the fence than any square john out there can ever understand or begin to suspect.

You take a place, a hard-nosed max joint like our happy little home, with all the security systems they've been able to figure out, all the nice electrical gadgetry and Big Brotherhood, where you can't help but hate the hack and you get nothing more than the minimal requirements of survival. Nobody expects anything of you and there's not a thing they can take from you. That's freedom. The things that bind and prison a man are his own hopes and fears. When you've surrendered them, there's no way they can ever hold you, there's just no way for them to grab hold of you.

So it's all a question of sitting out the darkness, sitting here in the cell that's a cave and a dark womb, knowing the darkness that lives like a sad fire on an empty hillside where the gathered masses have at last fallen silent and the dead past has no more reality than all the songs trailing across the air.

The Toledo Madman is gone now. Eventually he became so free of all this lurking darkness that he sat in the back corner of his cell for hours, then days, at a time, radiating a warmth and brightness that pushed back the edges of the night and all of us here in the cellblock could begin to see. The hacks began to tremble a little, just to have to walk past his cell; to meet the placid smile and feel the glow of his eyes on them. They finally took him back there for two weeks — guy coming out of there said the hacks were beating him every night, trying to put out his lights. Anyone in the place could've told them they were throwing water at the sun, but they never bothered to ask.

Two weeks of that was enough — that infuriating smile that branded them while they were breaking their shitsticks over his shoulders and head, they couldn't take that — a knife in the balloon. It's hard to hit a man who doesn't cringe or cry out or at least hate you. They called it madness — the Toledo Madman in the full radiant glory of his time-disguise! — and shipped him off to a place where the shrinks could look at him and not feel the eyes of a hundred cons like shanks pressing at their backs, questioning them every second.

I got a letter from him yesterday. He said the damn sparrows followed him up there and they sit on the fence, laughing at him still. And he asked about Hercules — who I flushed down my toilet two days after they shipped the Madman out. This is no life for a cute little mouse like that.

1975, London Correctional Institution
London, Ohio

Routines and Ruptures

Learning to do time, according to PEN writers, is to weather a series of harsh lessons. New prisoners often refuse to accept their actual surroundings and cling emotionally to lost realities — for men, typically, the world of the streets, for women the family. The dream of early release — through legal relief or otherwise — dies hard and typically leaves depression in its wake.

By stages prisoners acknowledge their new surroundings and adapt to prison culture. When they settle in, many — especially long-termers — survive by structuring their lives around religion or some other productive or creative activity. For some men, doing time means aggressively pursuing their appeals or entering into lawsuits protesting their conditions. For others, it means, according to one writer, "giving in or buying in to the jailin' lifestyle of pumping iron, hanging with gangs, kicking back." Women take to the courts less frequently. And, where men find protection, identity, a sense of belonging, and companionship in gangs, women find these more often in multigenerational surrogate families.

Meanwhile, daily institutional routines — like the count, work shifts, meals, yard time — supplant habits and expectations people bring from the world outside. For better or for worse, they order the prisoner's day. But some routines, like the delivery of mail, permit a recipient like Jimmy Santiago Baca a fleeting transcendence of all constraint.

Nature, too, has routines that can't be entirely locked away. New seasons, breaking the routines of old seasons, also color prison routine and may convert a prison guard into a dreaming fisherman, as in Michael Hogan's "Spring."

Prisoners' performances, displays of personality by which they assure themselves of their own humanity and put their personal stamp on their surroundings, can also be called routines. Thus a new inmate, like Lori McLuckie's "Trina Marie," flaunts her style in an effort to navigate the enigmatic new society and discover whom she can trust, while clinging to fantasies of happiness. In "After Lights Out,"

Barbara Saunders sets such brave performances against the real —
and routine — threat of predators. Doing time is made of uneasy combinations of such competing routines.

Music can evoke familiar worlds of freedom and their cherished
routines. The beat of a conga drummer in D Yard stirs the answering
rhythms of poet Raymond Ringo Fernandez. *"Contratiempo con el
tiempo"* — one beat, one time, one way of doing time calls up
another, and the dissonance of a lone instrument in "culturally
deprived" Attica plays against the many-voiced harmonies of a
Nuyorican jam-session and home. "Lies and gossip"* (as Fernandez
characterizes prison discourse in another poem) are routines that help
domesticate steel-and-concrete corridors. "In the Big Yard," by
Reginald S. Lewis, catalogues the competing routines of yard gossip
circa 1988. His poem ends with a tribute to Pops, the runner who has
seen it all and acts as guide. But by 1997, the survival of a similar old
con is menaced by the heedless young in Patrick Nolan's poem "Old
Man Motown."

Inherent in all routine is the possibility of its rupture. Prison routines are shadowed by the mental mutinies that would destroy them.
Hostility between prisoner and guard becomes reflexive, along with
the repression of rage — and other feeling — in both. In Scott
Antworth's "The Tower Pig," institutional routine is ruptured by a
brief venture of keeper and kept into free air; the encounter between
these two very different prison-hardened characters permits a slight
but crucial opening, a moment of surprising recognition. In Daniel
Roseboom's "The Night the Owl Interrupted," an alternative utopian
solidarity briefly emerges with the near-miraculous intervention of
nature. It provides the men inner fortification against the return to
institutional routine.

Spring

Michael Hogan

Ice has been cracking all day
and small boys on the shore
pretending it is the booming of artillery
lie prone clutching imaginary carbines.

Inside the compound returning birds
peck at bread scraps from the mess hall.

Old cons shiver in cloth jackets
as they cross the naked quadrangle.
They know the inside perimeter is exactly
two thousand eighty-four steps
and they can walk it five more times
before a steam whistle blows for count.

Above them a tower guard dips his rifle
then raises it again dreamily.
He imagines a speckled trout
coming up shining and raging with life.

> 1975, Arizona State Prison–Florence
> Florence, Arizona

Autumn Yard

Chuck Culhane

I sit bundled in the peaceful sun.

To my right, a slip of colored sail
  goes downriver
   behind the old death house.

Two prisoners circle a dirt path
    bordering a green field
    double-fenced and walled
    with liberal layers of barbed wire.

Buck, a Lifer, works on the bars
    doing chins and dips
    building his house trim and strong
    against the long years.

George, hands scrunched in wordless pockets
    walks with recent loss
    of his young brother.
    We nod hello, and faded pennants
    snap in the wind along the fencetop.

    1985, Sing Sing Correctional Facility
    Ossining, New York

Letters Come to Prison

Jimmy Santiago Baca

From the cold hands of guards
Flocks of white doves
Handed to us through the bars,
Our hands like nests hold them
As we unfold the wings
They crash upward through
Layers of ice around our hearts,
Cracking crisply
As we leave our shells
And fly over the waves of fresh words,
Gliding softly on top of the world
Flapping our wings for the lost horizon.

    1976, Arizona State Prison–Florence
    Florence, Arizona

Trina Marie

Lori Lynn McLuckie

Walking down the prison hallway
With your scarlet-lipstick Norma Jean smile,
Green eyes inviting;
Deliberately so.
A woman-child
With translucent white skin
And the impetuous manner
Of a street child
Who knows the drill;
How to smoke cigarettes
And see people for what they really want from you.

These gray walls,
These dirty floors,
This cynicism and despair
Set off
Your vivacious and vulnerable glow;
And the deep gruff sounds
Echoing between these stark walls
Are mere background to the clear
Sweet tones of your childlike voice;
To your bold laughter
That defies anything less.

You forge your way
Through this confusion every day,
Burning your candle at both ends
And loving at whim;
Not quite sure
Who to count on,
What is solid
Or what you want to be solid.
And in your concrete room at night,
Among your cigarettes and lipstick tubes,
Your letters and pictures,
You sit on your steel bunk

And wonder when you'll be able to settle down
To that one great love
You have always imagined.

1991, Colorado Correctional Institution for Women
Cañon City, Colorado

After Lights Out

Barbara Saunders

Lonely, all angles and bones
knobs and knees and
eyes like saucers.
Fat Nugie, a billiard ball
in a baseball cap and
tennis shoes.
Rhonda, the 400 pound flasher
letting it all hang out
"not shamed o' my body."
Pie, strippin' and dancin' and
swinging a towel
and mooning the C.O.
as he walks away.
Night wraiths.
Dancers in the dark.
Forms move together, coalesce
separate and re-form.
Some singing, some laughter.
The scurry, the sneaking.

Predators come silently in the night
and whisper
"come with me."
Those who watch
immobilized, struck

dumb
pretend not to know
pretend not to see.

1997, Eddie Warrior Correctional Center
Taft, Oklahoma

poem for the conguero in D yard

Raymond Ringo Fernandez

on warm summer evenings
i hear the tumbao
of your sky blue conga
declamando
carrying your inspiration
over the wall
like a refreshing
caribbean wind

if it weren't for
the culturally deprived minds
in the gun towers
i'd swear
i was in Central Park
chilling out
by the fountain
con un yerbo and a cold
can of Bud
or

tumbao: a Caribbean rhythm played on the conga; *declamando:* reciting; *un yerbo:* Nuyorican for a joint (marijuana; Sp. *hierba,* pron. "yerba"); *haciendo coro* at *un bembé:* singing in chorus at a jam-session; *repica vida:* make life ring (in hand percussion, hits in rapid succession are called repique); *contratiempo con el tiempo:* lit. counter-rhythm with the rhythm. (RRF)

haciendo coro
at un bembé
on 110th street
where even the children
understand clave:

cla-cla/ cla-cla-cla

repica vida conguero
contratiempo con el tiempo
que with each slap
on the conga's skin
you bring me closer
to home.

1982, Attica Correctional Facility
Attica, New York

In the Big Yard

Reginald S. Lewis

Rumors abound Inmate So-and-So done gotta parole date.
Last Monday, but sucker don't even
Know his woman done run off with "sweet Cadillac Willie"
Who spent her
    welfare check on gasoline an' blow on a new pair of skins.
An' that scary lil' wimp locks on B Block ain't cool, man.
Snitched on his rap-partner 'bout that rape-kidnap-homicide-
robbery back in '76.
Hit goin' down in the Big Yard.
    Stay away, Homey.
'Cause bookies layin' ten-to-one odds some lieutenant finds
    the rat with his head propped up on the end of a long shank.
When they find the body what they do is ship it home in a
    cheap plywood box, tag with his number on it swinging list
    lessly on his big toe an' a

"Whut have I done to deserve this?" look on his dumb ugly
face.
Other day seen new blood shambling through
    the reception gate talking loud an' all cocky like he Mr. T.
    So a big mean lookin' con doin' life for
        mutilating his pregnant wife walks boldly up to Young-
blood an'
whispers somethin' soft an' sweet to 'im an' next day Young-
    blood's lips are
        red an' glossy an'
    his hair is long an' straight an' he's switchin' 'round the Big
Yard
Like he Diana Ross
An' the big con man says, "Hot young punk for sale, y'all!"
Squinting into the sun, Old Man "Pops" say he been down so
    long he done lost count.
"Kinda git used to it afta while, son," Pops says: the big time
    hoods an' their paper Cadillacs on cruise control.
The Hos on the stroll down the endless lightless white-clay
    strip.
Crack junkies chillin' out on smoke-marshmallow clouds.
Pseudointellectuals over there rappin' about the struggle.
An' the hapless chorus of crooners tryin' to sound like the
    Temptations.
        Pops says he don't pay 'im
        no mind an' he ain't listenin'
Don't even care 'bout nothin' cause he ain't neva had a woman
    noway.
Old bones runs the Big Yard through
    Chugging along like a locomotive that neva stops.
Runs all day long —
Bookies layin' ten-to-one odds old Pops plannin' to fly right
    over the big wall.

    1988, State Correctional Institution
    Pittsburgh, Pennsylvania

Old Man Motown

Patrick Nolan

Old Man Motown
dances toe to toe
around the prison
exercise track
throwing jabs
as he bobs and weaves,
dressed in cutoff
denim shorts
and hard soled boots,
while young cons lie
like rock lizards
bemoaning the three
digit heat.

Old Man Motown
alone with his thoughts,
shoots short combinations,
counters blow for blow
with some imaginary foe,
his five-foot-five frame
heavy with age,
pushing forward against
the concrete upgrade
that emanates a wall
of rippling heat.

Old Man Motown
his raven wing skin
streaked white with dried
sweat, knees pulsing pistons
of determination — to see
this silver haired grandpa
with the blue cataract eye,
one can't help but smile
as he dances his dance
in the sweltering northern
California sun.

Old Man Motown
times have changed
The once noble beasts
of this barren Savannah
are almost extinct,
ravaged by the vicious sweep
of rat packs that make prey
of the aged, sick, and weak.

1997, California State Prison–Sacramento
Represa, California

The Tower Pig

Scott A. Antworth

"Caine!" One of the East Wing hogs called after me through the crash and clamor of lunch release. I couldn't even see the guy, lost as he was in the flood of inmates surging past him for the chow hall, but from the tone of his voice he had to be a block officer. Rookie guards actually take classes: Speaking with Authority 101.

"Caine!" he barked again because I was acting like I'd not heard him, trying to be just another face in the stampede. "Stop by the SOC office. Captain Kruller wants to see you!"

Subtle, I thought. Tell me that when I've got two hundred cons packed around me to wonder what business I've got at the Security Operations Center on a Saturday afternoon. No one goes to the SOC office for good news. Standard convict paranoia — who's ratting who out — is enough to get at least some of them thinking.

"Spell my name right when you give your statement." My neighbor, Hodgson, chortled from deep inside his walrus neck as he lumbered down the stairs.

"Sure." I sneered at his back. "You spell it how, d-i-c-k-h-e-a-," I began, but he was already gone.

Captain Kruller was six feet of spit-shine and razor-creased blues with a leathery hide looking like it'd been cut from a rhino's ass and Superglued over an Erector Set. He kept his Marine citations and ribbons velvet-backed and under glass on his office wall to let everyone know he'd perfected his bearing on Parris Island and not behind the walls of Thomaston.

"Come in, Caine," he said. He'd pulled my file before I showed up and glanced at my mug shot. "Take a seat," he said, to give us the illusion of familiarity. I'd been sitting on folding chairs and wooden stools for the better part of a decade. My ass didn't know what to make of naugahyde and cushions.

"I've got some bad news, John," he said. Suddenly we were on a first-name basis.

"Who was it?" I asked.

"Your grandmother passed away yesterday morning," he said, his hands flat and precisely spaced on the blotter in front of him. "I'm sorry," he added as if such sentiments were foreign to him.

"Thank you," I muttered, only half believing I'd said it. Please and thank-yous pass between cops and inmates like bricks through a keyhole.

"You're taking it well."

I said that I'd known it was coming. She'd been sick for a long time. Truth is, I wasn't about to show him anything. Pain, joy, worry — whatever can be denied them — are shielded away from them until the cell doors slam and we're secured in our solitude. I'd weathered my first chunk of grieving for Nana when she was still mostly alive. For ten days in the hole, I had nothing to do but hate Strazinski, the Tower Pig, for putting me there and to mourn a grandmother finally too sick to visit.

"I can let you call your folks," he offered, gesturing to the phone.

"Thanks anyway," I told him, figuring they wouldn't know what to make of me calling them. We had nothing to say.

"But they're letting you go to the funeral, right?" Hodgson asked, leaning against the bars of my house and trying to sound consoling. He could skip deftly from one prison heartache to the next as if they were footprints stenciled on a studio dance floor, but real world problems would always catch him short.

"Kruller told me I could," I said. "In full equipment."

"Are you shittin' me?" he whined. "Full equipment? You're minimum security, bro. They should give you a car to go up there, not chain you up like a, well, you know."

"That's what I told him. He just gave me his that's-just-the-way-it-is speech. Said it was up to me if I wanted to go or not."

I was sitting at the head of my bunk, my back to the wall, feeling like I should be doing something but not having a clue. Hodgson's company with Nana's hands so firmly on my shoulders was intolerable. I wanted to be left alone but knew the minute he wandered off I'd be crushed by the silence.

"It ain't right, Caine, chaining you up like that when you're so close to getting out." He shook his head in disgust, warming to his subject. He was back in familiar territory; inmates treated like dogs and pigs riding roughshod over us because they were the ones with the dimestore badges and the power-trip egos.

"Full equipment." He sneered, lighting another roll-your-own cigarette. "You know they're just busting your balls over Strazinski."

"Naw," I said quietly. "They're screwing with me because they can is all. The pigs like that friggin' Straz about as much as they do us. Did you ever see him when he's off that wall? They damn near shake their drawers loose acting like he's not there."

He grins his best Hodgson smirk, the one that looks like it's been slashed in with a rusty straight razor.

"It must be a stone bitch," he said, "to be a pig and have even your own kind think you're a piece of shit."

I figure that's why Strazinski stays up on the wall whenever he can, sequestered in North Post, the gun tower that commands the prison street from where the road arches inelegantly past the craft shop, from the cell house to the yard. The only times I've ever seen him among the living was when he was pulling extra shifts. He clings to the periphery when he's not on his wall, glowering disdainfully at the inmates and avoiding the knots of officers gossiping and playing grab-ass. He looks as out of place in a crowd as he must feel, pressing his back to the wall and trying to be invisible. Older cons will argue how long he's been the Tower Pig, but none deny he's been on that wall longer than most of us have been inside it. His brother officers, doing their eight hours in the towers and loathing their isolation, don't know what to make of him. He's a freak, just like the mental cases who stand in the middle of their cells for hours at a go, staring at nothing.

"You ever wonder what he's like at home?" I asked presently.

"All the time," Hodgson purred, waiting for me to bite. "The hell's the matter with you? I ain't thinking of him at all when I ain't got to. Besides, I don't figure he's any different there than he's here. Donnelson tells me his ol' lady ditched him years ago. He ain't got no kids. The friggin' guy must put in sixty hours a week. Might as well stick a cot in the tower and crash there."

"I didn't know he was married," I said.

"He ain't, at least he ain't been long as I've been here. You're getting sentimental on me, Caine. Save it for your folks. All that guy's done for you is get you ten days in the hole."

Hodgson was hoping he'd get a rise out of me. He knew I was thinking of Nana again and was doing his best to try and keep me distracted. "All I'm saying? You can go on thinking that their making you go to the funeral all chained up ain't got nothing to do with you and Straz, but they still thought enough of him to put you in the Seg Unit over it. You hear what I'm saying? Just because he ain't real popular with them doesn't change his being one of their own kind."

He was right, but I didn't want to be thinking of any of it; not pigs and inmates, not the last of my bridges over the wall collapsing with Nana's passing — things as unyielding as the metal bunk, bolted to the wall, on which I sat. I don't know how long he stayed there talking, jumping from one subject to the next. The more I listened, the more his voiced dissolved into a drone. I offered monosyllables and halfhearted grunts to try to convince him I wasn't shutting him out completely. Finally, he drifted off with a "see you in the morning" and a sympathetic thump on my bars. I listened to the scuff of his footsteps and then I listened to nothing, already dreading the caverns of a Thomaston night.

I would not cry for Nana, but I would want to, wringing myself out through the hours after lock-down with all the recriminations and should-have-been's chanting in my head. I'd shed all my tears in the hole and in the weeks before.

Though Hodgson blamed Strazinski for my stretch in the hole a month ago, I'd gotten myself in that jam. It began the day Cassidy, the aspiring vegetable — who'd huff dry cleaning solvent if it was the only way to get high — stalked into my cell and pulled out a joint the size of his finger. "You want to burn this with me, just say the word," he said, tossing a book of matches down onto the table like a dare. Cassidy's the kind of refugee who ambles through life like everything's casual, drifting in unannounced at the oddest moments to flash enough dope to get us both an extra year as if it were a candy bar. He must have tried to get me stoned fifty times through the year, but that day I didn't want to brood anymore about Nana wheezing from her hospital bed, those tubes in her arms, alone with the night. I didn't say no.

An hour later and on the way to the craft shop, anyone would have thought we were the best of buddies, telling war stories. I felt freer than I had in a very long time, bouncing down that road with a stoner jounce. I didn't feel the walls of Thomaston crushing me, leaving me unable to do more for Nana than wait for her to die.

Pausing at the foot of the craft shop stairs, out on the road and in the shadow of North Post, Cassidy was going on and on about this lady friend of his, a flaked-out hippie chick. I was digging it, and I was more interested in letting him finish than I was in getting upstairs to spend the afternoon acting like I was working. The river of inmates on their way to wherever had thinned to a trickle.

"You!" Strazinski roared from the wall above us, looking like he was having a raging hangover. "Yeah, you! How many times have I got to tell you people to get moving?!"

"Me?" I asked, my hands on my chest. I always play dumb with the pigs. It makes them nuts.

"Who the hell do you think I'm talking to, you moron?!"

"He's talking to us," I snickered, turning to Cassidy, but Cassidy had turned to vapor, bolting up the stairs when Strazinski started his tirade.

"What do you need, someone to hold your hand to get you upstairs? Or do you need to be locked in for the day? What's your problem, Caine?!"

"What my problem?" I shouted back at the wall, "What's your problem? I'm the one that's going to work and you're the one acting like a headcase about it. Go on back inside your tower, Straz. You wouldn't know real work if someone rolled it in sand and shoved it up your ass!"

His face, chalky and time-furrowed, went the sweetest shade of vermilion.

"That's it! God damn it, that — is — it! Back to the blocks! You're tagged in!"

Seething, I managed to laugh at him as I turned back for the cell house with him still raging behind me.

"Have a nice day!" I yelled back over my shoulder while I snatched at the waistband of my sweat pants. I figured if he really wanted to see my butt headed back for the blocks, he might as well get the fifty-cent view. So I gave it to him. Both sun-starved cheeks and a vertical smile to remember me by.

Reviewing my case a week later, the chairman of the disciplinary board actually giggled when Straz's statement was read into the record. It had been months since anyone had mooned an officer. But amusement didn't prevent him from finding me guilty of a Class B Provocation charge and giving me ten days in the hole to contemplate my sins.

I didn't cry for my Nana the night before her funeral. Neither did I sleep. I rolled and tossed and jerked in disgust on a mattress little wider than my shoulders until, exhausted, I lay very still and watched the night pass on the bricks of the cell house wall. Across the way the steam pipe sputtered on, spitting hateful secrets to the twilight. I knew all the accusations, chapter and verse. I could already hear the hissing murmurs of the dozen remaining in my family as they gossiped busily in the pew, darting glances over their shoulders at me, shocked that I'd been allowed to attend and not in the least bit surprised that

I'd disrespect my grandmother by showing up handcuffed to a chain around my waist, with a guard hovering to make sure I didn't bolt for the door. I could even hear the bolder ones giving me their glad-you-could-make-its and offering me their insincere bests after the service, convinced I'd never amount to more than all the hardware hanging off me. I couldn't blame them. Junkie thieves are rarely a prized seed among those who worked themselves to death for everything they owned. Every last one of them had given up on me a year before I managed to get myself thrown in Thomaston for a ten-year sabbatical.

Only Nana refused to surrender me to the void, for only she was too stubborn to let me go. She played ambassador right till the end, giving me all the family gossip and browbeating my parents into their annual Christmas visit, only to keep the conversation going when the silences got so thick you couldn't hack through them with a machete.

The morning of the funeral began with my toilet plugging up with the first flush of the day and ended with the intake officer wrapping a belly chain around my waist and cuffing my hands to it. Between was the chaos of scrounging and making do. I finally got something of a shine on my weathered biker boots and spent half an hour pawing through the wardrobe of the prison commissary until I found a suit that was a close-enough fit. Having found no needle for the thread I'd managed to scrape up, I tacked up the hems of the trousers with an office stapler.

"Caine," Strazinski greeted me curtly as I was escorted into the intake area to find him not in his uniform but in a proper suit at least a size too small. "You're with me. Strip."

No inmate enters or leaves Thomaston without a thorough strip-search. I've gotten naked for more cops than I have for former lovers. I stripped down mechanically, knowing the drill, all the while searching the room for someone else in civilian clothes, hoping this was some sort of joke. There were four officers in that room with me, and only Straz wore a suit. He'd pulled the short straw to be my escort home.

In the prison garage, he neither spoke to me nor looked me in the face. He held the car door open long enough for me to fumble into the back, then buckled the seat belt over me.

Strazinski wedged himself into the driver's seat, the wheel shoved into his starched white shirt, cleaving his belly. Growling and grumbling, he tried to adjust his seat, but the security mesh between us kept it permanently in place. He kept glancing into the mirror to see if I was amused by his predicament.

"It's going to be a hot one," he said, addressing me for the first time since I stripped for him in Intake. "When we get to where we're going, you might want to take that jacket off and carry it inside."

"I'll be fine," I told him. "It might get warm, but it still covers most of the hardware."

"Yeah, well," he said. "Kruller said full equipment, so you get full equipment."

I wanted to tell him to go screw himself as he pulled the Chevy into brilliant sunlight. By blaming it on the boss, he didn't have to admit he was loving it. I slouched against the door and rested my cheek on the glass, watching the cracked asphalt of Route 1 hurtle past with cars in the opposing lane racing east. We were better than two miles down the road before I realized it was me and not they who were moving too quickly, their rush amplified by my starved perceptions and by the years I'd been inside.

"I got a messed-up question," the Tower Pig said after we'd turned onto 17 and were torpedoing for Augusta and the places I once called home. "You do know where we're going, don't you?"

"You get us to Augusta and I'll get us to the church," I told him, wanting to rub his nose in his ignorance.

"Fair enough," he grumbled. "You've been away a long time, haven't you?"

"Eight years," I said, watching the trees whirr past in kaleidoscope glimpses. Eight years, five months, and . . . eleven days, I thought.

"Long time," he announced, studying me in the mirror. "I bet it ain't changed all that much, has it?"

"Not much," I muttered to the window, still watching the trees and the undergrowth rioting in so many forgotten shades of green, green in a flood, all so impossibly thick and lush. They could not have been this dense when I bounded through them like a deer, the black earth and wet leaves like a sponge beneath ten-year-old feet. Through the hum of the Chevy I could hear the summer cicada shrill, knifed through by the buoyant cries of half-remembered friends frozen in child-voices.

"No," Straz said presently, having thought it over. "Home never changes much."

I said nothing. My stare drifted from the window to the security mesh to the floor.

"I'm sorry about your grandma," he said.

I flinched. Back behind the walls, if he wasn't barking at inmates he may as well have been a mute. I didn't want him talking about her; I didn't want him talking. It seemed the farther we got from Thomaston the harder it was for him to keep his mouth shut and leave me to my silence.

"I lost my mother last year," he said quietly. "This stuff's the worst, but what're you going to do, right? Get up, go to work, do your time. It gets easier someday."

"I'm sorry about your mom," I offered weakly, looking at him for the first time in miles. I stared at the back of his head the rest of the way into Augusta, watching the roll of fat at the base of his skull, pinched by the threadbare collar of his jacket, and waiting for him to speak.

Like every other city in Maine, Augusta bounds from the urban to the suburbs to the sticks in seconds. The broad wedge of St. Andrew's — the Roman Church meets seventies architecture — is shoved into the spine of a knoll wreathed in the conifers and hemlock walling out the erratically spaced lots and sagging roofs from the proper monotony of homes with identical floorplans and freshly mowed lawns.

I watched the church growing from its hill, remembering the masses I attended with Nana and how we'd go out for ice cream afterward. I scanned the faces of the mourners moving solemnly up the narrow asphalt path toward the rectory, recognizing none of them. Dumpy white-haired ladies in orthopedic shoes and old men in homburg hats despite July like a blast furnace. These were Nana's friends, I reckoned, pinochle players and retirement community denizens, all the faces who gathered for twice-weekly High Mass and for all the funerals as their members slowly fell away.

In the lee of the hill, in the broad oval of the parking lot behind St. Andrew's, Strazinski hid the Impala in among the hulking Buicks and salt-rusted Toyotas.

"So this is it?" he asked, and craned his neck to study the shingled cliff of St. Andrew's south wall.

"Funny-looking church," he said, glancing back at me when I didn't comment. "I guess I'm just used to them big stone Franco churches they got around here."

"I think that's why I liked this place when I was a kid," I told him when he opened my door and the heat hit me like a wall. "It wasn't like everywhere else."

At the base of the wall, ignoring the mourners drifting past them from the parking lot and hiding from the padre, two altarboys in black cassocks and white bibs pecked at a forbidden cigarette as if the filter burned their lips. I tucked my wrists in closer to my waist and pinched the tails of my jacket in with my arms, hiding what I could of the chain. Straz stood off away from me, his hands parked on the roll where his hips should be.

"We going?" I asked.

"Give me your hands," he said presently, decisively, as he fished in his pocket for his keyring.

I flushed, exultant and trying not to show it, and shoved my wrists as far toward him as they would go, six inches from my waist.

"You shouldn't have to be going in there like this," he said as the cuffs popped free and he turned his attention to the padlock on the belly chain. The hot summer air chilled my wrists where the steel had been.

"I appreciate it," I mumbled as the chain fell away from my waist and Straz bundled it into the back of the car, leaving me standing there unfettered in my borrowed suit, like anyone else in the parking lot. For the first time in eight years I was on the right side of the walls of Thomaston and looking like a free man. Nana would have loved it.

"If you really appreciate it," Straz said, looking me in the eye, "you'll remember one thing: This never happened. If Kruller catches wind of this, then it's my butt that's hanging out. Still, no one should have to bury their grandmother chained up like that. Got it?"

"I got it. And, look, whether you believe it or not, it'll sure mean a lot to my family not seeing me like that . . . and maybe it means a lot to me, too, you know? Thanks."

His fleshy brow crinkled, not knowing how to take being spoken to like that.

"Yeah, well," he said, opening his jacket to show me the gleaming butt of his .38 in its cross-draw holster. "Just you remember that it's too friggin' hot for me to be running after you."

"I love you too, Straz." I grinned, stepping off for the path ahead of him.

Nana's casket was white and shone like ivory on its gurney before the altar. The priest had not yet made his entrance. There had to be a hundred people in there, massed in a semicircle around the coffin, lined up in the pews with their heads bowed. I could hear only the whispers of pages as the organist, hunched at her bench and hidden beneath her hat's broad brim, flipped through her hymnal, bid-ing her time. Strazinski dipped his fingers in the holy water at the door and crossed himself.

"What?" he whispered, catching me watching him. "You figure I got to be French to be a Catholic? Hell, even the friggin' Pope's Polish." Then his hand was on my shoulder. "Go on and sit with your folks. I'll be back here by the door. Don't get lost now."

Taking a seat by himself, he left me standing in the aisle at the back of the church, scanning those gathered for a place to sit. My family was assembled in the pews immediately in front of Nana. My father, grayer and more railish than he'd been when I saw him last Christmas, was the first to notice me. The wrinkles of his crow's-feet pinched, his eyes hardening as he whispered in my mother's ear. Her shoulders trembled and sagged. I could just hear her sobs from where I stood in the rear. I watched the news of my presence ripple from them and through the pews with quick curt glances and feverish whispers. My sister leaned more deeply against the husband I'd not yet met, the crown of her head in the ginger of his beard as he sized me up from over his shoulder.

Through the ride up from Thomaston, bouncing around in the back of the prison's Impala, I'd steeled myself up to march right in, ignoring my chains, and impose myself on them because that's what Nana would have wanted. I barely acknowledged them before I turned from them and slipped into the pew beside Strazinski, knowing she'd understand. He tensed awkwardly as I sat, then nodded sympathetically. I watched his vast bulk relax from the corner of my eye. He shook his head and watched the altar, waiting on the organist and "Just a Closer Walk with Thee."

1998, Maine State Prison
Thomaston, Maine

The Night the Owl
Interrupted

Daniel Roseboom

Dixon said he'd lost his pump already, curling his arms profoundly, scrutinizing the bulge of biceps. Big snowflakes fused to the burrs of his green knit hat and melted over his warm sweatshirts.

I let the heavy lid slap closed over the weight box and sighed at having made it through another cold routine. The winter workouts were becoming lethargic in the blinding spotlight beams of the prison yard. I inhaled and the air crystallized and tickled my moist nostril hairs.

"It's these cheap weights," Dixon said, squeezing out one last curl.

He was right. It was the futile equipment, the warped barbells and spurred cables and rusty plates. It was the wicked weather and the absence of motivation. Ultimately it was the monotony of prison ambience: the razor-wire fences, the dirt and concrete ground, the Great Wall stacked with gun towers resembling tiny huts lit with big round spotlights. It was a battle with confinement and fatigue.

A flock of pigeons perched on the Great Wall and the gun towers' shingled peaks. There was an instant ripple of feathers as they abruptly flapped away toward the black sky. It reminded me of when I used to go hunting with my father before my incarceration, when our presence in the woods was momentarily powerful and our prey sensed it fearfully.

I noticed other inmates closing up their weight courts and weaving through the maze of bulky weight boxes and machinery to get to the main yard. The routine was over and it was time to go.

I slipped into my state coat but left it unzipped, as did Dixon. It was imprudent to zip it, especially after a workout when one's muscles were tired and tight. It was wise to stay as loose and flexible as possible, ready for the unpredictable dangers in the political battleground of the main yard.

I followed Dixon off the weight court and we siphoned into the stream of inmates lumbering along the main walkway through the tables divided according to racial or political decree. They sat at tables or stood in a huddle around a television drinking cup after cup of coffee to stay warm, cheering as the last minutes of a football game ticked away. Others rapped in rhythmic harmony to a metal tabletop and snap of many fingers. Some merely waited, standing erect in the snowfall with their hands stuffed in warm pockets, rocking on their heels, wondering if the announcement to "return to the blocks" would ever crackle over the weathered speakers. The need to get into the prison blocks, into our cells, and beneath wool blankets always intensified as the cold long evening stretched on.

A damp snowflake settled on my eyelash and, just as I blinked to cleanse the blur, a feathered creature of brilliant white sailed across my path. I froze beside Dixon and other astonished inmates. The bird flapped its powerful wings and climbed to the prison block windows. It curled its steel talons into the wire mesh, adjusting thick wings against its body. Its feathery head bobbed and swiveled as it surveyed the area.

The yard was quiet. The eternal hype of rap lyrics, the shouts and whistles of football philosophy, the political arguments and subtle threats of inmate reasoning were all scooped up and tossed away. It was as if a magical wind had swept the yard of its life and carried it off to the dark sky, where it remained suspended, its essence lingering in bulky suspense.

I felt euphoric. My heartbeat thumped in my ears as adrenaline spurted into my bloodstream. Then suddenly the heavy bird plummeted down. Inches from the ground, its wings unfolded and caught a breeze that lifted it into a sensuous arc of freedom. Inmates parted for the bird's flight up the main walkway and then turned to watch it gracefully settle on the shingled peak of an officer's watch booth.

We gathered around the little booth and watched the owl twitch its wings. Shuffling its feet on the snow-dusted peak like a cat padding about a pillow, it found its perch. It curved its muscular neck and, with its beak, scratched the tuft of feathers on its chest. Then, with its dark round eyes, it looked at us and blinked.

Two officers inside the booth gazed at the hundred or more inmates encompassing their little haven.

"They look nervous," I said.

Dixon elbowed an inmate at his side and they grinned in unison at the two officers. Not long after, the announcement exploded from the rusty speakers.

"THE YARD IS CLOSED . . . RETURN TO THE BLOCKS."

The snow continued to layer our shoulders and hats as we remained steadfast. One of the officers spoke into a phone; the other twitched like a trapped mouse, eyes bulging and rolling from one group of inmates to the next. The officer hung up the phone and nodded to his partner.

If we refused to enter the blocks what would they do? What law were we breaking by watching a snow owl? Would they rush at us with batons and shields and beat down every last one of us? Would an officer emerge from the dark cove of the gun tower and fire hot bullets into our flesh?

Then I realized something very peculiar about this formation of inmates, this aggregation of whites, blacks, and Hispanics. We were a unit of power. There was no racial discrimination to inhibit our combined strength, no political force to determine what would go down. We were the elite of this cramped atmosphere, able to strike back if struck upon.

Inmates gazed with unblinking eyes at the fixed monument on the booth's shingled peak. I wondered if they, too, were aware of our power. Would this power emerge as a riot where a few would take charge and eventually lose, or would everyone participate and stand proud against the threat of the system?

"THE YARD IS CLOSED," the speaker crackled. "RETURN TO THE BLOCKS."

And they did. Inmates smiled at the great bird, shook their heads, then turned away and headed for the blocks. The powerful elite dwindled before my eyes. The suspense split and the elements we knew so well — prejudice, ignorance, self concern — sifted back down from the void like snowflakes onto our shoulders.

Dixon nudged my arm. "C'mon, Danny." He wiped the snow off his shoulders and gazed at the trapped officers. "We got ours."

I followed him up the slushy steps of our block and turned to look one last time. The two officers had emerged from the small booth and were now herding the last of the inmates toward the blocks. The booth stood detached from everything else.

On its peak snowflakes settled on the white owl that had provided me with an existential moment that would last forever. Dixon's last statement was now clear. I flexed my biceps and felt the swell of blood in the tight muscles: energy reborn.

An officer waved for me to enter the block. I realized he was one of those trapped from before. I smiled and nodded, then followed the last of the inmates into the reality of confinement.

1993, Auburn Correctional Facility
Auburn, New York

Work

You ought to come on the river in nineteen-four,
You find a dead man on ever' turn row.
You ought to been on the river in nineteen-ten,
They's rollin' the women, like they drive the men.
"Ain't No More Cane on This Brazis"

In the wake of the American Revolution, Quaker reformers repudiated the colonial practice of public and corporal punishment, creating in Philadelphia's Walnut Street Jail the first institution to combine isolated confinement with labor. The idea of extracting labor from prisoners took deeper hold than the notion of penance, especially after the abolition of slavery. Some historians argue that prisons have sustained slavery by other means. In his essay, "From the Plantation to Prison" (1990),* Easy Waters noted that the New York legislature considered bills on the emancipation of slaves and the creation of the first state prison on the same date in 1796. In "Chronicling Sing Sing Prison" here, Waters narrates the shipping of convicts, virtual "galley slaves," to build their own prison in the early nineteenth century.

In the South, too, the link between prison and slavery was more obvious. After the Civil War, the labor-lease system (whereby prisoners were leased to private contractors) sprang up. Leasing gave way to prison farms, some like Angola in Louisiana built on the former Angola slave plantation (named for the African origin of the slaves who worked it). As late as 1933, songs like "Ain't No More Cane on This Brazis," cited above, sung in a South Texas prison farm on the Brazos River, followed the pattern of slave work-gang songs. In Avoyelles Correctional Center, in Cottonport, Louisiana, the hard work, tension, and hair-trigger responses of keepers described in Michael Saucier's poems here evoke slave labor. Under these conditions, although the exercise of skill and concentration of mind can be steadying, the solace is short-lived and the aftertaste bitter.

Contract labor performed inside prison, initiated in the South, was taken up in the North around 1900 to help make prisons self-sustaining. But the labor movement's protests resulted in legislation containing industry in state prisons. UNICOR, the trade name for the Federal Prison Industries Corporation run by the U.S. Bureau of Prisons, whose employ is so desired by "Big Bird" and Colombian immigrants in Richard Stratton's story, is highly controversial. Founded in 1934, it now employs about 27 percent of all federal inmates and produces about $200 million in goods annually. Since 1990, thirty-eight states have legalized the contracting out of prison labor to private companies. This development has come just in time to help states dealing out more and longer sentences meet escalating costs of the new and expanding prisons. In a 1998 essay*, Larry Bratt writes that he has learned marketable skills and takes pride in his performance in his prison job in Maryland. Others, considering a larger context, criticize private prison industry and suggest that imprisonment is becoming a facile "solution" to the grave problems of poverty, poor education, unemployment, and racism.

Most inmates are assigned prison maintenance jobs, and it is not easy to find a prison job that is neither dehumanizing nor dangerous, let alone useful to the worker. But it is not impossible. In "Death of a Duke" (**Players, Games**), the protagonist has to exercise diplomacy to finagle a job that uses his skills and enables him to help his fellows. In Robert Kelsey's story here, the protagonist finds a niche that proves fulfilling to himself and others. Therapeutic programs can provide niches, as can academic or creative programs, which are described in the next section.

Chronicling Sing Sing Prison

Easy Waters

First on a canal boat
Later on freighter steamers
One hundred men made an historic trip
Down the Hudson River in 1825
They weren't called galley slaves
But they were weighed down with chains
They arrived in Sing Sing
The village named after the
Indigenous Sint Sincks
Popular history says they sold
Their land in 1685
The name, which has been interpreted
As "stone upon stone"
Is all that remains of those Algonquins
And the prison, of course
An awesome mausoleum
Peopled with 614 tombstones
Monuments to the Chair
But all of that was later
After the foundation stone was laid
The prisoners labored
To build their own cells
7 feet deep, 3 feet 3 inches wide
And 6 feet 7 inches high
What could be crueler
To dig their own graves
Or to suffer the added indignity
Of having the graveyard called
Mount Pleasant State Prison
Stone upon stone
Granite known as Sing Sing marble
Prisoners
Cutting stones for public corporations
Stones for a courthouse in Troy
Stones for the statehouse in New Haven
Stones for the city hall in Albany

Stones for Fort Adams in Rhode Island
Convict labor
Offered at a premium price
Working
From dawn to dusk
Cutting stone
Stone upon stone
Granite known as Sing Sing marble
Poor production severely punished
Shower baths
Hair cropped close
Darkened cells
Ball and chains
Yokes — long iron bars
Four inches wide
Weights up to 40 pounds
Strapped around the outstretched arms
Of the prisoners
With staples for neck and arm
An awesome burden
For crime — and punishment
Cutting stone
Stone upon stone
Granite known as Sing Sing marble
In 1926 more stone upon stone
Two more cellblocks
A capacity of 1,366
More than 2,000 total
In 1994, the gutted remains
Of the old Sing Sing stands
A monument to a time
The Stone Age
When prisoners were sent
Up and down the Hudson River
If you get close enough to the shore
To the granite known as Sing Sing marble
You can hear the ghosts of prisoners' past
Chronicling the history of Sint Sinck
Stone upon stone
Granite known as Sing Sing marble
The building hasn't stopped yet

Million-dollar contractors
Replace convict labor
Slowly dismantling the stone upon stone
Replacing it with fences
Triple-layered razor wire
Heat sensors around the perimeter
Perhaps a mine or two
Floodlights have it on center stage
Sing Sing on the Hudson
What an eyesore
An eerie monument
Boats on the river
No longer freighter steamers
No longer carrying prisoners
Galley slaves
But the memory remains
Shackled prisoners still call the buses that transport
Them to Sing Sing —
And all the other stone monuments —
Boats
Boats
Up and down the Hudson River
In early spring and throughout the summer
And on into fall
Boats
No longer peopled with convicts
But pleasure-seeking passersby
Boating
And water-skiing
And wind surfing
Beautiful women
Weighted down with two-piece bathing suits
Smile and wave and sometimes flash
As they dare to come close to the shore
Defying the guard towers
And the awesome history of the place
A punishment perhaps as cruel as the yoke
Watching their bare-back retreat
The waves lapping against
The stone upon stone
Granite known as Sing Sing marble

If you listen closely
You can hear the howls
Of the 614 people
Who walked the last mile
Step by step
Stone by stone
To eternity
If you listen even closer
Over the waves lapping against
The stone upon stone
You can hear the other howls
The howls of men enduring different punishments
Punishments nonetheless
Severe in their own way
In keeping with contemporary standards
Still
Some bang their heads against the stones
Stone upon stone
Granite known as Sing Sing marble
Still standing
A monument for the chronicler
To pull apart stone by stone

    1994, Sing Sing Correctional Facility
    Ossining, New York

Cut Partner

Michael E. Saucier

His eyes search among the hundreds of men
crowding the fence
for someone he's worked with before
or someone whose work he knows
who isn't afraid to catch his cut

    You got a work partner this morning?
    Yeah. Where's your boy?

Medical call-out.
Trying to get hisself a doody statik[†] , huh?
Yeah, the sell-out.
Go ask homes there. I hear his boy
got blocked last night.

Four inmates exit the toolshed
arms loaded with hoes
to chop clean a summer
of dirt, weeds, and trees;
dropped in a tangled heap on the roadside
his eyes run along the stout and steel,
trying to see the good ones

Free man spits a long red stream,
his signal . . . First five, pick 'em up.
He races with the others across the road
a flurry of black and brown, sun-peeled white hands
examine, choose, discard, choose another

> This one got a good, long handle, but
> the head be swiv'lin
> Handle here already split.
> Best drop that one, homes. Hit it wrong
> against one of those palmettos
> you'll be stuck out eight dollars, sure
> If it ain't my fault!
> Shi', free man don't care —
> figure nigger trying to get out o' work
> It'll cost you eight dollars, homeboy,
> or ten days on the rock . . . believe that.

In the second he has
he grabs the best two he can find
and returns to the line; cut partner looks worried
so he hands him his choice
Cut partner runs his thumb along the edge

> Dull, he says . . . but not as bad as that thing
> I had yesterday . . . bitch killed me.

† Doody statik: "duty status" is a medical exemption from hard work, good for a
day, a week, or longer. (MES)

They take bites and slices at the earth,
testing for sharpness
amount of energy that'll be required
then he remembers: today is file day
twice a week Sarge sends the file man around.
Hours pass. Finally he comes, lays a few, deep strokes
with the heavy rasp
the weeds, grass, palmettos, and thin willow trees
give easier, and it angers him —
the small joys he has had to settle for;
throughout the long, burned-up day
he mutters . . . what a waste . . . what a goddamned waste.

1991, Avoyelles Correctional Center
Cottonport, Louisiana

Gun Guard

Michael E. Saucier

The gun guard sits
squarely in the saddle
broiling in the Louisiana sun
silent atop his big red horse.

His eyes squint
through salt and sweat;
carefully maintains the proper distance
should he have to run us down
or shoot.

Meanwhile,
we chop chop chop
our hoeing has a rhythm
our mouths dry and dirty
the water cooler, empty
fewer words are spoken;
we're looking for the headland.

With his shotgun firm
against his hip
and Big Red hanging a droolin' lip
they're looking for it, too.

The gun guard's eyes sweep the line
alert to any disturbance;
carelessly, I take an extra step
his 12 gauge
pumps up — KA KLAK
steel-barreled voice, blue and hot
"Get off my guard line. NOW!"

Cut partner jerks me
back into the safety zone,
off the gun guard's holy ground
who
rubs Big Red
gently with a sweaty
palm "Whoa, boy . . . whoa, now."

> 1991, Avoyelles Correctional Center
> Cottonport, Louisiana

Skyline Turkey

Richard Stratton

No one saw the actual ascension. Big Bird — a huge black, well in his fifties — just appeared there one morning, roosting on the catwalk atop the lofty water tower in the middle of the compound. He made a nest of blankets and parcels and, like a bag lady, settled in for a long siege with magazines and his portable radio, perched in his rookery like some daft old crow who suddenly moves into the neighborhood.

"Reminds me a when I was in Texas," said the Old Con at breakfast.

We sat at our usual table in the front of the chow hall. In the limpid early-morning sky the water tower was silhouetted high above the buildings of the prison complex; we could sit sipping coffee and watching Big Bird through the window. It was an event, something to distinguish this day from hundreds upon hundreds just like it.

"Texas? When was you ever in Texas?" asked Red, who'd done almost as much time as the Old Con. They'd been together at Marion back in the sixties before that joint was locked down. They'd been together at Lompoc in California when that institution became a maximum-security penitentiary. Red had been in so long his full torso and arms were covered with intricate tattoowork that had faded and was sagging like a wrinkled old paisley shirt.

"They had them turkeys out there," the Old Con went on. "Big ol' turkey buzzards they called 'em."

"You was never in Texas," Red insisted. "Old fool's been in jail all his life."

"So? They got jails in Texas, don't they? An' prisons, too. Lots of 'em. You never heard of Huntsville? Rough stop. An' federal joints. La Tuna. Bastrop. Seagoville. I got out one time in Texas. Went to work out there in a place near San Antone. Yessir, turkey ranch, they called it. Had all these turkeys runnin' around a big fenced-in area, jus' like us. All day they'd hang out in flocks like waitin' for food. Then at night, I never saw 'em, but somehow they must a hopped up in the trees. Them scrubby little trees, live oaks, they call 'em, an' mesquite. 'Cause in the morning when the sun come up, that's where I'd see them turkeys. Sittin' in the trees all along that big ol' skyline. Jus' like that there fellah."

The Old Con lifted his coffee mug and pointed out the window and all our eyes went back to the water tower.

When the whistle blew at seven thirty and the prisoners came streaming out from the cellblocks and living units, Big Bird hadn't moved. Groups of prisoners lingered on their way to work in the factories and stood around laughing and pointing up at the water tower.

Word circulated like an electric current. Big Bird, whose feet were so big his shoes had to be specially ordered, was an eccentric, wild-eyed man who wore trench coats or overcoats and a knit wool watch cap in the dog days of summer and carried on heated arguments with himself or sang and laughed lustily as he walked about flapping his arms. A refugee from the streets of Washington, D.C., he was forever in and out of prison, doing life on the installment plan. This was the kind of guy who, in your worst prison nightmare, ends up being assigned to bunk in your cell, and you live in fear not just because he's so big his hands look like oars, but because you know at a glance he's completely mad and you have no idea where he's coming from or what it takes to set him off.

He had a whole slew of nicknames: Camel (because of his loping stride and a hump high on his back caused by bad posture), Lurch (after the TV show character), and the Strangler. But upon his occupation of the water tower none seemed to fit so well as Big Bird.

The staff knew all about him, as they knew about all of us, and treated him with a kind of amused indifference reserved for those whose names are on the "Pay Him No Mind" list with the rest of the malingerers, charlatans, and stir-crazy old jailbirds.

After breakfast, as the compound cleared and we began our workday, two lieutenants strolled casually to the base of the water tower to see if they could convince Big Bird to come down and join the rest of us.

By lunchtime the Bird still had not flown. The Old Con, a prison archetype who had mysterious sources of information and knew everything that was happening not only in this prison but throughout the system, told us Big Bird sent word to the warden that he did not intend to jump. Groups of prisoners had been standing around the water tower heckling Big Bird and yelling at him to take off. But he had his radio (presumably the reception was good up there), he had some food, and he had his overcoat and his cap and a blanket or two, even though it was early September and the temperature was in the high eighties. He told the lieutenants he was just there and come count time at four o'clock they could count him on the water tower. We wondered how that might sound when the count was called in to Washington: "One thousand eighty-one in their cells and one on the water tower."

"He wants somethin'," said the Old Con at lunch as we sat watching the distant aerie. "He ain't up there for the view."

The water tower stood behind the vocational training shops and looked over the rec yard and weight pile on one side and, on the other, the complex of buildings that made up UNICOR, the prison's cable factory, printing plant, and warehouses where most of the prisoners worked. We walked to and from the factories, past the water tower, day in, day out without a second thought. Only today it was significant.

The workers labor for pennies per hour; the highest-paid make a dollar an hour. Still, with overtime, some of them earn two or three hundred dollars a month, which to the Colombian and other Third Worlders might be as much as they could make in a year in their homeland. They can send enough money to their wives each month to support a family of twelve and still have plenty left over for their allotment at the commissary. Upon arrest, these men flock to the factories. Some say when the wind is in the right direction you can stand on the beach in south Florida and hear the Colombians out there on the motherships calling: "A bottom bunk, a pair of Reeboks, and a job in UNICOR."

UNICOR is the backbone of the system. Without the factories, which do government contract work and bring in untold millions each year, the system might buckle and collapse under the strain on taxpayers of having to clothe, feed, and amuse the tens of thousands of new prisoners, many of them foreigners, coming into the American gulag each year. But the bureaucrats in Washington know how to deal with social phenomena: They turn them into businesses. In the words of Chief Justice Warren Burger, let the prisons of America become "factories behind walls." And it works. Men and women are coming to prison in droves, as though some well-kept secret about how good life is in here leaked out. Though shunned as slave labor by many long-term, old-school convicts and the wealthier criminals who come to prison to relax, there are long waiting lists for jobs in the UNICOR factories.

As usual, the Old Con was right: Big Bird wanted something. By three forty-five when the whistle blew to end the workday and the compound was cleared for the afternoon count, Big Bird had sent a list of his demands. The list consisted of one item: a job at UNICOR.

They'll never go for it," said the Old Con out on the rec yard. From where we sat we could hear tunes from Big Bird's radio carried on the evening breeze. He was still up there, like some brooding god pondering life from above the fray, his thick legs like logs dangling over the edge of the catwalk, his cap pulled down over his forehead, his arms folded across his barrel chest.

"His name's been on the list for over a year," Red said and lit another generic cigarette. "I guess he finally wised up to the fact that guys been comin' in after him and gettin' hired there an' his name jus' don't seem to move up the list."

"Damn, that's pitiful." The Old Con shook his bald, wrinkled head. "Imagine bein' too crazy to work in UNICOR."

"Well, they got a lotta tools down there," Red said, his watery blue eyes watching Big Bird. "The Bird's all right, but sometimes he gets his ass in an uproar for no reason. They're probably worried he might club somebody over the head with one a them tools."

"Whatever happens, I can tell ya one thing," the Old Con said. He looked up at the Bird and stroked the gray stubble on his chin. "No way they gonna let him spend the night up there. Somethin's gotta give. He may be a nut job, but I can guarantee ya, these people'll come up with somethin'. They'll have that turkey off the skyline by the nine o'clock count if they have to shoot him."

Red chortled and waved a hand toward the gun towers looming at each corner of the prison. "Talk about a sitting duck!"

No one knew exactly what Big Bird was in prison for, but we knew he was from D.C. That meant he could be in for anything from petty theft and cashing bogus welfare checks to rape or murder. The D.C. prisoners were the most despised element in the system. New York blacks, blacks from Baltimore and Philadelphia, were quick to point out they "ain't no D.C. nigger." Most of them were wild young men who'd been doing time since they were kids. Many banded together for protection and because they knew each other from the streets of the capital and from doing time together in other prisons. Like all prison gangs — the Colombians, the Mexican and Italian mafias, the bikers, the racists, the Puerto Rican street kids — in numbers they might make you tense with anger and fear; but individually, if you could ever break through their studied personae, they could sometimes amaze you with the complexity and depth of their characters. Some of them knew so much about the dog-eat-dog world of the street and little else. They were daring and enterprising and recognized only the scruples of survival. They came to prison not because they were failures at crimes, but because in their contempt for the law they were not trying to get away with anything.

But Big Bird was a loner. Whenever we saw him bounding around the compound with that lunging stride of his, as though his feet were so big and heavy he had to heave with his whole body to move them, his arms flapping winglike at his sides, he was nearly always alone and carrying on a discussion with unseen companions. Whites avoided his wide-eyed gaze and cleared out of his way. His own homeboys teased him unmercifully and tried to provoke him. Big Bird would laugh at them with a booming guffaw that was scarier than any threats. He grinned at them with a mouthful of huge gleaming teeth that looked strong enough to chew off an arm.

Only once did we see him buddy up, and that was with a kid we called Dirt Man or the Janitor because he ate dirt, dust balls, pieces of trash, with the voraciousness of a billy goat. We knew that Dirt Man understood what he was doing wasn't right because he would do it on the sly. His favorites were the old mop strings that got caught and broke off beneath the legs of the tables in the chow hall. We used to watch him when he stood in line for his chow but really he was on the lookout for mop strings. When he'd spot one you could see a little quiver of excitement go through him as he sized up the situation. He'd leave the line and sidle up to the table, then in a swift series of moves he'd catch the piece of mop string with the toe of his boot, drag it out, reach down and snag it, roll it into a ball, and nonchalantly pop it into his mouth.

Big Bird took Dirt Man under his wing. Dirt Man also wore a lot of heavy clothes even during the hottest weather. We would see them out in the rec yard playing chess, the Bird with his radio, Dirt Man snacking on dust between moves. For a while they even celled together. The Old Con said Dirt Man was the ideal cellmate because he would lick the floor clean and eat all the rubbish. But really he was a sad case and finally a couple of us grabbed the shrink, who was also wacky, and asked him how they could let a young man walk around here all day eating cigarette butts and mop strings. Soon Dirt Man disappeared, which was also sad because then Big Bird was alone again.

And now Big Bird was bivouacked alone on the water tower, nesting like some giant swallow. We all knew the Old Con was right, somehow or other they would get him down by nightfall, even if they had to shoot him.

And sure enough, by morning Big Bird had flown. There was all sorts of speculation as to how they had enticed him to come down. But those of us who've been here a while knew only the Old Con would have the real story, and so we waited until he came shuffling into the chow hall for his morning coffee, sat down, and gazed out at the now curiously stark water tower.

"Well, they negotiated a settlement," said the Old Con, and he blew on his mug of steaming coffee. "Ol' Big Bird, that fella's got an appetite. He ate up all his food the first twelve hours of the sit-in. An' sure 'nough, come nine o'clock, the Bird was hungry. Lieutenant tol' him if he'd come on down they'd send out and get him any kinda food he wanted. Bird wanted to know about the job in UNICOR. Lieutenant tol' him, 'Don't worry about that job now, your name's on the list.' Well, Bird wasn't goin' for that. He knows what list they got his name on. Still, the fella was hungry. He needed to eat. So finally he said he'd come down if they promised to send out and get him a Big Mac."

"A Big Mac!" Red exclaimed in disbelief. "You're serious? This idiot coulda asked for anything he wanted an' he tells 'em to get him a Big Mac!"

"What can I tell ya?" the Old Con said. "That's what the fella ordered, a Big Mac. He said if he couldn't have his job in UNICOR, he'd settle for a Big Mac."

Everyone at the table was silent. We looked at the Old Con, who sat sipping his coffee and stroking his whiskers.

"Well?" said Red at last, his curiosity getting the better of him. "Did they get him a Big Mac?"

Now everyone was laughing.

"Well, Red, you know how that goes. Give 'em a Big Mac this week an' next week you'll have fellas up there demandin' Kentucky Fried Chicken. In no time the *I*-talians'll be up there sayin' they want Mama Leone's pizza. No, no Big Mac. I'll tell ya what they did give him, though. They gave him a baloney an' cheese sandwich when they come 'n got his ass from the hole this mornin' an' shipped him to that nut joint they got over there in North Carolina."

1989, Federal Correctional Institution Petersburg
Petersburg, Virginia

Suicide!

Robert Kelsey

"Suicide on the gate!"

I yelled it loud as hell and gave the gate a rattle, but it didn't really matter; the C.O. would come and open it whenever he was good and ready to. I'd just rung the doorbell, sort of. But the sound of my voice was buried in the din of sixth-floor noise bouncing off steel walls: tinny TV speakers blaring, guys shouting from cell to cell to day-room — "Yo, homeboy" — "*Vaya*, Chino" — "Hey, dude" — I took a seat on my square Tupperware bucket stuffed with blanket, pillow, book, writing paper, coffee, and cup, and — I jumped back up, realizing I was squishing — a package of Oreo cookies. I smiled when I thought of how it resembled a kid's pajama party: Bring your own sleeping gear, the cookies, the horseplay. I was going over to the M.O. tier. The Mental Observation Unit. The nuts, the bugs, the loony-tunes. My post for the night as a Q.H.D.M.-S.P.A. Queens House of Detention for Men — Suicide Prevention Aide. "Suicide" for short. That's what they all called me — "Suicide."

"Yo, Kerry — give this to Big Chas," Hunter, the guy in the cell next to mine, had said as he slipped a *Penthouse* mag in under the blanket in the bucket. His hand lingered in the folds of the blanket.

"Get outta my cookie stash, thief. I'll have you thrown in jail!" I said and picked up the bucket, forcing him to retrieve his hand and laugh. The C.O. came finally, unlocked the gate, and I stepped out into the gallery, where the noise became quadraphonically balanced — A Side, B Side, C Side, D Side. Then I signed the sign-in sheet on the C.O.'s desk, indicating I had just left C Side to work the 10 P.M.–6 A.M. shift on B Side, and the C.O. led me to the B Side gate, M.O. land, where he opened it and I passed in. *Clang.*

I'd gotten up in the afternoon to wash my suit. I was the only guy on the whole floor who had a suit in his possession. It was a matching jacket and vest, with a pair of gray slacks I'd already had when my sister sent the jacket and vest from San Francisco. She'd found them in a thrift shop. It was like magic, the way they matched the pants. "You look like a fucking lawyer!" guys would say and laugh. They mostly went to court dressed in Guess jeans and high-dollar sneakers, a gold chain or two, except for the one or two guys who had relatives bring them a suit for court appearances — guys who were looking at fifteen or twenty-five to life. *They* got serious.

Washing the suit was an ordeal. I took it upstairs to the dorm and the big long utility sink there. I watched the water get darker and darker with the grunge of the many years of dirt embedded into the bars, the floor, the wire mesh, the elevator walls, the bus seats; everything that the suit touched on its journey of elevator-bullpen-bullpen-bullpen-courtroom.

I hung up the suit in my cell to dry on my clothesline: a ripped-off edge of sheet stretched from rear-wall vent to front bars. I had fashioned a coat hanger out of more sheet scrap and a rolled-up newspaper for the cross member, like one of the jailhouse veterans had shown me. The wet jacket and vest would hang heavy, bringing the clothesline low. It looked empty, like hollow company, the way it hung there. Somehow it reminded me of how I would feel the next day, wearing it, standing before a judge who would wrangle with the D.A. and my lawyer while the family — the family of the kid who ran in front of me and I killed while driving home drunk one night — jeered at my back. I never turned around.

I'd even ironed the pants because they dried pretty quick, and when I went up to the little barbershop room that looked down on the gallery, where they locked us in and let us iron, Fitzgerald was there. He was 15 Cell on the M.O. tier. He had killed his wife and was about to get sentenced after blowing trial — found guilty. He was ironing his pants too, but he didn't have any jacket or tie or anything, just a nice shirt and a sweater his son had brought him. His son had testified against him. Fitzgerald looked like he was going to play golf — just a casual sweater and slacks, brown loafers, distinguished gray hair — whenever he went to court.

"Fold them like this, make sure the iron isn't sticky, Kerry — doesn't have anything burnt on it. These guys . . . " Fitz's voice trailed off as he shook his head a little and showed me with his strong fireman's hands how to iron: It was obvious I didn't know how. "These guys don't know how to care for *anything*."

"Whadya think you'll get, Fitz?" I asked him, trying to make conversation. He had to wait till I was done anyway — the C.O. wasn't going to let us out one at a time.

"Fifteen-to-life, I guess — that's what my lawyer, the D.A., everybody is sayin'." He seemed disinterested in the topic, like it was about someone else, but he kept his eyes on the creases I was attempting. "Whadya think you'll get?" Then he added, "Here," reached out for the iron, and started fixing my botched ironing job.

"I don't know, not a whole lot . . ." I knew the maximum I could get was five-to-fifteen. Seemed like nothing compared to what Fitz faced the following day. "Maybe a three-to-nine or somethin'. Not a whole lot for a life." It didn't come out like I wanted it to, and I was worried how Fitz would take it.

"You didn't mean to kill anyone; you were just drunk," he told me as he ironed, not looking up. "Me, I *shot* my wife, and if I had it to do over again . . . I'd shoot her again." His face skewed momentarily. When we were both done, Fitz walked to the front of the barbershop cage with his pants, crisp-edge and delicately folded over his outstretched arm, as I plucked mine from the board and held it the same way. He yelled for the C.O. by his name, not shouting "see-oh" like all us young turkeys.

"Fuckin' murderer!" It was said loud enough to be heard throughout the courtroom. I stood with my hands cuffed behind me, watching the judge who was emceeing "Let's Make a Deal" with the D.A. and my attorney. My suit was still damp and felt cold and clingy, giving me the feeling of not being in my own body. I switched my concentration to the line of dirty masking tape at my feet, where the bailiff had pointed, telling me where to stand. After a while, I let my eyes wander the courtroom walls, giant mahogany panels that swallowed up the low-toned voices of the players before me so that I couldn't make out what they were saying, just horrific tidbits that branded that night: eyewitness, direction, headlights, excessive . . . Postponed. Resumed in six weeks. The bailiff opened the twelve-foot-high doors and I exited as I heard quiet sobbing. The handcuffs were removed and I was sent back up two flights of narrow stairs to the bullpens full of people I didn't know. A young Colombian kid was miming out a robbery for some others, showing what had happened. Before I had left the sixth floor back at Q.H.D.M., Fay, an M.O. from the dorm upstairs, told me, "Don't worry, Kerry, that suit is good luck." I'd loaned it to him for one court appearance and he had snapped up an offer of two-to-six for bank robbery. He'd used a bicycle for a get-away vehicle for the first few rush-hour robberies, then switched to a car and got caught. His wife was furious. And I was dubious of his superstitious predictions. I felt like every kind of luck was passing me by, except bad.

My attorney, Tom, arrived huffing and puffing from the stairs.

His suit fit snugly around his portly body and his tie was loosened. The C.O. stuck him in the Plexiglas booth adjoining the bullpen, then put me opposite him so we were separated inside by a Plexiglas dividing wall with round holes in it.

"How ya doin', Kerry. I filed for the Rosario Hearing . . ." he began.

"Tom — what's with the D.A.? You got any offer from him yet? Something to cop out *to?*" I was sick of bus rides and bullpens, and the family's screams echoed in my head a little longer after each court appearance. This had been my third one. "I'll take anything, I just want to get this *over* with . . ."

He gave me a "Then why did you hire me?" look. There was a long pause. The Colombian kid mimicked a gun with his fingers, pointing them at another guy with a Mickey Mouse T-shirt and heavy acne scars. They both laughed. We looked at each other through the smudged Plexiglas.

"I'll see what they say." The Colombian kid genuflected as he left the bullpen to go down the stairs.

"See-oh! Ten-ta-six Suicide on the mutha-fuckin' gate!" I shouted it loud and slow like the announcer at the beginning of a prizefight. This time the C.O. was nearby and led me quickly through the routine of sign-in and gates until I was secured on B Side. *Clang.*

First I went into the dayroom, where I set down my Tupperware bucket, which again contained cookies and whatnot. The M.O.'s were watching *Penitentiary III* for maybe the fourth time that week. "No way *anybody* could jump that high . . ." Ernesto said in a slightly effeminate voice, looking at my face, hoping I would defend him in an argument about one of the characters: an animallike, nonspeaking, chained-up black dwarf with superhuman strength. Later on in the movie, he would be chained up in the penitentiary basement and made to watch violent movies while smoking crack. Some of the M.O.'s were dozing in their chairs, tranquilized on Thorazine, Prolixin, Sinequan . . .

"You're right, Ernesto, no way — he ain't smoked that crack yet," I told him and some guys stirred in their seats and laughed. Ernesto stamped one foot in anger, and then turned away with a hurt look. He prided himself on being a cut above the others, with more vocabulary and suave mannerisms. He had been robbing cabbies while strung out on crack himself, using a cap pistol. It was a miracle he hadn't got shot. He'd slit his wrists once while he'd been on the M.O. tier, but it hadn't been a real deep wound, and they had simply bandaged him up and sent him back from the infirmary a few hours later. I warned him never to pull a stunt like that on my shift.

I couldn't watch the damn movie — it was just too bizarre for me, so I took a walk down the tier, like it tells you to do in the S.P.A. manual. You come in, go take a simple test the first Monday. Guys help each other openly; if you can't read, the C.O. reads it *to* you, you pass — everybody does — and presto! you're an S.P.A. I stopped at Stymie's cell. "Sui-*cide*!" he said cheerily. He was a young black kid, stringbean tall with one unbendable leg, the result of being hit by a car as a small child. He was afflicted with grand-mal epilepsy. He sold a lot of crack; this was his third time in, and he'd go upstate for sure. Standing up off his bed, he hopped up to the bars. "Suicide, tell the C.O. crack my cell, I'm gonna go watch the movie." I told him I'd get it done on my return run.

Next I went by 8 Cell, with Lemar, a huge, lumbering southern black man who'd strangled his wife. Lemar was listening to his radio, monitoring the news. He suffered from Parkinson's disease. He shook as he reached to remove his headphones. "H-h-how z-zit g-goin'?" he asked. I smiled at him.

"How ya doin', Lemar? Any *good* news?" Lemar had once gotten fifty dollars from his lawyers for Christmas. It was a fifty-dollar bill stuck in an envelope with a card. The C.O. that did the mail that day — a boozy, red-nosed, balding nobody — watched Lemar as he shuffled up to the gate upon hearing his name called out.

"Wanna *touch* it, Harris — feel the money?" He handed Lemar the bill through the bars like a peanut to a monkey, and watched as Lemar grinned, clutching the bill and shaking it with his Parkinson's tremble. "Feels good, huh? Might be the last money you ever touch." The C.O. took it back to put in Lemar's account, and went on with the mail call, unable to disturb Lemar's peaceful smile. Fifty dollars is a lot of money in prison. Sometimes I let Lemar wear my vest off of my suit setup. He'd walk down the cell runway, feeling real dapper, though the vest was awful tight. It seemed to brighten up his day. Lemar had been at Q.H.D.M. for a hell of a long time.

"Lock it in!" the C.O. bellowed precisely at ten fifty-five. He unlocked the gate and entered the runway in front of the cells, walking along and slamming shut the cell's gate if the occupant was inside. I grabbed my Tupperware bucket out of the dayroom and took a spot in front of 1 Cell, where a shaft of light hit so I could read. After every-one was locked in, I spread out my blanket on the grimy cement floor. The C.O. checked his cell-locking panel on the gallery — old Decateur cable-and-pulley hardware from the 1930s, controlled by levers and wheels. "Thirteen cell! Take that off back-lock and don't do that shit again!" he yelled and was answered with a clang. "That's better."

A lot of yelling and kidding came cascading down from the dor-mitory upstairs, its wire-mesh wall shared with the cell runway down-stairs, creating no audio resistance. You could hear everything. A couple of guys upstairs were teasing Shakey, a down-and-out street bum, who begged for cigarettes constantly and smoked the butts off the floor. "Hey, Shakey — do my laundry tomorrow, I'll give you three cigarettes . . ."

"Five . . ." Shakey called back up, and the dorm broke into con-vulsive laughter. Ernesto called out from his cell, and I walked over. "Kerry, I wish they'd get rid of Shakey, ship him to Brooklyn General — he's such a dirt bag," he whined.

"Hey, Ernesto — he's got a right to be in jail, just like you and me. Get arrested, get three hots and a cot, medication to boot — this is a great country, Ernesto." This got him laughing, but suddenly he stopped.

"You know, Kerry, if they try to send me to a max when I get sentenced, I'll kill myself, I swear I will . . ."

"Listen — *nobody* kills themself on my shift — besides, suicide is a C felony, they take you *back* downstairs and book you again, up your bail . . ." I heard Fitz laughing from 15 Cell. Then, from the middle of the tier I heard an ominous thud.

I ran down the line peering into each cell, but already I knew what was wrong. Stymie was having a seizure. I stood in front of 6 Cell holding both my hands over my head and pointing at the cell like a beach lifeguard, yelling "See-oh! Crack six cell! See-oh! Crack six cell!" The C.O. ran down the D Side catwalk and to his Decateur con-trol panel. I heard the cell door unlatch. *Click.*

I ran in and squatted down. The foot attached to Stymie's stiff leg was beating a fast, chaotic rhythm on the stainless-steel toilet. I took his head in my hands, then grabbed a blue N.Y. Giants knit cap that was lying on his bed and stuffed it into his mouth to keep him from biting his tongue. Then I found a sweatshirt also within easy reach and fashioned it into a pillow, the whole time holding his chat-tering head in my lap. His legs twitched spastically. The C.O. stuck his head in the cell. "Good job, Suicide. I'll call upstairs . . ." We'd all been through this before.

Stymie surfaced into groggy consciousness just before the nurse and captain came to take him to the infirmary. "Suicide — I dreamed you was playin' cards . . ." he said in a soft, disoriented voice. ". . . You had jacks and queens. Did . . . did I have me a fit?" he asked, and I told him yes. They helped him into the wheelchair and took him upstairs for the night.

I talked with Fitz afterward, about fighting fires, marriage, raising kids, and sentencing, and shared some Oreos with him. Ernesto asked for some aspirin. Then Shakey asked if I would pick up a few butts off the floor for him — I refused and conned a cigarette out of 2 Cell instead. Finally everyone went to sleep, some calling to the C.O. to turn out their cell light from the control panel, some asking *me* to ask him.

I lay on my blanket, head propped against the bucket with a pillow, all butted up against the filthy bars. I stuck my book in the shaft of light — *Bonfire of the Vanities*. When the C.O.'s nighttime snack wagon came, he gave me an ice cream. I dozed off at one point, and woke up suddenly to a fluttering at my eyelid: a mouse was checking me out at close range. The mouse looked huge, larger than life, in the moment that I opened my eyes. It ran off quickly, more frightened than I was, and scrambled into each cell, then darted out, unhampered by bars and shopping for tidbits. Morning came with the noise of the nearby expressway's traffic buildup, and I helped with the chow wagon and breakfast, ending off by cleaning trays. I went and locked myself in my cell, and lay down for sleep to come over me. Another day.

I sat with Chris one day, a young white kid who worked the upstairs M.O. while I worked the cells downstairs. The M.O.'s were lined up at the gate for meds. Each one would hand an I.D. card through the bars to an attractive Jamaican nurse, and in return receive a Dixie Cup with pills or liquid Thorazine or whatever, then maybe a cup of water to wash it down. The whole time the nurse would answer their remarks with varying responses, most distilling to "Just take your medicine, please."

Chris sat glued to the TV, always making stupid comments like "I'd like to fuck her . . ." at the Excedrin commercial spokespersons. After saying something profound he looked up at me. "Hey, maybe someone'll hang up tonight, we'll save 'em, split the fifty dollars . . ." His face beamed the bright shine of too many acid trips.

"There ain't no fifty-dollar reward. That's just a goddamn myth," I told him, picturing him at a Grateful Dead concert — which was where he was busted at — talking about Jerry Garcia or intergalactic travel plans. He was a real piece of work. I watched him refocus on the TV after I had squashed his attempt at conversation: It was a movie — *Death Wish* with Charles Bronson.

From downstairs came a thud. Not very loud in itself, but loud enough within the relative quiet that developed whenever the nurse's wagon appeared. I didn't like the sound of it. I dropped the newspaper and ran down the stairs. There was still a line for meds, and I saw Stymie in it. I walked briskly down the line of cells, one, two, three . . . I got to 12 Cell, and rushed it — luckily it was unlocked.

A young Arab guy lay with his head bleeding into his Puma sweatshirt and a long-sleeved shirt tied tight around his neck. I loosened it. He breathed. Chris looked over my shoulder. "Get the see-oh, tell him to call the infirmary," I told him. It was a half-assed suicide attempt: Evidently the kid had tied the shirt around his neck so tight he passed out while standing up on his bed. The thud I had heard was his head cracking against the sink as he fell. He'd be all right. "Twenty-five each, right?" Chris said and vanished before I could curse him out. I was sick of hearing about the supposed reward for saving guys. I doubted the jail was giving fifty dollars to anybody for anything. I wiped the Arab's temple with another shirt handy. "He all right?" came Fitz's voice from 15 Cell, locked in, which he preferred.

"Yeah, he'll be okay," I said. I heard an M.O. complain that Chris was cutting in line as he sought to get to the gate and grab the C.O.'s attention among the thrusting hands clutching I.D. cards and raucous ribbing of the pretty Jamaican nurse. I stood up and looked out the window at some trees whose leaves were turning, and it occurred to me I'd been here, doing this, for ten months.

Going back to court later that month, I wound up being shackled to one of the M.O.'s from the upstairs dorm. He kept singing the refrain from a currently popular song: "The girls, the girls they love me, the girls the girls they love me." I stared out the bus window at morning traffic I used to detest.

Back in the courthouse bullpen, I felt the dread of the appearance pulling my stomach apart. The suit jacket felt like a straitjacket. I'd gotten my vest back from Lemar the night before, working my shift even though I didn't have to the night preceding court. I always did — it kept my mind off of it all. "Are y-y-y-you g-g-going t-to trial?" he asked. "I don't want to," I'd told him.

I didn't get taken to the courtroom by lunchtime, and lunch was highlighted by my bus partner setting on fire the little Styrofoam cups our tea came in. The black smoke pissed off a few guys, and the mood in the bullpen grew ugly and tense.

My attorney came up just before I was to go down. He told me nothing, really, just shook his head and complained about the unwavering D.A., who "wouldn't play ball." I felt homesick for the sixth floor, that's how bad it was.

I went down finally to face more screaming, more crying, more nothing. Postponed. I wanted all this to come to an end. Bad.

There was someone new in the bullpen when I got back up there, and he stood looking out of one of the windows to the street below, the sun radiating through his dirty long blond hair and darker beard. He turned around and looked at me as the C.O. shut the gate. "How'd it go?" he said, real polite-like, not bullpen jaded or tough. Two black guys were beating out a rap rhythm on the bench — "You, you got what I needed . . ." The long-haired freak almost seemed to know me. "Not good," I told him. His eyes were clear blue like mine.

"What happened?" he asked. He wasn't asking about the preceding courtroom drama, but my crime.

"I got drunk, driving on the wrong side of the road, and this poor kid ran out in front of me . . ." I said.

"You'll be okay. I can tell you never meant to hurt anybody," he told me matter-of-factly. We stood quietly while the pounding continued, both now gazing out the window. He lifted his arm and pointed to a mother with a baby carriage, fussing with the infant's little blue hat as they sat in the courthouse square among the park benches and drunks. The rappers came to their chorus and sang, ". . . say he's just a friend, say he's just a friend . . ."

I moved off to a corner and took off the suit jacket, spread it out on the dirty bullpen floor and lay down. I'd been up a long, long time, what with working the nighttime suicide shift. I shed my vest and used it as a pillow, and dozed off for what must have been a couple of hours. When I woke up, the C.O. was jangling his keys and opening the gate. It was time for the bus ride back. The long-haired freak was gone. I asked the rappers. "Went back to Brooklyn General." He'd come from the hospital, evidently. Probably a "bug."

"What are you, crazy?" Ernesto was playing chess with Lemar. But he was speaking to a guy named Checkers. He was called Checkers because he was always picking up a checker piece off the playing board, putting it in his mouth, and grinning. Now he deviated a little from his regular modus operandi, and had the black queen peeking out from his grin. He could screw with the checker pieces all day, and guys would just replace the piece with whatever was handy, a scrap of paper, a matchbook, or whatever.

"M-m-m-my q-q-q-quwween!" Lemar yelled, furious. His big arms trembled as he stood up and grabbed the slightly built Checkers by the throat real hard, and lifted him up in the air, feet dangling. Left alone, Lemar would kill Checkers. The black queen became a projectile that hit Lemar squarely in the chest and clattered to the floor. Checker's face tried to form a scream but couldn't, and saliva ran down his chin while his face turned beet red. I bumped Lemar real hard with my shoulder and distracted his murderous choking. "C'mon, it's your move — you're holdin' up the game." He let go, still trembling, and Checkers hit the floor and took off like a cat out of a bathtub, out of the room and up the stairs to the dorm. Most of the time, Checkers never spoke, except for once in a while he'd be clinging to the bars like a koala bear, arms and legs wrapped through and up off the ground, and he'd scream, "Where's Petey?" followed by a Hollywood madhouse laugh. He was on a lot of medication.

The chess game resumed and soon Lemar was content to lose, moving foolishly as Ernesto proceeded to checkmate him. Ron returned to his cell and put on his headphones to listen to the news. Ernesto scouted the dayroom for more challengers. Everybody was absorbed watching *The Price Is Right* or dozing after meds. I was over there during the day because the regular daytime S.P.A. had court and I had decided I just plain *liked* it over on the M.O. tier better. I'd become state property soon, get transferred into the State Correctional System. I was sentenced, packed, waiting for the call any day. I'd given my vest to Lemar because he would probably go to a hospital for the criminally insane where he might still wear street clothes. I wanted to move on — it felt like I'd been on the sixth floor forever.

Stymie limped in and sat down. "Nineteen thousand five hundred twenty-nine dollars for the Chevy Blazer," I heard from the TV; I had always wanted a Blazer.

"Who's gonna watch me after you go, Kerry?" The look on Stymie's face was one I'd never seen before. He was dead serious.

Ernesto chimed in. "Yeah — who's gonna take the night shift, bring us cookies?"

I almost started to cry, but I caught myself. I think it was because, just at that moment, I remembered Stymie, one of the first nights I was there, saying to me, after listening to me tell the story of the night of my crime, "You the one needs a soo-cide watch on yo' ass." The words, spoken in that downhome ghetto accent, slashed through me then, and I swore I'd never appear to be anything but . . . strong.

"Don't worry, gang, they'll find somebody. It ain't like you clowns are *that* crazy," I said, reached out and grabbed the white knight, stuck it in my mouth, and spit it out at Ernesto.

"That's dis-gusting," he said with a flourish and a foot-stomp, and we all laughed loud as hell as bells went off, announcing that somebody had won the Blazer.

1994, Mid-State Correctional Facility
Marcy, New York

Reading and Writing

"If you give a nigger an inch, he will take an ell. A nigger should know nothing but to obey his master — to do as he is told to do. Learning would spoil *the best nigger in the world. Now," said he, "if you teach that nigger [speaking of myself] how to read, there would be no keeping him. It would forever unfit him to be a slave."*
— Narrative of the Life of Frederick Douglass, 1845

In his classic autobiography, Douglass overhears his master thus instructing his wife. "From that moment," Douglass says, "I understood the pathway from slavery to freedom." In a similar way, for the dispossessed young Jimmy Santiago Baca, coming to own language and to inhabit it, was overwhelming and repeatedly empowering as his tumultuous memoir here attests.

In prison, 19 percent of adult males are illiterate, and 40 percent "functionally illiterate" — which means for example that they would be unable to write a business letter — as opposed to the national rate for adult Americans of 4 percent and 21 percent respectively. Learning disability rates, too (11 percent in prison compared to 3 percent in the general population), have contributed to the fact that over 70 percent of prisoners in state facilities have not completed high school. If illiteracy, as some believe, is a major cause of crime, literacy provides a means to see oneself, one's life and condition, and to imagine alternatives.

Education lowers recidivism more effectively than any other program, and the more education received, the less likely an individual is to be rearrested or reimprisoned. The internal growth made possible by higher education is incalculable; most writers in this collection took advantage of college courses offered behind bars. For this reason, the defeat in 1994 of federal Pell Grants for higher education to prisoners was particularly devastating. One of the thousands of beneficiaries of post-secondary education behind bars, Jon Marc Taylor has been a tireless fighter for the continuation or restoration of such programs.

Education can make an extraordinary difference in the way one does time. Literate convicts with a trace of conscience are kept very busy, as O'Neill Stough of Arizona attested in two prizewinning pieces. In "Deliberate Indifference" (1994),* Roland, a man with AIDS, surprises the narrator into activism. As Roland is illiterate and timid, his requests for adequate blankets, food, and vitamins are ignored. The narrator writes his complaint for him, and when it fails, organizes assistance from other inmates. Later, writing Roland's obituary in the form of a grievance lands him in isolation, but brings about reform. Stough's essay "Cruel and Quite Usual" (1993)* narrates how a cruel guard was exposed in a prison newspaper.

Women in prison who have gotten together to address their medical needs (including AIDS), parenting, and the needs of their children, sometimes publish the results. Many men and women write about becoming jailhouse lawyers. Victor Hassine used his legal background to bring successful conditions-of-confinement lawsuits against two Pennsylvania prisons. Other writers have described how hosts of educated men and women become teachers of classes in literacy, AIDS, or whatever they can — work even more vital with the deep cuts in education and other programs.

Poet and teacher Joseph Bruchac analyzes the extraordinary transformative power of creative writing. "A lack of empathy may be one of the characteristics of the man or woman who commits a violent crime against another human being. Having been brutalized themselves as children, they pass on that violence to their victims. But when a person begins to write poetry, to create art, several things may happen. One is a birth of self-respect . . . Another is the ability to empathize." Many prison writers suggest that coming to feel compassion has saved them from being brutalized; the exploration of the self through writing breaks the hold of the institution and opens the writer to growth (See **About the Authors**). In "Colorado Kills Creativity" (1994)* J. C. Amberchele recalls "a scared biker handing over a poem about love and loneliness" to a prison magazine (since suspended), "revealing a secret he had guarded most of his life." Writing "was our first attempt to give something from within rather than to take from others," he writes, "to act instead of react."

While for some creativity makes sense only as a solitary refuge, others work well collectively. In Hettie Jones's writing workshop at Bedford Hills Correctional Facility, women meet for what they sometimes describe as three hours of unlimited freedom. Six of them here offer a "tetrina." (A tetrina is a variant on the sestina, using four end words instead of six, which are repeated in a specified sequence.) When their work appeared in the book *Aliens at the Border,* the poets offered the facility's first poetry reading. Later, a sextet composed of workshop members — Iris Bowen, Kathy Boudin, Judy Clark, Lisa Finkle, Miriam Lopez, and Jan Warren — collaborated to set down what the workshop has meant to them.

One of the most complex pieces in this volume, "Behind the Mirror's Face," by Paul St. John, is at once an attack on prison writing and a superb example of it. The sardonic monologist vents suspicions of the self-serving cynicism and sentimentality at the heart of "creative" ventures in a site of coercion. In his corrosive view, prison magazines are tokens that serve the administration's agenda, writing teachers have overblown and naive expectations of the power of writing to change author and audience, and inmate authors seize on writing only to deepen their self-deception. His assaults on the abuses of writing reveal his hunger for an honesty and commitment he despairs of finding. Then, feeling reproached by another inmate's suicide, he exits the scene in a narcotic flight, assigning classic names — Plethora, Hedone, Cacoethes (excess, pleasure, and bad habits) — to the rescuing drug.

Many writers in this book have been thrust into segregation (the "hole," the "box," the Special Housing Unit) or transferred because of their writing. Many have had their books and papers confiscated. Michael Saucier's "Black Flag to the Rescue" here presents an unusual, comic — but true — writerly predicament. Incensed by reading this poem in the prison newspaper, the warden challenged Saucier to show him the roach casings he had found in his battery-operated typewriter. Saucier complied, to the warden's chagrin.

Coming into Language

Jimmy Santiago Baca

On weekend graveyard shifts at St. Joseph's Hospital I worked the emergency room, mopping up pools of blood and carting plastic bags stuffed with arms, legs, and hands to the outdoor incinerator. I enjoyed the quiet, away from the screams of shotgunned, knifed, and mangled kids writhing on gurneys outside the operating rooms. Ambulance sirens shrieked and squad car lights reddened the cool nights, flashing against the hospital walls: gray — red, gray — red. On slow nights I would lock the door of the administration office, search the reference library for a book on female anatomy and, with my feet propped on the desk, leaf through the illustrations, smoking my cigarette. I was seventeen.

One night my eye was caught by a familiar-looking word on the spine of a book. The title was *450 Years of Chicano History in Pictures.* On the cover were black-and-white photos: Padre Hidalgo exhorting Mexican peasants to revolt against the Spanish dictators; Anglo vigilantes hanging two Mexicans from a tree; a young Mexican woman with rifle and ammunition belts crisscrossing her breast; César Chávez and field workers marching for fair wages; Chicano railroad workers laying creosote ties; Chicanas laboring at machines in textile factories; Chicanas picketing and hoisting boycott signs.

From the time I was seven, teachers had been punishing me for not knowing my lessons by making me stick my nose in a circle chalked on the blackboard. Ashamed of not understanding and fearful of asking questions, I dropped out of school in the ninth grade. At seventeen I still didn't know how to read, but those pictures confirmed my identity. I stole the book that night, stashing it for safety under the slop sink until I got off work. Back at my boardinghouse, I showed the book to friends. All of us were amazed; this book told us we were alive. We, too, had defended ourselves with our fists against hostile Anglos, gasping for breath in fights with the policemen who out-numbered us. The book reflected back to us our struggle in a way that made us proud.

Most of my life I felt like a target in the crosshairs of a hunter's rifle. When strangers and outsiders questioned me I felt the hang-rope tighten around my neck and the trapdoor creak beneath my feet.

There was nothing so humiliating as being unable to express myself, and my inarticulateness increased my sense of jeopardy. Behind a mask of humility, I seethed with mute rebellion.

Before I was eighteen, I was arrested on suspicion of murder after refusing to explain a deep cut on my forearm. With shocking speed I found myself handcuffed to a chain gang of inmates and bused to a holding facility to await trial. There I met men, prisoners, who read aloud to each other the works of Neruda, Paz, Sabines, Nemerov, and Hemingway. Never had I felt such freedom as in that dormitory. Listening to the words of these writers, I felt that invisible threat from without lessen — my sense of teetering on a rotting plank over swamp water where famished alligators clapped their horny snouts for my blood. While I listened to the words of the poets, the alligators slumbered powerless in their lairs. The language of poetry was the magic that could liberate me from myself, transform me into another person, transport me to places far away.

And when they closed the books, these Chicanos, and went into their own Chicano language, they made barrio life come alive for me in the fullness of its vitality. I began to learn my own language, the bilingual words and phrases explaining to me my place in the universe.

Months later I was released, as I had suspected I would be. I had been guilty of nothing but shattering the windshield of my girlfriend's car in a fit of rage.

Two years passed. I was twenty now, and behind bars again. The federal marshals had failed to provide convincing evidence to extradite me to Arizona on a drug charge, but still I was being held. They had ninety days to prove I was guilty. The only evidence against me was that my girlfriend had been at the scene of the crime with my driver's license in her purse. They had to come up with something else. But there was nothing else. Eventually they negotiated a deal with the actual drug dealer, who took the stand against me. When the judge hit me with a million-dollar bail, I emptied my pockets on his booking desk: twenty-six cents.

One night in my third month in the county jail, I was mopping the floor in front of the booking desk. Some detectives had kneed an old drunk and handcuffed him to the booking bars. His shrill screams raked my nerves like a hacksaw on bone, the desperate protest of his dignity against their inhumanity. But the detectives just laughed as he tried to rise and kicked him to his knees. When they went to the bathroom to pee and the desk attendant walked to the file cabinet to pull the arrest record, I shot my arm through the bars, grabbed one of the attendant's university textbooks, and tucked it in my overalls. It was the only way I had of protesting.

It was late when I returned to my cell. Under my blanket I switched on a pen flashlight and opened the thick book at random, scanning the pages. I could hear the jailer making his rounds on the other tiers. The jangle of his keys and the sharp click of his boot heels intensified my solitude. Slowly I enunciated the words . . . p-o-n-d, ri-pple. It scared me that I had been reduced to this to find comfort. I always had thought reading a waste of time, that nothing could be gained by it. Only by action, by moving out into the world and confronting and challenging the obstacles, could one learn anything worth knowing.

Even as I tried to convince myself that I was merely curious, I became so absorbed in how the sounds created music in me and happiness, I forgot where I was. Memories began to quiver in me, glowing with a strange but familiar intimacy in which I found refuge. For a while, a deep sadness overcame me, as if I had chanced on a long-lost friend and mourned the years of separation. But soon the heartache of having missed so much of life, that had numbed me since I was a child, gave way, as if a grave illness lifted itself from me and I was cured, innocently believing in the beauty of life again. I stumblingly repeated the author's name as I fell asleep, saying it over and over in the dark: Words-worth, Words-worth.

Before long my sister came to visit me, and I joked about taking her to a place called Xanadu and getting her a blind date with this *vato*† named Coleridge who lived on the seacoast and was *malias*‡ on morphine. When I asked her to make a trip into enemy territory to buy me a grammar book, she said she couldn't. Bookstores intimidated her, because she, too, could neither read nor write.

Days later, with a stub pencil I whittled sharp with my teeth, I propped a Red Chief notebook on my knees and wrote my first words. From that moment, a hunger for poetry possessed me.

Until then, I had felt as if I had been born into a raging ocean where I swam relentlessly, flailing my arms in hope of rescue, of reaching a shoreline I never sighted. Never solid ground beneath me, never a resting place. I had lived with only the desperate hope to stay afloat; that and nothing more.

† In Chicano dialect: dude. (JSB)
‡ In Chicano dialect: strung out. (JSB)

But when at last I wrote my first words on the page, I felt an island rising beneath my feet like the back of a whale. As more and more words emerged, I could finally rest: I had a place to stand for the first time in my life. The island grew, with each page, into a continent inhabited by people I knew and mapped with the life I lived.

I wrote about it all — about people I had loved or hated, about the brutalities and ecstasies of my life. And, for the first time, the child in me who had witnessed and endured unspeakable terrors cried out not just in impotent despair, but with the power of language. Suddenly, through language, through writing, my grief and my joy could be shared with anyone who would listen. And I could do this all alone; I could do it anywhere. I was no longer a captive of demons eating away at me, no longer a victim of other people's mockery and loathing, that had made me clench my fist white with rage and grit my teeth to silence. Words now pleaded back with the bleak lucidity of hurt. They were wrong, those others, and now I could say it.

Through language I was free. I could respond, escape, indulge; embrace or reject earth or the cosmos. I was launched on an endless journey without boundaries or rules, in which I could salvage the floating fragments of my past, or be born anew in the spontaneous ignition of understanding some heretofore concealed aspect of myself. Each word steamed with the hot lava juices of my primordial making, and I crawled out of stanzas dripping with birth-blood, reborn and freed from the chaos of my life. The child in the dark room of my heart, who had never been able to find or reach the light switch, flicked it on now; and I found in the room a stranger, myself, who had waited so many years to speak again. My words struck in me lightning crackles of elation and thunderhead storms of grief.

When I had been in the county jail longer than anyone else, I was made a trustee. One morning, after a fistfight, I went to the unlocked and unoccupied office used for lawyer-client meetings, to think. The bare white room with its fluorescent tube lighting seemed to expose and illuminate my dark and worthless life. When I had fought before, I never gave it a thought. Now, for the first time, I had something to lose — my chance to read, to write; a way to live with dignity and meaning, that had opened for me when I stole that scuffed, second-hand book about the Romantic poets.

"I will never do any work in this prison system as long as I am not allowed to get my G.E.D." That's what I told the reclassification panel. The captain flicked off the tape recorder. He looked at me hard and said, "You'll never walk outta here alive. Oh, you'll work, put a copper penny on that, you'll work."

After that interview I was confined to deadlock maximum security in a subterranean dungeon, with ground-level chicken-wired windows painted gray. Twenty-three hours a day I was in that cell. I kept sane by borrowing books from the other cons on the tier. Then, just before Christmas, I received a letter from Harry, a charity house Samaritan who doled out hot soup to the homeless in Phoenix. He had picked my name from a list of cons who had no one to write to them. I wrote back asking for a grammar book, and a week later received one of Mary Baker Eddy's treatises on salvation and redemption, with Spanish and English on opposing pages. Pacing my cell all day and most of each night, I grappled with grammar until I was able to write a long true-romance confession for a con to send to his pen pal. He paid me with a pack of smokes. Soon I had a thriving barter business, exchanging my poems and letters for novels, commissary pencils, and writing tablets.

One day I tore two flaps from the cardboard box that held all my belongings and punctured holes along the edge of each flap and along the border of a ream of state-issue paper. After I had aligned them to form a spine, I threaded the holes with a shoestring, and sketched on the cover a hummingbird fluttering above a rose. This was my first journal.

Whole afternoons I wrote, unconscious of passing time or whether it was day or night. Sunbursts exploded from the lead tip of my pencil, words that grafted me into awareness of who I was; peeled back to a burning core of bleak terror, an embryo floating in the image of water, I cracked out of the shell wide-eyed and insane. Trees grew out of the palms of my hands, the threatening otherness of life dissolved, and I became one with the air and sky, the dirt and the iron and concrete. There was no longer any distinction between the other and I. Language made bridges of fire between me and everything I saw. I entered into the blade of grass, the basketball, the con's eye and child's soul.

At night I flew. I conversed with floating heads in my cell, and visited strange houses where lonely women brewed tea and rocked in wicker rocking chairs listening to sad Joni Mitchell songs.

Before long I was frayed like rope carrying too much weight, that suddenly snaps. I quit talking. Bars, walls, steel bunk and floor bristled with millions of poem-making sparks. My face was no longer familiar to me. The only reality was the swirling cornucopia of images in my mind, the voices in the air. Midair a cactus blossom would appear, a snake-flame in blinding dance around it, stunning me like a guard's fist striking my neck from behind.

The prison administrators tried several tactics to get me to work. For six months, after the next monthly prison board review, they sent cons to my cell to hassle me. When the guard would open my cell door to let one of them in, I'd leap out and fight him — and get sent to thirty-day isolation. I did a lot of isolation time. But I honed my image-making talents in that sensory-deprived solitude. Finally they moved me to death row, and after that to "nut-run," the tier that housed the mentally disturbed.

As the months passed, I became more and more sluggish. My eyelids were heavy, I could no longer write or read. I slept all the time.

One day a guard took me out to the exercise field. For the first time in years I felt grass and earth under my feet. It was spring. The sun warmed my face as I sat on the bleachers watching the cons box and run, hit the handball, lift weights. Some of them stopped to ask how I was, but I found it impossible to utter a syllable. My tongue would not move, saliva drooled from the corners of my mouth. I had been so heavily medicated I could not summon the slightest gestures. Yet inside me a small voice cried out, I am fine! I am hurt now but I will come back! I'm fine!

Back in my cell, for weeks I refused to eat. Styrofoam cups of urine and hot water were hurled at me. Other things happened. There were beatings, shock therapy, intimidation.

Later, I regained some clarity of mind. But there was a place in my heart where I had died. My life had compressed itself into an unbearable dread of being. The strain had been too much. I had stepped over that line where a human being has lost more than he can bear, where the pain is too intense, and he knows he is changed forever. I was now capable of killing, coldly and without feeling. I was empty, as I have never, before or since, known emptiness. I had no connection to this life.

But then, the encroaching darkness that began to envelop me forced me to re-form and give birth to myself again in the chaos. I withdrew even deeper into the world of language, cleaving the diamonds of verbs and nouns, plunging into the brilliant light of poetry's regenerative mystery. Words gave off rings of white energy, radar signals from powers beyond me that infused me with truth. I believed what I wrote, because I wrote what was true. My words did not come from books or textual formulas, but from a deep faith in the voice of my heart.

I had been steeped in self-loathing and rejected by everyone and everything — society, family, cons, God and demons. But now I had become as the burning ember floating in darkness that descends on a dry leaf and sets flame to forests. The word was the ember and the forest was my life. . . .

Writing bridged my divided life of prisoner and free man. I wrote of the emotional butchery of prisons, and my acute gratitude for poetry. Where my blind doubt and spontaneous trust in life met, I discovered empathy and compassion. The power to express myself was a welcome storm rasping at tendril roots, flooding my soul's cracked dirt. Writing was water that cleansed the wound and fed the parched root of my heart.

I wrote to sublimate my rage, from a place where all hope is gone, from a madness of having been damaged too much, from a silence of killing rage. I wrote to avenge the betrayals of a lifetime, to purge the bitterness of injustice. I wrote with a deep groan of doom in my blood, bewildered and dumbstruck; from an indestructible love of life, to affirm breath and laughter and the abiding innocence of things. I wrote the way I wept, and danced, and made love.

1991, Reflections on Albuquerque County Jail, New Mexico
and Arizona State Prison–Florence, Arizona

Pell Grants for Prisoners

Jon Marc Taylor

Prisoners are the black sheep of our societal family, and thus discussions of their treatment are relegated to back-room deliberations of how they should be punished. A common opinion is that we are too soft on criminals and that whatever rehabilitation (or lack thereof) they receive is more than they deserve. An example of this disposition was the congressional effort to bar inmate eligibility for Pell Grant higher-education financial assistance. Last year, both the Senate and the House of Representatives passed legislation prohibiting offenders from qualifying for such aid. Before surveying this attempt at *capitol* punishment, a short history of college programs for prisoners is in order.

Not until 1953, when the University of Southern Illinois matriculated its first class of inmate-students, did higher education enter the nation's penal institutions. U.S.I.'s radical experiment was slow to take root, for by 1965 there were only twelve Post-Secondary Correctional Education programs in the country. The largest constraint facing these programs was the same as for any type of rehabilitative program — lack of funding.

In 1965, however, Congress passed Title IV of the Higher Education Act, which contained the Pell Grant program entitling student-prisoners who met certain criteria to receive financial aid for college-level studies. With the implementation of this funding, PSCE opportunities flourished; by 1973 there were 182 programs, by 1976, 237 programs and by 1982 (the last official count), 350 programs offered in 90 percent of the states. Yet with the continued growth of the nation's correctional population, at most 10 percent of the country's prisoners were enrolled in PSCE.

Even so, prison officials could see the effectiveness of these programs. Correctional administrators, facing ever-growing numbers of offenders whom they had to house and control, found that those enrolled in them were easier to manage and better behaved than the average prisoner, provided a calming effect on the rest of the population, and served as positive role models.

What is more, beginning in the mid-1970s, studies of inmate college students (especially those earning degrees) revealed that they recidivated at much lower rates than nonenrolled prisoners. Between 1974 and 1979, three programs in Alabama, Maryland, and New Jersey reported substantial reductions in offender-students' recidivism, compared with standard return rates. These reductions ranged from a drop from 57 to 37 percent in one case to a dramatic difference of from 80 to only 10 percent in another program.

Perhaps the most widely reported evaluation was published in *Psychology Today* in 1983. The study noted that "recidivism . . . among college classes at New Mexico State Penitentiary between 1967 and 1977 averaged 15.5 percent, while the general population averaged 68 percent recidivism."

The positive reports continue into this decade, with the District of Columbia's Lorton Prison College Program noting a recidivism rate for students of only 6 percent, compared with an average that exceeded 40 percent. In 1991, the New York Department of Correctional Services reported on its four-year study of the state's PSCE — the second-largest program in the nation. The study found a "statistically significant" difference in the return rates of those who earned degrees and those who did not complete the college program.

Today it costs $25,000 annually to incarcerate an individual, whereas one year of PSCE programming can be purchased for $2,500. In other words, for only 10 percent of the cost of a single year of imprisonment, an offender can enroll for two semesters of postsecondary education. If such education is continued for two to four years, society more than likely will receive ex-offenders whose chances of recidivating are in the low double- or single-digit range, compared with a national recidivism range of 50 to 70 percent.

Besides providing substantial savings by reducing the costly rate of recidivism, prison college programs produce educated workers for the economy. Studies in New York and Ohio in the early 1980s, at the height of the Reagan recession, revealed that PSCE graduates were employed in substantially higher numbers than other parolees in the area (60 to 75 percent compared with only 40 percent), suggesting that the education earned by the offenders favorably influenced employers' decisions in hiring them and offset the social stigma attached to their ex-con status. Parolee unemployment is a prime contributor to recidivism, so any program that enhances an ex-offender's employability is of benefit to the community.

The Corrections Program of the College of Santa Fe, New Mexico, has had great success in turning around its inmate-students. Examples include a graduate who went on to become a physician, another who became a vice president of an international company, and others who became personnel directors and teachers. A former death-row inmate rose to the directorship of a state corrections industry department.

These success stories give added emphasis to the words of former Chief Justice Warren Burger: "We must accept the reality that to confine offenders behind walls without trying to change them is an expensive folly with short-term benefits — winning battles while losing the war."

On July 30, 1991, Senator Jesse Helms rose to introduce Amendment 938, which read: "No person incarcerated in a federal or state penal institution shall receive any funds appropriated to carry out subpart 1 of part A of Title IV of the Higher Education Act of 1965." Helms fulminated that "American taxpayers are being forced to pay taxes to provide free college tuitions for prisoners at a time when so many law-abiding, taxpaying citizens are struggling to find enough money to send their children to college."

The Helms Amendment was grounded in two assumptions: (1) that a significant diversion of grants from needy young people to prisoners is occurring, resulting in a large percentage of traditional students failing to receive aid; and (2) that inmate-students are not "needy." Both are false. Only 1.2 percent of the total number of Pell Grants issued went to prisoners. By any stretch of the imagination, this is not a significant diversion of funds.

As for prisoners not being "needy," a 1986 Bureau of Justice Statistics bulletin noted that 60 percent of prison inmates had earned less than $10,000 the year previous to their incarcerations. In other words, they would have been below the poverty line and thus eligible for educational financial aid had they not been imprisoned.

With African-Americans, Latinos, and other minorities composing 55 percent of our country's prison population, and with 60 percent of inmates coming from the lowest economic levels of society and 41 percent having less than a ninth-grade education, compared with 16 percent of the nation's adult population, there can be little doubt that student-prisoners are "needy." "If you want to educate black men, if you want to reclaim the talent out there," observes Robert Powell, assistant vice president for academic affairs at Shaw University in North Carolina, "you have to go into the prison." The sad reality in the United States today is that PSCE is one of the few remaining means by which minority youth can receive a college education.

The same day Amendment 938 was introduced, it passed the

Senate by a floor vote of 60 to 38 and was attached to an appropriations bill. Helms later attached his amendment to the Higher Education Reauthorization Act. By then, the legislative action had shifted to the floor of the House.

On March 26, 1992, Representative Thomas Coleman and Representative Bart Gordon presented a joint amendment that would prohibit "any individual who is incarcerated in any Federal or State penal institution" from qualifying for Pell Grant assistance. The basic argument propelling the measure was the same as the one Senator Helms had promulgated the previous July. Many "facts" and "figures" were bandied about during proponents' orations over the issue, most of them inaccurate.

Representative Coleman, for example, claimed 100,000 prisoners received Pell Grants. This figure would mean that one out of every eight inmates in the nation is a college student! Such a notion is preposterous. In 1982, researcher John Littlefield and Bruce Wolford estimated that 27,000 inmate-students were enrolled in 359 prison college programs, representing less than 4 percent of the national penal population. Another study conducted the same year reported that PSCE funding was arranged through a myriad of sources, but Pell Grants were the primary tuitional financing for 37 percent of the inmate-students. Even with prison populations doubling in the interim, projecting a matching increase of inmate-students and guesstimating a doubling in the percentage of Pell Grant use by this population, a reasonable assumption is that fewer than 40,000 offenders received federal higher-education assistance in 1991.

During the House debate, Representative Steve Gunderson tossed more false facts into the mix. He stated that only 3.1 million students out of 6.3 million applicants received Pell Grants, and that this imbalance of aid "to the most needy of students among us" could be substantially corrected by barring inmate eligibility.

Actually, 3.6 million students receive Pell Grants, not 3.1 million. Furthermore, the Senate's version of the Higher Education Reauthorization Act significantly increased the appropriation for the Pell Grant program, enabling an additional 600,000 students to receive aid. The increased funding of the program will raise the family income ceiling from the current $30,000 to $50,000, with grant maximums raised as well, from $2,400 to $3,700 and eventually $4,500 by 1999. Ironically, Senator Helms cast the only dissenting vote against the very program he was so concerned about the year before.

The Coleman-Gordon Amendment easily passed, 351 to 39, and

was sent to a joint House-Senate conference, whose duty it was to resolve the differences between it and the Senate's version.

Meanwhile, outside Congress, opposition to the Helms and Coleman-Gordon amendments was gathering. On July 31, 1991, the day after Senator Helms introduced his amendment, a one-page alert, head-lined HELMS AMENDMENT WOULD DROP INCARCERATED PELL GRANT PROGRAMS, went out over the national Post-Secondary e-mail net-work. The bulletin briefly explained the proposition and included some of the debate's highlights.

This rapid notification of the impending disaster facing Post-Secondary Correctional Education galvanized a wide array of insti-tutions, organizations, and individuals. College presidents and university deans, professional associations and political action com-mittees, friends and family of prisoners as well as prisoners them-selves — all organized campaigns and lobbied Congress to vote against the prohibition of Pell Grants for prisoners.

In September 1991, the fourteen universities and nine private colleges that compose New York's Inmate Higher Education Program (IHEP) convened their semiannual conference with the Pell Grant cri-sis as the main item on the agenda. They agreed to form a political action committee to oppose the amendments.

The newly formed PAC collected information and disseminated it both within and outside the New York IHEP association. It also cooperated with other concerned organizations, including Educators for Social Responsibility, the Fortune Society, Literacy Volunteers, Minorities in Corrections, the National Education Association, the NAACP, the New York State Correctional Association, the Coalition for Criminal Justice, PEN, the Urban League, and Wilmington College. Additionally, the PAC contacted the offices of representatives who sat on the joint congressional committees and provided exten-sive PSCE data.

Another group active in the fight was the Correctional Education Association. Founded in 1946 by Austin McCormick, the man who established correctional education as a fundamental part of prison reform in the 1930s, the CEA is the only professional association ded-icated to serving educators and administrators who provide services to students in correctional settings. Steven Steures, the CEA executive director and legislative network chairman, organized the association's extensive response.

Also active was Citizens United for the Rehabilitation of Errants (CURE), which was founded in Texas in 1972, was expanded nationally in 1985, and now has more than seven thousand members. The organization's position is that prisons should be used only for those who absolutely must be incarcerated and should have all the resources they need to turn prisoners' lives around. The national office in Washington has extensive contacts with congressional representatives and worked closely with Senator Pell's staff.

Across the nation, inmate-students also worked to defeat their funding exclusion. On some prison-college campuses, such as in New York State, the faculty and institution staff organized the students' reaction, while on others the students themselves marshaled their response.

The men enrolled in Ball State University's extension program at the Indiana State Reformatory were such a self-motivated group. Members of the prison's debate team utilized the semester's various speech and communications classes, which had enrolled over 70 percent of the 138-member student body, as a forum to get the word out.

With the cooperation of the teaching staff, students in the speech classes were allowed to fashion presentations in accordance with the courses' structures to provide information on the Helms Amendment. These presentations ranged from simple lectures to round-table discussions to mock debates. The students imaginatively employed cost-comparison charts, experts on PSCE, and audience participation as debate judges to bring home the point of the value of PSCE and the seriousness of the legislative threat. Other students wrote letters directly to the state's representatives, or to friends and relatives urging them to do so.

The combined efforts of the nation's colleges and universities, professional associations and political action committees, individual voters, as well as the erudite pleas of the prisoners themselves, effected the defeat of the Helms Amendment in two separate joint committees. The process was repeated against the Coleman-Gordon Amendment.

In this effort incarcerated persons learned that they were not powerless. They could lobby Washington politicians just like any other special interest group. What the men and women who wear numbers on their chests lack in political clout and financial resources, they can make up in cunning and determination to succeed. Across the nation, the motto of prisoners needs to become *nec aspera terrant* (frightened by no difficulties).

1993, Indiana State Reformatory
Pendleton, Indiana

Tetrina

Bedford Hills Writing Workshop

Six women argue with their lives
as they write among their dreams
chasing shadows down streets
and reaching for words

like fruit, like stars, words
to save their lives
to snatch them from the streets
defend their dreams

Don't we deserve our dreams
our hard borne words
labor of our lives?
We have taken in our streets

the clash, the color, the broken streets
and shaped them into dreams
and then to words
to change our lives

six lives held by dreams
a world of streets, our luminous words

1996, Bedford Hills Correctional Facility
Bedford Hills, New York

Sestina: Reflections on Writing

Bedford Hills Writing Workshop

"Write about something inside that wants to get out — a poem, a bitch, a muse, something *tethered*."

It's six fifteen on a Wednesday evening. Six women, pens in hand, are gathered around a table. The lesson has come from Hettie Jones, who runs the writing workshop at Bedford Hills Correctional Facility. This "inside-out" exercise is only one of the many assignments she has brought us over the nine years the workshop has been in existence. We've written about "night," about "an encounter with a stranger," about persons, places, and events. We've even responded successfully to the challenge to "write a poem that makes no sense."

Each week's lesson comes with many examples of published work. We take turns reading these and then talk about issues related to writing — techniques, style, form, content. The hope is that the work will inspire us and that we'll find a starting point to begin our own.

The writing workshop has had a profound and lasting impact on each of us. Some of our writing is taken from personal experience, both in and out of prison, a lot of it comes from the pain of being incarcerated, away from family and especially children. Sometimes the writing just comes from a place never visited before. We all agree that being in the workshop has made a distinct difference in how we see ourselves. To explore this, we decided to respond to a series of questions about it.

What brought you to the workshop initially?

Iris: "I knew I liked to write and wanted to learn the proper techniques."

Lisa: "I'd come from a battered relationship. The group appeared to offer a safe place to start to figure out who and what I was."

Jan: "I went because I was looking for anything to do that would help me forget where I was. The first time I attended I didn't feel able to write, although I wanted to. My mother had a gift for words. She could express herself very well and I wanted so much to be like her.

But I wasn't like her. In class that first night, Hettie had to lead me through the experience of visualizing a story. I imagined a tinker who drove a battered car on a dusty road. I could see the place he traveled. I could smell the sagebrush and hear the lullaby of the ocean. But I couldn't put it on paper."

What was it like the first time you read aloud something you wrote?

Lisa: "I was scared to death."

Jan: "I was afraid my words wouldn't be understood."

Iris: "Scary. I didn't like it."

What has the workshop done for you?

Lisa: "Hettie took what I thought of as personal and private and made me see it as potentially an art form."

Kathy: "When I was in the women's movement, and a whole generation of poetry was *created* out of the rising identity of women, I found myself writing some poetry, but I never thought that I could do it as a regular part of my life. I grew up clinging to the rational. Emotional currents had, for me, the terror of loss of control. Yet poetry always called me. It was my way of letting go and feeling those inner currents — dreaming, hoping, crying, and fearing. With the writing workshop, I had found a space that would, on a regular basis, give me permission to look at the inner self and walk in it."

Miriam: "I've learned to express myself better. If I write anything that hurts, it's like getting it out of the way. I don't have to worry about it again. I used to hold things in and lash out. By writing, I can actually calm myself and avoid hurting someone's feelings."

Precious: "Writing about my daughter gave me an opportunity to express some feelings I had about our relationship. I work with women in here who have children in foster care. Losing children is a tremendous psychological loss. My poems gave me the opportunity to write that pain out."

Iris: "I feel differently about my whole life now. Instead of getting angry, I just go and write it. That's a change for me. Through the workshop I've learned to let those feelings out in a productive manner. And as I write more, I've begun to discover another part of me."

Judy: "The workshop is a place in this environment where we let go of the distractions and just work. After we read what Hettie brings in, we sit quietly, preparing to write. The energy of that quietness, that collective quietness, is the moment creativity gets inspired in that room. What's interesting, looking back at the process, is that the content of what I write about often sneaks up on me. For example,

Hettie once gave us an exercise to write a short prose piece in which we focus on pacing by slowing down the action through use of minute detail. I tried to think of an experience where time seemed to stand still, and found myself telling a story of being molested by a French tutor. I was writing about an event that I had never been able to tell anyone about. I felt a rush of energy as something that had been moldering inside me was released."

Have you come to think differently about your writing process?

Jan: "I never wrote that story of the tinker. In fact, for a long time I did not go back to the workshop. But when I did, I found myself looking to learn. And I did. I'm not sure I can identify pace and rhythm and drama by pointing to an example of these in my writing. What I can do is sense that what words I have strung together have those qualities. I feel, I remember, I write. And sometimes I'm just very fortunate to end up with a piece that works."

Precious: "My earliest memories now are of how clinical my writing was when I started. I guess that was to be expected since I had just finished a degree in psychology. Still, I wasn't pleased with Hettie's constant reminders of just how dry my writing was. Wasn't poetry a mosaic of passion, sadness, and happiness — all psychological expressions of our experience? I wanted desperately to write wonderful words about my children and my family — it's important that we do things in here to let our families know we are okay. Then I read this line from another poet — 'hit from time to time with lonely postcards.' It moved me deeply and helped me to write a poem to someone from my past who was, like me, imprisoned. This one didn't get the usual 'too analytical' comment from Hettie, and I was very pleased. It gave me hope, convinced me again that even if I'm incarcerated, my mind isn't."

Judy: "At first, I would balk at taking any word out, as though each word represented a piece of my soul. But gradually I learned that a flood of words can muddy up the picture, that often less is more. Making a poem is like carving a sculpture out of rough rock. I get this intense pleasure out of carving away words. It feels like a spiritual experience. Once that happened, that's when I felt, you know, I'm a poet."

The workshop has published two books — *More In Than Out* in 1992 and *Aliens at the Border* in 1997. There is an interesting story behind the title of one of these publications. One night, Hettie brought into the workshop a photo with a caption "Aliens at the Border," and one of the women wrote a poem about it. The title seemed to be a perfect description of the group. As Miriam said at the time, "I think it is perfect because sometimes I feel as if I'm looking out from the other side of the world." What were some of your reactions when you finally did see your work published out in the world?

Iris: "It felt good that I had written something well enough and purposeful enough to be brought to the attention of the public."

Lisa: "I was proud of myself — and that was a strange feeling. It also felt encouraging, I think. It's one thing to have Hettie say you have potential, that you're a great writer. Then to have your work published and know that people are buying it — that's a whole different thing."

Jan: "When I was young and full of dreams, I used to tell my friends in school I was going to 'make the books.' It was my way of saying that I would achieve some wonderful thing in my life that everyone would know about. Seeing my work, pieces of my life laid out in our book, made me feel I had fulfilled that prophecy."

What lasting effects has your experience in the workshop left you with?

Lisa: "Many, but one is a real desire for writing — not just a desire, but a real *joy*. I consider myself a writer, a good writer."

Kathy: "Poetry and my work in the workshop have become a part of my life in the way some people meditate or pray. I go to poetry to help me discover the mysteries of my thoughts and feelings. It is a path into the world that is always present but whose presence we are not always aware of or do not always value. Poetry is also a craft. After struggling with emotions that I should be able to spontaneously write a poem from, I am slowly learning the patience to take a thought and work with it."

Iris: "I can disperse my pain through my pen."

Judy: "My poetry has also been a way for me to express feelings of loss and shame and hope as a mother in prison, and my growing sense of remorse for the terrible losses I have caused others by my crime. I don't think I'm exaggerating when I say that the workshop has played a role in my reclaiming myself and my humanity."

For all of us the writing workshop has been a joy, a burden, but most of all a release from the cinderblock walls that surround us year after year. We assume that we will be there, to release ourselves, every Wednesday. When we presented a reading of our poetry to the prison population for the first time, everyone wondered why we hadn't done it sooner. But first we had to learn to take ourselves seriously as writers. Not only finding our voices, but also believing that these voices mean something beyond our private world.

1998, Bedford Hills Correctional Facility
Bedford Hills, New York

Behind the Mirror's Face

Paul St. John

Charlie says to me, "We gotta get ready for that new facility mag, get us our voices heard." He's chewing on a nip of his cigar, which I despise, the stogie like a pen on the tripod of his hand.

"This is prison, Chuck, not a facility. In here they don't facilitate a friggin' thing."

Charlie can't listen and talk in the same context. "Prison writing, man, that's where it's at." He's staring at a blank screen above my shoulder.

My brain lines up a reasonable response: How long you been down, you big stupid ape? "It makes no difference, bro," I say instead. This is one redneck I won't offend.

From here on in it's a one-way conversation, two hundred and eighty pounds of duress humming on about Jack Henry Abbott writing his way out of the joint because he had the guts to speak up, how prison writing breaks down the walls of isolation, how the pen is mightier than . . .

The thoughts begin to soar V-formation:

Funny that in the end the sword proved to be Abbott's master. / With Mailer for an editor I'd write my way out of hell. / He also did a little snitching there, if the truth be told. /

But they just dive off and fall away. I wave my hands at the curtains of smoke Charlie has installed in my cell, and he knows that's enough of him for one morning.

I ride the inside track, and within an hour I find out why the warden has seen fit that a few caged birds should go to print. As every con knows, democracy in the prison setting is just another word for "never," so when each inmate group petitions to put out their own newsletters, the warden has an aberration to prevent. (Manifold printing costs, new jobs for x inmate staffs to type, edit, and lay out page after page of burning prose and slick graphics on blazing 486 computers. Forget it. They end up smarter than the guards. Then the salaried censorship squad for all whiners who will harp on and on about an evil system and skewed justice, dire living, exploitation, Bill of Rights violations and conspiracy theories ad nauseam.) So what is a reasonably sly warden to do? He will locate two or three lifers who would have been Nobel laureates if not for lack of opportunity, to offer them the chance of their lifetime. It is time his prisoners be heard!

He will leave out one small detail: This is to be a one-time venture, something he can show the inmate groups so their nagging will rest. You will have one facility-sponsored publication, one single vehicle of choice for all your groaning pains and visions. Come and spill out your guts, dudes, in unity of song!

There will be plenty of Dostoyevskys and Malcolms in this number, but from the groups Mr. Warden will hear a single chorus: RUB IT ON YOUR CHEST 'CAUSE WE AIN'T RIDIN' SHOTGUN. His calculated effort will be thus consummated, and he will smile to the portrait of Reagan on his wall. Hey, guys, I handed it to you on a mess hall tray and you declined.

For Charlie it will be the beginning of great things. Charlie got soul. If I could synthesize the heart of his verse it would be this: the longing of looking through iron bars at the real world. Real touching stuff once you get past the trademark ache / break and dove / love rhymes. Next time around he would probably push his more radical stuff, things like "Why the Parole Board Should Be Abolished" and "Why Media Coverage of Violent Crime Should Be Abolished" and "Why the Random Cell Search Should Be Abolished." I just hope he won't start acting up when he discovers there isn't going to be a second time.

Prison Writing. The term reverberates in my brain case like kettledrums. The anger returns. I can't recall the psycho-speak, but I know it's like a form of Pavlov's. People are set off by certain sights, sounds, even smells, that affect them in very special ways.

Suddenly the gallery feels awfully quiet. I stare at my typewriter, which turns into a missile-control board. It's time to fire away.

I will call her Mother Nature, an artist who came into the prison to "find flowers where others saw only weeds." I taped the Author's Release to the wall two weeks ago. I feed a blank sheet to the machine.

Dear Mother Nature,

Thank you for the opportunity you have given us to videotape our work for a showing at the Cultural Center. I think you are a unique spirit for daring to tap into the voices of this miserably dark place. However, I regret to say that you are on the wrong track if your intentions are to use this so-called Prison Writing Experience as a means for reform, simply because prisoners, although they understand what is wrong with the system better than any criminologist, judge, cop, or outsider, have the credibility of elves. In this sense prison writing's dead wood.

The only other way to look at prison writing is as a way of expression. And, frankly, who wants to hear about loneliness, hopelessness, despair, loss of autonomy, harassment, contempt, or civil death, except to feel real good that things aren't as bad out in the world? Please don't think that I will allow myself to be used as consolation for a civilian audience.

Finally, if you are on a true healing mission, seeking to change the minds and hearts of prisoners through a revolution of the pen, I will appreciate it very much if you'd begin with sending me some real food and vitamins to counterbalance the negative effects of the garbage I am fed. I could also use real medical care, you know, the kind that steps right to the business and doesn't doubt the patient, and doesn't wait for rigor mortis in order to proceed. That's all I got to say.

Very truly yours,
Dr. J.

Sorry, Charlie, I think you better take all your "I hurt" trash and your impossible solutions and rub them on your fat redneck chest. I will be a writer in prison, for now. You be all the prison writer you wish. Be a white gorilla in your cubicle bush with iron fronds and rock-hard soil. Moan your nightly if-onlys and grunt your morning sores of broken luck alone, my man, 'cause I'll be traveling light with the Daughters of Sin. Their silken manes fall down their rears like pouring silver, and their moans are all I need for a cloak. Their touch is a tingle of mercurial dew, their panting a hot leaden mist on a desert of glass. I won't tell you about their kiss, not tonight, Charlie.

Charlie would never understand that nothing they do here is for his benefit. The language of his philosophical cutlery will be toned down, watered down, rekneaded to retain the basic dignity of the system, or rejected if he doesn't go along. Would any prison foster a printed attack on its own ways? Prison writing is as free as the author. Again I engage the machine and begin to spin out a little speech I have prepared for my prison writing group, which I polish up as I go.

On the Subject of Prison Writing

Good evening, fellow writers. I would like to take a few minutes tonight to discuss prison writing and its place in the larger world of letters.

As we know, writing comes in many kinds. There is fiction writing, journal writing, junk mail writing, copy writing, textbook writing, speech writing, news writing, film script writing . . . you aim, I shoot.

Subject, genre, specialty — the writer enters it by choice. But prison writing is a matter of status. It comes with the bid and that's that. It must take as subject matter life in prison. Prison writing is literally forced upon the writer, who, incidentally, has been stripped of just about everything else. Now, that's supposed to liberate.

Hey, Charlie, you dumb ass! You big cigar-puffin' ignorant crass sack of southern white trash! You bemused witless serf!

A con may write fiction, but everybody will know where it comes from. His fiction wears the stink of prison for a belt. Her fiction is pregnant with loss disguised as possibility. His outlaws always get the better of a wicked status quo. Her heroines grope through a jungle of shame for their stolen womanhood, and perhaps a piece of heaven. A convict may write about Mars, the sea, rebirth, cats, needles and pins; without the "convict point of view" there is no prison writing. Take this goddamned place out of your art is what I am trying to tell you all.

My concentration is assaulted by my boombox-proud neighbor, who jacks up the rapper cacophony until the presence of the guard, like some magical wand, directs him to turn into a punk. (Whatever happened to cool smooth good ol' American jazz?) As soon as the guard leaves the gallery, he is King Kong again.

King Punk is confined to his cell for talking to another inmate two steps out of character. Although he got the brunt of it, violence has no victims here. Self-defense is without justification. If you're hurt, you shouldn't have been there. If you do not defend yourself, you're on a stainless-steel table with a sheet over your head, it's that simple.

And yet sometimes I think prison violence is all overstated, amplified, dramatized, *mythicized,* mostly by outsiders. Mybe I'm desensitized but prison life isn't really as dangerous as it's commonly portrayed. Much of the tension on the inside comes more from the perception of danger than from danger itself. That's why the sneak attack is the preferred mode of action — the little guy sticking a pen in the big guy's eye after the latter jokingly threatened to make him his girl. Although most cases of violence involve aggressor and prey, prison managers are unwilling to recognize assault because of the lawsuits. So they do their damnedest to make everyone look guilty or well-deserving.

Their process is succored by an important rule: Never believe what an inmate says except when he's snitching. In the old days telling was an abomination. Sooner or later the snitch would be found out and have to face the music. Today, telling is something of a sport and the facing up usually doesn't happen, as the snitch may conveniently check his cowardly ass into protective custody.

Underlying this apparent confusion is a beautiful symmetry. In the street, where self-defense is a legitimate act and telling is the bread of concerned citizens, crises tend to ripple off toward agreement. Behind the mirror's face, the littlest disturbance bears the seed of chaos.

After mopping the gallery catwalk that stretches like a giant steel blade past forty cells, I ease into my slippers and robe. On my way to the shower I pass Captain Lafane, whose harrowed look makes me wonder if it's me who is doing the time. He knows that my transition from systems analyst to prison porter has not been easy, but that is not the reason for his grief. His oldest son has AIDS.

I awaken to the chirping of birds. With all the nooks on the outside, they had to nest in here. There are dozens of them, lodged in the stone bowers high above the uppermost gallery. Jailbirds. Now it happens that prison is also a state of mind.

Will there be any stabbings today? Any rapes? Who cares? No one will ever know the half of it. Just as I rake the stubble off my chin two guards rush past my window into the deep of the gallery. A minute later, two more guards go by with a wire mesh stretcher. Here we go.

Except for the crackle of radios, the gallery is dead-still. No one has been out yet. We must have an overnighter. The portable mirrors go into peeking mode.

The guards are slow on the catwalk. Two are old and overweight;

one just looks sick and tired. Their walk is like a funeral march without an entourage. As they approach my cell I pull my mirror in and look down at the stretcher. It's Jimmy G. I better hurry up and finish shaving before they yell for chow.

* * *

Questions are being raised about the night guard's rounds, which should go on every two hours. The coroner has established that Jimmy took his life sometime after two. Even after this leak, we know that nothing will be done beyond tightening up the rounds for a while. No jobs will be in jeopardy, even when Jimmy had been talking suicide a few weeks in advance. Even after he was taken twice for observation to a psychiatric center, and advised that there was nothing wrong with him. Even after he flashed his suicide card to his pastor.

In her letter of thanks to his church for having run a fund collection, his mother stated that Jimmy had a chemical imbalance, foreclosing any possibility of a negligence action. Anyway, thank you, Mrs. G. Now all of us who did nothing to prevent your son from giving up will feel better. It was all in his genes as luck is in the stars, we will say.

Jimmy was four-fifths of the way through a sentence for murder. If the truth be told, I can think of one thousand better candidates for Hades just on the basis of their bearing. Jimmy had found religion. Jimmy had found a good church girl to elope with.

We all knew that he had been distressed over his failed marriage, but in here a man is pretty much left alone with the affairs of his heart. It was a union blessed by God, not to be set asunder by another. Why did she have to have "a male friend" at her house almost every time he called . . .

It couldn't have been you instead of Jimmy, could it, King Punk, you rappin' tappin' slappin' wind-up moppet-faced big bad mouth cybernaut stooge. Even you, farther down, who would have your voice heard by the prison machine. How much are you willing to renounce? A noun-slice here, a verb-tuck there, perhaps a sentence-graft or two? Why don't you just sing praises to the Beast? Something might click. A new trend. Charlie, it might just make a difference!

Jimmy, perhaps you should have come to me. I would have told you their names:

I saw your humbled heart filling your mouth with hardened bread, and I kept silent. You should have known her, too, the one holding the wineskin, that fine hostess of spoils. Plethora will give you of her sac of ambrosia, and you will be made new. I will not risk offending, else I would bring her to you.

When I heard you smite your chest in penitence, I thought, *Jimmy, that ain't no way of doin' time.* Hedone will give you relish, comfort, a new zest. Frolic between the happy slopes and valleys of her Eden, for no one needs saving from love. Rest, Jimmy, rest now, and pound your chest no more.

But of the three, Cacoethes is the crown. She's the baddest, the goodest, the sweetest, the tartest, the hostess of play. She's the lifeline, the night life, hops, cheers, saturnalia again. Fandago, tango, fling, and boogaloo.

They say that she's full of bad habits. Not true. She's sport, gala, picnic, and game all the same. Overall, she's a labor of love. In a cinch she's Ways and Means, my man. For you, she would have plucked the hand that held the knife of infidelity, before it ripped your heart. When Mars directs the rouge over her lips, and paints her eyes for the battle cry, you know there's no staying and no praying for more. All in all, she'll save you from a two-timer wife. Cacoethes is the blood of my pen, liberation without the prison writing.

You won't be needing religion in the bowels of Earth. Neither do I in the belly of Baal. You may judge me unwise, but at least there is no falling from grace in this bed. One day I might tell you the meaning of their names, if you should resurrect.

But tonight I'm riding with the wind.

1994, Eastern New York Correctional Facility
Napanoch, New York

Black Flag to the Rescue

Michael E. Saucier

It's a race between the roaches and me
to see which of us is going to win
final and total control of this typewriter
        Will I finish my Great American Novel
with all its inherent, time-consuming rewrites before
these filthy things that huddle in the dark recesses
of my battery-powered machine, scurrying in twenty
different directions when I remove the case
that swarm all over the printing head as it zings back
along its track, sometimes jamming it
that impudently crawl up and down a sheet of prose
right in the middle of a tender love scene . . .
I mean I'm trying to write some literature here,
you repulsive !#@¥+**&! bugs
        . . . before they eventually chew through the electronic
ribbon — the lifeline of my machine?
Will I be able to complete my book before they do all this?
In past days I've noticed they've gathered in greater numbers
on this critical ribbon as if planning a final campaign;
it's worrying me sick

        I've noticed too during this unseasonably warm and
humid
winter at the Louisiana Correctional Center from where I write
that a whole new generation has hatched —
now there are tiny tot roaches inside my typewriter
growing toward full roachhood
What do they think this is, a brooder?
        The plastic coated ribbon must be emitting
some hellaciously appetizing radon odors
or something else equally as sensual that drives
these vile creatures into a breeding frenzy
because every time I snap the case shut — *they're at it!*
        How do I work
with all this gross activity occurring just inches
from my fingertips — ? With much grimacing and teeth
grinding.

What we writers have to endure
sometimes
ain't nothing nice

   I wonder how many other roaches,
older, wiser, and warier are crouched in the farthest
most inaccessible spaces of my Canon
feeding on these nutritiously addictive command wires,
disemboweling the computer circuitry byte by byte?
Inexorably they're forcing me to condense my long, languorous
tender love scenes into cheap, artless quickies
forget foreplay — there's no time
a bunch of stupid roaches are pushing me
perilously close to writing pornography
Is there no hope? No remedy? Is my art to be sacrificed
to these wanton, concupiscent creatures?

   If only I had some bug spray —
I'd douse those mothers good and proper!
Black Flag would do the job
but lethal stuff like that is absolutely prohibited
to us inmates
A pest control man does come around occasionally,
spraying the baseboards, which only drives the little vermins
deeper into the sanctuary of my locker and typewriter;
they love it here — and why not?
They've got everything they need for a happy life:
darkness, dampness, and lots of hard juicy plastic to munch on
I tell you, it's a battle.
I've got to hurry and finish this novel
before they completely overrun my machine
I swear I'd forfeit a month's Good Time — really!
maybe more
for just one small can
of that deadly stuff

   1993, Avoyelles Correctional Center
   Cottonport, Louisiana

Players, Games

Big shots on both sides of the razor wire are often called "players," and their games are legion. Prisoners favor the street jingle: "X is my name and Y is my game." Games in prison can be rap, routine, or hustle. The two worlds of hustling, inside and out, overlap, especially where gangs are concentrated. New inmates must learn how to recognize and respond to prison games if they are to navigate a course among treacherous allies or protectors and outright predators. This means adopting, or simulating, an appropriate role. In one way or another, all prisoners become players. For some, "doing time" and playing games are one.

In "I See Your Work," the protagonist Willis — prison green-horn, political activist, and coming computer-game entrepreneur — tells his story in the overheated and telegraphic patois he is trying to master: "Jammin'. My cool still chillin'? Do I know what time it is?" Mentored by a supreme gamesmaster — the law librarian and jail-house lawyer — Willis prowls the multicultural maze of prison hustles while practicing his own. At the same time, he is plotting out a computer game about prison life. The story peels back the title's layers of meaning, from I-see-what-you've-done to I've got your number.

As in other "total" institutions like the army or boarding school, solidarity among peers is an option in prison, but conditions militate against it. Prisoners' desire to curry favor with the staff and — among men — commitments to macho image intensify disunity. In "solidarity with cataracts," Vera Montgomery (whose use of "k" to spell "camp" betokens her allegiance to the black power movement), laments her sisters' deafness to one another's cries for help, their collaboration in wantonly destructive cell searches, and their readiness to snitch for privileges. Fourteen years later, Marilyn Buck spins out a fantasy of a rebellious solidarity built on woman-love.

Convict culture in men's prisons appears to be dominated by ornate systems of games — ranging from handball, poker, and business deals to scams and deadly gambles — which are often interlinked. The byzantine plots of the stories by Jackie Ruzas, David

Wood and Dax Xenos seem dictated by the very atmosphere of scheming and calculation that pervades the cellblock. Yet unexpected moral complexity blossoms in each tale. In "Ryan's Ruse" both the handball game and interethnic rivalry are manipulated to heat up the betting, which in turn serves the friendship of Irish Ryan and black Hap. Having AIDS locks the inmates in "Feathers on the Solar Wind" into a prison within the prison until a gamble with death confers a wild kind of liberty on some and propels others to seek forgiveness. The narrator of "Death of a Duke" has mastered the rules of the doing-time game: the joint "is like quicksand," he says, "like one of those Chinese finger stretchers. The more you struggle, the deeper you go or the tighter it gets. But you can be cool and make your way through it and get out." But the passion of the bigtime player, the Duke of Earl, makes him strain against such rules. Like "Lee's Time" (**Race**), this story inquires whether morality can be reconciled with doing time coolly in prison.

I See Your Work

Joseph E. Sissler

The C.O. at the front gate was idly watching Willis with government issue long-barreled Nikon binoculars. He had noticed Willis up close on the compound, noticed how he was different from the rest, immune it seemed, with a distinctive kind of observer's calm, as if he were here for the waters. He seemed more purposeful if a bit clumsy and inexperienced. And in fact Willis *was* on an expedition of sorts, both killing time for a moral stance and conducting research for a project long on his mind.

He was down for taking a hammer in a destructive unpatriotic manner to the tail of an Air Force jet. Going to jail was the purple heart of Willis's activist group led by the well known Fathers. Willis's companions were not with him, having distanced themselves at a critical time and receiving only a trespassing charge and the symbolic one night in jail. Willis, though not awash in remorse had, admittedly, been unsettled at his sentence, which was quite a bit longer than the group legal theorist had predicted. His sentence of a year and a day translated in federal computation to ten months.

Educated fringe dweller Willis had, in his work with a Catholic relief agency, run a soup kitchen and rubbed scabbed elbows with enough alley dwellers to grow boldly curious about their street life. The fruit of this curiosity had emerged as his first independent software production, a simulation game called *Homeless*. For his field work he had immersed himself in the cold city of Washington, D.C., scavenging the alleys of late autumn until almost Christmas. Except for the regular postings of his notes he remained isolated and unfunded. He utilized what he learned: the picking of a pizza dumpster lock with a pop-top from a soda can, panhandling stolen morning papers, the heating grate territories, choice outdoor places to shit, and he packed these details into software that explored this world in an engaging and moving manner, one simpatico with his activist roots. The game became a cult favorite and now he was prospecting for details to pack into a followup that would make a serious name in the industry and fund some serious kitchens for those urban outdoors people. He owed it to them; he owed it to himself. Only Fulton, his software distributor, knew of the plans.

* * *

Willis stepped into the prison law library. Russ, the legal librarian on duty, stood behind the interior dutch door taking delivery of a half-filled mesh commissary bag, payoff for a legal brief. The bag jutted angles of coffee jars and oranges, a plastic bottle of hot sauce, and many packets of rice and beans. On the top was a clump of green bananas. Facing Russ across the door-shelf was a jockey-size man smiling broadly and shaking a sheaf of legal papers over his head as if he held a Bible.

"I seen your work with Shorty Bighead," the man said. "Now got my own. Be like throwing a dead dog in the backyard of that car company. And better, that worthless bitch will piss all over herself. Gonna rock her little world."

Russ nodded his head in time to his customer's praise. It was good to get paid. It didn't always happen. "Make your copies first," he said. "Remember, Hollis, you owe me two bucks for the postage. Envelope all set up and good to go." Russ winked at Willis. "And next time your old lady sells a car, you can't owe on it."

"Not no next time with her. She smoked the damn money up less'n a week. D'int send a dime. Cabs to the dope corner, sometime on the hour, was how my cousin said. Then them fuckin' letters from the car people. Tapping into my paycheck. Gonna ruin my good credit."

"We can start that divorce anytime," said Russ.

Hollis rubbed his bristly chin. "After my furlough we do it. Getting twelve hours this weekend. My ex–old lady got a tiny sister name Dee-dee. She gonna check me out, pick me up. Still counts as family on the paperwork. Gonna knock over some of that. We been eying each other for years, see, and Dee-dee don't like her sister neither. She gonna take back a Polaroid of my johnson, see if the bitch still know it."

Russ shook his head. "Hollis, you gonna need me plenty more, that's my prediction. Just keep rollin' with that commissary" — he shook the bag — "I'll keep the typewriter hot. Hey, and jump on one time for me."

"Yeah," Hollis said, tilting back his head. "Saturday I'm gonna be lying in the crib and you be thumbing them thick books wishing."

They laughed, slapped hands. "On time about that," said Russ. Hollis was out the door smiling.

While he waited, Willis gazed around the walls at the musty paper inventory of LAW. This room was a repository heart-deep in the iron beast, a pool of magical chants which sometimes, when strung in perfect order, went poof and everything changed, all the bureaucratic locks snapped open, legal cancer cured like from above. But mostly these arcane and blunt instruments were used against the researcher, the petitioner, the ever hopeful.

"Next," Russ said, pointing a pinkie at Willis.

"Just a little off the top," joked Willis.

"What up?" asked Russ, slumping in a stylized manner. He made a street-gang signal with his right hand, forefinger, pinkie, thumb extended, hand inverted. The Conquistadors from Chicago. He'd shown Willis a dozen times and still Willis couldn't duplicate it.

"Jammin'," said Willis. "My cool still chillin'? Do I know what time it is?"

"Not exactly, you're still runnin' slow. Sound a bit like Zippy the Pinhead, but on the other hand there's been progress of a serious nature, I wouldn't kid you about that. You got potential. For now how about a shift to another gear? A practical task out in the wide world."

Russ reached behind some federal law supplements and extracted a bag. "What we have here is genuine sliced cheap cheese of the chow hall variety." He grabbed another bag and slightly shook it. "Here we got chicken breasts of the boneless persuasion nicely marinated; a rare and precious item. Take the cheese, walk through rec. A quarter a packet, a buck for the chicken breast, which we leave here for now. You get one packet of cheese just for strolling around, putting the product out there."

Willis was skeptical. "You sound like my distributor."

"You mean dealer?"

"I mean software distributor." Willis looked at the cold yellow lumps. "I don't know who to sell to."

"They find you." Russ grinned close to Willis's face, "You ain't pushing for a bigger cut are you? Look, it's the trip of living here. You tell me you want to know, here it is. Just walk around to people you know. Get close to them, look over your shoulder, get shifty. Be like the SOB sellin' watches in the bus station. Pass the word in a whisper. People go for the sly deal. Get them leaning. The price is right. No dealing. Credit if they seem straight to you. Let'm know in that case who's behind you."

"All right. You sold me. I'll try it. Probably be bringing the cheese back."

"Just try. This will be good for you. Remember. Slink around when you start cruising the customers. Zip here. Jit there. Point A to point B. People notice, it's advertising. On the way there shoot by the rec office and make sure them motherfuckers still on their dead asses."

Willis put the cheese in his coat pocket, hesitated. Did he really need this? Yes. He'd take his little notepad with him.

Russ shook his finger at him. "Go on with you. Mix it up with the kids."

The wide central hallway was quiet except for a pickup basketball game in the gym, ball dribble echoing out, some sharp exhalations, a curse. The auditorium movie had sucked away population, leaving the corridor unnaturally vacant. Further along the wall on the top of a low dusty glass trophy case two of the girls played some game, slapping down cards with a lazy indifference. The tall one, called Lick-lick Willis believed, red scarf around head, hip outshot, looked over the few people in the hallway. Willis angled toward the bathroom and Lick-lick shifted, head tossing the dangling scarf fringe. She prepared to intercept him. Belatedly Willis realized Lick-lick was a lockout so shifted his course to the other side of the broad hallway. Another behavioral twitch. Jot it down, program to silicon reality.

Willis looked through the double side doors into the rec area, near empty. No customers yet in the here and now. He'd wait until the movie let out, some cop flick with everyone rooting for the wrong side and waiting for the shootout ending. Meditate outside. The hall's glass exit doors halted him for a moment and he briefly viewed the girls' reflections as he left.

Outside a dead dark sky, a few smokers lounging against the rec wall thoughtfully exhaling. The sound of water over rock, the miniature rapids, soothing to Willis's ear. The temperature was hovering near freezing; snow that evening, late, it was predicted. A half a foot maybe. Start as rain. Change your space, thought Willis. Make the world anew. Put on another wrapper.

Some few brisk striders surfaced under the hanging globe lamps that carved up bits of the night, then disappeared back into the dark, their sock-capped heads swaying to headsets. Keep on the move and everything was all right. The creek flowed close and Willis walked beyond the wide sidewalk to the bank and peered into the blackness sliding by. The creek was slower here, placid, gurgles at odd intervals rather than the signature hiss of the rock-combed waters up near the ballfield, the very end of his legal landscape. The creek came from beyond where he had never been and emptied, according to the library map, into some river he'd never seen and couldn't yet pronounce. Not to follow it, that was prison.

By these barriers, and others invisible, is my life defined, thought Willis. He remembered the immigrants from Central America he had assisted, principally the Salvadorans, but also the Guatemalans. He thought of how they were overwhelmed in so much landscape and here Willis was trapped in a postage-stamp patch of it. They had crossed dangerous borders on their bellies; he stood like a sheep in a gateless pen.

Light flowed from the top of the rec area's steamed glass panels. Willis could hear the inside transformed into a noisy circus: some Ping-Pong, the crack of a pool ball break, other petty competitions with a pushup payoff from the losers. "Man down" was shouted, and the loser hit the floor for settlement. "Gimme good money" shouted his tormentor, no doubt standing over him. "Crack those elbows. Go deeper, touch that bird chest to my fist."

Willis knew that in the far corner would be a clandestine poker game with worn old playing cards notched *just so* functioning as camouflaged chips. There was a lookout for the roving compound officer. The poker people would be the usual rapt ruined faces with noses long ago mashed, little hats shoved back on heads, a rodent concentration even from the bystanders: nothing minded but the game.

Everything a gamble here: boccie ball, pro football, which piece of floating bread in the pond would be pulled down first, which duck landing would stumble. Stir the monotony. Most wagers were an ice cream here, a can of tuna there, a shoeshine. It all added up.

In the chilled, windless air Willis heard the ducks holed in a tight pack inside one of the big PVC drain pipes. Muffled quacking sporadically cracked the night air. Willis put a hand into his pocket. He was surprised by the cheese . . . the task.

He passed through a misted door to domino games and tonk, with poker and chess in the distance, all ringing the central carpeted area with its pool tables and Ping-Pong. A mutated boy's club, graying and profane.

There was Bow-Wow standing by himself, and Willis walked to him, growling "Real dog. You okay?"

"Ruff-ruff," barked Bow-Wow. "Gonna be greater later."

"I got some cheese I'm looking to move." Willis tapped his coat pocket.

Bow-Wow made a face. Shook his head. "No man. Binds me bad since I ate it with goat in Jamaica. Anyway, I'm down broke, no bone in my pocket 'til payday."

"You change your mind, catch a few bucks, I might locate some chicken too."

"Can a dog eat a hot-dog?"

Willis walked to the TV area. He had forgotten to slink, to side talk, to jit . . . whatever that was. Maybe these maneuvers were important. They weren't when he was living homeless, stealing and selling newspapers near the subway. Then he had played it straight, and the businessmen had usually given him a buck for the quarter paper, maybe for not running a game, for not slowing them down. He had easily sold the papers in the cold, he ought to be able to get rid of the cheese and chicken. He grinned about the cheese, the government cheese. On the outside, at the public kitchen, he had given it away. How things turn inside out.

There came a sudden shadow hanging over him, accusing. "Laughin' over nothing now, Willis? Could get you shipped to Kansas. They already think you crazy." Half & Half, the bondsman from Pittsburgh, was momentarily away from his seat at the poker table. He carried a thick stack of red-backed marker cards, which he reflexively shuffled hand to hand. "I'm giving the fools a breather, let'em pass the money around to each other until I get a smoke outside. Then I go back to work. Payday."

Willis looked over his shoulder, then dropped his voice. "I'm just walking around tryin' to sell this cheese."

"Cheese! I look like a rat to you? What else Russ got?"

"Russ?"

"Yeah, Russ. You just another of his scouts. I know what time it is. He trains 'em all look over their shoulder." Half & Half winked at Willis, gave the gang hand signal. "Hey, it's cool, everything be everything. Me and Russ been to school together down Leavenworth. I run an account. Send him homeboys for the legal shit. Now, what else he got?" He held up his hand. "Wait, let me guess. The chicken for lunch today. Probably the better pieces, staff stuff. That his special. Gimme two of the breasts. Have him throw them between some bread he always has, slap the cheese on it. Some mayo too, I know he got in the back book room. I'll skip by after another run on the bank, or you bring it by, whatever. Maybe we want more if somebody else get lucky and have anything left."

Willis tried to pass him the cheese but he shook his head. "Put it on the sandwich with a little mayonnaise. Russ know. He the best burner on the compound even working on cold cuts."

Willis walked toward the door, where he stopped for a few minutes and watched two Nigerians engaged in a powerful long-distance game of Ping-Pong. No sense in going back too soon and making Russ think it was easy. Standing next to Willis was Nawaba, another Nigerian, also watching, waiting, custom thick rubber-faced paddle in his hand rhythmically tapping his palm.

"How did you guys from Africa get so good at this game? Was it the Chinese advisers I hear you got over there?"

Nawaba shook his head and laughed. "You got my country confused. Africa much bigger than you Americans think. The Chinese were in the east. You have Cubans in Angola, and, of course, the Texans in Nigeria, and they know nothing but oil and beer and our girls in their hotel beds. But I tell you what makes my countrymen so fine at this sport. We are just many miles of bush and poor villages. The people in their little huts take tin cans and flatten them out, put them on a stick. They stretch a fish net between two milk cans. We get here and it is like a paradise with these paddles and balls, these smooth, fine tables. So now you know and forever can spread the word."

Willis always enjoyed talking to the Nigerians. "So now, Nawaba, that you got pants pulled over those tribal ballsacks, tell me how you come to speak better English than the hillbilly staff. Also tell me how you lucked into those two Pizza Huts the newspaper said you had. The three cars and boat. The condo at Ocean City."

"I am just a simple man the government wants to deport to the lions."

The two of them watched the ball slammed back and forth, the contestants standing impossibly far away from the table swinging hard and accurately. Beyond the Ping-Pong along a far wall were weight machines swarmed by lifters, their extremities blood swollen and heavily veined, some strutting chest out, posing awkwardly, rigidly getting their breath, pushing each other out of the way to peep themselves in the mirror.

The high ceiling collected sounds of the smacked Ping-Pong balls, racked pool balls, the sharp clack of the weight stacks, the background drone of the corner TV, the hollers of homeboys. It was an atmosphere, if not exactly carnival, lively, a swirl Willis would be challenged to re-create. A pick-up-stick snarl, which deliberate programming could perhaps encompass, utilizing the rec hall as a kind of spinning hub that altered the player's course. Inject a lifelike randomness to it all. It didn't have to affect immediately, five moves later would work the fork to another routine. Day has become night. Your name has been called to report to the lieutenant's office. You have an impending appointment with the incompetent medical professional who will perform a painful procedure . . . go back three spaces. These junctions, Willis thought, were switching stations. The chow hall would be another. It was almost as if these gathering places were waterholes for predator and prey. He scribbled a few notes and strolled through the door toward the law library.

Across the hall by the bathroom the two girls had been joined by a third, the beautiful, heavily hormoned Michelle. Two raincoated serious fellows, toothpicks moving side to side in their mouths, rocked on their heels. There was no friendly chatting up.

"You don't know?" Michelle shook her head. "I see your work. Know all about it. Seen your work is why. You dig?"

The two raincoats looked at each other and shook their heads slowly. One spit his pick on the floor and ground his heel over it.

Lick-lick, red head scarf coming unwound, said, "Mac game over, man. Mac game gone even for you country ass."

Willis walked back to the law library. Russ was still standing behind the door, elbows on shelf, chin resting in his palms, smiling. Willis relayed Half & Half's order.

"He was a bondsman," said Russ. "Got set up by a customer. Imagine that. Who would believe the deceit rolling loose in this land. Half & Half had this specialty of working with the Dominican dealers. He learned a little bit of Spanish like 'Don't worry,' 'Talk to no one,' 'Who do I see about the money?'

"The way he had it worked out he usually got full bond with a ten percent edge, so when they skipped, which was often, he made out fine. The Dominicans had the money, the whole bond in cash, but they knew they just couldn't go down to the station house themselves with it. Police take it, laugh, tell them to come back with more. This one time he took a couple of bales of pot as deposit and it was a set up. When he returned the stuff the Feds came out of the bushes and they laid trafficking on him. Tried to turn him, get the scoop on his customers. He didn't . . . and here he be. I know. I did a twenty-two fifty-five for him."

Russ opened the Dutch door and ushered Willis through to the rear and pulled down several thick law books. Inside were chicken breasts in individual poly bags. "Three bucks, three breasts and three cheeses. Special deal. He always hits me for the bread and mayo. Pays his tab. We look out for each other."

"Yeah, he seemed fine," said Willis, his mind moving on. "Ah . . . what's the Mac game?"

"The Mac game? It ain't you, Willis. It's something been over for all but the idiots. Over since crack hit the streets."

"Yeah, I heard it was over, but what is it? was it?"

"The pimping thing. You know, running whores. Pimps were mostly put out of business by freelancing dope fiends of all sexes. Crack has them sucking on anything to kiss a pipe. And now there's all those escort services in the yellow pages so convenient for Mr. Businessman. All you got left is some fools hustling nowhere, counting nickels and dimes and wondering who stole their hat."

"I heard an argument in the hallway between the he/shes banging cards and a couple of country homeboys."

"Yeah, some of these new boys broadcast tough when they see a few flamers. Big visions of cornering the market, think they're the first ever got the idea. They dream of a locker full of cigarettes. You got more gays here than you see. A lot more. Respectable ones keep to themselves, keep to their own. Meet their gentlemen friends privately. Do the gump bump in the shower at midnight. But there's always some few parading like they still working the street, batting them long fake eyelashes, livin' the life, slow dying from whatever, bodies a bomb of virus. They rub against some of these dumbfuck's minds. Overheat them. Always trouble dancing around them. Use them to cut your hair, but otherwise stay away."

Willis packed his coat pockets with the food and walked back to the card game. In the hall he saw through the outside glass doors where the girls were gesticulating at the two toughs receding into the dark along the sidewalk. The girls were laughing and taunting, holding their noses. One of the toughs turned back and flicked a cigarette at them, red arc lost in the door lights. Red scarf picked it up and tossed it back weakly overhand, just like a girl.

1995, Federal Correctional Institution Morgantown
Morgantown, West Virginia

solidarity with cataracts

Vera Montgomery

at 3:25 yesterday mornin'
i awakened to staccato wails of
a sister in sky-high pain and
the kamp was sister packed
i screamed
i shouted
i banged
i yelled
i hollered
i cursed and
the sister of yesterday's wails
carry surgical scars today
all the while
i wondered as
i screamed
i shouted
i banged
i yelled
i hollered
i cursed
where was solidarity?

one afternoon
a sister wept and
i wept inside for the
wreckin'-crew sisters
i can't erase this scene:
a water-soaked mountain of
broken/empty toiletries
shredded literature
cut up garments and
atop the heap
our sister's love one's
pictures hate torn
to bits
all the while

i stood and wondered
where was solidarity?

all kamps install a
stool pigeon snitch box
the box is never idle
'cause louise stole an
extra slice of bread
jeanette is high
how can dotty go on
a furlough when she
has walked on grass
ann bought
commissary for
rose 'cause they
play chicks
rita stole a pair of
chartreuse state sneakers
vivian smokes in bed
how can kisha go
home to attend her
dad's funeral while
not-in-good-standin'
maria was playin' stink
finger in the movie and
as i robbed the kampkeeper's
stool pigeon's snitch-box
notes
i wondered
where was solidarity?

1976, Edna Mahan Correctional Facility
Clinton, New Jersey

Clandestine Kisses

Marilyn Buck

for Linda and her lover

Kisses
blooming on lips
which have already spoken
and now await
stolen clandestine kisses

A prisoner kisses
she is defiant
she breaks the rules
she traffics in contraband women's kisses.

A crime wave of kisses
Bitter sweet sensuality
flouting women-hating satraps
in their prison fiefdoms
     furious
     that love
     cannot be arrested.

1990, Washington, D.C. Jail

Ryan's Ruse

Jackie Ruzas

The hot August sun and pea soup humidity set the temperature in Sing Sing's yard somewhere between simmer and boil. It was the second day of hell-like heat, and the normally energized cons were playing in the shade on the old death house wall.

Out on the Hudson, sails hung limp for want of a breeze; the current alone carried boaters down river to "The Apple." All in all it was a beat down drag-out uncommon Sing Sing day, and the only thing that saved it from resembling a convict burial ground was the sound of action across the yard.

His gray-headed body moved with surprising grace across the concrete floor. It bent, stretched, and darted side to side in terpsichorean display, belying the lines that crossed his face like cracks in a shattered windshield. From forehead to chin the sweat ran free down the crisscross pattern, causing him to wipe it clean after each volley.

The game was handball. Two out of three games, at twenty-one points a pop for three cartons of smoke. He had lost a tough first game against the young Latino, Carlos, with a 21–18 score, and this second game was pumping repeat where he trailed by three at 16–13.

Carlos's next serve careened off the wall to the old-timer's left, causing him to return it high center wall. He then watched helplessly as Carlos stepped up and buried it low in the right-hand corner for point 17. Disgusted with his return, he called, "TIME" and stepped off the court to the sound of hostile voices from a group of partisan Latinos. "*Tu no eres nada, viejo!*" "*Tu necesitas aire, viejo, y no descanso!*" With the hostile shouts came hostile laughter, served in a way that made him smile, but only inside. Taking a green bandanna from his back pocket, he tied it Apache style around his forehead and stepped back on the court. "Serve," he said.

Jimmy Ryan was his name and handball was his game. At age fifty-one he had spent the last twenty-two years moving from one "max" prison to another, and where some cons spent their time on any number of prison hustles, Jimmy used his handball skill to supplement his prison wages. Handball to him was like junk to a junkie, and insulin to a diabetic. It got him high and kept him alive. Sure, the money was a means of survival, but to Jimmy it was much more complex than a simple hustle for capital. He needed the physical and emotional output provided by a game of one-on-one. All important was the drama and drain of competition, along with the crowd of back-slapping fans and back-stabbing enemies, looking for any edge to bet with or against him. Those were the things he fed on, the things that made Jimmy tick.

Carlos's serve was adequate but nothing to strike fear, and on point 17, it came knee high to Jimmy's left hand. Although right-handed, Jimmy's dexterity with both "smitties" was a talent honed long ago, and as Carlos moved right to control center court, Jimmy fired a return low to the left corner. Carlos's attempt to reverse his direction came up inches short and the serve changed hands at 17–13. Friendly voices helped strike a balance. "Way to go, Pops!"

"Take it easy on him, Jimmy!"

"You da man, mighty whitey!" Recognizing the last voice, Jimmy looked in that direction and caught the wink in the wrinkled black face.

Lucius "Hap" Lewis had been a rival of Jimmy's back in their Dannemora prison days, when integrated sports were administratively discouraged under a divide-and-conquer philosophy. On his way to becoming a handball legend, "Hap" (short for happy) caught a bad decision on a Dannemora court from a Harlem homeboy. With a shank in his hand and murder on his mind, the homeboy laid four inches in Hap's back, consigning him to a life on crutches.

Jimmy returned Hap's wink and stepped to the serve line. "Where do you want it, kid?" he challenged Carlos.

"Anywhere on the court, *viejo*. Anywhere, any way."

Jimmy's movement was fluid. Bending over low he bounced the ball inches from the ground, and on the third bounce his right arm swung down in an arc, smashing the ball on a straight line to the wall. Like a rocket it ricocheted low off the wall and zeroed in on Carlos's left ankle. Stepping quickly to avoid it, the kid managed only a feeble right-hand return to center wall. Jimmy followed the ball in and tapped it lightly as it came off the wall. The ball struck low and rolled back along the ground. 17–14.

With a little smirk, Jimmy called, "Where do you want the next one, kid?"

Embarrassed but still confident, Carlos replied, "Put it in my right hand, old man, so I can drive it up your nasty old ass."

The Latino cadre whistled and yelled their pleasure at Carlos's bravado, and Jimmy used their display to make his move. Looking directly at Papo Nuñez, he challenged, "Hey, Papo! You think that's funny? You're the Brooklyn Big Willie, you want some of this action?"

Dismissing Jimmy with a wave of his manicured hand, Papo added, "Ju know I don need ju *cigarillos, viejo blanco,* play and lose."

"You're smarter than you look, Papo," Jimmy replied, knowing the slight was not lost on Papo or his posse.

"*Qué pasa,* man, you gonna play or bullshit?" Carlos prompted.

Jimmy's next serve was a repeat of the last, but the young Latino timed it perfectly. Stepping up and to the left he took it on a fly with his right hand and tried to hit a "kill shot" in the right-hand corner. The shot landed too high, causing an ample bounce, which Jimmy easily returned low cross court to the left corner, on an angle Carlos couldn't reach. 17–15.

The noise of the action had caused the curious to leave the shaded wall, and the crowd grew larger with black, brown, and white faces. Out of this Sing Sing melting pot the sentimental favorite among ebony and ivory was the old dude playing his ass off against youth and nature's clock. "Do that shit, Pops!"

"Slap that rubber, Jimmy!"

"Yeah, man, you jinglin', Jimmy!" Ever the showman, Jimmy acknowledged the fans with a "thumbs up." Then, looking Carlos in the eye, he turned his thumb down. The crowd whooped and whistled at the gesture, while the Latino fans yelled insults of "*Cabrón!*" and "*Maricón sucio,*" with ever increasing emotion.

Fighting off heat and exhaustion with a mental image of a cold beer on a Rockaway boardwalk, Jimmy gauged the Latino temperament and stole a peek at his watch. It was 3:45 P.M. At 4 P.M. the loudspeakers would blare, "The yard is closed! The yard is closed!" causing each man to return to their cell for the prison count. It was all a matter of timing now. At 17–15, he was six points from a win and Carlos was four.

While Jimmy's mind drank beer and computed time, Hap Lewis made his move. Easing closer to Papo Nuñez, he picked up the pitch with ethnic taunts, and punctuated each with a menacing wave of his left crutch. "Can't no Rican play handball, man. Ain't nuttin' but mud walls and booty bandits in dey prisons. Paddle that *culo* for us ol' folks." Hap's gibes, when blended with the heat and waving crutch, were like yeast to a cake, and Papo and his posse's tempers began to rise. Seeming to ignore Hap's folly, Jimmy wiped sweat from the ball and smiled at Carlos. Bite, Papo, he thought, while he listened to Hap cut deeper into Latino pride.

The serve was inches short of the short line, and Jimmy wasted a few more seconds before he served again. He stood straight up this time and served the ball high to Carlos's right side. Too high to attempt a kill shot, Carlos sought to play out of position and get him running side to side. The strategy caused a volley back and forth, until Jimmy caught Carlos coming in and lobbed a shot over his head just inches above his upstretched left hand. 17–16. The crowd's roar of approval gave Hap a little boost.

Hap cased the crowd to make sure no guards were near, and when satisfied, his gravel voice challenged Papo's pride and pocket. Almost in Papo's ear he shouted, "Man, spank that cuchifrito ass. Ain't nuttin' but chump change an' scared money here." Papo whirled on Hap with blood in his eye. "Ju got a big mout, wooden legs. What chu wanna bet? Whatcha got, eh?" Papo's posse wanted his tongue, not his money, but they echoed Papo's words like good soldiers. "Yeah, nigga, what chu got, man?" "We ain't bettin' no chitlins, motherfucker." "Show money or shut da fuck up."

The crowd was enjoying both shows, the one on the court and the one on the sidelines. While Jimmy played one, Hap played to the other.

With eleven minutes left Jimmy served again, and this time the ball went over the long line. Carlos laughed and chided Jimmy, "*Qué pasa, viejo?* That ball gettin' too heavy?" Jimmy ignored the comment but allowed the crowd to see him take a few deep breaths as he wiped the sweat from his face. None of this was lost on Papo.

Jimmy's second serve was waist high with less zip, and Carlos tagged it for a kill in the right-hand corner. Looking disgusted and drained, Jimmy walked slowly to the back court as Carlos's fans clapped and shouted their approval. "Ju dead, *viejo,* now lay down," Papo shouted.

"DEAD!" Hap roared with derisive laughter. "Man lay four-to-one, 'n' I'll bet dis hundred on the corpse right now!" He flashed the folded Ben Franklin in his sweaty palm.

Papo saw the three figures, then it was gone. "Ju crazy, nigga? Ju no stick me up no four to one, man." Every con within earshot listened in.

"Crazy! Man, I be crazy if I don't get dem odds," Hap responded. "The dead man's twice his age, he's losin', he jus' los' da serve, an' da game's almos' over. It's all your way. Ohh! Maybe you wan' da odds too," Hap teased.

Caught on the short side of macho, logic, and the crowd's stares, Papo said, "Ju got it, big mout'. Three-to-one."

"Bet! Bet!" Hap's gravel voice roared, and they both slapped five to seal it.

On the court Jimmy heard Hap's "BET!" and watched the five slap seal. My turn, he thought, and he called to Papo, "Hey! Big Willie! It's about time you found some heart. Now what about me? Can the player get a play?"

"Ju show me *cien dolares, viejo,* an ju got it too."

"It's in my stash," Jimmy replied. "If I lose you'll get it tonight."

Antagonisms aside, Papo and Jimmy were convicts whose word you could take to the bank, so the bet was sealed with another slap five, and the game resumed with Carlos changing strategy.

Thinking he could take advantage of Jimmy's weaker left side, Carlos walked across court to serve from right to left. Jimmy clocked the move as desperate, but glanced at Carlos's feet and eased toward his left as the Latino went into his serve. The ball angled sharply to the left side, but Jimmy was already in motion and with a crisp left hand he returned it to the same spot that Carlos had served from. Carlos, who had moved to center court for control, was forced to lunge right. With equal parts skill and luck, his fingers just tipped the ball and it sailed in a slow arc to reach the wall and die: 18–16.

Papo's posse roared their pleasure, "*Vaya,* Carlos . . . *vaya, mi 'mano!*" Whistles mixed with applause, and one homeboy, Chino, ran on the court to slap Carlos a "high five" support.

Jimmy quickly took advantage of the move. "Hey! Whoa! Wait a minute!" he shouted. "You can't run on the court stopping play with that bullshit."

Chino, still burning from Hap's insults, shouted a litany of Spanish curses, and Carlos said, "The play was over, *viejo.* He didn't stop shit, man. What about when you called time before and stepped off?"

"The point is, he ain't in the game, he don't belong on the court," Jimmy fired back.

"All right, *muy bien.* You caught your breath now, *viejo,*" Carlos chided. "Let's play." Papo called Chino off the court, and the game continued with Carlos returning to his strong side to resume play.

A peek at his watch showed 3:52 P.M. I need a serve, Jimmy determined. On the sideline, Hap thought, his ass shoulda been on a tightrope.

With every ounce of energy he could corral, Jimmy waited and clocked the kid's feet. When Carlos went into a low arc serve, Jimmy was on the balls of his feet ready to pounce. The ball shot low to

Jimmy's far right side, but the old-timer was on it. He scooped it up in a side-arm arc and sent it pumping cross court to the far left corner. Anticipating the return and angle perfectly, Carlos did not anticipate the ball's bottom spin caused by Jimmy's snap of wrist and fingers, and instead of an easy point, he lost the serve.

Jimmy figured that with a series of serve changes he could freeze the score at 18–16, and maybe scare up a few more bets on tomorrow's conclusion, but his plan went belly-up when Carlos killed a low return for point nineteen just as the speakers blared, "The yard is closed! The yard is closed!"

Some cons caught up in the drama and personalities at play shouted, "Fuck you, throw the tear gas!"

"Play it out!"

"Count this!" shouted a guy grabbing his crotch.

Papo, just two points short of a win with Carlos serving, shouted, "Rápido! Rápido!"

But Jimmy, never so happy to have a fast watch, had a different agenda in mind. He walked over to Papo and motioned Carlos over also. "Carlos, you might get two fast points, but I doubt it. There's no way I can get the five I need and neither of us can take a lockup for delaying the count. So we'll finish this in the morning as it stands." To Papo he added, "I'll show you the hundred tonight, like I promised." With no choice but to agree, they shook hands and dispersed.

On the walk up to A Block, as Jimmy passed Hap in the tunnel, he heard, "You shoulda been a barber with your close shavin' ass."

Without a hitch in his step Jimmy shot back, "And you should've watched your back years ago, so I could work the crowd today. Call a cab, we might need it." He shot a thumbs-up, and disappeared.

A Block was a large concrete warehouse of convict condos in a nine-by-six-foot single-occupancy design. Opened in the first quarter of the nineteenth century, its recycled stock of castaways lived in four double-sided tiers that stretched over eighty cells or two city blocks long. By 9 P.M., the din from the over seven hundred tenants had settled to a murmur, and another day was only a wake-up away. Freshly showered and shaved, Jimmy grated soap chips from a bar of state soap, while a low strain of Coltrane provided memories and escape. Birdland in the fifties was his favorite haunt, with Coltrane then and now his favorite genie.

"Hey, Irish! They sell Tide in the commissary," the voice on the bars offered. Not missing a grate, Jimmy replied, "They sell salami and cheese, too. You got any?"

Vincent "Vig" Vigliano was a "Goodfella" who ran numbers and book for one of New York's five families; but for the past three years he was an A Block clerk, a sometime shylock, and an all-time good man.

"You want mustard with that order, O'Toole?" Vig joked.

"Yeah, Pal, mustard and the hundred back."

"Mannaggia, la Madonna!" Vig exclaimed, smacking his forehead for effect. "You just gave it back two days ago. Whatta we doing here?"

"Keep your Ballys on, Vig. I just need it to flash Papo Nuñez. And since I'm locked in, I need you to be my flasher."

"Hey, hardon! Ya want me in a raincoat too?" They shared a laugh and Vig added, "I had a visit today from Barbara and the kids, but Louie told me you and Hap had some fun in the yard. Is that what this flash is all about?"

Jimmy scooped the soap granules into a container. "Fun! I'd rather sandpaper a lion's ass than do a repeat of today. But yeah, that's the deal. The score is nineteen-sixteen his way, and he's serving. Hap embarrassed Papo into a tough-to-get-three-to-one on the kid."

A low whistle sounded from Vig. "Nineteen-sixteen?" That's playin' it a little close ain't it, maestro?"

Jimmy gave a wee smile. "Ahh, you know me, pal. If it ain't rough, it ain't right," and he added a wink.

Vig gave a knowing nod. "I'll go flash Papo, then make the sandwich."

"Grazie, Godfather," Jimmy mumbled in fun and respect. Vig had taken a few steps when Jimmy called, "If you flash a little green of your own, don't forget to tip the mechanic."

Still stepping, Vig called back, "You're a schemin' bastard, O'Toole. Ya sure you ain't Sicilian?" His footsteps and words were swallowed in the concrete warehouse.

Jimmy put up a pot of hot water, dropped a teabag in his cup, lit a Lucky Strike, and laid back on his bed. The hot shower had chased most of the ache from his body, but little pockets of soreness still remained. It gets harder every year, he thought. While Coltrane and Elvin Jones dueled to the delight of Birdland's patrons, Jimmy eased into a reflection on the day's hustle and how it came to be.

It was Hap who marked the kid as a possible route to Papo's pocket two weeks ago, and as usual, the old hustler was right. Jimmy had clocked Carlos's play. He was young, fast, and cocky with two good hands, but his strategy and ball control were weak, with his serve just a notch above. At a time when Carlos was enjoying the fruits of a successful afternoon with Papo and his posse, Jimmy happened by. After exchanging greetings with Papo, he was happily surprised when Papo opened the door. "*Qué pasa,* Jimmy? Ju wan' to play Carlos? He's good."

"Yeah, they're all good at his age, Papo, but can he win?" Jimmy teased. That was all it took.

Jimmy lay there with Coltrane in the background while his mind played back every serve, volley, and nuance of today's games. He knew it was only a matter of regaining the serve and keeping it, but he also knew that "shit happens," which was how Carlos had gotten the nineteenth point. He ran a few mock plays in his head and charted their probable result. Vig broke his reverie. "I saw Papo. Here's your sandwich. Hap said to soak your feet. There's a cab strike. Good luck *mañana.*" Then Vig was gone. If I had to depend on luck, there would be no *mañana,* Jimmy thought, as he reached for the sandwich on the bars.

The ten o'clock morning promised an action-packed Sing Sing summer day. The humidity had disappeared into Mother Nature's handbag, and the temperature was a comfortable seventy-two degrees. The crowd was slightly larger than the day before, and so was Papo's posse. No words were exchanged between participants, but Vig and Louie cornered Jimmy to say that there was healthy action on the sidelines. Jimmy looked to the gallery of cons. "You had a busy night, I see. No wonder you dropped off the sandwich and ran. Tonight I want lobster tails." Louie laughed, and Vig pinched Jimmy's cheek, then both stepped off.

It was not a pretty sight, unless you liked train wrecks and reruns of Ali v. Wepner. The 19–16 score was too close to do anything but attack, and Jimmy wanted to keep Carlos's fans subdued and out of the game. The opportunity came early on Carlos's first serve. After a low killer serve that Jimmy handled easily, an eight-shot volley saw both players scrambling cross-court. Jimmy literally dove for a low ball, and came up with a badly scraped forearm, and the serve. The play caused a trickle of blood, a roar from the crowd, and a gag order on Papo and his people. Jimmy's face acknowledged nothing. In silence he walked to the serve line, giving thanks to the handball gods who sent him that shot, while Hap on the sideline just nodded and smiled.

Jimmy scored three quick points with a repertoire of left/right corner-catching killer serves that weren't on display the day before. The crowd ate it up, and Louie yelled, "Hey Jimmy, where'd you get that serve?"

"In a salami sandwich," Jimmy joked back. Some cons laughed, but none were Latino, and Jimmy went back to work. With the score now tied at nineteen, Carlos broke Jimmy's serve with a lunging backhand return of a shot that could've given Jimmy point seven. Papo & Company came alive with whistles and applause, but it was a fleeting celebration. The old-timer broke the kid's serve again, and went on to score two consecutive points for the game win.

The sound of applause echoed across the yard, attended by whistles and shouts of "I told ya so!" that stung the ears of the nonbelievers. Jimmy approached Carlos with his right hand extended. "Good game, kid," he offered. "Whataya wanna do about game three?"

Carlos's cockiness had given way to a sudden awareness. "Thanks, *viejo*, I'll get back ta ya," he managed as he shook Jimmy's hand, then split.

After the back slaps and congratulations had run their course, Jimmy sauntered over to the bench and lit a Lucky Strike. Looking toward the court, he watched one of Papo's posses smack Hap's palm, and then come walking his way. "From Papo," is all he said as he repeated the smack on Jimmy, and strolled away. Vig came over and pinched his cheek. "No lobster tails, but Barbara brought me spare ribs, and I'll make a salad." Looking down at Jimmy's worn sneakers, he added, "You're a funny bastard, O'Toole." Then he was gone.

The lone figure sat against the handball wall, with his crutches standing guard. Jimmy flicked his Lucky in the breeze, and closed the distance between them. "Pull up some concrete, cracker, 'n' I'll have my maid bring a mint julep," Hap joked in his gravel tone. Jimmy kept silent and slid down the wall. Quiet seconds passed where the two old friends jockeyed thoughts about in private.

Finally Jimmy queried, "You got any plans for that three hundred?"

"Yeah, I'm gonna buy me a lot in Scarsdale 'n' plant watermelons. How 'bout you?"

"I'm gonna buy all the trees in that neighborhood so they can't hang your silly black ass."

They were quiet again until Jimmy said, "Let me see it, Hap." The old hustler's fingers slid into his sock and came out with the carefully folded Ben Franklin. The fast glance of a greedy eye would see the one inch square 100, but examination would reveal only half a bill, skillfully folded over paper.

"Someday you're gonna get me killed," Jimmy said.

"Don't worry," Hap replied. "I'll bury ya on my lot."

1994, Great Meadow Correctional Facility
Comstock, New York

Feathers on the Solar Wind

David Wood

A heavy winter rainstorm drummed the buildings of Hesiod Correctional Institution the night Daniel Martin Pinkston finally died in the AIDS Dormitory. It was 2 A.M. when four corrections officers in protective clothing wheeled him on a gurney out the iron door for the last time. Kenneth "South Philly" Johnson and Willie Norton looked up from their card game. John Mohammed "Deathrow" Rollins spared one last glance at the closing door before he began his cleanup duties.

"That's two we lost since midnight," Willie said as he began shuffling cards. "First Parker Calloway, now Pinkston. You know when it goes like this there'll be a third."

"Third time's a charm," Johnson said. "I'll put up a pack of Lucky Strikes that Morgan will go next."

"Be quiet, man," Deathrow snarled. "You don't respect death and you don't respect God." He was stripping off Pinkston's soiled sheets and double bagging them in red contagion bags. "And keep it down! These sick men are trying to sleep!"

"Sorry, man," Willie said. "We just can't sleep."

Deathrow looked up as he scrubbed the waterproof mattress with bleach. "I can get you some sleeping pills if you want."

"No need, brother," Willie said. "I'll just play with South Philly here and let him tell me his life story. I'll be asleep in fifteen minutes." He nodded at Johnson, who'd spent most of his life in South Philadelphia before coming to Florida and landing a bid for armed robbery and kidnapping. Now in his mid-forties, he was an animate human skeleton, his neon-white skin spotted by Kaposi's sarcoma. Willie, at fifty, was just as thin, his black skin dry and flaky, most of his graying hair gone.

"But if you need something, you tell me!" Deathrow said, pointing his thumb at his chest. "You got a problem, I'll take care of it."

He returned to his duties, and the older men watched him for a moment. Like them, Deathrow had HIV, but he was still big and black and bald and muscular, his voice deep like James Earl Jones's, his energy and patience endless. At nineteen he had killed two police officers, and spent twelve years shooting one writ after another into the courts from death row, doing all he could to keep from making that last walk to Old Sparky, Florida's electric chair. He'd finally got his sentence changed to life, but after one year on the compound he had the virus.

After six months of bitter denial he converted to Islam, and though he could have spent years on the compound until full-blown AIDS set in, he volunteered to live in the AIDS dorm to work as a nurse's aide. He humbly performed all the duties shunned by the officers and the doctors and nurses, who visited the dorm as little as possible. He emptied the catheter bags, changed soiled linen, gave bedbaths to men too weak to bathe themselves. He held men up and fed them, checked them for bedsores, and his muscular killer's hands massaged sore spots to keep them from becoming bedsores. His prison job duties required him to work eight hours a day, five days a week, but he never stopped working as long as he wasn't asleep.

"I wish I had that kind of energy," South Philly said, watching Deathrow carry the contagion bags to the laundry.

"You got plenty of energy," Willie said as he dealt the cards. He noticed Jimmie Long across the dorm climbing out of bed into his wheelchair. "Look at you, up all night partying and playing cards. You're as lively as a feather on the wind."

"Give me three cards," South Philly mumbled. "And hold your sarcasm. You're full of shit and bad jokes, and your farts stink like roadkill when they float over to my bunk." He examined his cards and bet two tailormades — Lucky Strikes — while he puffed a cigarette he'd rolled himself. "Deathrow had to slide my locker between our bunks so we could play. My strength is draining."

"At least you don't have to wear adult diapers," Willie said, reaching for his Chesterfields. "I'll see your two and raise you three. Now, when you ask me if I'm going to wear briefs or boxer shorts tomorrow, I answer 'Depends.' Jimmie's coming for a visit."

"What got you up?" South Philly asked, nodding at Jimmie. "You're usually sawing logs about now."

"Can't sleep," Jimmie mumbled, stopping by their bunks.

"Deal you in?" Willie asked.

"I'll watch," Jimmie said. Though he looked healthier than the two older men, his legs were quickly growing weak. The doctor couldn't figure out why. His face looked as if it had a rash under the red ceiling nightlights.

"I call," South Philly said, setting his cards down, two queens, ace high. Willie showed him three deuces before scooping up his cigarettes. "Damn."

"You never traveled enough to play against good players," Willie said.

"Well, I won't get a chance to travel now."

"Oh, you are, in a way," Willie said. "The earth is twenty-four thousand miles around, and it spins like a sonovabitch. You're going about a thousand miles an hour and don't even know it."

"Who gives a shit," Jimmie mumbled.

South Philly looked at him. "Homey, you in a bad mood or something?"

"I know what it is," Willie said, putting on his state-issued glasses and gazing at Jimmie. "Pinkston died tonight, and he's the one who gave you AIDS, isn't he?"

"Man, I'm no fag!"

"You two were cellmated," Willie went on. "You can't tell me you didn't get some mud on your turtle."

"Man, just shut your fuckin' mouth!" Jimmie yelled, his cheeks redder than normal.

"Watch your mouth, bro," South Philly said, scooping up the cards. "We didn't invite you over here, so if you want to cop an attitude, take it back to bed."

"And don't get defensive," Willie added. "None of us got in this dorm by sharing a needle or getting a blood transfusion."

"Man," Jimmie shook his head. "I just don't want to die like this. This place stinks like a busted meat locker, people dying every other day, we're fenced off from the rest of the compound, and all we can do is wait to die. I don't want to die like this, I want to die like a man!"

"Shut up, punk," South Philly hissed, rising up on bony legs hidden in nylon pajama bottoms. "This *is* how a man dies. Look at me. My mother writes me every week, but here I am, I got myself locked away from her and dying. You think she's proud of me? You think I'm proud of myself? My father has Alzheimer's, and she's trying to take care of him, and she probably wonders every day who's going to die first, me or my father. But this is how a man dies, with the Ninja or Alzheimer's, or cancer. If you wanted to throw yourself on a grenade and save your buddies and die a hero's death, you should've joined the Marines."

"South Philly, stop running your jaw," Wyman Reed said, walking through the maze of bunks toward them. "If Deathrow comes back and catches you waking up his patients, he'll gag you and tie you to your bed."

"You guys are waking the dead over here," Carl "Smokey" Dukes said. "Can't you keep your voices down?" Both men wore their blankets over their shoulders. Like Jimmie, who had on a sweatshirt over his pajama top, they couldn't put up with the cold air in the dorm. The heaters were in the ceiling instead of the floor, and the slow-turning ceiling fans couldn't quite get the warm air down. Willie and South Philly both had fevers that night, and sat on their bunks shirtless, their ribby chests like washboards.

"I'm sorry, Smokey," Willie said. "We won't holler and hoot again. This was supposed to be a quiet party. Go ahead back to sleep."

"Hell with that," Wyman said. "Deal me in." He held up a pack of generic cigarettes.

"You up to a game this late?" South Philly asked, shuffling the cards. Wyman nodded. "Smokey?"

"I'm all out, homey. I'll just watch." He pulled an empty wheelchair closer as Wyman sat on the bed next to South Philly. Wyman was a tall black man who hadn't yet shown signs of the virus, but three long bouts of pneumonia had weakened him. He couldn't live in open population anymore. Sometimes he'd go outside and stand by the fence, watching inmates play basketball in the distance. He never stayed out long, because it was only a matter of time before he'd be noticed and become the target of insults and catcalls. This irritated him no end: At least a third of them were also infected, though outwardly healthy, and they, too, would be landing in the AIDS dorm.

"You know they took Pinkston and Calloway out tonight," Willie said, rolling a cigarette.

"Hospital?" Smokey asked.

"Morgue," Willie answered.

"Two?" Wyman whispered. South Philly nudged him to cut the cards. "Jesus Christ, that's not good."

"Don't take the Lord's name in vain, man," Smokey said.

"Save your church for Sunday," South Philly snapped.

"Philly thinks someone else will go before the dawn comes up," Willie said.

"This is too morbid," Jimmie whispered.

"Why three?" Wyman asked.

South Philly began dealing. "It goes in threes, Wyman. If two die during the week, it's a sure bet a third will go before that week is up. Just listen." He held up his hand for silence. The sounds of snoring men, mixing with the whirring of the fans and the steady tattoo of rain on the roof, but behind it was the rattling, deep breath of several men struggling through pneumonia.

"You hear that?" South Philly whispered. "We got Death waiting in the wings. It's that kind of night."

"Man, you're getting a bad attitude," Smokey said. He was feeling uneasy, as were Wyman and Jimmie. "You're not psychic."

"I don't know," South Philly said. "But that's the way it goes, people die in threes. I used to work in a nursing home in Pennsylvania. Weeks would go by, and then three old people would go in one week. It was strange, no reason for it, but there you are."

"C'mon, man, let's play cards," Wyman said. "Your talk's getting too creepy. And I don't believe it anyway."

"What?" Smokey whispered. "That someone else will die tonight?"

"Far as I'm concerned, that's a given," South Philly said. "I propose we each bet on *who* will die."

"Man, you're sick," Smokey growled.

"Ashes to ashes, dustballs to dustballs," Willie said. "Even the Bible admits that, Smokey. I read my King James daily, too, you know."

"So we pick someone in the dorm?" Wyman said. "One of our sick patients?"

South Philly slowly set his cards down, his face serious. "No, that's too easy. Way too easy. I predict it will be one of us here." The other men gazed at him in silence. Even Willie looked shaken. "I say we bet one pack of tailormades each, we each choose a different one among us, place our bets, and wait for the dawn."

A dreadful silence fell over them, a silence like an arctic night. Smells of the dorm wrapped around them, smells of sickness and sweat. "It's sinful," Smokey said.

"Sin got us here thus far," Willie mimicked, "and sin will lead us home."

"Don't try me, Willie!"

"You fucked a punk like the rest of us," Willie said. "Don't give me any of your self-righteous crap, Smokey. South Philly has hit on something, I don't know what, but I'm game."

"You want to die?" Smokey asked. "Is that it?"

"No, it's not," Willie said. "But I'm going to die anyway, whether I like it or not. And if I gotta die, I might as well play one last game with Death himself."

Wyman nodded. "Yeah, maybe. But I don't think no one's gonna kick off in our little circle. What if it happens, Philly, and it's not one of us?"

"Then nobody wins, and we all keep our cigarettes, and die of lung cancer instead." South Philly looked from man to man. "In fact, the way I see it, winning and losing are both desirable. You win, you get the cigarettes. You lose, you get out of the goddam dorm."

This time Smokey didn't complain. Jimmie was looking into his lap, gripping his wheels. At twenty-five, he looked like a little boy awaiting the whipping of his life. Wyman looked from man to man, intrigued but scared, as though he had just been invited to play a game of Russian Roulette, and he knew he was too tempted to refuse. "All right," he said. "Let's go for it."

"It's not right!" Smokey yelled.

"Shut the fuck up!" someone yelled from across the dorm. "I'm sleeping!"

"You're all a bunch of fools!" Smokey whispered. "No wonder you're in this mess."

"You're in the same predicament, my man," Willie said. "And you fall as short of the pearly gates as the rest of us. I know more about you than you might think."

"And what's that supposed to mean?"

"It means you don't have much leeway to complain about anybody else." Willie took off his glasses and stared at him. "Now, if you don't like what we're doing here, go back to bed, I'm tired of your mouth."

Smokey was silent, but he stared back until Willie looked at the others. "Boys, I don't know how real this all is, but I swear I feel spirits in the air. I've been scared of dying since I popped out of my momma's womb, but just tonight I'd like to look Death in the eye and prove I'm a good sport."

He put his glasses back on. "Now there's science and there's the spirit world. According to science, we are mostly made up of water, but we are what's known as a carbon-based life form. Carbon is that black stuff left over after we burn something, and a friend once told me that no planet naturally has carbon on it anywhere. Carbon comes from the sun and other stars."

"So what's your point?" Wyman asked, still holding his cards.

"My point," Willie said, examining his hand, "is that we are made of stardust. And when we are dead, our carbon molecules go into the soil and become part of other life forms. So you see, part of us goes on, just like the carbon molecules of other living things that are in us now, and all of it comes from the big burning stars in the sky."

"So there's bits and pieces of dinosaurs in us, too," South Philly said.

"Something like that," Willie agreed. "But now we're heading slowly back to our old carbon selves. I like to think we're heading back to the sun myself, we're going back to be cremated into nonexistence, nothing but that damn stardust. And if I go, I might as well play over the sunspots, and this little bet is how we can do it, how we can be feathers on the solar wind for awhile, floating and dancing on the music of the cosmos before the final incineration."

"Willie, you sure know a lot of big words and ideas for a black man," South Philly snorted.

Willie grinned at his old friend. "If it makes you too uncomfortable, Philly, I could talk like Aunt Jemima for a while."

"It's still all a lot of bunk," Smokey said.

"If you think so," Wyman answered, "then you make the first bet."

Smokey opened his mouth, about to refuse, when he looked around. "A pack of smokes, you said?"

"Exactly," South Philly answered. "But you got to pick one of us."

Smokey stroked his chin. "Okay, I bet a pack of rip that old Willie here will die first."

The other men looked at each other.

"Man, that's slimy," South Philly said. "Just because he told you about your ass . . ."

"He done right," Willie said. "And he chose well, I look like I'm halfway to the crypt, the way I see it."

"And who do you choose?" South Philly asked.

"I place my bet on Wyman," Willie said. "No offense."

"None taken," Wyman answered, though he looked a bit shaken. The game was too real to him.

"Wyman's the healthiest one here, and I got the feeling too much health is not always a good thing," Willie explained.

"That's crazy," Smokey said.

"Yeah, it sounds sorta crazy, but I figger I'll go against the odds."

"And you, Wyman?" South Philly asked.

Wyman looked around from face to face. "I don't think any of us are going to die, leastways not tonight. And I'd hate to name someone and actually have them die and me win cigarettes on their body. I just don't know."

"Yeah, it feels a little dirty, I admit," Willie said. "But I feel the spirits kicking tonight, and me, I gotta dance with Death, just one slow dance. If you don't feel up to it . . ."

Wyman shook his head. "Philly, I put my pack on you. God knows, I hope I lose, but I'm gonna play this game."

South Philly smiled at him. "No hard feelings, brother. Tonight I don't feel afraid. I don't even care. But I put my smokes on Jimmie."

"Oh, no, man," Jimmie gasped. "Hell no, man! I'm not gonna die tonight!"

"Well, if you don't, then I lose. You got nothing to worry about."

"Change your bet, Philly. Change it!"

"You're my pick, bro. Now your turn."

"I'm not gonna."

"Smokey's left," South Philly said. "Though he looks like he'll live a good long time, but you can never tell."

"Back off, man," Smokey said. "The boy doesn't need any help."

"Man, I'm through with this shit," Jimmie said, and wheeled off.

"We scared him," Wyman said. "Maybe we shouldn't have done this."

"It's done," South Philly replied. "The boy needs to cope with what's happening."

Jimmie's wheelchair clipped a steel bunk as he turned and headed for the shower room. They watched him disappear through the door.

"Sirius is high in the sky tonight," Willie mumbled, "and the natives are restless."

"Sirius?" South Philly asked. "What's that?"

"Sirius, the Dog Star, the harbinger of death. The brightest spot in the sky, if the moon isn't out."

"Putting out carbon molecules," Wyman said, picking up his cards. "Maybe if we get enough carbon molecules, we can all be made whole again."

The shower room was a long hallway illuminated by filthy neon lights. The walls and floor were covered by worn white and tan tiles. A chest-high wall ran along the middle, with sinks and mirrors on both sides. To the right were a dozen stainless-steel toilets and an equal number of metal urinals. To the left were a dozen showerheads, with two specially built showers to accommodate the handicapped.

Jimmie rolled his wheelchair through the meatlocker-cold room to the farthest sink. He looked into his own haunted eyes in the bent steel mirror, his rash-covered cheeks. He turned on the cold water and let it run while he reached beneath his sweatshirt and pulled out two bottle of pills — Pinkston's pain pills, which he'd stolen before the officers had come to take Pinkston away. When he heard somebody come in, he quickly stuffed the bottles out of sight between his legs.

One of the showers came on. Someone couldn't sleep, he thought. He was shivering from the cold, but he got one of the plastic bottles open and poured six pills into his palm, tossed them into his mouth and leaned over the sink, scooping water into his mouth. He had dumped six more pills into his hand when he noticed steam filling the room.

Something seemed out of kilter. He gripped the pills in one hand and with the other pulled himself up to a standing position. He gazed at the naked figure under the spray of hot water, and his weak legs nearly gave out. "Oh my god," he whispered.

"Give me two cards," Wyman said, setting two cards on the locker. "I know what you're talking about, us under the influence of that star."

"Sirius," Willie said. "Canis Major."

"Just a star," Smokey said.

"With stardust," South Philly added.

Smokey pulled his blanket closer around him, glancing at Deathrow, who was going from bed to bed, emptying catheter bags into a plastic urinal bottle, writing down the amount, then pouring it into a bucket before moving to the next bag.

"We'd be in a bad fix without Deathrow," Wyman said, following Smokey's gaze. "That man's a saint. If I could choose one person to survive this dorm, it would be him."

"Maybe in the parallel world, he's out free and clean of the virus," Willie said. "Erwin Schrodinger once mentioned that there might be a whole series of different dimensions where the same people were living different lives."

"That doesn't help me none now, does it?" South Philly said. "Maybe next time I'll try a different dimension."

Wyman looked over his shoulder. "Jimmie must be off beating his meat, he ain't come back yet."

"He's just taking a dump," South Philly said.

"He could've passed out," Smokey said. "Let me check on him." He rose from the wheelchair and stalked off, his blanket dragging the floor.

"He needs to deal with things," South Philly said. "Maybe we all do. I'll see your two cigarettes and raise you two, Willie."

In the shower room, Jimmie stared over the wall at the naked inmate in the steam. The two bottles dropped to the floor. Pills fell from his sweaty palm. He was staring at Daniel Pinkston, very much alive, young and muscular as he was when they'd first met, not in his later emaciated state. Jimmie felt he was hallucinating, but Daniel stared right at him, smiling. The tiny metal ring pierced his left nipple, and over that was the team emblem of the Florida State Seminoles tattooed where it always had been.

"But you're dead," he whispered.

"What does a small thing like that matter to anyone?" It was Daniel's voice.

His mannerisms, his movements, everything; Jimmie felt sick. "I never even tried to say good-bye."

"I never did like that word," Daniel said.

"My god, Dan, do you forgive me?"

"For what?"

"For every way I wronged you. For ignoring you in this dorm while you were lying there, dying and pissing your bed, and you wanted to talk, I could see it in your eyes . . ."

"There's nothing for me to forgive," Daniel said. "It's you who must forgive yourself." He turned, and Jimmie followed his gaze. Smokey stood in the doorway, his mouth open, his eyes wide. Steam filled the room in billowing clouds. "Only you can forgive yourself. Nobody else." He said this while staring at Smokey.

South Philly picked up the cigarettes, his winnings. Wyman shuffled the cards. They turned their heads when Deathrow gave a yell, stepping out of Jimmie's way as he wheeled into the room. "Next time you run over my foot I'll pour this bucket of piss on your damn head!" he shouted before continuing to the shower room.

"I saw him!" Jimmie banged against the bunk, gripping Wyman's arm. The cards fluttered to the floor. "I saw Danny's ghost! Danny Pinkston!"

"Brother, what got into you?" Willie asked.

"Danny didn't give me AIDS, I gave it to him!" Jimmie cried. "I swear! It wasn't his fault! I was punked out when I first came to prison. When I started doing Danny I didn't even know I had the virus! I should've died first, I had the virus first!"

"The truth comes out," South Philly mumbled.

"Easy on the boy, Philly," Willie said. "I believe he really did see a ghost. I told you the spirits were restless tonight."

"I asked him to forgive me," Jimmie gasped, his voice trailing. "But he said I had to forgive myself."

"That's the first thing you said tonight that makes sense," South Philly said.

"Wyman, I need your help."

Deathrow stood silhouetted in the doorway. His voice was soft, almost a whisper, but the authority in it carried over the roomful of snoring men. "After I tell the bosses." He nodded at the two officers sleeping on chairs in the Plexiglas-enclosed officers station. "After I tell them, I'll need you to help me with the body."

"Body?"

"Smokey — he cut his throat with a razor blade," Deathrow said.

Jimmie stared after him, dumbstruck, as he went to wake the officers. Wyman gazed sadly at the empty shower room doorway. South Philly angrily picked up the cards. "Third time's a charm," he mumbled.

"Why?" Jimmie whispered.

"He had a dirty little secret," Willie said. "Parker Calloway told me before he died. Smokey turned state's evidence on his brother, got his brother the chair, when it was him who did the killing. When you saw Daniel Pinkston's ghost, he probably saw his brother's ghost. Only he wasn't capable of forgiving himself."

"You shoulda took that bet," Wyman said bitterly. "You'd have scored a few packs of cigarettes." He rose and headed off to help Deathrow.

"That could've been me," Jimmie said, feeling tears well up, remembering Daniel when he first met him. He leaned over, weary. Willie, suddenly cold, pulled his blanket over his bare shoulders. South Philly shuffled the cards.

1997, Hardee Correctional Facility
Bowling Green, Florida

Death of a Duke

Dax Xenos

The face was strange. The voice vaguely familiar.

"Hey, Fox. Ol' Foxy, come here."

I was heading into the gym to work off a little tension when I was distracted by a thin black dude in the lock-up section. The concrete slab serving as the gym's floor was split in two equal plots by a walkway lined with heavy gauge chain-link fence. One side teemed with convicts busy at basketball, handball and lifting iron weights. The other side was vacant except for the gaunt stranger and another black, locked behind the double mesh. I started to pass.

"Fox. It's me, man!"

I felt it wise to check out the voice so insistent to attract my attention, and walked over. Two liquid brown eyes swam above baggy lower lids dressing an angular face. Sweat streamed from his steel wool hair and ran down to collect in a pair of kerchiefs tied loosely about his throat. A red and a blue. This was significant because you couldn't buy them at the commissary and they were contraband on the unit. They would get you a case if the boss was feeling bitchy.

"It's Earl, man," he said. "From the Dexter Unit."

"Earl?" I still wasn't believing him. The Earl I remembered from Dexter was bigger, lots of flesh and fat and a jolly face.

"I knew an Earl Peterson. 'Earl the Pearl' we called him. But we changed it to —"

"Duke of Earl," he cut me off. "After the song 'cause I was such a bad dude! I lived in H-2, Twenty-one Cell, bottom bunk. You were next door in Twenty-two on top. Your cellie was Ebbie something. Big blond guy who worked in the laundry."

It was Earl all right. I began to piece it together — the voice, the face, the mannerisms — but the changes were numerous.

"You look different," I said. "Thinner, lean even. You've got some muscle tone, a raw edge to you. Before you were flabby. Used to walk with a cane."

"Yeah, well, I been workin' out. See."

He flexed his muscles and made a face like a movie actor. I had to admit he had improved himself considerably. His biceps knotted up into high mounds and lines of separation outlined his individual muscles in fine definition. I also noticed stretch marks left from the weight he had dropped.

"You lost some weight, Earl."

"Seventy pounds."

"That's pretty radical. But it's been a year."

"Yeah. Lots of changes, m'man."

It was a cold crawling kind of smirk he flashed me then, right at home on a face with hate-filled eyes. Something had changed deep inside him. He had been a jiver and a player, but he used to be able to enjoy himself too. All that was gone now, replaced by a dark violence I could feel through the air.

"What are you doing over here in lockup, Duke?"

"Had some trouble on the chain. Got into it with a dude goin' to the hospital."

I remembered Earl liked to ride the hospital bus. He was a master hypochondriac and an expert at manipulating the doctor. Earl had managed to convince him through the years to get him checked out by every specialist the state had in its prison healthcare stable.

"So, what's the deal?" I asked again, wanting an update on the mental condition of a fellow convict some regarded as unpredictable at best.

Earl the Pearl displayed the basis for his early nickname as his facial muscles pulled his cheeks tight over the bones. He was smiling, but his eyes were cold and mirthless.

"The other dude stayed at the hospital. Doctor's orders. Something about broken bones. I think he'll be there a while. Brought me back in shackles and stuck me in lockup. Took away all my shit. Haven't even got a fan. The run is loaded with crazies who scream all night, throw food and piss, break out the windows, and run around like psychos at shower time. Last night they tore up their fuckin' sheets and jammed up the shitters and flooded the place. I wake up and step right into a fucking puddle."

Earl was getting agitated. Foam started to form at the corners of his mouth. His eyes were steady but wild. He stuck his fingers through the woven mesh and squeezed his knuckles white.

"You got to take it easy, Earl. Cool down. Already they've got you in lockup. They can turn the screws to you, Earl."

"Let 'em start turnin' then, 'cause I had about all I can take. Time to fight back, I been thinking. The Duke is takin' it no more. From anybody."

Talk like that always unnerves me, because I understand what can happen when a man reaches that point. The point where a man doesn't care any longer to exercise control and restraint over himself. The point where he feels he is backed into a corner and has nothing to lose. The point where a man starts to become dangerous — unpredictably, savagely dangerous. Earl was near to reaching that point, if he hadn't already. I got the feeling an old homeboy like myself would not be immune from his fury should it break loose at anytime soon. Suddenly I realized the sanity of the chain-link fence.

"I don't see it that way, Earl. This place to me is like quicksand, like one of those Chinese finger stretchers. The more you struggle, the deeper you go or the tighter it gets. But you can be cool and make your way through it and get out."

"Yeah, unless you're man enough to bust that finger stretcher right off. Tear it up. Rip it right off your fingers and your hands will be free."

"Only it's not straw in here, Earl. The chains in here are tempered steel. You're not Superman."

"Yeah? Who the fuck says I ain't?"

Earl had an answer for everything. I was beginning to see that my words were having no effect. His hatred was too deeply rooted and was growing like a cancer inside him. As if to bleed off some of the tension forming in the air around us, the silent mulatto inside the cage with Earl got up and started to work the heavy bag with his fists. His blows thudded like quick snaps of thunder. Earl looked pleased at the support for his tirade. The one-man rebellion had been increased to two.

A job came open in the Major's office, and I sent in the proper form for an interview. Ol' Jonesy had made his parole third time up after doing six flat on twenty. The Major called me down for an interview at six o'clock in the morning. I stood outside in the hallway for half an hour before I heard him boom "Come in" through the closed door. I entered quickly and stood in a respectful position before his desk. The Major was struggling to assemble some kind of printed report into a colored tagboard binder. Lieutenant Green, a younger white field boss, sat off to the side scraping mud from his boot into a trash can.

"What did you have on your mind there, Ol' Fox?" The Major questioned me condescendingly.

"Bookkeeper's job, sir. I'm strong in math, good with ledgers, numbers. Can type sixty words a minute, have a college degree, sir. Used to run a construction company in the world."

The brief summary of what I thought would be pertinent credentials seemed to irritate him. The stack of pages burst from his hands and spread out all over the floor of the room.

"Damn!" The Major glared at me like it was my fault. I sensed my opportunity was at hand.

"Let me help you, sir," I said, bending down to gather the sheets. I worked rapidly and in a moment had the offending pages ordered and bound. I set the completed report before him and employed my best imitation of obsequiousness.

"There you are, sir. No problem."

Lieutenant Green looked up over his buck knife. I noticed his big toe was poking through his sock on the foot where the muddy boot was missing. He articulated his version of a command.

"There's a stack of them books that needs puttin' tagatha." He spit into the trash can, releasing a stream of dark amber from the wad in his cheek that dribbled on his chin.

"Yes, sir. Right away, sir." I sounded like a new recruit eager to please his superiors. I sat down at a small table against the wall and began to silently organize and collate copies of a report on sexual harassment complaint procedures. The two prison officers verbally evaluated my person in their own brand of code.

"You know 'im?" The Major inquired of the Lieutenant.

"Naw. Seen 'im around."

Pause . . . Buck knife scraping mud. Desk chair rocking, squeaking.

"Looks like he's got some snap."

"Yup."

"Be pretty hard to replace Ol' Jonesy."

"Jonesy was a good hand."

Pause . . . Buck knife folding. Foot squeezing into boot.

"Jonesy minded his own business. Never gave us any guff."

"Jonesy was awright."

"This one looks pretty good, too."

"He might be able to cut it, Major."

"Why don't we give him a shot, L.T."

"Okay by me."

The flow of words changed direction to include the one being observed during the dialogue.

"Where you workin' now, Ol' Fox?"

"Garment factory, Major," I said.

"What's a convict like you doing sewing overalls?"

"That's where they assigned me, Major."

"Makes a lot of sense, doesn't it, Fox?"

I sensed a test of some kind in his question. It seemed designed to measure my true opinion of their system. From my answer they would be able to tell whether or not I would fit in as the new book-keeper. A sincere, comprehensively evasive answer wrapped in respect was my ticket out of the garment factory.

"Well, sir, they process a thousand or so men through Diagnostics every two weeks. They have to analyze a lot of data and make the best decisions they can. I'm sure it's hard to find the perfect slot for everybody. I think what they do is just try to get close and once you get to your unit you're supposed to use a little initiative and find the right spot for yourself. That's why I'm here this morning, Major. I'd like to work in a capacity that utilizes some of my skills, where I'd be of maximum service to the institution. That way we both benefit."

When I turned around and set the completed stack of bound reports on his desk, the Major's eyes were wide and his expression blank, as if he was attempting to fathom some great mystery.

"There you are, sir," I said calmly, eagerly. "What's next?"

The Major glanced at the reports that had baffled him, then up at me. He seemed to be perceiving me from a renewed perspective.

"Get down to the laundry, Fox," he ordered. "Get yourself some pressed clothes. If you're going to work in this office you can't look like you just fell off the turnip truck. What your number?"

"H-17-223-83."

The Major made a move for the phone.

"Take off, Fox. Get the clothes and come right back. Ol' Jonesy left things a mess and you seem like the one to get them straight. I'm callin' garment right now and having you transferred."

"Yes, sir. Thank you, sir." A closing expression of anticipated gratitude. I skipped out through the heavy plate door and headed for the laundry. This was going to be easier than I had thought. The Major needed me.

Weeks rolled by and I adjusted to a somewhat civilized setting. The main difference was being out of earshot from the hatcheting machines and lint dust that, in two minutes, would settle a quarter-inch thick on a cup of coffee. The Major was right about things being a mess. Whether it had been Jonesy or someone else, it was hard to tell. But Jonesy took the blame. It's always that way when a guy goes home. He was the dumbest clown to have hit the unit that decade.

It took a while to gain the Major's trust — and that was, at best, dependent upon his coarse vicissitudes of mood — but soon I was able to help effect certain changes. Little things, like moving one-legged men off top bunks, weren't too difficult to convince the Major about. Getting a guy with recurring hepatitis out of the food-preparation area was a little harder. But with backup from medical records, and case law indicating how the unit could get in trouble with the federal examiners, the Major grudgingly saw his way clear to make the change.

In prison, the status quo is the rule — no procedures ever change except under duress of emergency. Only emergencies receive extra attention, and in them lies the only hope of modifying procedure for the good. To see the Major was hard, at best inconvenient. It was purposefully made that way. If you were hurting bad enough, you would stand on the wall for hours waiting, or come back four and five times to see him. Twelve years in the prison business had given the Major a certain wariness. Working as his bookkeeper, I was party to many of his interviews and over time developed a special respect for his perceptiveness. But once in a while a convict was able to get over on him. The Duke of Earl was just such a convict.

I had not seen Earl since that day in the gym, but had been able to track him though the move slips that crossed my desk. About three weeks after I took over Jonesy's job, Earl was moved from lockup over to D Building, the skid row block, home of the most violent and incorrigible prisoners. Our unit was classified as medium-minimum security, and Earl would have been on a maximum unit like Dexter but for his medical problems. This was the infirmary unit, and when inmates like Earl had to be here they were sequestered in D Building.

The problem was Johnny Boy. The pretty mulatto had been moved from lockup to A Building and this interrupted what I found out was a heavy sexual thing he had with Earl.

Earl had held out for the first three or four years, thinking his appeal would come through, but when it got denied and caused him the futile anxieties of climbing the judicial ladder to the Supreme Court, Earl needed sexual release. A need that grew stronger day by day in reverse ratio to his desire to wait for a woman. With a seventy-five-year sentence, Earl would have to do at least twelve flat to come up for parole, but with his lengthy record of prior offenses, he could bet on several set-offs. That was fifteen years without sex, and Earl soon became convinced that a pretty young boy was a hell of a lot better than his fading memories.

Johnny Boy had not been the first, but was the current favorite, of the Duke. Earl was actually in love with Johnny and was insanely jealous and possessive. I was getting out soon and could wait for a woman's touch, but I guess I could understand Earl's fascination. Slim but taut, cafe au lait coloring, dazzling green eyes and ripe full lips that frequently parted into a smile that must have said "I dare you" to Earl when they first met. Johnny loved Earl too, in his own kind of way, and was down with twenty for killing a pimp. They needed each other. They were good together. I saw that the first day in the gym.

So, Earl came to see the Major about a move.

"What is it, Peterson?"

"I want to integrate, Major," Earl said after waiting six hours on the wall. "Need your permission for the move."

Getting moved in with a friend was next to impossible, or the Major would have daily lines waiting a hundred deep. Integration was another story. It looked good when the races were mixing voluntarily. The federal monitors ate it up. Made the prison's socialization process appear to be working.

I looked up from my computer when I heard Earl come on with his approach. It was a brilliant tactic.

"Who's the other inmate, Peterson?"

"John Randall, sir. Lives in A4-21."

"Randall . . . Randall. Doesn't ring a bell. Pull his tag, Fox."

I went over to the master board that filled an entire wall. Every bunk in the entire unit was located in a complex diagram. I pulled the tag under bunk A4-21 and brought it over to the Major.

"Randall, John," the Major read. "Caucasian. Steward's Department. Why isn't Randall with you, Peterson?"

"Sick call, Major. He's having medical problems. That's why I want him with me. He needs someone to look after him. He gets these fainting spells, Major. Has to take special medicine."

The Major scrutinized the Duke. Something was amiss, but he couldn't put his finger on it.

"Who is your cellie now, Peterson?"

"Don't have one, sir. He went home yesterday."

Earl had all his ducks in a row. He made things attractive to the institution and thus the Major. No third party to move, an integration. How Earl had gotten Johnny's race designated as "Caucasian" was another indication of his skill as a politician. Earl had bribed the night bookkeeper with a taste of some good weed.

"Make out a move slip, Fox," the Major commanded.

I rolled it through the typewriter, imprinted both names, numbers, and cell locations. The Major took it, checked it, and slid it across his desk.

"Okay, sign it."

Earl Peterson made his obligatory mark.

"Have Randall come by and sign it, and I'll authorize the move."

"But, Major," Earl said. "You're going on vacation tomorrow.

If you would, sir, could you sign it while I'm here and I'll have John come in later? Lieutenant Green will be here."

The master stroke. The Major would never lay eyes on mulatto Johnny. He grabbed the paper and scrawled his signature.

"Okay. Dismissed, Peterson. I got better things to do than spend another minute with your goat-smellin' ass."

"Thank you, Major," Earl fawned. Only I saw his sly smirk as he slid through the door . . . Duke of Earl.

Johnny went in the next day as planned and signed the move slip before Lieutenant Green, consenting to the integration. Green was stumbling around, power-tripping and trying to fill the Major's shoes. The Major's signature on the slip was all he needed to pass it right through. I made up some new bed tags, slid them in the proper slots on the big board, and went about my business.

An hour later Earl and his mulatto were hot after it behind a bedsheet hung up over the bars. This was the beginning of the end for both of them, but you never would have known it then. They were just another happy couple.

Earl had been having his toenails cut out one at a time at a month's lay-in from work apiece. Johnny Boy kept them supplied with goods from the Steward's Department they traded on the block. Earl gambled at dominoes in the day room while Johnny cooked for the guards. In the afternoons they'd go to the gym, pump iron for a couple hours, then shower and be back on the run for the evening's business. D1-25 was on ground level at the very end of the run — the perfect location as headquarters for all kinds of illicit activities.

The Duke ruled fairly over his minions and enterprises, but came down iron-handed on those who broke their word or crossed him in any way. Maintaining control was a matter of image, and the Duke was frighteningly adept at inducing loyalty and respect in those with whom he had dealings. He had given up on his appeal and had steeled himself to do the long run. If he had to do fifteen or twenty years flat, he'd do it on his own terms. He felt he really had nothing to lose. Earl was discreet in his dealings, and the bosses left him alone. He was new on this unit and hadn't caused any trouble since the hospital chain. Little things like that are quickly forgotten. D Block was rough anyway, and the guards didn't like to come too far inside without official business. And then they never came alone.

Earl was a natural leader and organizer. He had boundless energy and an unlimited capacity for managing his ventures designed to beat the Man at his own game. Once he got going, Duke's reputation spread quickly. Before long he had established working relationships with everybody who was anybody. He didn't deal with short-timers or fools, but every solid dude knew the Duke and treated him with respect. There weren't many inside who would back up their play with their life, but the Duke of Earl was concrete. Minor players hung around him like flies. He got big, real big, too fast. And that was the problem.

Competition. Things had been operating fine long before Earl arrived on the unit, and the old power structure didn't like the rapid rise of the new kid on the block. Steaks had always been available on D Block for three decks, but Earl provided them hot and seasoned. Marijuana joints were four decks of freeworld cigarettes, but the Duke's stash would stone out three or four guys instead of one. Duke had prettier punks, many he had turned out himself. During football season, parlays paid five-to-one with the Duke, while Bumblebee still paid four-to-one.

Bumblebee. Six-foot-four, two-forty, could bench press 460 pounds and wore size thirteen triple-E brogans. Bumblebee had inherited D Block from Wolfman four years back when Wolf finally discharged an eighty-year sentence after serving twenty-five flat.

Bumblebee — so called because of his dark saucer-sized sunglasses and teeth of pollen gold — lived at the roof of the world in D5-25, right above Earl five open tiers upward. Bumblebee had felt the drain caused by Duke's action from day one but, to save face, blew it off to his runners and supplicants. Inside the lava was beginning to flow.

It wasn't until Magpie, Bumblebee's cellie and educated bookman, did some figuring and found that business was the lowest ever, that Bumblebee dispatched Highside, his A-number-one handyman and all-around snoop. A few days later Highside had uncovered an exploitable crack in the Duke's organization that bubbled with the emotional intensity necessary to get the Duke to blow his cool.

Earl was at the hospital getting his sixth toenail removed when Highside slid up next to Johnny Boy as he was coming back from the kitchen.

"Johnny Boy. Where's the Duke?"

"Hospital. What's up?"

"Something special jus' come in. Gotta find Duke or he's goin' miss it."

"He won't be back 'til afta chow."

"That's too bad, 'cause it's real pretty. Too bad you can't handle it."

That was the barb that finally got to Johnny Boy. He was tired of people thinking he was just the Duke's "gal" and nothing more.

"Sure. I can handle it. What's the deal?"

"Sinsemilla. Fresh and strong. Two ounces."

"You know the Duke always likes to test it first himself."

"Thought you said you could handle it."

"Who's the man?"

"Bumblebee. But Streaker from C Block is on his way over to take a look."

Johnny Boy drew himself up to a new height.

"All right. Let's go."

I know this dialogue is accurate. A little bird told me. His name is Fossil and he sweeps the runs and has powers of hearing equal to a sophisticated eavesdropping device the police might use. Fossil is half snitch, half self-appointed peacemaker. He's been known to give up a minor asshole to the Man so bigger fish can swim and feed in the deep. He's been around since before half the guys in here were born and is considered almost a tradition, an exhibit like in a museum.

According to Fossil, Johnny Boy followed Highside up to D5-25 to see Bumblebee and test the weed. Bumblebee came on real cordial, had a fat one already rolled and told Johnny Boy, if he liked it, could make the deal in Duke's place. He'd been watching, and thought Johnny's talents were going unappreciated, that he had more potential than was being utilized. Johnny Boy enjoyed this banter, and as he smoked the reefer, his feelings of self-importance soared. Johnny Boy played the big shot, smoked the joint deep and fast, said he could handle it no matter how strong it was. What he didn't realize was that Bumblebee had laced the joint with a heavy hit of hog tranquilizer, angel dust, a hit that would have knocked a donkey's dick in the dirt. A few minutes later the pretty mulatto slid down glassy-eyed in Bumblebee's bunk, like his body was suddenly robbed of all its bones.

Bumblebee brutalized that poor boy that afternoon, asserting his territorial rights again and again for over two hours. Later, the autopsy report would show that most of his internal organs had been ruptured. That was before Bumblebee stood outside his cell with Johnny Boy held high over his head and rattled the barred windows with his blood-curdling yell. The echoes continued after the body had fallen five stories and landed in front of cell D1-25, just as Earl was entering the run. He threw his cane aside and started running toward the blur of tan flesh. When he reached the body the shrieking started and didn't stop until the Duke was dead.

A call came into the Major's office from the building officer about then, and I watched Lieutenant Green's face go white with fear.

"Seal off the block," he barked into the phone. "I'm calling SWAT."

The Lieutenant began dialing furiously, bracing himself with thoughts of what the Major would do. I slipped out the door and eased my way down to D Block. The crash gates were locked tight when I got there, and I joined the crush of inmates looking up through the bars at the open stairway. I heard a noise, but couldn't place it. Then Earl ran by and I saw that he was screaming. It was an inhuman sound, one a hyena might make after tearing off its leg in the jaws of a steel trap. The riot squad ran up, but not one of them wanted to go inside the block.

"Let 'em cool off a little," said a helmeted corpsman as he slapped a stout oak club into his other palm.

The Duke took the stairs three at a time, even though one foot was swathed in bandages. He carried a length of hollow pipe, flattened and sharpened like a spear. In his other hand was a shorter shiv with a double-sided blade shiny at the edges. The Duke didn't see me. He didn't see anything but the broken body of Johnny Boy magnified by his rage.

Duke met Bumblebee halfway down 5 run and drove the spear through his mouth and out the back of his head. Bumblebee was weakened by his sex and other exertions, but still managed to drive a shank under Earl's ribcage before the Duke toppled him over the railing. He landed about twenty feet from us inside the bars with a thud I could feel through my shoes.

A moment later Duke stumbled down the stairs, eyes wide and spitting up blood. He wore Bumblebee's shank rooted in a wet stain on his left side. Red gauze bandages trailed from his foot like an obscene tail. He reached the body and everyone was stunned to silence as he went to work with the short knife. Metal scraped concrete and the Duke stood up and walked toward us where we stood watching. He dragged his left foot and held up Bumblebee's head by the black knotty hair. He approached the bars and pointed at the head with his bloody shiv.

"This guy has been fuckin' with me," the Duke said. Then he fell against the bars and slid to the floor.

1985, Walls Unit, Texas Department of Corrections
Huntsville, Texas

Race, Chance, Change

U.S. racism is nowhere more inescapable than in the brute facts and figures of our criminal justice system. In the general population, African-Americans constitute less than 13 percent, yet 51 percent of all prisoners nationwide are black. Thirty-two percent of black men in their twenties are under some form of criminal justice supervision. While blacks and whites are murder victims in roughly equal numbers, 82 percent of prisoners executed since 1977 were convicted of the murder of a white person.

How does racism operate behind the walls? "I've heard some men say prison made them much more racist than they were when they went in. The opposite was true for me. I never thought of myself as a racist, yet we all have our fears," writes Richard Stratton, who is white. "Unless we have the courage to break through the carefully structured fear that works so well in prison, we merely reinforce old biases."

"First Day on the Job," Henry Johnson's dramatic monologue here, shows that guards face the same choices about handling their fears as prisoners. An old white guard at Attica is breaking in a new one. Reminiscing about the time before the 1971 uprising, repression, and ensuing reform, the speaker conjures up a time when leaders like Martin Luther King, Malcolm X, and Jomo Kenyatta, first president of Kenya, stirred the pride of African-American male inmates and the fear of their white keepers. We see how racism may be fostered to bolster the confidence of the keepers.

While some guards like Sam in Michael Wayne Hunter's story here overcome racial fears, others, like those who urge inmates to make "hits" in the same story, manipulate racial strife between inmates. Jesse Lopez reported in "Arrival at McNeil Island" (1978)* that some prisons even put into solitary confinement those "guilty of interracial association." Some prisoners report on having been encouraged to practice racism openly inside. Others assert that the administraton causes more racial tension, for example, by exaggerating the extent of gang activity, keeping the races at each other's throats, and thus deflecting anger from the administration.

In Southern Ohio Correctional Facility in Lucasville in 1993, the administration forced members of different races — often from areas foreign to racial intermingling — to cell together, according to Paul Mulryan, author of "Eleven Days Under Siege." This often resulted in one or both parties being sent to the hole, labeled a racist and hence a gang member. Black and white prisoners, knowing that forced interracial celling caused more hatred than it prevented, organized an uprising to demand, among other things, that the practice cease. Relying on the public's assumption of racial strife and disregarding its interracial leadership, corrections officials told the press the uprising was a race riot. Of the several hundred riots in U.S. prisons since 1970, Lucasville was one of the most catastrophic: prisoners killed one guard and nine prisoners.

Trapped with hundreds of others in L Corridor with no way to exit during the riot, Mulryan was transferred to Mansfield Prison and held in the hole until he was cleared of any participation in it. There he wrote "Eleven Days," seeking to "describe the experience as candidly as possible" without inviting repercussions. The "very real possibility" of his "narrative being used by the state as supporting evidence to prosecute someone" prevented him from using names. Later, with others cleared of responsibility for the riot, Mulryan joined a class action that ended double-celling.

Prison has become that rare place where, through pure demographics, African-American men clearly seem to wield power. Their real or perceived threat can fire the animosity of white gangs. Although many new prisoners feel virtually forced into gangs for protection, this survival strategy can backfire. In Lance Fleming's play *Lockdown* (1995)* an Aryan gang buys drugs from a black gang and deliberately refuses to pay for them. By thus violating the code, they "force" the black gang to save face by killing two white gang members. Though the white protagonist knows the Aryans are planning a retaliative strike, he feels powerless to avert it, because snitches end in the morgue.

"Lee's Time" by Susan Rosenberg narrates a variant on this kind of moral crisis, with the difference that the prisoners are women and the issue is the highly charged one of interracial sexual contact between a prisoner and a corrections officer. Rosenberg reports that the case on which her story was loosely based was used with others to pass the federal law that makes it a felony for a C.O. to have even consensual sex with an inmate. No such law existed at the time of the event, Rosenberg says, but the extraordinary twenty-year sentence of the C.O. was actually imposed.

Chance — his being in the path of a riot — causes Paul Mulryan to be doubly punished, yet also impels him to bear his careful witness and to join a suit to redress some of the underlying wrong. Chance — her overhearing a sexual encounter — obliges Lee to decide to change the way she does time. Similar chance contacts change the odds for interracial friendships in Charles Norman's memoir and Michael Wayne Hunter's story, "Sam." Sam and the narrator also share opposition to the death penalty and grieve for Bobby Harris, the first man to be executed after California's five-year moratorium on the death penalty. It's surprising to find such triumphs over prejudice in such a violent environment. It would be profoundly ironic if the supposed dregs of our society can produce a higher standard of human responsibility than its "respectable" citizens.

First Day on the Job

Henry Johnson

*I have learned this: it is not what one does that is wrong, but what
one becomes as a consequence of it.*
  — Oscar Wilde

"Twenty years ago when I was young, kid,
we kept a special room in the basement at Attica —
ripe as any butcher shop, soundproofed.
Wild Bill, your squad commander,
shackled nigger convicts to the wall
and we beat hell out of them
with rubber hoses 'n such.
Lord, the screams in that place,
the heat and smell of blood.
Don't step on that junebug near your foot.
Had that same look in my eyes
my first day on the job,
like a child separated from his mother in a department store.
The Sergeant assigned me to work in D Block,
had to feed the cons waitin' to appear
before the adjustment committee.
It was like feedin' hogs. I watched
the trustee pour hot coffee for each of 'em
from a three-gallon tin can.
One of the cons in lockup begged me for a match,
dashed a mug of scaldin' hot coffee
in my face. The doctors saved my eyes,
but the skin on my face never healed right.
Friends told me they found the bugger hangin'
in his cell, one Sunday. One of his friends
must've slipped him some rope, God bless'm.

This here's your locker.
used to belong to old Deke Miller —
he shriveled up like a burnt piece of bacon
before he passed. Heard it was cancer.

When my wife ran off with a mechanic
from the next town, I staggered around for a while
like I was dazed from a blow to the heart.
Look here. See the girl with the blond pigtail?
that's Ellen, my daughter. Put her through
one of them fancy nursin' schools myself.
She's in Denver now, don't see her much
except for Christmas. Old Deke and his wife
clothed and fed her while I drank.

I was proud, hard.
But how hard is a man? —
pushed around against his will,
that King boy
tootin' his communist ass in our faces,
and singin' his heathen songs
in our streets.
And in anger, kid, in anger he swears
that no door in America will be closed to them
even if it means breakin' us
law by law.

So you see, you have to treat these bastards right.
See the con moppin' the rotunda floor?
Used to wear one of them afro haircuts
almost a foot high, and cobra-quick with a knife.
He'd call you cracker so often you'd answer
as though it was your Christian name.
But look at him now: bald, shaky in the knees.
Wild Bill pounded his head like a T-bone steak
with the south corridor keys,
slipped him back into his cell before mornin'.
Go on, ask him who Malcolm X is, or
Jomo Kenyatta. He'll shit all over himself.

You look pale, but you'll be just fine.
Cain't use the room no more, dammit.
So you gotta be smart.
They need to know the discipline of a guard's club,
the keys jangle like death bells ringin'.
We got to control their words, break 'em

and fling 'em into the mud like we did that King boy.
And we have to feed 'em right always
if not pork
then with an education that will send 'em marchin'
into the fire. Know what I mean, kid?

Here, bite a chew of this tobacco —
it keeps you calm.
Don't think it's over, kid, believe me, it ain't.
There'll be another one of 'em
screamin' and preachin' and scramblin'
for the mountaintop one of these days.

Heh heh. We should have a prison or two up there
by then, kid; maximum security.
Jobs for us all, and maybe
a special room somewhere."

      1988, Sing Sing Correctional Facility
      Ossining, New York

Eleven Days Under Siege: An Insider's Account of the Lucasville Riot

Paul Mulryan

"Hey, Paul!" I heard my road dog calling me from the other side of the fence dividing the blocks from the yard. "I just heard that some rollers got downed outside L Corridor! Keep your eyes open, rap, some strange shit is going down."

I didn't give much thought to what he had said. Fights between convicts and guards weren't exactly uncommon here. But I told him I'd keep my eyes open.

Then I heard the two guards in charge of my block yell, their voices full of panic and urgency, for the porter: "Lock up! Lock up now, damn it!"

Someone in the cells called out, "The guards are locking themselves in the bathroom! What the hell's happening?"

"They've got control of L Corridor! There are guys running around with masks on! They've got the keys! They've got the fucking keys!"

The rumble from the corridor began to grow like a rolling thunderstorm: muffled screams, the pounding of feet running through the halls, glass shattering and showering the floor, and echoes of loud ramming sounds as though heavy steel bars were battering down the walls. There was a louder crash, and then orders were yelled. "Open these cells! Let's get these doors open, and get these people out!"

By now I knew that the block I was in had been taken over, but I didn't know by whom. An icy dread swept through me. My first thought was that there must be a racial war.

Keys that the block officers had abandoned were thrown to the prisoner now manning the control panel. The eighty cells in the L Corridor were instantly opened. I grabbed a metal tray for a weapon and headed out of my cell. Down the range I could see several teams of masked convicts converging on the block. Each man was armed to the teeth: baseball bats, chains, and shanks of stainless steel, two foot long and honed to a point as fine as an icepick. These men meant business.

"Everyone out! Get the fuck out of your cell!" they yelled as they moved from cell to cell. "If anyone is caught trying to hide in their cell, kill the motherfucker! Let's go! Let's go!" I watched each man closely, trying to read his intentions from his eyes and body signals. If they tried to move in on me I'd go over the range to the first floor. The jump was nothing, and there were too many of them to even think about dealing with them head-on. My adrenaline shot to flight mode. I put my foot on the edge of the range, ready to go over. They came closer checking me out, and clearly not rattled by my metal tray. Then I saw both black and white skin showing through their masks. I was relieved. Blacks and whites wouldn't be working together if this was a race riot. "Everything's cool, brother," one said. "But we still want everyone out in the hall, so if you need to get some of your things together get them now and leave the block." I didn't recognize any of them, nor did I want to. Still I inched closer to the edge of the range.

"Be cool, bro. You've got no problem here," another said.

With that, I moved out, heading quickly down the range and out of the block. Something this big and unbridled could quickly get out of hand. My best bet was to get out to the rec yard where my road dog was. I knew what he was about and that we could look out for each other.

I stepped into L Corridor and into a world of chaos. Each of the 632 cells had been opened, and hundreds of convicts, some masked and armed, swarmed through the hallways like angry hornets. Faces were intense with fear. Eyes darted from face to face, face to hand, looking for weapons or any signs of danger. When eye contact was made, it was brief and concealed. No one wanted his concern to be misread as a threat or challenge.

"You men get something into your hands!" one guy kept shouting. "Let's get busy tearing this fucking place down!" He ran from window to window swinging a steel bar and smashing glass. I moved closer to the gym, hoping to find the exit door open, then spotted my friend Val from one of the other blocks. "Val!" I hollered as I worked my way toward him. "What the hell is this shit?"

"I don't know what's up, Paul. I just got out of the shower and the place was crazy!"

I told him my plans to head to the rec yard and he fell in beside me. Down the hall we came upon a body lying in a puddle of blood. There were punctures all over the guy's face and upper torso. Someone had pinned a guard's badge through his skin, a sign this was a snitch and that snitches would find no peace in L Corridor this day.

"Who is it? Can you tell who it is?" I asked my homey as I stepped around the blood.

"No, rap. Too much blood."

By the time Val and I made it through the hallway to the gym, it was too late. The exit door was already barricaded, wired shut, and guarded by several masked and armed convicts. Since this was the only available exit, it meant that Val and I were locked in for the long run.

We knew that the riot could erupt into a full-scale bloodbath at any time, and it was imperative that we arm ourselves as quickly as possible. We grabbed the first suitable thing we saw: pieces of heavy pipe. As we made our way back up the corridor, the heat and closeness of danger hung like a wet wool blanket.

"We're stuck in this shit for however long it lasts," I said to Val. "We've got to watch each other's back."

Val looked around, nodding his head. "Cool, rap. Let's get our asses out of the mainstream." This was too big to be safe.

"Listen up! Everyone shut the fuck up for a minute!" yelled one of the Masks as he marched through the hallway. "Everyone move against the wall! We gotta keep the middle of the corridor clear. Let's get together on this!"

The crowd flanked the wall as two other Masks walked down the center and announced: "Lucasville is ours! This is not racial. I repeat, not racial. It's us against the administration! We're tired of these people fucking us over. Is everybody with us? Let's hear ya!"

Hundreds of fists shot into the air as the prisoners roared their approval. I felt relief sweep over me. I was now a little clearer about what was happening. What I didn't know was that we were locked into what was soon to be one of the nation's longest and bloodiest riots.

Teams of men were assigned to barricade and guard each block. Two men were stationed in the day rooms to watch the rec yard; two were stationed in each of the range's top cells to watch the roof. L-2 was the only block that hadn't been opened. I overheard someone say that one of the prisoners had broken a key in the lock to keep the rioters from taking over. One of the Masks found pickaxes and busted the glass and the steel frame from the window casing. Twenty minutes later, L-2 was taken.

"Okay, get the bitch who broke the key in the lock! He wants to play police? We'll show him what's up!"

The prisoner had locked himself in the stairwell with the block officer, hoping that the brick-and-steel enclosure would keep him safe until help arrived. The Masks attacked the block wall with forty-five-pound weight bars and a heavy pickax, and within minutes the concrete wall gave way. The guard and the prisoner were dragged out. The guard was blindfolded, but the prisoner was hit with bats, weight bars, and shanks. A coroner's report later revealed that not only was his skull crushed, and numerous other bones broken, he had also been cut from neck to belly and gutted. His body was dragged to the end of the corridor and dumped on a pile of wet blankets near another body, both of which would later be hauled out to the rec yard.

Meanwhile, guards were being grabbed wherever they could be found. Several managed to break away and make it to safety, but others weren't so fortunate. Some were thrown onto the floor and hit so hard that they couldn't get back up. I didn't know if they were alive or dead as they were dragged into one of the cellblocks. During the first hour eleven were seized, blindfolded, and dressed in prison blues, inmate uniforms. The convicts beat some of the guards so badly they released them for fear that they might die. Of those seized, seven would be taken hostage for the duration of the riot; one would be killed.

The rioters covered all of the windows with blankets and then searched every cell for food. With more than four hundred prisoners and seven guards to feed, food would be essential. Everything we found was stored in an empty cell that became the kitchen. That first night cookies, chips, and cake were given to anyone who was hungry. Although I hadn't eaten all day, I wasn't hungry. I remember thinking that I'd get something to eat when it was all over. Little did I know it would last another ten days.

On the second day the prison authorities shut off the electricity and the water. Soon, all food was gone. The deprivation of food and water, coupled with the stress, began to take its toll. People lost weight at an alarming rate. Several men got so thirsty they drank from the fire extinguisher. Men began to divide into factions and surround themselves with their roads dogs for protection in case the unpredictable happened. It was impossible to get any sleep. I would lie on a mattress, my mind racing. Just as I was on the edge of sleep, my eyes would pop open and I'd sit up to make sure no one was creeping up on me. I'd go through this routine over and over.

By now, state highway patrolmen, SOCF (Southern Ohio Correctional Facility) security, and FBI agents had circled the prison, along with more than a thousand heavily armed National Guard personnel. Army helicopters flew overhead. Sharpshooters lined the roof.

We were concerned that the troops would launch a full-scale assault as they'd done in the 1968 uprising at the old Ohio Penitentiary. If that happened many of us would be killed indiscriminately, bystanders shot dead with no distinction between them and the ringleaders. I also knew that somewhere inside L Corridor there were seven hostages, and they were the only thing that stood between life and death, bullets and negotiations.

A team of convicts set up a phone line and established contact with the prison staff and the SOCF negotiator, who got things off to a bad start by calling the convicts "a bunch of clowns." The convict negotiators connected a tape recorder to the phone line so that those inside could be kept informed of the progress.

Eventually, however, the state woke up to the seriousness of the situation and flew in a special adviser from Georgia. He turned the talks around with a high degree of professionalism and won the guarded respect of the prisoners.

"We want every stage of these talks covered by the news media, sir," said one of the convicts. "We know how the prison administration operates, and we don't trust any of them. If this isn't covered by the media, the state will do nothing but stall and renege on any progress made."

News coverage would restrain the outside troops from either rushing the prison or killing the convicts once this was over. But the state wanted the situation kept under cover, with only select information reaching the outside through their own public relations office. Not surprisingly, the state released a story alleging that the riot was a racial war and that the prisoners refused to let the media talk to a convict spokesman. When they did allow one of the major Ohio newspapers to speak to a convict by phone, they quickly pulled the plug when he began to list the prisoners' demands.

Inside the prison, the convicts rigged up a PA system using a tape player and two large speakers taken from the rec department. They set these up near the windows facing the large media camp in front of the SOCF. A tape recording was played: "The prison authorities want you to think that this is a racial war. It is not! Whites and blacks have united to protest the abuses of the SOCF staff and administration. We want the FBI and we want a peaceful ending to this . . ."

The tape played on, listing demands. A SWAT team was sent to remove the system, but the speakers of the battery-operated tape player were set up so that they could be reached only from inside. Every time the tape would start to play, officials sent up helicopters, hoping to drown out the sound of the message.

Another group of convicts began painting messages on bed sheets and hanging them out the windows. Prison authorities tried to move the media out of the area, but it was too late. The cameras of the local and national news caught all of it. The next day, the painted sheets made front-page news.

Meanwhile along the hallway inside the prison, several prisoners were laid out with broken bones or other serious injuries. A few of the convicts built a makeshift infirmary and went to every cell collecting any medication or medical supplies they could find. Using the stage area of the gym, they rolled out a dozen or so mattresses for those too fucked-up to walk. That first night all of the mattresses were full. One of the wounded was bleeding so profusely that I didn't think he'd last the night.

A self-appointed medic found a needle and thread and went to work stitching up the guy's neck. In an hour he was stitched and laid out on a mattress. He was one of the lucky ones who would live to tell his story. The unlucky ones were piled on top of each other like a heap of dirty laundry. A few days later the bodies were wrapped in blankets and dragged out to the rec yard. Two of them thought to be dead jumped up as soon as they were laid on the grass. They ran straight toward the National Guard, who didn't know whether to shoot them or run from them. A guard thought to be dead lay in the yard for several hours while numerous convicts who had clustered there kicked and assailed him. When the coast seemed clear, he hobbled over toward the fences, where armed guards covered him as he made his way across the yard to the K-side gym. One of the prisoners who was running across the yard was the prisoner Val and I had seen earlier lying in the corridor with a badge pinned to his body. How he managed to lie perfectly still for all of those hours, including the painful moment while the badge was being stuck to his body, is still a mystery.

When the prison authorities saw all of the bodies dumped in the rec yard they began to realize that this was more serious than they'd thought. So, when negotiations continued, attitudes were more strained.

"We want food and water! You people think we're playing games. We'll bring this fucking place down!" the convicts demanded.

"Listen up!" the negotiator responded. "We're working on food and water. We'll get it together and I'll call you back as soon as it's ready. Just hang on for a couple of hours."

Several hours later the supplies came and were left in the yard. A team of Masks brought food and water to the prisoners and rationed them, greatly reducing the tension inside. The downside was that prison authorities would now try to use food as a bargaining chip. Their mistake was in thinking that now they were in a position where they could call the shots.

The negotiations continued over the next several days like a Ping-Pong match, back and forth, neither side wanting to lose the first point. Prison authorities still wouldn't agree to live media coverage.

"You either get the news media in here or else these talks will end!" the convicts yelled. "We don't have to talk at all!"

But the officials acted like it was all just a game. "We can't let a TV crew inside for security reasons. It can't be done!"

Several more bodies were dumped into the rec yard. The phone began to ring.

"Okay. We're working things out with an Ohio news network for a live TV interview. Can we get a hostage in return, as a show of good faith?"

"A hostage is no problem. We'll bring one of your people out when we come to do the interview. Set it up and call when you're ready."

The following morning, before the interview was scheduled, a group of masked prisoners explained to those manning the phones that more food and water was needed.

The authorities saw this as a chance to show who was in control. "We can't change the original deal. You said all you wanted was a TV interview and we got it for you. Now you're playing games. We'll give you the interview but nothing else. If you want the food and water you'll have to give us two hostages." A few minutes later another group of Masks, who called themselves the "hardliners," came to the phone.

"Here's what's gonna happen," said a spokesman for the hardliners. "You people are going to bring us more food and water with the TV interview for one hostage. This is not negotiable. If you play games, we'll send you a hostage — but he won't be walking out!"

The authorities denied the demand and asked to talk to the original negotiator. Returning to the phone, he said, "All we're asking for is food and water. We know this won't cost you a thing. If we don't get it, the hardliners will take over! There's nothing I can do. You could lose a hostage for something as basic as food and water!"

A local radio station, hearing of the exchange, expressed concern that the hostage might be killed. A spokesperson for the prison authorities released a statement to the media: "We don't take this too seriously. We believe it's a serious threat, but it's a common ploy used during a hostage situation."

Later that day a hostage was killed. His body was placed on a mattress and carried into the rec yard by six convicts. Everyone waited for the National Guard to hit the joint, guns blasting at anything that moved.

Suddenly, one of the convicts at the back window yelled out: "They're crossing the yard! The state boys are in the rec yard heading this way!"

I ran to the window to see how much time I had before they reached the walls of L Corridor. Outside a light fog had begun to roll in, and from the center of the rec yard about thirty National Guardsmen marched forward in V formation.

"Get your motherfucking asses back across the yard, boys, or you'll get one of these hostages hurt!" a rioter yelled at the police.

All movement came to a halt. The phone began to ring. Before the prison officials could say anything the prisoner manning it yelled, "Get those police off the yard now! What the fuck are you trying to do?"

They cleared the yard. It was later discovered that they were only on the yard to serve as security while the news media set up a conference table and moved their equipment into place. Though tragic, the murder of the hostage had served as a catalyst. From that moment on, things moved forward quickly. The special negotiator from Georgia was now supervising most of the talks. A horde of thirty-five "experts" swarmed the prison authorities who were manning the phone banks.

The state wanted the siege to end without further bloodshed. They wanted the prison back under their rule, the remaining hostages released unharmed, and themselves out of the national media. The takeover had been dragging on in a slow blur, and people on both sides wanted to get on with their lives. Live TV and radio coverage was soon arranged. To show good faith, two hostages were released. The remaining five would be held till the day of surrender. One of the rioters' demands was that the 409 prisoners inside the L Corridor be represented by competent legal counsel to assure their safety and the protection of their rights. The authorities quickly agreed and flew in an attorney from Cleveland, who hammered out a contract with the convict negotiators. It was decided that they would surrender the following day.

Inside, the mood changed dramatically and activity shifted into high gear. Demolition crews were formed to destroy as much of SOCF as possible. Unit managers' offices were gutted, files destroyed, and windows, walls, and ceilings bashed. Each cell was hit. Toilets, sinks, and windows were busted; cell doors were removed, plumbing destroyed, and cabinets ripped off the walls. The control panels in each block were dismantled, and all the wiring and electrical components were ripped out or set ablaze. The sounds of destruction could be heard by the troops surrounding the prison. They stared as though expecting the walls to fall and the prisoners to come pouring out into the rec yard.

The prisoners packed up their personal property, preparing to leave a bad memory behind. High fives, laughs, and jokes filled the air, and the last of the food was given out in generous portions. It wasn't so much celebration of what had been accomplished as an expression of incredible relief that the thing was finally coming to an end.

The next afternoon, prisoner negotiators went through L Corridor collecting names of convicts who were willing to transfer to other prisons. As part of the agreement, the prison authorities had approved mass transfers. L Corridor would be closed for a couple of years or at least until all the damage had been repaired. This meant that hundreds of beds had to be found in a system already working at 185 percent over capacity. I didn't care where I ended up. I just wanted to leave SOCF; Val felt the same way. Our names were added to the transfer list. We knew anyplace would beat the shit out of Lucasville.

Val and I walked into one of the opened blocks and sat next to a fire. Our property was packed into large plastic trash bags and we were ready to walk out.

Out in the rec yard, state officials, media, legal counsel, and prison negotiators sat facing each other at the conference table. Each was furiously signing copies of the twenty-one-point agreement that the lawyers and prisoners had prepared.

I watched everyone shake hands and laugh, a false show of fellowship. Hell, I knew they held each other in contempt, but it meant that the agreement had been reached. If the package was wrapped in blatant hypocrisy, so be it.

TV cameras were trained on the door that would release the surrendering prisoners. The sick and the wounded went first. Some were busted up so badly that they came out on stretchers. Bloodied T-shirts and dirty makeshift bandages hung off their bodies like rags off scarecrows. Those able to walk on their own limped or hobbled as fast as their feet could carry them, eager to put distance between them and their assailants. Convicts watched the process from behind covered windows. If anything happened to the first group, the exchange would no longer be honored.

The surrender went smoothly, and at 10:30 P.M. Val and I walked into the rec yard with a group of thirty other prisoners. The special negotiator from Georgia escorted us to the state patrolmen.

"All right, men, listen up! When I direct you to come forward, you are to walk over to that officer there," said a state official pacing in front of us. Pointing at me and two other prisoners, he shouted, "You, you, and you. Move up!"

I walked forward.

"Listen carefully to every word I say! Put your hands on your head, interlock your fingers, look straight ahead, and don't move!"

I stood there while one man held my hands on top of my head and another searched me for weapons. After tying my hands behind my back with a nylon rope, the officials escorted me to the K Corridor gym. My shoes swished through the wet grass as I walked away from the most bizarre eleven days of my life.

Two hours later over a hundred other convicts and I were put on three prison buses and shipped to the Mansfield Correctional Institution. The bus stopped at a red light in a small town, and through the steamed windows of the bus I could see a digital clock glowing a distorted 4:00 A.M. I looked over at Val. He was off in a world of his own, probably thinking of home and family. It seemed like the right thing to do, so I closed my eyes and went home too.

1995, Mansfield Correctional Institute
Mansfield, Ohio

Pearl Got Stabbed!

Charles P. Norman

I needed a request slip, and as I walked out of my room on my way to the laundry I stopped by the officer's station to ask for one. There's a heavy metal drawer that slides in and out, where you can put your ID tag to get Tylenol, cold pills, envelopes, or requests. I was about to lean over and speak into the drawer, until I looked through the bulletproof glass window and realized that both guards were asleep sitting up, both their mouths hanging open. I could never sleep that way. I stood there for a minute or so. I hated to wake them up — they might cop an attitude and shine a flashlight in my eyes when they came around on midnight shift to get even — but I needed that request slip, and if I didn't hurry, the laundry would be closed. I figured that if I just stood there one of them was bound to wake up soon on his own.

Just as I was about to tap on the glass, this sissy named Jerome came screaming down the stairs from the second floor, yelling at the top of his lungs, "Pearl got stabbed, Pearl got stabbed! My God, you gotta help her! PEARL'S BEEN STABBED . . . !" It was bloodcurdling, Jerome's screeching, so panic-stricken and desperate that I thought for sure I'd see a butcher knife sticking out of Jerome's back as he raced past me. Jerome screamed into the drawer to the sleeping guards, "PEARL GOT STABBED, PEARL GOT STABBED," and the shock of those words caused the guards to almost jump out of their socks. They snapped awake like they'd been shot. Confused and befuddled, not knowing what to do, they stared at Jerome as he hammered on the impregnable glass with his fists, hollering over and over, "PEARL GOT STABBED, PEARL GOT STABBED."

I knew this wasn't a good time to ask for a request slip, so I stood there for a moment, frozen, like everyone else. The guards were arguing over who would call it in on the telephone, and who would go back upstairs to see what happened. Neither one of the guards seemed to want to race up the stairs to investigate. Survival instincts are strong.

We all went back up the stairs together. As the guard came out of the control room, Kilgore, Pearl's chain gang boyfriend, pushed past him and walked out of the building, the blood on his hands unnoticed. When I got up to the second floor, I saw a crowd of prisoners looking down the hallway. I didn't need to see any more, I'd seen enough of death and dying in prison, and I didn't want to see poor Pearl butchered up. I turned away, walked downstairs, and headed to the laundry to drop off my clothes before it was too late.

As I walked down the back road, I thought of the last time I'd seen Pearl, the day before. I had been by the window of the upstairs TV room when I looked out and saw Pearl spreading his freshly washed underclothes out on the grass to dry. Pearl had on a bleached-white T-shirt and white cutoff shorts, stark contrast to his jet black skin. Pearl was small and slight, like a young boy physically, but toughened beyond his years by the time he'd spent in prison, playing a woman's role in a little man's body, trying to get along and live a normal life in an abnormal environment. I had known Pearl since we'd both been at "The Rock," Raiford Prison, and I had signed him up for the GOLAB (Growth Orientation Laboratory) program, for which I was working at the time.

I knew him then by his given name, Emerson Jackson. In the GOLAB, prisoners spend eight days talking together without any free people observing them, going through a series of events that give them the chance to talk about their lives, to hear other people's stories, and to gain insight into their own situations. I remembered Pearl talking about his early life. He was reticent, shy, unwilling to share his experiences at first, then finally opening up, talking and talking, about his childhood, how he came to prison, how he'd come to that point in his life. We listened with rapt attention. Pearl and I had virtually nothing in common, it seemed, besides being prisoners, and under normal circumstances in prison we'd not likely have even so much as spoken to one another, but in the GOLAB we developed a mutual respect and camaraderie that transcended racial, ethnic, cultural, and social boundaries. I came to know Emerson Jackson as a sensitive human being, a decent person, a man who had endured incredible hardships, who had survived and succeeded in the harsh prison environment, and as Pearl, who had pursued a lifestyle that was alien to me. It was Pearl's life though, and I respected him. He was my friend.

Years went by. I left The Rock and went on a tour of Florida prisons after making the mistake of thinking that filing grievances would have any effect besides causing me to be bused from one prison to another until I wised up and shut up. I finally made it to central Florida, thirty-eight miles from my family in Tampa, and decided that for their sake I'd keep a low profile. My mother was getting too old to drive out to swamps in the middle of nowhere trying to find where they'd shipped her son this time.

When you're serving a life sentence, and you've served a chunk of years, no matter where you go you find people you've done time with before. It was no different this time. When I got off the bus and hit the yard, it was like old home week at the reformatory, seeing men I'd known for years, when we'd all been younger, thinner, with more hair and fewer tattoos. We laughed, talked, compared notes, asked about mutual acquaintances, who'd gotten out, who'd come back, who'd died, who'd escaped.

A day or two later I saw Pearl standing in a line. He glanced at me as I walked by, averting his eyes, and we both continued on. There are barriers beyond the razor wire that surrounds us and keeps us in, racial barriers, gay versus straight barriers, homeboy barriers, among others, that constitute an etiquette of sorts in prison. I didn't want to embarrass Pearl in front of his friends by letting it be known that some white person knew him, and perhaps Pearl didn't want anyone to think the wrong thing if he spoke to me.

One day I was walking some laps on the back field when I saw Pearl running the opposite way, coming toward me. I remembered that at The Rock Pearl had logged many miles on the prison track. A lot of men jog in prison, some just barely shuffling along, others moving a little faster, not much more than walking speed, but not Pearl. Pearl was a runner. I used to wonder what demons were chasing Pearl to make him run so fast, and for so long. He was watching the ground ahead of him as he approached me, his face showing the exhaustion, rivulets of sweat running down his ebony cheeks, lost in his world, oblivious to any outsiders.

As he came abreast of me, I said, "Pearl," in a sort of acknowledgment, like the "Howdy," or "Good Morning," that normal folks in society might say to an acquaintance on passing. People are on guard in prison — you never know where or when something might jump off — and my saying "Pearl" was just enough of a shock to cause Pearl's eyes to dart upward from the ground to mine, a moment of panic, then a breathless "Hi," as he registered "no threat," and continued on. On the next lap Pearl was smiling as he came around, his glistening countenance completely different from the previous lap, recognition shining through as he ran past. It was amusing to me in a way, how we hadn't spoken or acknowledged each other for a week or so, then when we did, every time Pearl made a lap past me he'd smile real big and say, "Hi."

That episode broke the ice, and from then on, whenever we passed each other we'd speak, and Pearl would say to his companions, "That's my friend, Norman, from Raiford." Pearl was very courteous and polite to his old acquaintances and took pride in being friendly and gracious. Not everybody in prison is a Neanderthal.

Every now and then we'd be walking the same way and we'd talk. Pearl would remind me of the GOLAB, of someone I'd forgotten, and I'd tell him about someone we'd known then, where he was now. "I was so scared, at first, Norman, on that trust walk, with that blindfold on, I never liked to trust anybody." I suppose we were being a bit maudlin, two prisoners trapped in the Twilight Zone time warp of prison, recalling a lost youth. Times had changed, we were all older, but the invisible bonds of that other time still linked us together.

I heard the whole story later, about the chain gang love triangle, how Pearl hadn't been true to Kilgore, how Kilgore threatened to kill him if he caught him with a certain individual again, how Pearl had ignored the threats.

Kilgore had it all planned out. He got a knife somewhere and hid it outside our building. The day before, he'd gotten some paint thinner from the chair factory and hidden it in a trash drum. On the day of the killing the guards were asleep, catching a little rest before the midnight shift got off at 8 A.M. Kilgore sauntered right past them, loaded for bear, with murder on his mind.

He'd stabbed Pearl first, several times, as Jerome and other prisoners stood and watched. Pearl fell by the shower, and Kilgore poured the paint thinner over his face and body, intending to burn him up. He tried to light a book of matches, but his hands were so bloody that the matches got wet and he couldn't light them. Another, larger, stronger prisoner took the matches away from him, perhaps thinking enough is enough, saving Pearl from flames. Kilgore walked out, leaving Pearl there on his back, dead.

It was 8:05 A.M. when they wheeled Pearl into medical on a stretcher. About the same time Kilgore turned himself in to the guards, they cuffed him and escorted him to confinement. Pearl went out for the last time in an ambulance, slow, no lights or sirens for a dead man. Kilgore went out in the back seat of a deputy's car to the county jail and a first-degree-murder charge.

They did an autopsy on poor Emerson Jackson, the Black Pearl, violating his lifeless body one more time, verifying that he'd been murdered, intimating that the volatile liquid killed him before the stab wounds did. They said Pearl tested positive for AIDS, so he probably wouldn't have lived long anyway. That institutional "oh well" justification didn't minimize his death to me. Even after witnessing years of mind-numbing atrocities, after enduring incident after incident of dehumanization, after building up walls to hold back emotions, Pearl's death had a profound effect on me. I was silent that day, lost in my own thoughts, facing my own mortality, grieving for a friend. I wondered if anyone would grieve for me when my turn came.

1992, Polk Correctional Institution
Polk City, Florida

Sam

Michael Wayne Hunter

While trudging from the exercise yard today, I saw in the distance a tall, thin, green-clad black man, and thought for a heartbeat or two that it might be Sam. But, if it is Sam, I chuckled, silently, grimly, I should just forget my legal appeals because I'm dead already. But then, if ghosts really exist, I reflected further, I suspect that they tend to hang out in places like the dungeons of the castle that I call home, San Quentin's death row.

As I approached the black guard, I saw that it indeed wasn't Sam. Passing by with a simple nod of my head, I jogged up the stairs to my cell. Once my body was locked inside, the handcuffs were removed from my wrists. Still standing by the rusty, pitted iron bars, I peered out the filthy windows of the cellblock and watched the wind whip white crests across the blue swells of the San Francisco Bay. As my eyes studied the scene, my mind spun back to the first time that I'd encountered Sam.

Leaning against the yellow cinderblock wall that separates the condemned men's exercise yard from the world, I was contentedly puffing a rollie Bugler cancer-stick. As I pulled the smoke deep into my lungs, I felt real good about the kick-butt workout routine that I'd just put in on the weight pile. Stretching my arms out slowly, I hid behind my 187 sunglasses while feeling the sun's rays softly massaging my sore muscles. I was waiting to be called by the guard conducting yard recall. When my name pierced the air, it would be my turn to move to the yard's gate for handcuffs.

Penetrating my happy fatigue, I heard the murmuring of other dead men complaining: "Da canine's fuckin' it up! Jesus Christ, the damn five-oh can't even get the muthuhfuckin' list raht!"

Laughing at the curses, I watched the rookie canine struggle on and on with the yard recall lists. It didn't flash in my head for even a half a beat to help the mutt out, wasn't my day to babysit any infant coppers.

"Can't ja read!" bellowed an irate, pot-bellied sergeant while stomping out of the condemned-men cellblock and advancing on the helpless puppy cop. "Whad da hell do dey teach yeh at da ah-cademy, ennyway?"

The baby-guard that I came to know as Sam answered quickly

in a half-strangled voice, "Of course I know how to read. The inmates aren't coming to the gate when I call their names."

"Call 'em twice!" snapped the sergeant. "Dey don't show, write 'em!" Spinning on his patent-leather heel, the top dog walked.

My amusement over Sam's inexperienced fumbling changed to anger in a quarter beat the next day, when I found out that I was "Confined to Quarters." Turned out Sam had claimed that I'd screwed up yard recall by not coming to the gate when he called me — a damned lie! Then, out of the kindness of his Kool-Aid pumping heart or to cover his butt, the mutt had written me a "Rule Violation Report."

When Sam walked by my cell during yard release that day, I called to him in my most tactful, diplomatic manner. "Hey fuckhead! What's your mothuh-fuckin' problem? You blow the gig and you write me! For Christsakes, yard recall ain't rocket science. What are ya, anyway? Another example of affirmative action gone wild?"

Sam hesitated for a beat and then looked like he was going to flee the scene. But to his credit, he stepped to my bars and said softly, "Wasn't just you, I wrote Anderson, too."

That's when my fury jumped from a rolling, boiling three to a nine plus — pretty near nuclear-explosion ground-zero time. For you to comprehend the full depth and intensity of my emotion, you'd have to understand prison from the inside. I'll do my best to lay it out for you, but describing doing all day long behind bars in a hard-core prison is a lot like explaining sex to a virgin. Words, pictures, diagrams just ain't a real good substitute for the real thing.

Anyway, S.Q. had been rocking and rolling for months. Whistles, alarms going off all over the place, violence as common as the cockroaches crawling around on the peeling, faded walls. Almost daily you'd see a bleeding body lying on an orange stretcher en route to the hospital or morgue. So many guys have been going down stabbed, shot, that the entire prison had been locked tight one out of every two days for the past year.

Six weeks before, the prison officials assigned to my housing unit had called the leaders of different gangs together, allegedly to try to work out a truce. At the conference, a Mexican gangbanger pulled out a shank, and yanked and cranked it into the body of a black leader until he was dead while the badges ran for cover.

Rumors (rumors I believed) abounded around the prison that the killing had been engineered by a high-ranking Mexican-American prison official, and the state legislature was holding hearings to determine whether this was true. If you weren't aware of racial tensions, you were too stupid to be walking around inside the walls of S.Q. without fuckin' training wheels.

White guards had offered me weapons if I'd agree to hit black or Mexican gangbangers. The canine would offer to search me himself to make certain that I got the shank to the exercise yard, and even guarantee a warning shot from the mutt with the assault rifle on the catwalk. In theory the warning would give me a chance to drop the shank, go to the ground, and keep from getting my head caved in with a bullet. Didn't really buy the warning-shot deal. Figured that once I made the hit, the canine with the assault rifle would bust open my skull with a .223 and laugh his ass off about the stupid dead man who believed in free passes and other such fairy tales.

A man would have to be a fool not to believe that black coppers weren't making the same offer to black prisoners, and Mexican coppers to Mexican prisoners. The badges fill our heads with their personal brand of vitriol, supply the implements of destruction, and then we get locked down again and again and again while they pull down the lockdown overtime pay.

Now, amid all that craziness, I got a black canine telling me not to take it personally that he wrote me up on a bogus beef, cuz he wrote another white prisoner too. Shit! Ain't that stupid, jus' look this way, man!

After lasering the canine with hate-filled eyes for a moment, I said, "Whatta coincidence, yah bagged two white guys."

"Probably won't come as a news flash to you," Sam mouthed quietly, "but I am brand new, fresh out of the academy. Didn't know what I was doing with the yard lists, and when the sarge jumped on me for messing it up, I told him that you guys weren't coming in when I called your names. When the sarge tol' me to write the inmates who didn't show right away at the gate, I panicked; then I just pointed to two names at random. You know I don't know your names yet, or the color of the men behind the names. You got to believe me, it wasn't a racial move.

"Yeah," he said, "I should have come clean with the sarge, but I am still on probation, and I really need this job. Need the paycheck. If you want," Sam sighed, "I'll go tell the sarge right now that I screwed it up, and get you back on the yard list. But I'd really appreciate it if you let it slide for today. I'll owe you one, okay?"

Funny thing about the truth, you don't hear it often anywhere; in prison it's pretty damn near extinct. But when truth rings out, it rings clear, rings true, and sounds so beautiful that it is real hard to disturb the melody with a bunch of petty static. "Okay, man," I heard myself answering as if from a distance while I wondered where my voice was taking me. "I'll get with Anderson and quash it with him, too. But you owe me. I don't just want some extra raggedy lunch bag sometime."

"Deal," came from behind flashing teeth, and the canine was gone.

On the yard the next day, I told Anderson that Sam had blown it, but I didn't think it was racial, just a new cop tripping all over himself. Even as I quashed it with Anderson, I wondered what the hell I was doing.

Guards on their nine-month probationary period are moved all around the prison, and just fill in wherever a badge is needed, so I didn't see very much of Sam. When our paths did cross, we'd just nod in that ritualistic way that people do when they know each other's faces, but aren't close. Never did we speak of his debt to me.

A year later. On the exercise yard, a Mexican hit-man conjured a shank out of nowhere and tried to drive it through my sunglasses into my right eye. Luckily, I was wearing Ray-Ban Wayfarers. Instead of falling apart, the shades took the blow, deflected the blade upward, and it stuck into the bone above my right eye socket, just below the eyebrow. In the next few moments I was raining blood from my socket and blows filled with evil intent from my fists, when I heard the mechanical clack of a bullet slamming into the chamber of a canine's assault rifle. Even in the fog of my pain and rage, I realized that if I didn't stop fighting, in less than a beat a .223 would be tracking toward my skull. I raised my hands and backed off the assassin.

Later I wondered where in the hell were all my homeboys while I was getting blindsided and bleeding all over the concrete? I didn't ask them, though; they'd have some damned excuse — prison's full of them. My eye and vision returned to what they'd been before, but my view of my homeboys was changed forever. Oh, I still hit the iron with the fellas, but when the workout was done, I started double-tying my shoelaces and heading out to play basketball with the black guys. It blew the minds of the homies, but I didn't give a damn. I wanted to find out who the hell were some of the other guys hanging out on the condemned yard with me for years. So I told my workout partners, "Don't beat on my trip, and I won't beat on yours."

"Yah git in trouble out there, ya on your own!" snarled one of my putative buddies.

Think I been on my own for quite awhile but jus' didn't know it 'til now, flashed through my brain. But I just nodded and went to hoop it up.

On the round-ball court, I'd hear some trash talk, but it was mostly directed at my two-inch vertical leap. So I got white man's disease, but I can put the damned rock into the hoop at least one shot out of every ten.

One bright shiny day, I was having a monster day on the court. I was in the zone, everything I tossed toward the bucket was falling in! Mook Man, who was guarding me, couldn't believe it, and seemed even more delighted about it than me. The man didn't guard me too tough, probably just figured that I'd chill and start banging bricks off of the side of the rim — as usual.

Out of nowhere some psycho on the sidelines hollered, "Ay, Mookie! Don't let that white boy tear you up! You're making a muthahfuckin' all-star outta the wood!"

Everyone laughed but the Mook Man. Thought about telling him it was just my turn for fifteen minutes of fame, but the game started up again before I had a chance.

Catching the ball in the lane, I felt Mook Man's body on mine for the first time that day, crowding me for the ball. Flashing an up-fake at him, I showed him the ball. When he soared into the air, I spun the other way and softly laid it into the hoop.

Next play, Mook Man caught me in the forehead with his elbow. Wincing in pain, I rasped out, "Hey, Mookie, it's only a game, man. No one's makin' a livin' out here."

"Men playing." Mook glowered at me. "Can't take it, get your punk ass to your end of the yard." He bit off the words as he violently gestured toward the white boys against the far wall.

Flashing my eye around, I saw that all of a sudden I was alone. No one, not a single soul, was meeting my eyes. I'd seen these looks before in the county jail. The Deputy Dawgs would slam a score or more guys into a tank built for a dozen. Jammed in like rats, the pack would begin to form, all of a sudden someone would become a nonentity as the mob got ready to roll. If the victim fought back, he'd just get beaten. If he laid down, it was all about the gang bang rape scene. After awhile, I came to realize that this wasn't about sex, it was about anger, evil, and most of all, power!

As my eyes continued to move to each of the black men around me, I found that my hand was involuntarily rubbing the scar above my right eye. I heard a voice and was startled to discover that it was mine. "Forget it," I said in an eerily normal tone of voice. "Let's play ball."

Next play when the ball went up, I got up as high as I could into the air and ripped my arm toward Mook's skull. Realizing in mid-flight that I couldn't soar high enough to tag him, I snatched his shoulder, and yanked him down to the concrete. Landing lightly next to him, I booted him in the side of the body while snarling, "You get the fuck offa da court, ASSHOLE!" Just stay down, man, I thought, as I stepped to the side.

Rolling with my kick, Mook Man bounced to his feet, fast, real fast! Throwing a right hand that barely missed my jaw, as I jerked my head in the other direction, his fist smacked hard into the side of my neck.

Out of the corner of my eye, I spied that Mook Man's homeboy, J.T., six feet three inches, two hundred fifty pounds of weight-driving muscle, was pounding directly toward my body. Spinning away from Mook to face his homey, I knew that it was futile. J.T.'s just too damn big for me! Bracing myself for the avalanche, all of a sudden J.T.'s passed me and snatched up Mook Man like he was a two-year-old, and simply walked away with him.

My mind blown apart by J.T.'s move, my eyes looked over and immediately flicked up to the gun canine on the catwalk. As I watched, the badge swung the business end of his assault rifle toward the yard. Behind the mirrored sunglasses, I saw the canine's face — it was Sam. Standing quietly, I waited to find out what he was going to do about what just went down.

Sam looked down at me, and then his eyes moved to Mook Man, who was walking the other way as J.T. intently packed words through his ears and into his head.

"Rough ball game," Sam called from the catwalk. "I'm calling on the radio for escorts to take you and Mookie to your cells. Get your stories straight in case the sergeant interviews you. No punches, no fight, you were just playing a bit too rough. You with me or you want to spend the next six months in the hole?"

Damn! A free pass! The notion rocketed through my head as I collected my workout clothes getting ready to leave the yard, J.T. came at me, blotting out the sunlight with his huge ebony self. "Mook cheap-shotted you, and got his lumps to make it square. Now it's over, man. No reason to start a war over a petty scuffle."

"I hear that," I answered as I nodded my agreement while starting to figure that this might work out.

Escorts made the scene. Handcuffed, I walked into the con-demned housing unit. Kidnapped, I'm not taken to my cell. Instead, the escort canine took me to a black cage outside the sergeant's office and locked my body inside.

I've been through this before, the sarge will keep us locked in the cages for a couple of hours to soften us up. The canines figure (cor-rectly) that the wait will prey on our minds while we wonder what they're getting ready to do to us. I always try to argue with myself that since I know and understand their tactics, they won't affect me. That's an argument that I always seem to lose. Sitting with my eyes hidden behind my sunglasses, I just kept telling myself, "Worry about what you can control, homeboy, forget about the rest."

Sergeant Dana walked by me and strode into her office. I've known her for a couple of years. She was one of the first female guards at San Quentin, and she's also openly lesbian. Sergeant Dana belongs to a leather-wearing, Harley-riding biker club called "Dykes on Bikes," and she never misses a Gay Pride parade in San Francisco. For her to survive and make sergeant in the macho male environment of San Quentin that's openly hostile to her is quite an accomplishment. She did it by being flat-out smarter and better at her job than anyone else.

My thoughts of the sergeant were interrupted by the sight of Sam marching toward Dana's office. Evidently she's called him down from the catwalk in order to make his report in person. Seemed like the female canine was her usual efficient self.

After minutes tick-tocked by, Sam emerged from the office with a grim look on his face. As he walked by he stole a glance at me, but kept right on motoring. I took the quick look as a good sign.

More minutes trudged by before Sergeant Dana sent a guard to escort Mook Man into her office, but Mook wasn't having any. "Tell that bitch I ain't got nuttin' ta tell her, 'cept to get herself fucked by a man!" Mook Man muttered angrily at the canine.

Deciding that he didn't want to deliver the message, the escort canine called Sergeant Dana to the cage, and Mook Man repeated his words.

Tilting her head away from Mook Man, Sergeant Dana nar-rowed her eyes at me and snarled, "You refusing your interview too?"

Thanks a lot, Mookie, I thought, you really softened the chick up for me. Smiling, I answered, "Kind of bored hangin' out here. Conversation sounds cool to me."

"What exactly happened out there?" Sergeant Dana inquired.

Hesitating a beat or two, I looked at the clock on the gray office wall behind her head. The tactic of leaving me in the cage to sweat had its penalty for Sergeant Dana too. By 3 P.M. she's hot to have me locked in my cell for count or write me a ticket for the hole. In the next thirty minutes, she's got to make a decision, and if I can fill that time with nonsense, I'll be home free.

"Can't really call it, Sarge," I answered in my most innocent manner. "Me and the fellas were jus' playing a little ball, and the cop tossed us offa da yard."

"Understand that there was a punch thrown," Sergeant Dana bluffed, at least I hoped she was bluffing.

"Naw, just a lot of contact. You know we play twenty-five-to-life ball out there . . ."

Finally, the sarge questioned, "What's that red mark on your neck? Looks to me like you got hit. Tell me the truth, was this a racial attack?"

"Yah know San Quentin's policy is to pull all da fellas with racial problems from the yards." I grinned at the sergeant. "Yah wouldn't be sayin' the classification committee is blowin' it, would you, Sarge? Letting gang members onto the integrated yard?"

For the first time Sergeant Dana smiled back at me because we both know that the classification committee is full of ugly, empty, acrylic suits that wouldn't be able to identify a gangbanger if he had the information tattooed on his forehead. And many gangbangers do just that, tattoo their gang affiliation on their foreheads. But, somehow, the classification committee misses it and assigns them to the racially integrated yards anyway.

"You're looking for what ain't there," I replied solemnly. "It was just a rough game, nuttin' more." With that last lie, the interview was over, and the sergeant decided that she didn't have enough to beam my body directly into the hole, so she had me locked back in my cell.

That night I received a "Blue Violation Report," written by Sergeant Dana. I'd been charged with "Involvement in a Physical Alteration," whatever the hell that meant. After being locked in my cell for three days, an escort canine came and took me to a disciplinary hearing. The lieutenant found me not guilty, partly because Sam stuck to the story of rough ball game, and mostly because the lieutenant hated Sergeant Dana.

Next day I returned to the exercise yard. Strolling across the concrete, I was more than a little uptight while I wondered what I'd find.

Looking around, I saw that Mook Man hadn't made it to the

yard, and my nervousness jumped up and multiplied by ten. The lieutenant found him guilty of disrespecting Sergeant Dana.

Eventually, Sam fell by my cell and said, "We're even."

"Yeah, we are." I smiled back at the sunglasses before he turned and walked.

After that day, Sam started dropping by my cell from time to time. Met his parents, his wife through the photos in his wallets, and his life through him. I learned how it was tough for him in the inner city of the flatlands of Oakland. Sam talked with pride about the first house that he'd just bought with his wife in the same neighborhood they'd grown up in.

"Now that you're making money," I remarked, "why don't you get out of there? Move on out to the suburbs?"

"Wouldn't want to do that," Sam replied. "Our house is close to the church my family's always attended, and besides, a lot of people in the community helped me when I was a kid. No one, and I mean no one, makes something out of himself in the ghetto — alone. You just don't do it all alone."

One day after one of our many conversations, I found to my surprise that I didn't think of him as a cop or a black man anymore, just as Sam.

Sam once asked me, "What're you doing in here? You don't seem to belong on death row."

Real uncomfortable with the question, I finally answered, slowly, softly, "Guess no one was ever there to reach down and pull me out, Sam."

Sam simply nodded his head and never brought up the subject again.

A couple of years ago, Sam asked me, "Do you think they will kill Bobby?" Bobby Harris had an execution date, the first one in California since the five-year moratorium on the death penalty.

"Don't know," I answered. "We'll just have to wait and see what happens."

Shaking his head solemnly, "Don't know about working here if they start killing you guys. Don't want to support my family on thirty pieces of silver. My wife is praying for Bobby, don't want to see anyone die."

The next day, a canine dropped by my pad, banged on my bars with his baton, and then said in a serious tone that caught my attention and quickly drew my feet to the front of my cell, "Sam's wife wanted me to talk to you."

"His wife? You sure?" I wondered in surprise.

"Yeah, Sam's dead," the canine told me as he began to explain what had happened.

Sam had invited some guards to fall by his house for a get-together. Some young men crashed the party, but Sam and his wife didn't care for the intrusion.

Sam didn't make a big deal out of their drugs, but he did ask one young man to leave, and all of his buddies decided to fly away with him too.

When they had just left, a stone crashed through the front window of Sam's home. Sam and his fellow guards went out to confront the young men. Shots were fired and Sam lay dead in the streets.

After hearing the story, I flipped on my television for the news. Sam's death got thirty seconds on the local news while Bobby's possible pending execution was analyzed in detail for five minutes on the national network news.

1995, California State Prison–San Quentin
San Quentin, California

Lee's Time

Susan Rosenberg

I was almost asleep when I heard the keys turn the bolt next door. Highly unusual: Unless someone is dying and they can get the guard's attention, the cells are locked and stay locked for the night, period.

Wilson was on duty. I heard his voice, smooth and enticing. "Okay, baby, there's no way out, nowhere to go. I'm gonna fuck you right now."

"What if I don't want you to?" Jane, my next-door neighbor, said.

"You know you want it, I know you want it. You've been wavin' that ass in my face for too long. I heard you like it black. I'm ready."

"You have to come and get it then." Even through the wall I could hear her voice getting husky.

"No problem." His tone thickened with desire.

Jane was a strange one. She threw herself at any man who walked in the door, but night after night woke up screaming from some internal terror. Ain't this a bitch, I thought. I did not want to hear her fucking Wilson. I did not want to be there. Somebody would peep it and the fallout would be heavy.

I closed my mind and drifted. After you do time for a while, you learn how to build your own wall. You learn to show nothing and hear nothing. After eight years I can shut out almost anything.

When Wilson came back at 6 A.M. to unlock the doors, it was business as usual. As everyone went to work, Jane passed me on the tier and nodded her normal hello. We weren't friends, but once in a while we'd run the track together. She looked cool, more dressed than usual, with more makeup, and she'd rolled her hair. I had a bad feeling about this.

Night came again and we locked down. Not one hour later I heard it happening again: Wilson opening Jane's door. I heard them laughing, then moaning. If I could hear, so could Maria on the other side. I thought about banging on the wall. I wanted to yell at them: "Don't put me in your shit!" But I didn't.

Wilson and Jane went at it for a few more nights and then stopped. I don't know why. Maybe they got spooked, tired, or their thing just fizzled. There weren't any rumors on the unit. I hoped it was all over. But a week later on my way to work in Mechanical

Services, I saw Jane at the officers' station leaning across the desk laughing with Wilson. He put his hand on top of hers in one sexy move. Keisha, my best friend here, walked by and saw it too. As soon as Wilson saw Keisha, he pulled his hand away, and Jane straightened up and walked out the door.

On the line at lunch, Keisha and Maria were talking. I picked up a tray and inched up behind them. "For sure, I hate that shit," Keisha was saying. "Wilson is fine, and he don't need to be with no white broad."

"Fuck her, she's crazy. That's why she screams every night," Maria said. We got our beige-colored slop and moved to the tables. Maria looked at me. "Lee, I know you can hear them every night, too. I get hot just listening."

"What are you talking about?" I hoped I sounded casual.

"Yeah right," Keisha shot me a look. "I remember how you can't hear. When Sally Barnes lived next to you and had that seizure, you heard enough to bang and yell, even though Maria slept through it. Remember what's-her-name, Miss, uh, Havers? She came a half hour later and Sally was blue 'cause she'd swallowed her tongue, and you were screaming at her: 'Where's the med team?' "

Yeah, I remembered. Havers had freaked out and let me out of my cell — very irregular — because she knew I could get Sally breathing. Then she'd turned around and locked me in the hole for being out of my cell after lockdown just to cover her simple-assed self.

Fortunately we couldn't find an empty table, so we couldn't continue the conversation. We had the "hate prison food talk" instead.

Every time I put on my khakis I think about my old life, my free life when I'd put on my whites, my nurse's uniform. It's always a passing thought, a second of longing. Then I do my crunches to get my blood flowing before I leave the cell.

I walked out and ran into the unit manager, Mr. Jason. He's one sick guy. No decision is made without his personal approval. He's king here and we're his "girls." Behind our backs, he calls us his "bitches." That gives the guards a green light to treat us like dogs. Whenever a guard cops a feel on me doing a pat search I think, "Mr. Jason, one day there will be divine justice." Jeffrey Jason, Bureau of Prisons, hack supreme: Mr. white suit, brown shirt, Brut-smelling, "family values man." I hate him and usually I stay out of his way.

But this morning he stopped right in front of my cell. "Lee McMann, this your room?"

"I live in this cell, yes."

"Get to work."

I did, but I looked back and saw that Jason was in my cell. At lunch I went back to see what was missing or if he'd found my petty contraband (cinnamon and oregano from the kitchen, a little Comet for my sink) but everything was exactly as I'd left it. The man had looked but not touched. Something had been violated, but I didn't know what.

I started back to work but bumped into Maria on the tier. "*Los puercos* were in my cell this morning," she said. "The vent between mine and Jane's was opened. That's the only thing they touched. Big Daddy Jason was in yours, too."

"Yeah, I hate that man." I wasn't going to discuss this with Maria. She talked a good line against the cops, but she was a government witness in her own case. As far as I was concerned, that meant she was a snitch.

Maria pushed it. "Do you think it's about Wilson? How could they know so fast?"

I shrugged. Maybe 'cause you told them, I thought. It was closing in on me, and I started to get mad. Fuck all this. Fuck Jane and her lying ass. Fuck the lieutenants. Fuck Wilson.

Well, maybe not Wilson. He'd always been all right with me, and everyone else too. When my coworker Cakes's mom had a heart attack, he'd called the hospital and let her talk with her brother. Another time he'd found two women in bed so he just counted them right there and never said a word. He was a human being first — and that can be dangerous for a cop.

When I got to Mechanical Services, my boss was at lunch, as usual. All the work orders were filled, the tools locked up, and there was nothing to do. Keisha, Louise, and Cakes were sitting around having a loud argument.

"I don't care," Louise was yelling — very unusual for her. "All these men walking around, patting us down, walking in the cells when we're on the toilet, pawing through our clothes. I hate it. I hate all of them. Talking to us any way they want, calling us bitches and whores. I believe her."

"You're one stupid, blind white girl. You just saying that 'cause he's black and she's white." Cakes heaved herself up from the chair and glowered. The sweat on her forehead glistened and her temper was about to blow.

"Lee can tell us. Right, Lee?" Keisha looked me straight in the eyes and smiled. "We all know you're a space case — but only when you wanna be, right? Cakes heard that Jane said Wilson raped her. How about it? Yes? No? Is the white girls' club gonna put on their robes, or what?"

I shot back: "I don't know what the KKK's gonna do. The white girls' club can tar and feather themselves to death."

Cakes was frowning, concentrating hard on a spot over Louise's head, trying not to let her fury run wild. Keisha had stopped smiling, but the smirk was still in her eyes. Louise was almost crying. She had pulled her knees up to her chin and slid down in her chair, looking even thinner than usual. I looked at her and said, "Stop crying. He didn't rape you, did he? He didn't fuck you, right?"

"No. But these men around here make me think of Jerry. He beat me up every time it rained. He said I was his and there was nothing I could do about it. When I got arrested, the first thing I thought was 'Jerry can't do me no more,' and I was happy."

"Ain't that some shit," Cakes said. "You gotta go to prison to get away from your old man. I wouldn't take that from any man. All you white girls are the same. Either you take it from your men, or you take ours."

My boss walked in and everyone shut up.

"What's going on, girls?"

"Nothing," everyone said almost at once.

"There's a special count. Everyone go back to your quarters. Come back at two P.M."

I was relieved. I wanted to talk to Keisha. If there's anyone I can talk to, it's Keisha. She reminds me of Tina, a woman I went to nursing school with who was always telling me to touch my patients. Tina said I'd never be a real nurse if I was afraid to touch, roll up my sleeves, and dive into their illnesses. One day in the emergency room a black woman who had overdosed was brought in. She had open wounds all over her arms and was lying in her own vomit. We had to clear the vomit from her throat, then pack her in ice and clean her sores. I hesitated, and Tina caught it. The shame burned as I turned red. It wasn't the vomit or the sores that made me hesitate. It was because she was black. I'd never touched anyone black. Tina never said anything about it, but she knew. After that I thought a lot about how fucked up I was, how I was a racist and didn't even know it.

When I met Keisha, she asked me why I wasn't in the white girls' club. At first I would only say I didn't want to be in any club, that I was a loner. But later I told her this story. She said at least I'd realized it. Most people would have let someone else treat the woman. I liked

Keisha for saying that. But after that she told me about her life, and how white people didn't know how racist they were, or they knew and enjoyed it. She told me about her father trying to organize the United Auto Workers union in Detroit, and how the whites fire-bombed her house. Keisha is really proud she's black. She is BLACK, almost blue-black.

She called us "the odd team," and we hung out because we worked together. We didn't need to talk all the time. We were comfortable with each other on some level I can't explain. It's just one of those friendships that happen in prison and wouldn't happen anywhere else.

We walked across the compound, past the rec field. Even though it was windy and the leaves were blowing, we walked slowly, because once we got inside it would be harder to talk.

"You know you're going to be called by the lieutenant," Keisha said. "Security is going to deal with this one. Jane said he raped her, and she's gonna go for it. The white girls' club has already started talking. They're talking to all the white girls who will listen. They're saying it's cop violence."

"Why me, damn it? I never talk to the police."

"Lee, don't be a jerk. You live next door to her. You and Maria are part of their investigation for sure."

"I hate this shit. All I want to do is my time and get on."

"What will you tell them?"

"It's none of your business what I tell them."

"Yes it is. If you tell them you don't know anything, they'll put you in the hole until it's over, and I'll have to send you stuff. If you tell them he raped her, then you'll be the white girl of the month. If you say it wasn't rape, then you'll be called a cop lover and a snitch. Any way you do it I'll have to decide where I stand with you. It is my business."

"But it's not my business. I don't care about Jane or Wilson. They don't care about me. They didn't give a shit about me when they did it in her cell."

"It may not be your fault, but now you're in it. So you have a problem."

The door to the unit was open and people were filing in. Half the unit was standing on the tiers or in the lobby. The count hadn't been called yet. On the top tier there were two lieutenants and two other men in sports clothes standing at the rail, taking pictures of cells — Jane's, Maria's, mine. Everyone was watching. I cursed Jane over and over.

At five the next morning I heard officers opening Jane's cell, telling her to get dressed. They took her out of the unit. The investigation had begun.

I wanted time to think, but I had to go to work. On my way, I saw Louise talking to Bonnie, this stone-cold racist. She and her husband had been part of some racist gang in Idaho that went on a terror rampage against Vietnamese immigrants. Now she's "born again" and leads an all-white self-esteem group. Seeing her with Louise gave me the chills; I realized that Bonnie was trying to find out what I was going to do about Jane and Wilson. I was going to have to start watching my back if this was gonna be a gang thing. It could get physical and someone could get cut up.

I got to Mechanical Services — out of the air, into the dungeon. Work was an overheated, dark basement office where I spent my days jockeying for a seat on the best of the torn-up trashed chairs we collected from the garbage to furnish our office. One of our jobs is to pick up broken furniture and equipment, but since there's no place to store it, and it takes months to get anything fixed, most of it sits in the basement hall rotting.

Keisha was going through work orders and pulling out the parts we'd need for each one. Louise came in right after me and walked to the desk in the middle of the room, looking more strung out than usual. I always thought all that whacking around and beating had made her dull. She was so skinny and she looked like she was scared to put food in her mouth.

Louise's jaw popped. "Everyone's saying that Wilson did it. Jane is really afraid the guards are gonna set her up. Unless we support her, she may have to go into protective custody. This woman in a state prison had the same thing happen to her. She got pushed off a tier and broke her back. Now she's paralyzed, I mean, a guard raped her and tried to kill her."

"Since when do you talk to Bonnie so much, Louise?" Keisha asked.

Louise stuttered, surprised by Keisha's challenge. "I, uh, that's not it. It's just that I believe Jane, and besides, he's a cop and it's her word against his. And we never win unless we stick together."

"Well, I don't think he raped her," Keisha said. "I think they were lovers. She was into him. I want to know why she's doing this. First she fucks him, then yells rape. Just 'cause she says it, don't make it so."

I wanted to know why she was doing it too. I also wanted to jump out of my skin and run.

Cakes walked in. "They just took Maria in handcuffs to the captain's office," she announced. "Four of them. 'Come with us,' they said. They didn't even wait 'til she was outside to put the cuffs on her."

When I got back to the unit, Jane was still gone and Maria was sitting on her bunk, staring at the wall. I knocked and went in. She didn't look good. She'd been crying and her wrists were swollen from the cuffs. I asked her if she was okay.

A long line of Spanish curses came out: *pendejo* this, *pendejo* that. "That was worse than all my talks with the U.S. Attorney, that *cabrón*. They were screaming at me and threatening me. They said I could get a new case for perjury, and no matter what, I'd go to a grand jury. I don't even know where the grand jury is. *Chingada*. They made me take a lie detector test. I kept asking to call my lawyer and they said, 'Fuck your lawyer!' They said I'd go to segregation and do the rest of my time there. Six of 'em kept saying, 'He raped her.' They said it over and over."

"Who was there?" I asked.

"I don't know — some lieutenants, that *pendejo* Jason, the captain, and two other guys who said they were from Washington, some agency I never heard of. They were the ones with the lie detector. Shit man, I didn't do anything." She was breathing hard.

"How long were you in there?"

"Three hours."

My heart dropped. Before I could stop myself, I said, "You were in there all that time? What did you say to them? I mean, that's a long time."

Maria cut her eyes at me and froze. Just that fast, I had stopped being someone to comfort her, someone she could confide in. Now I was an immediate threat. I'd blown it before I could find out anything she'd said. Spending three hours with the police meant she'd told them lots of things. I tried to save the conversation by asking if my name had come up, but other than tell me that they'd called her because she lived next door, Maria had had nothing else to say. She stood up, wanting me to leave.

I went to my cell. Since my cell will never be my home or "house," as the police like to call it, I don't keep a lot of things. But I do have a big, knitted blanket which I crawled under, trying to get warm and calm down so I could think. I was waiting for the police to call me in for interrogation. I wasn't going to say one word, but I knew they'd physically keep me there and threaten me with new charges and more time.

From what Maria had said, I knew there was an outside investigation. It wasn't just the prison. Unlike all the other investigations I'd seen or heard about, this time they were going after the officer, not the prisoner. A few years ago, this other officer had been fucking every woman he could. Everyone knew it. He and a woman prisoner got busted in the shower by the night orderly. When the administration found out about it, the officer got transferred. A few months later we heard he'd gotten a promotion. All the women involved went to the hole for months. The difference: He was white.

"Chow line. Last call." There was a rap on my door and Keisha barged in.

She stood over me, her arms crossed and her braid all messy. "No rest for the weary. GET UP!" she said. "I waited at dinner but I should've known you wouldn't show. We have work to do. You can't lie here like a vegetable. The whole compound is freaking out. Maria's wrists are black and blue and she's in the cafeteria crying. There are four extra cops on duty and the lieutenants are running around like there's gonna be a riot, and you're takin' a goddamned nap." Keisha was barely controlling her voice.

"Tough shit," I said. "I'm thinking."

"You're not thinking," Keisha said, her voice getting loud. "You're catatonic. You can't zone out now."

"I'm trying to figure it out, okay? So leave it." I could get loud too, if I wanted.

"No, I won't," she said.

"It's none of your damn business. You're the one always telling me to stay away from the crap."

"Listen here, and listen good. This isn't the same. One, this is about to become a lynching of one more black man, and two, you've been my friend and you're in it. So, it's a different case. Get it?" Keisha went on. "I know we always say you gotta do what you gotta do, but sometimes that just don't work. This is about race. A lynching. They're gonna take the word of that cracker Jane and screw Wilson to the wall. Don't you know that anytime a white girl says 'rape by a black man,' the mob runs for a rope?"

"But he's a cop, Keisha." My voice was catching.

"Yeh, he's a cop with a dick for brains. But he didn't rape her, did he?"

No he didn't, I thought. It got real silent. Then I said: "Look, I never told you about my case, and I don't really want to now, 'cause I don't like to think about it. But I murdered this old guy. I pulled the plug on his life support because he begged me to. I did it because he was suffering and he couldn't stand it and I couldn't stand it either. He probably would've died in a couple of weeks, I don't know. But I'm the one who ended his life. As soon as the monitors went flat and I plugged them back in, I knew I was in deep shit. The heart machine alarm started buzzing, and I thought I'd go to prison for this. But I didn't. The hospital didn't want a scandal, so I lost my job and my license instead. And then I started selling drugs, which got me busted. But I'm still glad the old guy didn't have to keep suffering. So, I just get by in here. I just want to live through it and see the free light of day again. That's it. I'm afraid of more time, of a new case, of having to get into some shit that isn't mine. I'm in my own shit and I've fucked up my life and can barely manage that. You know I leave everyone alone, don't bother anyone, don't talk to the cops. I just do my time."

Keisha sat down on the bed and put her arms around me. Sometime during that stream of words I'd started to cry.

"It's cool, Lee, it's okay. You're okay. What I'm trying to say is that I can't let it go down again. Every second of every day the shit I have to eat because I'm black ... sometimes I just feel like choking someone. To me this whole thing is a black-white thing. And 'cause I know you see it, even if you don't feel it, I thought you'd understand." Her braid had come undone and she had tears in the corners of her eyes. We sat there a while. Then she got up and said, "I'll see you later, okay?" She walked out before I could say anything.

I cried until I couldn't breathe and my chest hurt. Then something cracked. I felt light. I could catch my breath. A really deep breath. I hadn't breathed that deep in years. I lay there feeling calm, looking at the early evening light coming into my cell. Keisha was right; I couldn't ride this one out. I wasn't going to be part of a lynch mob. Most of the time it's all so twisted and sick, but sometimes there's right and wrong, even in here.

Lucky for me they came before I lost my nerve. Four guards hustled me out of the cell, cuffed my hands behind my back, and almost carried me out of the unit. But I was ready. I was even sort of looking forward to it.

Segregation. The hole. There was very little light and the air was dank. The walls oozed. It had become cold outside, and the water pipes upstairs froze, then exploded, and when I put my hand to the wall it came away wet. I was trying to read the time away, holding my book open toward the light that came through the food slot in the door.

After they'd brought in the fifth Harlequin Romance, I'd thrown a fit. Then this cop came to the door with four thick paperbacks and tossed them through the slot. Now I was trying to read *Hawaii*, by James Michener, but all I kept thinking about was how much I wanted to be in Hawaii.

We call the hole "three hots and a cot." Actually it's three of everything: cold food, cold water, cold weather; three hours a week outside and three showers a week. What I hate the most is never being able to get hot coffee.

Every time they come for me to go outside for recreation, I'm ready. Segregation's rec yard is the size of a basketball court, and it's chopped up into six little cages, each with a basketball hoop at the end. Sometimes, there's even a basketball. You walk into the cage one at a time, then the gate is locked. You put your hands through a slot and they take the cuffs off. Then you have sixty minutes. Beyond the cage is an open, grassy space, but it's off limits except for prisoners on landscape detail.

Keisha and Cakes appeared in that grassy area pushing an old hand lawnmower. They were hoping they wouldn't be stopped, but here it was forty degrees out and the snow was still on the ground. I could see my breath and had to jump up and down to stop my teeth from chattering. I had no coat. They came to about five yards from the fence.

"What's happening, my non-Nubian sister?" Cakes asked.

I smiled. "I feel like a fucking corpse, but what else is new?" I hoped they knew what was happening. Cakes said something to Keisha, then started stamping her feet. She took a cigarette and tried to light it, but couldn't because of the wind.

"I'd really like to get that whore," Cakes said. "I really would. Lee, it's all fucked up."

"They lynched him, Lee. They lynched him." Keisha sounded hoarse. "Jane got transferred to some cushy joint, Maria got parole, and your poor ass is lying down for a year. But Wilson, they gave him twenty years. It was on the news. We saw it on TV. His wife and kids were in the courtroom and they all came out crying." Keisha kicked the ground.

Cakes hollered: "What really pisses me off is watching all those happy crackers running around here like they won a prize or something."

Then Keisha said something, but I couldn't hear her because the wind ate her words.

"What?" I yelled at her.

"Oh shit, I feel like I should be there instead of you. My advice sure didn't help anyone."

Keys. I heard keys rattling behind me.

"Time's up, McMann," the officer barked

"Damn," I thought. "Okay," I told the cop. "Just let me tie my shoes." I turned back around.

"Keisha," I yelled. "Cut it out. I'm all right with it. I really am. It's cool. It's Wilson who got destroyed."

"Thank you," Cakes said. "You hear that, Keisha? I told you she'd say that. She's all right. Lee is all right."

And I was.

> 1993, Federal Correctional Institution Marianna
> Marianna, Florida

Family

Although men and, to a greater degree, women create surrogate families behind bars, in this section prisoners write of blood relations. Reconstructing childhood on paper is the consolation of hundreds. Tender mothers and grandmothers — the last to give up on prisoners — are everywhere in prison writing. Sometimes even evanescent fathers are honored, as in Jimmy Santiago Baca's "Ancestor." Diane Hamill Metzger recalls a great-uncle who doubled as her grandfather.

To comb through the wreckage buried with their youth, some writers, like Barbara Saunders, choose indirection. Increasingly, men take on such themes. Alejo Dao'ud Rodriguez's narrator hears out another prisoner's story of damage untold in court and barely understood by the teller. Though Rodriguez himself has not sat on death row, his poem draws on the fact that the majority of persons there had been abused. Others begin to restore themselves by confronting in verse those who betrayed their trust. In "You Wanted to Be My Protector" (1995),* Delores Hornick narrates the battering experience that drove her to seek protection orders against a lover.

Writers register mixed feelings about sustaining family ties. Clay Downing's "Jailin' Man" (1974)* stops opening letters from home in order to "get busy bein' where I was, forget where I wasn't." Some fear what they may become in prison. In the story "Hey, you, our holes aren't working" (1979),* Roger Jaco's narrator says that, despite longing, he is thankful that he may never again see his wife and son: "Who knows what these years of punishment, rejection, and having 40 ccs. of bitterness injected into me daily might do to my loved ones if I were to let it escape from me in large doses. I care too much for them even to contact them." Sinking deeper into trouble in prison and despairing of winning his appeal, Jesse Lopez, in "Arrival at MacNeil Island" (1978),* begs his wife to find someone else to help raise the kids. Other long-termers describe electing to cut their women loose rather than risk almost inevitable pain later.

Relatives who stay the course and visit win songs of praise. "Our

Skirt" is Kathy Boudin's subtle evocation of her enduring bond with her mother. The loss of parents is particularly hard to bear behind bars. Even if one is furloughed, like Henry Johnson in "Funeral Parlor,"* grief may be locked away: "the watery eyed women / Soaked his collar in tears," and "he burned that dead black face deep / Into his memory," and "tried his best / To shed a tear. He tried real hard, but failed." In "The Ball Park," Johnson's narrator recalls a lost brother while celebrating the liveliness of that man's son.

More typically single parents than men, women are more preoc-cupied with sustaining meaningful bonds with their children. (Yet Anthony La Barca Falcone's poem testifies to one father's poignant longing.) More often than not, children must travel great distances to see their parents. Prison rules — and arbitrary manipulation of them — can thwart meetings, as in Judee Norton's story. But some prison administrators are beginning to see the long-term wisdom of teaching inmates parenting skills. At Bedford Hills Correctional Facility, courses on childcare and parenting from a distance help inmates heal themselves and become responsible resources for their children, thus breaking the cycles of abuse and criminal activity. Judith Clark's ongoing contact with her daughter enhances the growth of each. The struggle of all mothers with the necessity of sep-arating from their children as they mature is in prison particularly acute. In "A Trilogy of Journeys," Kathy Boudin delineates the pecu-liar pains and pleasures of an incarcerated mother experiencing her child's coming of age.

Long-termers sometimes get a chance to work through family regrets. In an essay called "Doing Time" (1995),* J. C. Amberchele says that for some "the shock of prison is so great as to propel them in a new direction." When his children visit, they bring him news that his father has died years before. He regrets missing his father's funeral and, more, not having told his reserved parent at least once that he loved him. "But I was also thinking," he says, that "prison, with its rigid conformity and structured regularity, has taught me that time is cyclical, not linear. I see time now as a great spiral, corkscrewing out of the past and carrying with it all the complex moments of history, and always coming around, coming around. The world, I have real-ized, allows for second chances, but only if you create them." As he looks into his son's face, so like his own and his father's, he is sud-denly able to tell him how much he loves him.

Ancestor

Jimmy Santiago Baca

It was a time when they were afraid of him.
My father, a bare man, a gypsy, a horse
with broken knees no one would shoot.
Then again, he was like the orange tree,
and young women plucked from him sweet fruit.
To meet him, you must be in the right place,
even his sons and daughter, we wondered
where was Papa now and what was he doing.
He held the mystique of travelers
that pass your backyard and disappear into the trees.
Then, when you follow, you find nothing,
not a stir, not a twig displaced from its bough.
And then he would appear one night.
Half covered in shadows and half in light,
his voice quiet, absorbing our unspoken thoughts.
When his hands lay on the table at breakfast,
they were hands that had not fixed our crumbling home,
hands that had not taken us into them
and the fingers did not gently rub along our lips.
They were hands of a gypsy that filled our home
with love and safety, for a moment;
with all the shambles of boards and empty stomachs,
they filled us because of the love in them.
Beyond the ordinary love, beyond the coordinated life,
beyond the sponging of broken hearts,
came the untimely word, the fallen smile, the quiet tear,
that made us grow quick and romantic.
Papa gave us something: when we paused from work,
my sister fourteen years old working the cotton fields,
my brother and I running like deer,
we would pause, because we had a papa no one could catch,
who spoke when he spoke and bragged and drank,
he bragged about us: he did not say we were smart,
nor did he say we were strong and were going to be rich
    someday.
He said we were good. He held us up to the world for it to see,

three children that were good, who understood love in a quiet
    way,
who owned nothing but callused hands and true freedom,
and that is how he made us: he offered us to the wind,
to the mountains, to the skies of autumn and spring.
He said, "Here are my children! Care for them!"
And he left again, going somewhere like a child
with a warrior's heart, nothing could stop him.
My grandmother would look at him for a long time,
and then she would say nothing.
She chose to remain silent, praying each night,
guiding down like a root in the heart of earth,
clutching sunlight and rains to her ancient breast.
And I am the blossom of many nights.
A threefold blossom: my sister is as she is,
my brother is as he is, and I am as I am.
Through sacred ceremony of living, daily living,
arose three distinct hopes, three loves,
out of the long felt nights and days of yesterday.

    1977, Arizona State Prison–Florence
    Florence, Arizona

Uncle Adam

Diane Hamill Metzger

Uncle Adam
Had a brogue
And a doberman,
Hated being called Unk,
And made terrible scrambled eggs.
Sent me a ticket
Every Easter at spring break
To visit him in Coral Gables
Because I made him feel young.
Took me to restaurants,

The stock-exchange,
The not-for-public beach,
and slipped me fifty dollars
At the departure gate.
I was adolescent,
Never knowing what moved him
Or why he liked me.
Can't tell him now
That I never meant to be a brat,
or blame it on my youth,
Which like his brogue
And his life
Went away.

> 1985, State Correctional Institute–Muncy
> Muncy, Pennsylvania

The Red Dress

Barbara Saunders

Tiny white five-petaled flowers
embroidered along
a portrait-collar neckline.
Short bodice
full skirt, puffed sleeves.
Blood red dress
on a fragile blond child.
Her hair hangs to her waist
unlike the platinum blond
Toni doll whose hair only comes
to her shoulders.
The doll is straight and tall
and proper and hard edged
invulnerable, always smiling
and only closing her eyes
when someone puts her down.

She has a red dress too
identical to mine.
No one touches her
no one takes her red dress off.
She stands by my bed
Her eyes never close.

1996, Eddie Warrior Correctional Center
Taft, Oklahoma

Ignorance Is No Excuse for the Law

Alejo Dao'ud Rodriguez

From the cell ten ft. across from mine,
he told how he used to play chicken for money.
He played in bars where no other kid his age
was allowed to go, but he went
and the scars of cigar burns between his knuckles
testified that he won more money than he lost.
"Ever smelled burning skin?" he would ask. "It's enough to
make you sick."

And his stories were never tired
and I was never tired of hearing them.
After all, living on death row
it's only fitting to allow a man
to tell the story
that wasn't allowed by law
to be told in court.
Where the formalities were too complex
for that sixteen-year-old boy to comprehend,
and it seems the law really didn't understand him either,
but one thing was for sure
he wasn't going to cry,

his father taught him that.
His mother cried for him though,
cried all the tears that were held back
watching him grow, watching his father
make a man out of him
a man, before the child was able to be a boy.

"Mom never really understood" he told me,
"You know, male bonding, the rites of passage,
to become a real man."
And every part of that real man's bleeding heart
was on death row — spilling its guts,
but still holding on to proud memories
of how he threw up on his first beer.
He was nine, and it was his father who made him drink it.
"That'll make a man out of you, boy."
And how, when he was seven, his father
made him stay and fight,
"Or you'll get a whuppin' when you get home," Dad said.
It didn't matter that the other kid
was twice his age and size.
"You never run from a fight, boy."
And when he got home
he still got a whuppin' anyway,
because he lost.
But by the time he was fourteen, grown men
were self-conscious being in his presence.

"I don't want to make it sound as though
the old man was a Drill Sergeant,"
he told me. "We used to do regular
father-and-son shit too."
Took him to baseball games
and got him his first mini bike
and they used to go camping a lot too.
"But why did Dad always forget his sleeping bag?"
he would ask, "and why did he have to share mine?"

His hands, the only visible part of him
through the porthole of the cell door,
where they serve our food,

would pound the air and move with his words
as though they were the ones doing the talking,
but the scars of melted skin made it look like
his knuckles were crying
every time the talking stopped.

Then he would excuse himself,
because he had to finish cleaning his cell.
A ritual he performed meticulously three times a day,
as though it were an act of repentance.
"Nobody ever taught me how to pray," he said.
"One time I got on my knees and just sat there,
but I didn't know what else to do.
I never seen them do anything else
in the movies."
So finally, when they did come for him,
he just asked the preacher to just clean him
afterward, in case he shit on himself.
But he assured the preacher that
"I'm gonna try my best to hold it all right."
And then trying his best to wipe his eyes
in handcuffs, he walked out of his cell
seeming to be more afraid of having to leave
the cell than facing death.

Back then I never really understood
his last words to me when he said,
"I died when I was born."
But now, I'm next.

> 1997, Sing Sing Correctional Facility
> Ossining, New York

Our Skirt

Kathy Boudin

You were forty-five and I was fourteen
when you gave me the skirt.
"It's from Paris!" you said
as if that would impress me
who at best had mixed feelings
about skirts.

But I was drawn by that summer cotton
with splashes of black and white — like paint
dabbed by an eager artist.
I borrowed your skirt
and it moved like waves
as I danced at a ninth-grade party.
Wearing it date after date
including my first dinner with a college man.
I never was much for buying new clothes,
once I liked something it stayed with me for years.

I remember the day I tried
ironing your skirt,
so wide it seemed to go on and on
like a western sky.
Then I smelled the burning
and, crushed, saw that I had left a red-brown scorch
on that painting.

But you, Mother, you understood
because ironing was not your thing either.
And over the years your skirt became my skirt
until I left it and other parts of home with you.

Now you are eighty and I almost fifty.
We sit across from each other
in the prison visiting room.
Your soft gray-thin hair twirls into style.
I follow the lines on your face, paths lit by your eyes

until my gaze comes to rest
on the black and white,
on the years
that our skirt has endured.

1995, Bedford Hills Correctional Facility
Bedford Hills, New York

The Ball Park

Henry Johnson

Sometimes you get the kind of day
you deserve: lots of sunshine, wind,
blue sky stretched tight as a military sheet.
Flushed, I jump up and down in the bleachers,
cheering my eight-year-old nephew
around the bases. I am proud, so I lead
the shouting, beer sloshing over the rim
of my cup like stream water out of a helmet.
What more could anyone want than
what's right: the smell of cooked onions, franks,
knishes sold hot from the stand on wheels
just outside the ball park? Luigi owned it —
old tyrant — and we had to stand in line like
I did when I was six, the carnival lighting up
the city. At twelve, my brother had the touch,
could tag a bull's-eye with one eye closed.
Some nights he'd dump the pretty woman
above the tank of water so often, the carnies
would blackball him from the games. Back home,
he'd lie awake staring at the ceiling,
smoke curling blue in the moonlight
from the window. One night in July,
sure that I was asleep, he sneaked out
by the fire escape, a red ski mask
stuffed deep into the pocket of his black

bomber jacket. Close behind, I saw him
slip through their defenses
like a commando, do a bellycrawl
over to the Ferris wheel, the tent
leading into the freak show
where we slipped under the flap to see
the dog-faced boy, the bearded lady.
Slipping in and out of shadow, he splashed gasoline
over everything, tossed a match, and the flames
chewed up the night the way they would years later
in the jungles of Vietnam. Back in our room,
he smiled, and we watched the place
burn to the ground.
Later my brother joined the marines, but
all the government shipped back was a sealed casket,
a letter from the President, a medal. I thought
I saw him in midtown Manhattan, yelling, jostling
passersby, his frightening dreadlocks
hanging to his waist. How often does hope
hit you like a sniper's bullet right between
the eyes? I ran after him yelling his name,
but the crowd swallowed him up
like a swamp bog. I double-timed it out of there
on a train back to Brooklyn.
Sometimes the eyes can play tricks on you,
like when you've been out in the bush
for days without water, or here
in the scorching heat of the ball park,
my voice shooting up the scale by octaves, and my
nephew — little trooper — sliding home, kicking a red cloud
of dust over home plate, excitement in his eyes exploding.

1988, Sing Sing Correctional Facility
Ossining, New York

Norton #59900

Judee Norton

"ATTENTION ON THE YARD, ATTENTION IN THE UNITS! NORTON, FIVE-NINE-NINE-ZERO-ZERO, OBTAIN A PASS AND REPORT TO THE CAPTAIN'S OFFICE IMMEDIATELY!" the public address speakers boom. The sound bounces around the yard, boomerangs between the buildings and my ears again and again. I am standing outside the schoolroom, smoking and sweating in the 112-degree summer afternoon, squinting at the sun and wondering idly whether this kind of weather would be more enjoyable if I were lying on a Mexican beach wearing only a string bikini and a smile, holding a frosty margarita in one hand and a fine, slender stick of Indika in the other. I have just decided that it most definitely would be when the summons comes.

At once I am approached from every direction by fellow inmates asking, "Did you hear them call you to the captain's office, Jude?" and, "What's going on? Why does the captain want you?" I feign indifference as I take a long final drag of my cigarette, then flip the butt with practiced skill into one of the pink-painted coffee cans nearby.

"Who the fuck knows," I respond with just the right degree of flippancy. My voice is sure and steady, and that pleases me. I can feel my face rearranging itself into a mask of haughty insolence, a half-sneer claims my mouth, one eyebrow hitches itself a quarter-inch upward on my forehead to indicate arrogant disregard. It is my intention to appear poised, untroubled, faintly amused, and slightly bored. I am quite sure I achieve such a look.

My guts belie my measured outward calm. They twist and grumble and roil, threatening to send my lunch to the sidewalk. My heart is beating much too fast. My mouth is dry, my tongue feels like a landed trout thrashing about in that arid, alien place. My hands are trembling, my knees belong to a stranger, I am grateful for the first time ever that it is so goddamn hot in Phoenix. Everyone glistens with a fine film of perspiration; perhaps no one will notice that I smell of fear.

I affect a hip-slung swagger for the amusement of the gathered crowd, and head for south unit control to ask for a pass. It strikes me that I am asking permission to go to a place I haven't the faintest glimmer of desire to go to, and I giggle. The officer issuing my pass looks up at me and says, "Hope you still think it's funny when you get back, Norton." I shrug. The walk across the yard is a long one, made longer by my determination to stroll casually under the scrutiny of a hundred watching eyes. I can feel them on me, can almost hear the thoughts behind them:

"Poor Jude!"

". . . 'bout time that goody-goody bitch got hers."

"Damn, hope it ain't bad news . . ."

"Gir'fren', please, look who be in trouble now!"

"Sheee-it . . ."

I knock purposefully at the polished wooden door with the brass plate that announces this as the Mount Olympus of DOC. CAPTAIN, it says, in big carved block letters. Fuck you, I mouth silently.

After just enough time has elapsed to make me feel insignificant and small, the door is opened by a fat, oily sergeant. She is damp and rumpled in spite of the cool, air-conditioned comfort of the room. She turns wordlessly from me and installs her sloppy bulk at a desk littered with forms — applications, requests, petitions — paper prayers from the miserable and needy. She selects one and peers importantly at it over the tops of her smeary glasses, then picks up a red pen and makes a large unmistakable red X in a box labeled DENIED. I imagine a look of malignant glee on her greasy flat features as she does it.

Having not been invited to sit, I am still standing near the door, feeling awkward and displaced, when the phone rings. She picks up the receiver, says, "Yeah?" into it, and after a moment looks at me, nods, and replaces it. She jerks her head in the direction of the door through which I have just come and says, "Go back outside for a minute, if you don't mind." Fleetingly, I wonder what she would say if I responded, "Oh, but I *do* mind, I mind very much, in fact; it's hotter than the devil's dick out there, you see, and I *so* much prefer it inside." What I actually say, though, is, "Oh, sure, no problem," and am mortified to find myself blushing.

Once outside, it occurs to me that if this was sly, psychological weaponry, designed to unseat and disadvantage me, it is quite effective. I feel humiliated and disgraced in a way I cannot identify. I light a cigarette and arrange my limbs carefully into a posture of indolent apathy. I hook my thumbs in my belt loops and squint with what I hope is an air of monumental unconcern through the smoke that curls up into my face.

At last the door opens again, and I am ushered into the cool depths of the anteroom, and this time I get a nod from the sergeant to proceed into the next room, the sacred chamber where sits the captain, enthroned behind a gleaming expanse of mahogany desk. He is leaning back in a maroon leather swivel chair, rolling a gold Cross pen between his startlingly white palms. He is a black giant, all teeth and long-fingered hands and military creases. His hair is cut very short on the sides and back, and the top flares out and up several inches. It is decidedly and perfectly flat on top, as though his barber used a T-square. I am reminded of the enchanting topiary at Disneyland's Small World; he appears a well-tended shrub. Then he smiles at me and I think to myself viciously that he looks like the offspring of Arsenio Hall and Jaws. He motions me to a small chair, carefully chosen and placed so that I am directly in front of him and several inches lower. I feel like a beggar, prostrate at the foot of the king. I am determined that he should not know this. I meet his gaze with a cool look of studied dignity.

"You're Norton?" he asks.

No, you moron, I'm Smith, Jones, Appleby, Wellington, Mother Teresa, Doc Holliday, Jackie Onassis, anyone in the world besides Norton, at least I'd like to be right now, dontcha know, I think wildly. Aloud, I say, "Yes, sir. I'm Norton."

The chair creaks as he leans forward and picks up a piece of paper, pretends to study it. Without looking at me, he says, "Norton, I called you in to talk to you about your son's at-ti-tude," pronouncing all three syllables distinctly as though to a slow child.

"My son's attitude?" I repeat, feeling exquisitely stupid.

He gives a derisive little snort, as though to indicate that of course we both know what he's talking about and it's damned silly of me to pretend ignorance. Bewildered, I ask, "What attitude, sir?"

The captain closes his eyes and leans back again, rolling the gold pen in his hands. It clicks annoyingly against his rings.

"Your son, Adam," he begins with an air of great forbearance, "seems to cause a problem every time he comes to visit you. My officers tell me that he is rude and disrespectful, a troublemaker." He opens his eyes and looks at me expectantly.

I am dismayed to notice that my mouth is agape, that I have been caught so unawares as to be, for one of the very few times in my entire life, speechless. "A troublemaker, sir?" I say, realizing with no small degree of consternation that thus far I have only managed to echo what has been said to me.

"Ap-par-ent-ly," he replies, again dividing the word carefully into all its syllables, "he demanded a full explanation of the visitor's dress code a couple of weeks ago. And last Sunday, according to the report, he questioned the policy that forbids inmates or their visitors to sit on the grass."

I have a quick vision of an official report, complete with the Seal of the Great State of Arizona, titled TROUBLEMAKERS, and can see my son's name emblazoned at the top of a long list. His sins are red-lettered: DEMANDING EXPLANATIONS and QUESTIONING POLICY. Suddenly and against all reason and prudence, I have a powerful urge to laugh, to say, "You're kidding, right, dude?" But I fight it and win, and say instead, "Sir?" as though it were a question in its own right, and the captain obliges me by treating it as such.

"Your son, Adam," he says with exaggerated patience, "insists upon knowing the reason for every rule and regulation DOC imposes, which we are in no way obligated to provide to him. He disrupts my officers in the performance of their duties."

I am beginning to hate the way he says my son's name, and I feel the first stirrings of anger. The visitation officers' "duties" consist of sitting in a cool, dark room with a bank of closed-circuit TV screens, looking out onto the baked parking lot where a line of parched visitors wait for the regal nod of approval that will allow them entry into the institution. Their "duties" include watching us chat with our loved ones, making sure that there is no "prolonged kissing," no hanky-panky under the tables, no exchanging of other than words. The most arduous task they will perform all day in the fulfillment of their "duties" is bending over to inspect my vagina after I squat and cough and "spread those cheeks *wide*" for a strip search at visit's end. I fail to comprehend how my son's questions interfere with these odious "duties," and I say so.

The captain's response is brusque, and it is obvious that he, too, is becoming annoyed. "It is not your place, Norton, to determine whether or not the officers' duties are being interfered with. It *is* your place to ensure that your visitors comply with procedure."

"What 'procedure,' sir, says that my boy can't ask questions?" I challenge, against my better judgment, which has long since flown. A little voice inside my head says, *Oh boy, now you've done it, you smartass,* and the voice is surely smarter than I am, for the captain stands up so fast he nearly topples his chair. His breath is coming fast and his eyes blaze.

As quickly as he is losing his calm, I am gaining mine, and from some place deep inside I thought was forever closed to me, I feel a surge of fearlessness. I stand also, and face him squarely and unblinkingly, an intrepid lioness defending her cub. It is a sensation that will not last.

"Sit," he commands.

I sit.

A moment later, he sits, crossing one elegantly trousered leg over the other and picking up the ubiquitous gold pen again. "Tell me," he says congenially, "what happened in the blue jeans incident two weeks ago."

"What happened, sir," I begin reasonably, "is that my son came to visit me wearing a pair of gray Dockers, you know, men's casual pants, and he was told that he could not see me because he was not in compliance with the dress code that specifies 'no blue jeans.' He was understandably upset, and asked that a higher authority be consulted."

"And were they?"

"Yes, sir, someone called the OIC[†], who didn't want to take the responsibility for a decision; she in turn called the lieutenant, who ultimately allowed him in."

"So he *was* admitted," the captain says, in a tone which implies that, after all, the whole point is moot, and why ever in the world am I so agitated about it?

Warming to my subject, and not liking one bit the look of smug self-satisfaction on his face, I throw caution to the winds, full speed ahead and damn the torpedoes, devil take the hindmost. All pretense of civility leaves me, my instinct for self-preservation is gone.

"Oh, he was admitted all right," I say, making no attempt to disguise my disgust. I note with detachment that my hands and arms have bravely joined the recitation and are describing sharply eloquent shapes and forms in the air, punctuating my mounting fury, underlining my passion. The pitch and timbre of my voice have changed and the words rush from me, unstoppable. "He was admitted, sir, twenty whole minutes before the end of visitation, after taking a filthy stinking city bus all the way from Tempe and being allowed to stand in the blazing sun for three and a half hours without a square inch of shade or so much as an offer of a drink of water. He was admitted after he begged, pleaded, cajoled, and tried to reason with every know-nothing brownshirt in this whole sorry place. He was admitted after repeatedly pointing out to every available cretin with a badge

[†] Officer in charge.

that his gray, pleated, slash-pocketed, cuffed, pleated and creased, one-hundred-percent cotton *slacks* were, in fact, neither 'blue' nor 'jeans' and therefore did not violate the 'no blue jeans' rule. He was admitted after being chastised like a naughty schoolboy by that loser of a sergeant, after being called immature, impatient, juvenile, and demanding, after being threatened with dismissal from the premises, after being subjected to an outrageously erroneous judgment call on his goddamn *pants, sir.* Disrespectful? Oh, I hope so. With all due respect to you, sir, I hope to Christ he was disrespectful to them."

By this time, I am shaking with rage. I am remembering my fair-skinned boy's sunburned face. I am remembering the awful look in his sky-colored eyes, that bright liquidity that tells of a boy perched on the brink of manhood, trying not to cry. I am remembering my own inability to explain, to soothe, to mend as mothers do, as they must, for if not they, who?

It is an omission of some seriousness that I did not notice earlier the twin spots of color that had crept to the captain's cheekbones. On his ebony skin they are the color of dried blood, and his eyes snap and sparkle at me. There is a vein pulsing at his left temple. I have an abrupt vision of myself cutting out my tongue with his letter-opener and simply leaving it flopping about on his desk in expiation. Too late.

"Norton," he says slowly, "it is clear to me where your son got his attitude." I notice that he does not divide his words into all their separate parts for me now. He taps his chin thoughtfully with the pen. "It is my feeling that for the continued secure operation of this institution, it will be necessary to discontinue your son's visits until further notice. Perhaps he only needs time away from you to learn to deal with the fact of your incarceration in a mature and sensible manner. An attitude adjustment period." He smiles.

My heart lurches and I feel the color staining my own cheeks even as it leaves his. "Sir," I say, hating the quavering, desperate sound of my voice, "surely you're not saying he can't come to see me anymore." I can hear the humble, supplicating tone I use, and I despise myself for it. "Please," I say, strangling the word.

Having regained his equilibrium, the captain sits up straighter in the chair and allows a wider smile. "That is pre-cise-ly what I am saying, Norton." In control once more, he has gone back to hacking his words apart. I hate him for that.

I am consumed by impotent rage, I wrestle with a crushing and mighty urge to rise and beat that superior face of his into a bleeding pulp of unrecognizable jutting bones and torn flesh. The desire is so intense as to be palpable. I can hear the dull wet crunch of gristle and cartilage, can feel his warm slippery brains between my fingers, can smell the dark coppery odor of his blood, can see it splashing up, up, onto the walls, the carpet, the desk, my face, my hair, crimson and joyous.

I am dazed and shaken by this vision. I sit for a moment gripping the chair bottom with white-knuckled horror. Then I push the chair back gently, like a woman preparing to excuse herself from the dinner table and say softly, "May I leave, sir?"

"Certainly," replies the captain, ever the gracious host. He smiles at me. I do not return the smile.

With the grace and ironclad composure that have saved me from humiliation since early childhood, I hold my head high as I walk through the outer office past the inquisitive stare of the duty sergeant. I close the big door quietly, and slip unnoticed around the corner of the building.

I lean against the sun-baked wall and struggle with a host of emotions I cannot put name to. I feel the wall burning my shoulders through my blue workshirt. My knees become suddenly and utterly incapable of supporting me. They fold up and I slide bonelessly down the wall, heedless of the way its pebbled surface scrapes at my back. My teeth are clenched, but my lips part and turn downward. From them comes an awful keening sound I do not recognize. My eyes sting with the threat of unwelcome tears, I beg them silently not to betray me. But they do, traitorous things, and a great wash of tears pours unchecked down my cheeks, off my chin, into my lap, a flood of them, pent up all those years when to cry was a sign of weakness and to be weak was to be a victim. I lay my forehead on my knees and drop my hands loosely to the blistering cement beside me, like useless weapons that would not fire when so much was at stake. I am dimly aware that I am crying in the brokenhearted way of a small child, a sort of hitching and breathless uh-uh-uh-uh-uh, complete with snot running down into my mouth. I feel naked and wounded, unmanned by grief and hopelessness.

Finally I can no longer hear the sounds of my own weeping. I turn my head to one side and feel the sun begin to evaporate the tears, leaving my face tight and dry. I spit on the fingertips of my hands and scrub away the trails they left, wipe my nose on my sleeve, and pull a small black comb from my back pocket. I take my sunglasses from the top of my head and run the comb briskly through the matted and dampened strands and stand up. Straight. Tall. Shoulders back. Chin up. I put the dark glasses on my face and the mantle of hard-ass prisoner on my soul.

I saunter nonchalantly around the corner, past the door marked CAPTAIN, onto the yard. An acquaintance approaches me and asks in an excited whisper, "So, what happened in there? What's up?"

She is immediately joined by a second and a third and a fourth, all eager, questioning. I am comfortable now. This is my milieu, this is where I know exactly what is expected of me, precisely how to behave, what to do and say. I shove both hands jauntily into the hip pockets of my Levi's and allow a disdainful grin to own my face.

"Fuck him," I say with contempt. "He can't touch this."

We all laugh.

1991, Arizona State Prison Complex–Phoenix
Phoenix, Arizona

A Stranger

Anthony La Barca Falcone

Behind the circus clowns, puffs of cotton candy, and taffy
sprinkled with saltwater and served with lopsided grins,
I spot you, the doe-eyed girl, in pigtails and overalls.
There is no mistaking you.
You are my eye's mirror,
my reflection in dark rooms,
my shadow in candlelight.
Two tigers pass, one resembles the other;
I think of you again:
young and full of mystery,
full of light and oceans
and gardens of roses and morning orchids.
I know you, little one, my trait is dominant, but to you
I am a grain of salt, a small spark lost in a blaze.

If I kneel and ask you to stare into my eyes,
what would you say? Would Father slip through your thin
lips?
Would your arms circle my neck? Would you kiss my cheek?
In dreams you smile at me
and ask me to recite old poems
that mean little to some
but the world to you. You
clap your hands to clouds and laugh at dawn's snowflakes.
Have I told you no flake is the same?
Have I told you no life is the same?
Have I told you no pain is the same?
There you go, slipping by the monkey cage and clowns.
I watch you go the way you never saw me arrive, face flush
and full of confusion. I may have given you life, may have been
that small angel who breathes life into puppets, but now I am
only a stranger, lost in his strange world of words and woes.

1996, Otisville Correctional Facility
Otisville, New York

After My Arrest

Judith Clark

among the everyday
pieces lost
a bright pink Indian cotton shirt

    worn through months of
    nursing, quickly unbuttoned
    to bring the rooting baby to my breast
    her head in its
    soft, filmy folds

set adrift among the debris
of police searches, overturned lives
tossed into a pile of orphaned clothes
and taken to a tag sale

    where my friend,
    recognizing it,
    bought it
    to keep me close

and wore it one day
to bring my daughter for a visit,
greeting me cheerfully,
"Remember this?"

and I laughed,
scooping up my baby
to carry her into the
toy-filled playroom
where she rode me, her horsey
among the oversized stuffed animals
until visiting hours were over

when I stood at that great divide,
the visitor's exit gate,
and watched my shirt and my child

leave
with my friend

1996, Bedford Hills Correctional Facility
Bedford Hills, New York

To Vladimir Mayakovsky[†]

Judith Clark

History
has been unkind to you
               Mayakovsky
   making fools
        or lunatics of
us
      who chased the rainbow
          blinded by its shimmering radiance
            fading
               like dreams disappearing
                  into morning

Your life   a warning:
    poets who would be prophets
    may lose their lyrics
          their lives
History's stern judgments:
    he sold his soul to dictators
        his craft to technocrats
he loved too much   he loved too little
he gave in
      he gave up

[†] Vladimir Mayakovsky (1893–1930), a Russian poet and dramatist, was considered the "premier voice" of the Bolshevik Revolution of 1917. But his relationship to the Soviet government grew contentious. He died by his own hand at the age of thirty-seven.

Today
the New World you championed
    the dreams I fought for
are consigned to history books
    written
        in black and white
           bereft of poems

A middle school teacher
    in America
wraps it up neatly, to his pupils
in one simple sentence:
    Communism was bad
        from start to finish
           bad   and it lost.
A child
stands
    hands on hips
    chin out in challenge:
        "That's your opinion
           and too simple
        My grandparents were Communists
        It was an idea   a dream
        People tried
        but they made mistakes
        It's not so simple as good and bad."

In the prison visiting room
the child looks her mother
in the eye. She says,
    "Your intentions were good
    but you went about them
        wrongly."

And I
    her mother
        who grew up
dancing
    to your rhythms and rhymes
        Mayakovsky

then plunged

from poetry
    to war
find my way back
    to you

Reading your rebellious lyrics
I contemplate your end
                Mayakovsky
    caught
in the iron jaws of history
and your own intimate demons

This I know:
        despite my failures and defeats
            my sorry solitude
            the burden of guilt
            and the death of dreams
        despite the cold of a winter morning
            waking to cinderblock walls and
            rows of barbed wire
            robbed
                of every warm blanket
                        of illusion

Still
    I crave life
        Mayakovsky
child
    poems
        dreams

1993, Bedford Hills Correctional Facility
Bedford Hills, New York

A Trilogy of Journeys

Kathy Boudin

for my son on turning 18

I.

The day approaches
　　when I begin
my yearly pilgrimage
　　back in time,
the present no longer important,
only the exact hour and minutes on a clock.
They will bring me to that moment
　　when you began
　　the longest journey
　　man ever makes,
out of the sea that
rocked you and bathed you,
out of the darkness and warmth
　　that caressed you,
out of the space
that you stretched like the skin of a drum
　　until it could no longer hold you
　　　　and you journeyed through my tunnel
　　　　　　with its twists and turns,
propelling yourself
on and on until
　　your two feet danced into brightness
and you taught me
　　the meaning
　　　　of miracles.

II.

Somewhere in the middle of the country
　　you are driving a car,
sitting straight, seat belt tight across your well-exercised chest,

looking into the horizon,
the hum of the engine dwarfed by the
    laughter of your companions.
You are driving toward 18.
Two sets of parents
    on each side of the continent
await your arrival,
    anxiously,
And you leave them astounded
    by that drive,
always part of you,
to grow up as soon as possible.
You move toward the point
    that as parents we both celebrate and dread,
foreshadowed by leavings that take place
    over and over again.
That leaving for kindergarten,
    that leaving for camp,
        that leaving parents home on a Saturday night.
Until that time when you really leave,
    which is the point of it all,
And the sweet sadness.

III.

My atlas sits
    on a makeshift desk,
a drawing board
    between two lock-boxes.
It was a hard-fought-for item,
    always suspect in the prison environment
as if I could slide into its multicolored shapes
    and take a journey.
In front of me is the United States
    spread across two pages.
I search for Route 80,
    a thin red line
and imagine you,
    a dot moving along it.
You, an explorer now.
Davenport, Iowa; Cheyenne, Wyoming; then Utah; Nevada;
    until you reach

the Sierras, looking down on the golden land.
Roads once traveled by your father and me.
As I struggle within myself to let you go,
    and it is only within,
for you *will* go,
I am lifted out of the limits
    of this jail cell,
and on the road
    with you, my son,
who more than any map or dream
    extends my world.
My freedom may be limited,
but I am your passenger.

    1998, Bedford Hills Correctional Facility
    Bedford Hills, New York

The World

"The real world" some prisoners call it ironically. Some say, as our soldiers did in Vietnam, "back in the world." Extracted from it, prisoners have a unique perspective on "the world."

In Paul St. John's 1994 story "Behind the Mirror's Face" (**Reading and Writing**), the narrator asserts that prison marks most inmate writing, and for the worse. "A con may write fiction, but everybody will know where it comes from. His fiction wears the stink of prison for a belt. Her fiction is pregnant with loss disguised as possibility. His outlaws always get the better of a wicked status quo. Her heroines grope through a jungle of shame for their stolen womanhood, and perhaps a piece of heaven." Certainly a portion of PEN contest entries support this charge. Every year men send pieces about the perfect crime, the foiled execution, the superhero's ultimately satisfying revenge; and the "stink of prison" is inescapable in the uncensored wet dreams and virulent misogynist fantasies (sometimes merged) sent to the contest. Some of the writing by women is freighted with longing; some return relentlessly to scenes of loss and betrayal.

With a passion born of desperation, St. John's narrator cries, "Take this goddamned place out of your art is what I am trying to tell you all." The best writing about "the world" is neither stuck in the groove of crime-guilt-loss-revenge nor wheeling free in the fantasy of might-have-been. Not imprisoned, it yet bears the mark of the journey the prisoner has taken. Writers who have come to terms with who and where they are effect a triumph over those conditions. They use insight gained in "that goddamned place" to engage and illuminate the so-called real world outside — neither in an exculpatory nor an accusatory way, but by naming the human bonds that link us all. Thus, in "Prisons of Our World," Allison Blake's bid in prison gives her piercing insight into the social and psychological captivity her "free" neighbors cannot see. Robert Moriarty's "Pilots in the War on Drugs" draws us into the romantic cockpit of perilous entrepreneurship and goes on to show how everything in our disingenuous war on drugs has driven pilots first to the air and, if they survive, to prison, scapegoats for a problem he can see, but the general public can't or won't.

The world seen through the prism of incarceration is cleansed of illusions and often startlingly unconventional. The hiphop poem by J. L. Wise Jr., "No Brownstones, Just Alleyways & Corner Pockets Full," renders the cauldron of a St. Louis ghetto summer night, where lurking disaster coexists with resilient vitality. In "Americans," Jon Schillaci celebrates our polyglot, postmodern society for its very confusions. In "For Sam Manzie," his empathy becomes an ethical challenge to media-dulled citizens; it is the poet's searing response to a *Newsweek* article about boy-killer Sam Manzie, who had himself been seduced over the Internet. "Diner at Midnight," an Edward Hopper–like sketch by David Taber, limns a moment of failed empathy. In a retake of the diner scene in "The Film," the protagonist willfully wipes out feeling for both waitress and himself, as he fashions himself, in a sinisterly all-American way, the hero in a typical thriller. And the late Henry Johnson, a saxophone player, offers a thrilling riff on a real murder (of jazz musician Lee Morgan by his ex-wife in Slug's Saloon), set in a glamorized "5-Spot Cafe."

The stink of prison is converted into a gift of pure imaginative transcendence in a sequential pair of stories by J. C. Amberchele. He traces a victim's ongoing quest to understand and master what has happened to her. A sensitive and idiosyncratic loner, Melody hardens, after her brush with murder, into Mel, a woman driven to recover her life by reinventing it. The very creation of this remarkable figure is a gesture toward redemption, extending imaginatively as it does to the other side of crime. Mel's preoccupation with her would-be murderer, speechless as a result of childhood trauma, makes her in some way his double, seeking a way to master, by encountering again, their shared horrific past.

Prisons of Our World

Allison Blake

Mrs. Hennessy is getting a manicure
No matter her husband loves her no more
Been vain and spoiled so long
Can't leave these comforts now
Love is the only sacrifice it seems
Now she finds it in her dreams.

Sarah was to be a great artist
Her talents were noticed years ago
The street life smothered her dream
Now she lives in the could-have-been
Wonders each night if it should-have-been
Too afraid to think of the would-have-been.

Harry reaches for the bottle
Can't get through the night without it
Colorful pictures dangle before him
Floating in unison with the sounds in his head
Can't turn the music off now
It starts and stops without him.

Little Mary is hiding in the cellar
Doesn't want her daddy to find her
Still hurting from last night's beating
Can't figure yet why it happened
Plans to run away as soon as she's grown
Like Big Sister who works for Big Eddie.

We stand alone in the prison of our space.

1995, Bedford Hills Correctional Facility
Bedford Hills, New York

Pilots in the War on Drugs

Robert J. Moriarty

The brutal midday Caribbean sun beats down on the two men sweltering in their cockpit that long ago turned into an oven. Sweat drips down the captain's chin as he patiently waits for the ground crew to finish loading his cargo. His eyes scan all quadrants of the sky, looking for unfriendly visitors. The rear cargo door slams shut with a dull *thunk*. The chief of his loading crew moves out to the left wing and smiles a shy grin as he passes a thumbs-up, a slight salute to the captain.

The pilot gently, smoothly pushes the throttles forward to their stops while firmly holding the brakes. His eyes make a quick pass over the engine gauges in a final check. His partner, occupying the right seat, makes a hurried, nervous sign of the cross. Glancing at him out of the corner of his eyes, the pilot cannot prevent a slight look of disdain from crossing his features.

Takeoff is always the critical point in these flights. Off to the side of the runway lie the crumpled remains of the planes that almost made it. This runway would never qualify for any FAA safety awards. The pilot doesn't even want to think about what happened to the crews of the mangled pieces of aluminum. He releases the brakes abruptly. Slowly, almost too slowly, the airplane starts its takeoff roll. Time seems to stretch to eternity. Rumbling and bouncing slightly, the aircraft accelerates down the narrow dirt strip hacked from a long-forgotten jungle. Infinity passes as the far end of the runway grows more distinct.

No flight manual covers takeoff in 100-degrees Fahrenheit heat with an overburdened aircraft powered by long-past-prime twin engines. The airspeed indicator limps clockwise a knot or so at a time. Flying speed may just be a few knots past eternity. Mentally the pilot prays the load is far enough forward in the cabin to still be within the aircraft flight envelope. He will know for sure in a few seconds.

As the end of the runway passes beneath the nose of the plane, he smoothly eases the yoke back. He rolls a smidgen of elevator trim then quickly pops the landing gear handle upward. It isn't worth his time to snatch a quick peek at the airspeed indicator. Either he has flying speed or not. A slight increase in drag from the gear doors opening causes the aircraft to settle slightly.

The aircraft climbs upward a few inches at a time. As it bounces through slight turbulence, the stall warning horn bleeps its sound of terror. Flying a plane under these conditions is a lot like making love to a lady gorilla. The pilot eases his aluminum chariot into a gentle turn to the north. He sets the cowl flaps to the trail position and gently pulls the props back to climb power. Just to be safe, he turns the transponder switch to the left one more time and rechecks that the circuit breaker has been pulled. It wouldn't make a whole lot of sense to get caught because the transponder somehow was left on.

Another planeload of drugs is on its way into the United States.

When the plane finally reaches cruising altitude cool enough to ride in comfort but low enough to evade radar, he sets the power to the maximum endurance setting. A few thousand feet below, the haze layer ever present over the ocean marks the boundary between turbulence and smooth air. The pilot turns to his still nervous assistant. "Reach in the back and see if any of the soda is still cold." As his partner turns to the rear of the plane to complete his assignment, the pilot muses to himself. Wonder if that bozo realized how dumb it is to distract a pilot during a takeoff like that? Now and again he scans the engine gauges. The left engine runs pretty hot but at this weight it isn't the critical engine any longer. Each engine is critical. If one quits or sputters, his aluminum butterfly will turn rapidly into a submarine. The pilot comforts himself with the thought of paper bags filled with cash. The hard work, the dangerous work has all been left behind at the jungle strip.

> WANTED: PILOT — *Low time okay, we train. Smoker okay; drinker okay; no medical required. We supply aircraft, fuel, some expenses. Should be able to navigate, land on remote strips. No fringe benefits; possible government supplied food, lodging, retirement. Some risk. Pay $50,000–$500,000 per trip.*

Trade-A-Plane never printed this ad. It never showed up in the *Miami Herald*. But it's correct. Openings exist. The ad is perhaps a little misleading. The real truth about drug smuggling is a lot like picking at an artichoke. You have to pull off a lot of cover to get to the heart.

Neither *Forbes* nor *Fortune* magazine publish any special editions about the size and extent of the illegal drug industry in the U.S. They should. If they did, the figures would show the business of selling illegal drugs to be far and away the biggest and most profitable business in the country. No one knows the total number of players, but if you estimate the employment figures for occupations we track on the "anti" side we can gauge employment totals. We have eight hundred thousand lawyers, eight hundred thousand police, six hundred thousand jailers and fifty thousand employed in the judicial system. If almost half the people imprisoned in this country were charged only with drug crimes, easily a million Americans draw legal employment strictly because of the prohibition laws. Lots more Americans sell drugs. Total employment: in the millions. The drug trade generates somewhere between $100 billion and $300 billion per year in gross revenues. Somewhere between the total sales of AT&T, IBM, McDonnell Douglas, and the total sales of the entire auto industry.

This massive flow of illegal drugs into the U.S. continues for only one reason. It's big business with big profits. The government refuses to admit it, but spending $50 billion a year on the "war on drugs" only makes the situation worse. Illegal drugs remain a problem primarily because someone defined them as illegal. The prohibition of drugs creates a 99 percent profit margin, encouraging people of all ages and occupations to enlist.

Wars may be hell for the victims, but they do create jobs. No one — not the dopers, certainly not the government — wants the public to recognize what really goes on behind the screen of smoke. Figures divulged by Charles B. Rangel (D), Chairman of the House Select Committee on Narcotics and Drug Abuse, suggest that in 1985, some eighteen thousand flights carrying illegal drugs entered the United States. That's about one flight every thirty minutes of every hour, every day, every week, every month of the year. Once every twenty hours, a planeload was captured — a humiliating 3 percent of the total flights. How can a "war on drugs" be so ineffective? As Congressman Rangel said, "It is so easy to smuggle drugs into our country by air that it would take an absolute idiot to get caught." A brief history of the drug trade may help put the picture in perspective.

Marijuana forms, and always has formed, the foundation upon which the house of drug smuggling was built. To a certain extent, the polarization of the body public caused by the seemingly endless slaughter in Vietnam played a part in the expansion of the drug trade. Young people, tired of cynical government claims of victory after bloody victory, listened to prophets like Dr. Timothy Leary. They "tuned in, turned on, and dropped out" at a record rate. If the powers-that-be lied about Vietnam, was it not also possible that the government lied about the demon weed, marijuana? They tried it, liked it, and purchased record amounts.

Tractor-trailerloads by the hundreds and thousands passed from Mexico into the southern border areas of the U.S. through the late 1960s. Customs inspectors equipped with bulging wallets and very dark tinted sunglasses somehow missed most of these loads. As demand increased, a few World War II and Korean War vintage DC-4s, DC-6s, Convairs, and Martins made clandestine trips into long-abandoned Texas, New Mexico, and Arizona landing fields.

In 1970, the retail price for an ounce of grass ran about five dollars — "a nickel bag." A plane of locoweed might be worth $100,000 wholesale; hardly worth risking the value of an airplane. The still minimum value of the illicit cargo demanded low-cost ground transportation. Then the federal government stepped into the act, increasing not only the profit but also the demand for drugs.

Up until 1970, drug crimes actually fell under violation of tax laws, the Harrison Tax Act of 1914 and the Marijuana Tax Act of 1938. During the campaign for governor of New York in 1966, Nelson Rockefeller began using the term "war on drugs" to great political benefit. Never one to miss a political trick, Richard Nixon pressed Congress for sweeping new drug laws initiating the concept of mandatory sentencing for what had been in the past relatively minor violations of tax laws. By 1971, Nixon had slammed the door on the trailerloads of grass. The massive flow of reefer into the border states stopped — for about three and a half seconds.

In economics as in politics, nature abhors a vacuum. As long as demand exists, supply must follow. The price of grass shot up to fifteen dollars an ounce. When first turned back at U.S. border stations, the Mexican truck drivers shrugged a sigh of resignation and headed for the nearest airport. The fledgling bands of more-or-less amateur smugglers entered what would prove to be a golden age of aviation lasting years. What had been a tiny trickle of cargo planes across the border turned into a flood. As the price of grass went up, so did the price of planes. A DC-3 cost $50,000 in 1970 and $150,000 in 1985. You could track the price of either grass or airplanes just by knowing the price of the other.

From 1971 well into the middle 1980s, much of the Mexican crop crossed the border via airmail. The sophistication of the dopers increased as the efforts of the state and federal authorities increased. Larger profits allowed new investment in the latest transportation and communication equipment. As the price of illicit drugs continued to climb, the size of an aircraft necessary to fly a profitable load decreased as well. By 1985, a $30,000 Cessna 206 could easily carry a cargo of grass worth $400,000 wholesale and an ancient DC-3, costing $150,000, could deliver a $10 million load.

Meanwhile, the increase in price of grass had attracted new growers in all the Caribbean basin countries, and the center of gravity of the drug trade had shifted gradually eastward several hundred miles. The history of drug smuggling efforts in the Caribbean closely followed the Mexican model. Rather than tractor-trailers, at first fishing trawlers, then full-size oceangoing freighters carried marijuana north from the reefer-producing countries around the Caribbean basin. By 1985, the increased Coast Guard patrolling of the few natural ocean smuggling routes put a halt to the freighterloads of Colombian weed. A few trawlers tried to pick up the slack, but suffered unacceptably high losses. As the price escalated, cargo aircraft carried an ever increasing share of the contraband haul. The cost of an aircraft could be recovered perhaps tenfold with one successful trip. Decaying, well-worn, used and abused large cargo planes flew load after load of pot until every airstrip in the Caribbean was dotted with a fleet of worn DC-3s and other cargo planes. As their presence began to draw unwanted attention, a fleet of smaller, less conspicuous Cessnas and Navajos equipped with high-performance engines and long-range tanks started to converge on every airfield in South Florida and the Bahamas.

As the drug runners became increasingly slick, well-heeled, and experienced, the nature of the business started to change. Reacting to the natural laws of supply and demand, drug traffickers and smugglers realized that aircraft capable of carrying a load of grass worth perhaps $100,000 wholesale, could carry a load of coke worth $20 million wholesale. The traffickers started carrying trickles of cocaine from Colombia and heroin from Mexico to the primary drug markets of Miami, Houston, Los Angeles, and New York. The smugglers sort of figured that they might as well be hung for sheep as for lamb. Because of its increased availability, the much more dangerous cocaine and heroin continued to drop in price, thus increasing demand. So we traded a minor marijuana problem for a major hard drug problem.

During the 1970s and well into the early 1980s, a few well-financed, well-organized groups controlled most of the flow of drugs into the United States. On a clockwork basis, the DEA or Customs would make a highly publicized bust of a "major drug-smuggling ring." Much to their dismay, they found that every time they smashed one "drug-smuggling ring," ten more sprang up from the remains of the group. Maintaining an accurate account of the number of "major drug-smuggling rings" busted would require IBM's biggest and latest mainframe.

It is 1988. Dozens of flights leave Jamaica or Haiti or Belize or Cuba each day carrying planeloads of reefer. Many airdrop their loads to waiting fast boats off the coast of Florida. A few continue to make a low-level entry into the U.S. to land in Florida, Georgia, or South Carolina. The retail price of grass is up to $150 an ounce. Flocks of Cessna Turbo and Piper Senecas with up to three thousand miles in range carry paste from Bolivia and Peru to Colombia for processing into cocaine powder. Increased government intervention has only resulted in importation of far more of the truly dangerous drugs, in greater use of violence, and in runaway crime associated with drugs.

Few drug pilots make it to retirement. The chances of getting caught are slim. The chances of getting killed, whether in an accident, or by fellow drug gang members, are high indeed. Most drug dealers value pilots a little less than a good plane and little more, just a wee bit more, than a quart of lukewarm spit. Drug traffickers, those organizing smuggling attempts, are similar to every other sort of businessman. They seek minimum risk, minimum cost, and maximum profit. Pilots are viewed as rubbers — to be used and then discarded. Drug pilots are the first to be killed, the first to land in jail, the first to be snitched upon, and the very last to be paid.

The drug lords never advertise the whole truth about smuggling. For the one drug deal that succeeds out of three or four attempts, the pilot gets very well paid indeed. Sometimes. After all, anyone going to all the trouble to set up a drug deal has already broken numerous laws. Why not steal too? Who else is easier to steal from than the pilot? Who is he going to complain to?

Every smuggling strip in the Caribbean has a refuse pile nearby built from the remains of planes that "almost" made it. Every flight is flown overweight, often out of center-of-gravity limits, always right on the edge of the flying envelope, and most with submarginal equipment.

I flew in Vietnam from 1968 to 1970. I remember an area just south of the DMZ called Helicopter Valley. From a vantage point a few thousand feet in the air, you could look in any direction and see the wreckage of dozens of crashed helicopters. The thought of the hundreds of young men killed in battle over a few pockmarked hills no one really wanted anyway still leads to depression. And the ultimate crime in any pilot's mind is breaking an airplane for no reason at all.

Colombia is worse. Jamaica is worse. Bimini Island, some forty-five miles off the coast of Florida, keeps a bulldozer permanently stationed next to the runway just to clear the wrecks of drug flights. The authorities in Bimini created a mountain of the wreckage, which serves as a constant reminder of mortality. It's like walking into someone's home and seeing a casket used as a dinner table.

The winding down of the war in Southeast Asia marked the transition period of drug usage for Americans. As the war shifted from a battle to keep the Viet Cong from invading Hawaii to a holding action, bored and scared American troops began to consume hard drugs as never before. The stage was set for increased drug use, a crime level never seen before in American history, and corruption in government reaching every level. Just as with every prohibition.

The two wars share more similarities than differences. Few take the time to understand how we became entrenched in either. No one even discusses how we might get out of the "war on drugs." With both we have a history of atrocities, abuse of government power, and needless waste which goes hand in hand with all warfare. With Vietnam we destroyed the cream of one generation, with the "war on drugs" we seem destined to totally destroy generation after generation; leaving the bills for our great-grandchildren to pay.

At the start of any war it seems glorious. Maybe the good guys *do* wear white hats, just like on TV. Eventually, in the mud and gore of the battlefield, all uniforms tend to look alike. Nobody ever won any war. All that ever happens is that one side loses more than the other. Like all wars, this war is fought mainly by our young people: our most precious resource. Perhaps it's time to declare a victory and go home. For our kids' sake.

1989, Dade Work Camp
Florida City, Florida

No Brownstones, Just Alleyways & Corner Pockets Full

J. L. Wise Jr.

I.

Hot bothered nights . . .

street corner hype &
neon signs winking to def jams'
rhythms jumping
the juke joint;
Mad Dog
T-bird
& greasy fatburger's stench
reeks from sweaty pores
of nickel dime poolhall hustlers
busting nine-balls &
          OOPS
upside the heads of
bluesed out screwballs;
where fanged flies on a mission
ignore the
          ENTER AT YOUR OWN RISK
signs
like kamikaze daredevils
free-basing poppies &
practicing the serious art
of hara-kiri;
a 15-story highwire act featuring
odiferous mongrels howling unmolestedly
off key
in schoolless breezeways up 14th St.
sporting flat-top fades on second grade
boys rolling dice
drunks
          cursing like Popeye the Sailorman

& breaking down gats & Macs
as a skillful trade;
where cornrow-weaved
cornbread and swine fed
bow-bellied hoochies
double-dutch into labor.

Salvation dies too many deaths
in this palefaceless metro
where first-of-the-month checks
arrive a little & too late again
straight shooters
                    "jingle it, baby . . ."
& face-cracking Wet Willies[†]
flood Afrika's blood.

II.

The buck stops here
headlining Monday's toilet paper
after rendezvous in pissy gangways
between swingblade strawberries[‡]
doing their best James Cagney
impersonations &
                    oversexed
                    overweight
                    outraged corporate America
(The Brave?)

ganked
stunted
jacked and permanently dissed
screaming for mercy
911
        (it's a joke in our town!)
frigid wives

[†] "Face-cracking Wet Willies" are More cigarettes laced with PCP, which — if "good" — cause a grimace.
[‡] A "strawberry" is a woman who will do anything for a hit of crack, including selling her body. (JLW Jr.)

& the AIDS hotline;
where storefront philanderers
preach 666 Hail Marys
in atonement for satisfying sins

with an idea when the indoctrination
began
but none of where hell or this alleyway
end
determined to discover brownstones
still
in corner pockets full.

Hot bothered nights . . .

but unstrange bedfellows.

> 1994, Potosi Correctional Center
> Mineral Point, Missouri

Americans

Jon Schillaci

Mr. Srinivasan
instructs us to call him "Babu"
because no one can say
his name —

perverted letters mate
unnaturally, heretic
bloodlines (sex in high school
was like sports: we did our
best and hoped someone
important saw). This country

Absorbs into its blondness
darkness and we began
in darkness —

I wonder how a Hindu
falls in love in Texas.
I wonder where Ann Nguyen went
(who threw her books into my
hands and knew English
enough to say, "You are my
boyfriend," no matter what
I thought) —

who kissed engulfingly yet was
so tiny her ring sat only
a crown on my fingertip —
I thought I was the most
powerful chain-link boy
in school.

Mr. Srinivasan
was born in Rusk (a tiny
Texas town which still
dreams of the Republic)
and speaks only English.
His drawl is John Wayne or

Ross Perot and once in
Texas cows were sacred;
once in high school a girl
from Vietnam was more
beautiful than America.

> 1998, Ramsey I Unit, TDCJ-ID
> Rosharon, Texas

For Sam Manzie

Jon Schillaci

Who, at fifteen, raped and killed a boy

Rattled in daysleepdreams the taste of space
Filled with www.com and photographs
Of himself caressed by strangers.
The lady says (the lady with the hat
That says, "I am a lady,") Sam Manzie
Should be chained or photocopied,
Paper clipped to hell. Still I think
Of your fingers and think someone
Should hold your hand
            (should hold you down:
Did you think he would rise after the weekend
And harrow hell to retrieve you?) but they
Reappear. They rise and sign autographs, give credit

To James Cameron's Hollywood for their
Annual resurrection
                (was there something beautiful
Inside a teenage softskincandywrapper,
Art in smashed pumpkins?) or maybe he was
Much too boylikeyou for you? An instant
Eternal brief while (you felt) what about
How I or you trembled (what about
How you or I felt (tell me how we felt

And I know what the world lost. Not one child.
Two. Everyone is dead, and everything
Is lost, and everywhere is hell, and I
Blame wherethehellwasIanyway for the lady

Who says (yet has never deathtrembled) we should
Rather kill you than allow someone to hold
Your vacant palm, your curl-fingered hand.

1998, Ramsey I Unit, TDCJ-ID
Rosharon, Texas

Diner at Midnight

David Taber

Buildings rise around the waitress
that are of concrete and metal shadow, dark
beyond the silver black of night.

There is a moon.
Lunar mountains
shine on the jukebox

that hangs over my left elbow.
The moon begs a song through newspaper print
after a murder of the previous

night. I insert no spare quarter.
I cannot decide whether I am
like Hamlet; or the city is a parasite.

I note my own insignificance, drag on a cigarette.
The waitress bends over a Spanish omelette,
white American cheese, toast. The plate

clatters like death. I drink coffee
I shake ketchup onto eggs
though I notice the absurdity of my elbow

pumping tomato paste Eucharist.
I know the waitress: curled blond hair,
blue eyes of a Wonder Bread billboard

faded image of an industrial era.
When we were fourteen we kissed
in an antiseptic high school corridor.

Anna had an abortion last week.
I exhibit no sign
of how deeply

someone has reached into her soul:
I fear what
I may see, what I may feel.

1997, Massachusetts Correctional Facility–Norfolk
Norfolk, Massachusetts

The Film

David Taber

The highway lures me out of my house
at night, when lead-white faces mock
a black moon.

I get into an Oldsmobile.
Red lights blink.
I push in a tape
and follow the words of a song.
Nothing is real.

I look at my watch.
10:30 P.M. E.S.T.
I slant in my seat
an imitation of a cinema actor.

There is a gun under my front seat.

*   *   *

I pull into a diner
in the middle of Connecticut.
I order eggs and bacon.
I drink coffee.

The waitress is a cheap actress.
I ignore her.

She may be thinking of her tip
or she may not care.
It doesn't matter.
She is air.

I eat.
I put on a lead-white face.
Do you want anything else?
No.
My life is a cinema cliché.

*   *   *

I finish my second cup of coffee
and I am on the verge
of philosophical observation.

Highway lights pass.
It is 1:00 A.M.
Police follow me.
I am an owl.

Without doubt I am analytical.
I possess an introspective
bent.
I grimace through a lead-white face.

The lights of New York City
flash onto my windshield.
I am in a film
There is a gun under my front seat.

This is the part
where the criminal hero . . .

1997, Massachusetts Correctional Facility–Norfolk
Norfolk, Massachusetts

The 5-Spot Cafe

Henry Johnson

for Lee Morgan

Your latest lover sits at my table,
and I snap open my purse
as her lips smudge
the rim of her champagne glass red.
Your gun fills my palm
like something sexual
while all the nights I spent alone
beat black-wings inside my chest.
You raise your trumpet,
the stage lights shimmer like stars
while I watch you from the shadows
in the 5-Spot Cafe, damp hands
balled into trembling fists.
I schemed for days, imagining ways
to win you back, like the time
I met you at our apartment door
naked but for the red rose
in my hair. Once you even cried
on my shoulder, and I glowed inside
until the phone rang and you
rushed out the door, lies falling
from your lips like fruit.
I close my purse.

Halfway through your new arrangement
I sashay past tables with candles
in tinted red glasses, the slip of satin
like a cool hand against my back.
My anger like steam
knocking against pipes as I brush the shoulder
of a man leaning back in his seat,
eyes closed like a lover
waiting to be kissed.

I beg his pardon, step gingerly
past your lover nearer the stage.
Our eyes meet, and for a moment
I almost lose it, remembering you
hard and strong in my arms, black hair
slicked back like a silk cap
tight against your skull. But when
you turn away it's like steam
filling this room so full, the lights
dim, and each riff burns like the iron
you held near my face the night we fought
about a motel room receipt
I found balled up in your pants pocket.
Tonight I ride with you to the last measure,
where the music is pure, where applause
retards to a heartbeat, and
your lover calls out, "play it sweet
for me baby," and I bring the crowd
to their feet — with a single,
well-aimed shot
I compose my own arrangement
all over the white brick wall.

> 1989, Sing Sing Correctional Facility
> Ossining, New York

Melody

J. C. Amberchele

Mel is standing on the curb in front of her father's house, digging in her knapsack for the key and wondering how she could have misplaced it, or why she has misplaced it, wondering if maybe she has misplaced it on purpose. She is aware of the dream and thinking: I'll be a sibyl, a seeress, I'll see halos and auras, I'll predict the future . . .

It is noon and the cab has just dropped her off and she's had a headache since this morning when she left Omaha.

"I'll find the keys," she says out loud, surprising herself with her sarcasm . . . and immediately remembers an inside pocket on her windbreaker.

The house has been empty for a year. It is brick and stone, three stories under a red tile roof. There are turrets at the front corners, three-quarter round with bay windows on all floors, medieval structures that to Mel have always seemed an architectural afterthought. Out front on the lawn is the stocky red juniper her father planted before she was born, and at the curb, towering over the street, the roots so effortlessly heaving the pavement aside, is the ancient sycamore that has been around longer than the houses on the block. The hedge separating the yard from the neighbor's is frantic with growth, but the lawn has been mowed — the real estate company has seen to that — although the first thing Mel noticed from the taxi was that no one had taken down the blue window awnings this past winter, and now they look faded and sad. Sad windows and sad gray walls, the welcome mat missing from the front steps, ivy gone wild and snagging the rain gutters, the chimney fascia spilling its rust down the wall overlooking the driveway. Her father's castle, his crumbling fortress in the middle of the block.

On the porch, knapsack harassing her shoulder, Mel fingers the key from her jacket and aims it at the lock, noticing as she does that her hand is trembling.

She is here to meet the woman from the real estate company. There is a buyer for the house, and a good offer. Paul, Mel's brother in Omaha — where Mel has spent the last year recovering — has come to Denver twice this month to arrange the sale, and actually Mel didn't have to return. But the deal didn't include the furniture, room after crowded room of turn-of-century tables and chairs, antique wall hangings and rugs, thousands of knickknacks — and ostensibly Mel has come for this: to sell or store the furniture, or as she told Paul before she left, to check her room one final time, to see if there is anything she wants to keep.

Mel closes the door behind her but then swings it open again because the air in the hallway is stale. She eases her knapsack to the floor and looks down the length of the narrow room. To Mel the hall has always been the unfriendliest room in the house, a dim passageway of hardwood floors and empty walls, so unlike the other rooms. There are heavy sliding doors, closed now, to the parlor on the left and the dining room on the right, and farther along there are single doors to the den and to the closets under the stairwell. Toward the rear of the house is an entryway to the kitchen, and next to it, another door — the service stairs, a metal spiral in a narrow shaft from basement to roof.

Which was how he got to them, so quietly, she and her father light sleepers but never hearing the familiar creak of the staircase in the hall, the groan of the wooden banister . . .

. . . She awoke with the barrel of the gun pushed between her lips, icy metal against her teeth, the reading lamp turned above her and shining in her eyes. He wore a ski mask, a ratty blue parka that rustled as he moved. All she could think was that she was naked beneath the covers. He drew the gun from her mouth and pointed it at her head and with the other hand shoved a note in her face — so as not to reveal his voice? she wondered, squinting, trying hard to focus on the words. The safe, it said. Where was the safe, and what was the combination?

But there was no safe. She hesitated, and then couldn't speak. He motioned for her to sit up. She did, spilling the covers to her lap. Curiously, she wasn't afraid. She felt her heart race, felt her skin turn cold; her eyes stung in the brightness of the bulb and what puzzled her was that she knew this man would probably kill her — and yet she wasn't afraid, as if in her mind there wasn't room or even time enough for fear.

He took her arm and pulled her from the bed, spun her around, and jammed the gun in her hair — her wild hair, springy curls out past her shoulders — and pushed her to her father's room down the hall . . .

Mel opens the sliding doors to the dining room. Nothing has changed. The walls are cluttered with eighteenth-century engravings and elaborately framed mirrors. The Queen Anne dining set, the china case, look recently polished; the crystal glassware and figural silver are displayed exactly as they have always been.

She walks through and into the kitchen. The refrigerator door is open; the light is off. She closes the door and lifts the phone off the wall and holds it to her ear, knowing there will be no dial tone. Except for her bedroom, this was her favorite part of the house, here at the oak table in the breakfast nook where she'd read or do her homework, the afternoon sunlight angling through the bay windows. By the time she was twelve, she was mostly alone here. Her father could no longer afford the maid, and by then her brother had left home permanently. And so after school she would bring her books to the table by the window, and then with cookies or maybe a cake in the oven she would dream up salads or fix casseroles that too often her father wouldn't show up to eat, but even so, the idea of something ready on the stove or warm in the oven was a comfort to her.

Mel hangs up the phone and, returning to the hallway, hears a car pull up out front — and knows it is Beth, the real estate lady who is selling the house. This wasn't Mel's idea. It was Paul who had called Beth from the airport. But then in a way it was Mel's idea because it was she who had insisted on coming back, and selling or storing the furniture was the handy excuse, something Paul would understand. Paul who had ignored her all her life and who now acted as though he needed her, as though he needed to protect her.

Mel walks to the front door. Beth steps out of her shiny car and looks up at the giant tree spreading high above her, and somehow at that instant Mel realizes that the new owners, whoever they are, will cut it down, will decide it is too old and too big for the neighborhood.

"Such a lovely tree," Beth calls from the curb. She wears a white suit with low heels to match, a floppy spring hat that Mel thinks is silly. Approaching the porch she says, "I hope it survives. You know, this Dutch elm disease is rampant here."

"It's a sycamore," Mel says, and Beth shrugs and flips a hand in the air as if to say: Sycamore, elm, what's the difference?

Beth is a retired housewife, in her late forties, Mel decides. Her nose is too long and her mouth too wide but other than that she is attractive in a motherly way. Paul has been in touch with her since last fall, ever since he and Mel agreed to sell the house. Paul, at twenty-nine, is ten years older than Mel; he is a dentist in Omaha where he lives in a boxy suburban neighborhood and cares for his two young sons, a result of a recent divorce. For the past eleven months, ever since she left the hospital, Mel has been recovering at Paul's, taking

care of the boys when she was able. Paul has made trips to Denver
about the house, but Mel couldn't return, not until she was ready. And
then one night when he was away she dreamed a crazy dream, a dream
similar to the recurring nightmare but different because this time she
knew she was dreaming; like a spectator at a film, she saw herself
return to her father's house, watched as she moved from room to
room reliving the horror of that night — and abruptly the dream
shifted to a distant future in which she had arrived at an unknown
faraway place, and there in her mind had grown numb and therefore
comfortable and as a bonus had acquired these strange mental powers — she could read people's auras, she could see their lives unfolding, minute by minute — a future in which she existed in the same
spatial dimensions as everyone else and yet in a time slightly ahead,
so that even her own days were predictable . . . a future also in which
the nightmare of the past had ended, had vanished as, in a sense, she
herself had vanished.

. . . The man snapped the overhead light on, and her father sat up as
they entered the room. He sat up blinking, and there wasn't much else
he could do, not with the gun at her head, naked as she was and with
the man gripping her neck from behind. The man pulled her father
out of bed, motioned for them to lie on the floor, face down. He
grabbed a blanket and tossed it over her, a thing that surprised her,
but then he knelt above her and yanked the blanket down and forced
her hands behind her back where he taped her wrists, moved to her
ankles and taped them also, then started on her father. And her father
kept asking, Why? and Who was he? and What did he want? over and
over, with the tape tearing, screeching in Melody's ear. But the answer
when it came was only the note, this time held low to her father's eyes.
Where was the safe? What was the combination?

But there was no safe. Her father told him: There never was a
safe, not in this house. On the dresser — take the wallet, the watch —
take the TV, anything. Just don't hurt them.

And Melody kept thinking: He won't hurt us, he only wants
money, he'll take the wallet and leave . . .

He began with the paintings on the wall, tore them off one by
one and threw them to the floor, then moved to the closet, ripped the
clothes out and pulled all the boxes off the shelves. No safe. He
stopped, chest heaving, and Melody could feel his anger, could almost
see the air around him boil with rage. He stood above them for a
moment, then suddenly grabbed her father by the hair and pressed the

gun to his forehead . . . and Melody waited, wanting desperately to be afraid, wanting fear to release her, to feel it as a poison in her blood, pumping into her mind, pumping everywhere at once . . .

There was a life insurance policy, a few dollars in a checking account, a trust fund for her college tuition. Paul sold the car and gave her half the money, but she gave it back as monthly rent — even after the hospital bill, her half of the insurance policy and the money from the house would be more than enough.

As for the trust fund, her father had never mentioned it. But that was like him, not to tell her. Losing his wife when Mel was born, silent and brooding, a tall man with sunken eyes and permanently hunched shoulders, he rarely told her anything: There were entire days when he didn't speak to her, so that she grew up trying too hard, hoping to replace not only his loss but her own. There were financial problems. Eventually he sold the printing company that had been his grandfather's and his father's and took a job in the press room at the *Denver Post.* And Mel had finished high school and had attended her graduation ceremony alone, had spent a year after that working odd jobs and hanging around the library downtown — and he hadn't said a thing about a trust fund.

"You know what I like about this place?" Beth says. "It's so quiet." She pats the wall next to the front door. "It's so solid."

Mel considers smiling but isn't sure it won't come out as a frown. Although Beth is right: The house is quiet. Mel's paternal grandparents lived and died here before she was born; they were, as her mother and her mother's parents were, more of the silent family she never knew. Growing up, Mel embraced the silence, took it for her own, but Paul came up angry, hating this house and leaving as soon as he could. Now Mel isn't sure what to think — this was never a happy place, never a place for a child, really, but it is all she knows. And now she must forget it — she must walk through it, room by room, erasing it from her mind.

She slides open the doors to the parlor. The furniture is untouched — the sofa and loveseat by the fireplace, the octagonal table in the turret bay, the Estey pump organ against the wall. There are too many tables: coffee tables and end tables and corner tables, all busy with knickknacks that have never meant a thing to her but to which she now feels an unwelcome attachment, knowing they are hers to dispose of.

"Try the sofa by the fireplace," she says to Beth. She is aware of

having acquired a short fuse: since the hospital she has found it difficult to listen to her brother complain about his divorce, and today in
the taxi on the way from the airport she snapped at the driver when
he tried his small talk. Mel doesn't wish to be rude to Beth, but neither does she feel a need to explain — it is simply that she must do
this alone. "I'll be back," she says.

She climbs the stairs to the second floor, crosses the balcony, and
enters her bedroom. The room is sunny; the drapes have been drawn
from the window overlooking the backyard, probably by her brother
on his recent visit. Here, there is a thin layer of dust over everything:
the massive headboard on the bed, the heavy walnut dresser with the
teardrop pulls, the books piled on her desk and floor — it was never
a girl's room, never frilly, although when she was six her father
relented and exchanged the antique wallpaper for Pooh characters:
Owl and Eeyore and Christopher Robin, Pooh and Piglet following
in circles the multiplying tracks of a Woozle — the wallpaper that
seems faded and brittle now, about to peel from the walls.

She stops at the window. The lawn in the backyard is patchy,
blemished with debris brought by the winter wind, and the dogwood
tree, bursting with hundreds of clusters of brilliant white flowers,
seems delirious, abandoned to nature. Beyond the fence there is the
wide expanse of the neighbor's lawn, and across the street, the country club where as a child she would spend her weekends — alone on
winter Sundays she would test the frozen creek, hike the empty golf
course that became her private estate; the trees she would climb were
make-believe houses where she'd perch in her heavy coat like a silent
bird, watching frosted cars glide by on a nearby avenue. She was a
tomboy; she was more a boy than a girl; she thought of herself as odd
and graceless and at fault, and with her brother so much older and
her father hardly home even when he was, there was no one to tell
her different.

Mel turns and leaves the bedroom but stops just outside the door.
She is suddenly lightheaded, dizzy. She is fine, she tells herself — she
has come this far; she can go on. She takes a breath and steadies herself with a hand against the wall, walks to her brother's room and
looks in, then continues around the stairwell toward her father's
room. This is why she has returned — she has forced herself to this
room because she believes in the dream; she has rehearsed this a hundred times in her mind; she is convinced she can walk in and walk out
and in that fleeting turn bring it all back — everything: the senseless-
ness of it, the horror, the fear that would never come. And then walk

out and forget it, forget this room altogether . . . or perhaps remember it as it had always been so perfectly ordinary — his robe hanging on the back of the closet door, the collection of antique paperweights on the roll-top desk, the wisteria lamp in the corner with the tilted shade, the humid oversweet odor of pipe tobacco and cologne permeating everything — the Oriental rug faded where the afternoon sun burns through the tall windows . . . but there on the rug is another faded area, a large oval where someone has scrubbed, where a stain has been lifted by hard work and whatever chemicals . . .

. . . He walked out. He tucked the gun in his pocket and looked around the room as though deciding what to do or what to take, glared at them as if to say, You think I came for your wallet, old man? You think I came for the fucking TV?

And walked out. She heard him in her brother's room, knocking pictures off the wall, toppling the dresser. Then in her room, hangers springing from the closet, drawers yanked open and clattering to the floor. He ran downstairs, and she heard him in the parlor, furniture crashing, glass breaking. She tried twisting her arms to loosen the tape, tried slipping a hand out but couldn't. Her father lay next to her — if she could inch down, get to his wrists, she could chew the tape and free his hands. She rolled to her side, told her father what she was doing, expecting, hoping he would say Yes, hurry . . . but all he could say was Why? — Why was this happening to them?

Melody in her bathrobe, tugging her father through the snow in the backyard, over the fence and into the darkness of the neighbor's yard — she saw this in her mind: tiptoeing to her room for her bathrobe, the two of them hurrying down the service stairs to the rear door and out into the night . . . but the man returned before she could finish with the tape at her father's wrists; he walked in as she was lifting her head, a long strand in her mouth.

He did not hit her. He simply pulled her by the hair, back to where she'd been. And then leaned over them, his breath quick and labored now, nearly a wheeze, and held the note where they both could read it, held it with a young and shaky hand, tapping it with the barrel of the gun. And her father said, "Dammit, there is no safe. Can't you hear? There is no safe." And the man shot him. In a clap of thunder she saw her father bounce once and then leak his life onto the rug through a ragged opening in his head. And the last thing she felt was the gun in her hair, and a roar, not a sound but a pressure, a rushing as of wind in a tunnel, going away . . .

* * *

It is too much for her. With no warning she begins to retch. She hurries out the door and down the hall to the bathroom, reaches the toilet but can't throw up. She waits but nothing happens. She considers pushing a finger down her throat but can't do that either. This is how it has been since the hospital, this sense of choking, of something there but not there, something not in her throat but hidden in the damage at the base of her skull, poised as if to ambush her. And it will not come, it will not leave her.

She moves to the sink, and realizes — standing now at the mirror, seeing a face that is not her present face but a face from the future — that the dream was a sham, a hoax, that she was a fool to think she could walk in and walk out and rid herself of the past. She could almost laugh. She is both the joke and the joker, the dreamer and the dream itself. Oh, but the fear will come — she knows this now, she can see it in her eyes — it will leak from her slowly, drop by drop, year after year, as tears, blood from a wound that will never heal.

She splashes water on her face, hoping to shrink the endlessness of it all. She must grow her hair back, she thinks, her wild hair that saved her — so that he thought he'd shot her in the center of the head when in fact the bullet had only grazed her; she had turned to her father at that instant, turned her crown of curls out past her shoulders and halfway down her back — and he'd shot her hair instead.

Hair that is gone now, barely long enough to cover the crease in her skull. She had been a month in the hospital, and then the long, slow recovery at her brother's in Omaha. The police had arrested the man that same night, in another house a block away — a drug addict, or a mental patient, she never did get it straight. She had come to in a haze of pain, the left side of her face sinking in a pool of blood — hers and her father's, the sickening, fruity smell of it in her throat — and had pushed herself across the floor, then back with the telephone cord in her mouth until the old metal phone toppled from the desk. And later, out of the hospital and at her brother's house, the nightmares began: a man in a ski mask stalking her, catching her, the gun tangled in her hair — every night she'd wake up screaming, and her brother at first troubled, even frightened, and then later impatient, condescending, would tell her it was okay, everything was okay now, the man was in prison. As if that were enough.

Mel leaves the bathroom. She feels heavy; the gray light in the upstairs hall seems to press against her; the air settles in her lungs like ash. She forces herself past the bedrooms and down the stairs, and when she enters the living room Beth gets off the couch. The front door is still open, and now a chill is added to the gloomy silence of the house.

"There's nothing I want here," Mel says, and Beth blinks, looks around at the furniture and then touches the arm of the couch.

"This is very old."

"Yes, it's stuffed with horsehair," Mel says, impatient now. "And that's marble on the tables, and the chairs are antiques. So is the rug."

"Worth a fortune," Beth says, almost dreamily.

"Then maybe you should sell it for a fortune —"

Mel is about to add: And buy yourself a new hat ... and can think of a dozen other phrases too cruel to be witty ... but she is aware of an almost visible warmth from Beth, a concern that has nothing to do with the house.

Beth hesitates, and clears her throat. "Honey, all your books, all your clothes in your room. You don't want any of it?"

Suddenly Mel wants out. Out of the house, out of the city. She's had this idea about hitchhiking to Alaska, working construction or crewing a fishing boat, something hard and out of doors. Something far away.

"Are there papers to sign?"

Beth smiles. "Your brother took care of that. We're set to close in a month."

Mel lifts her knapsack by the strap, slings it over her shoulder. "Then can you give me a ride? To the freeway downtown?"

"Honey, of course." Beth stares toward her but stops abruptly when Mel turns. From behind Mel she says, "But why don't we have lunch at Andre's first? Or there's this cute little place on the downtown mall."

Mel can't answer. The idea of lunch is so absurd she feels like crying. She steps outside onto the porch. The sun winks through the upper branches of the sycamore in a way that is familiar. When she was small, five or six, she carried a serving dish from the dining room and filled it with dirt from around the rhododendrons in the front yard. Her father spanked her, struck her for the first time. And then on the porch he picked her up, and in a rare show of affection, and with the sun over his shoulder winking rainbows through her tears, he kissed her cheek and told her he was sorry.

Mel hands Beth the key and Beth locks the front door. The fragmented light has a hypnotic effect, and as they walk to the car Mel sees too clearly what will happen to the old sycamore — she sees them cutting it, limb by limb, grinding the branches in one of those infernal machines, the sawdust swirling high into the summer sky.

Beth opens the car door for Mel and says, "Can't I take you to a friend's place? Or a hotel? Listen, hon, I don't have to return to the office. You could come out to Cherry Hills. The last of my daughters is in college and my husband and I are all alone with too many empty rooms. It's such a lovely house, with a magnificent yard, with dogwood and cherry trees, and, oh, the flower garden, it's the perfect time of year . . . you can stay, you know, we'd love to have you. It would be a nice place to relax."

"No thanks," Mel says, dropping herself on the front seat of Beth's car and shifting her knapsack to her lap, hugging it to her chest as a girl would hug a doll. Because she doesn't feel like relaxing. What she feels like is running. Running and running until she runs out of herself. What she feels like is disappearing, though she knows it wouldn't help. What she really feels like is killing someone.

1992, Colorado Territorial Correctional Facility
Cañon City, Colorado

Mel

J. C. Amberchele

It is late winter . . . sun high in a pale blue sky, the air sharp with the scent of pine from the foothills to the west. Mel has been driving for three hours, from her home on the western slope to this city on the edge of the plains where the mountains have become wrinkled fingers stretching eastward, dry escarpments hugging the river, and where the highway no longer meanders with the lay of the valley but abruptly widens to become a busy thoroughfare into town — immediately to the left is the prison: high stone walls and tin-roofed guard towers, chain-link fences topped with concertina wire, a parking lot out front.

She locks the car door. It is Saturday, visiting day, nearly noon, and there are plenty of vehicles in the lot. She is here to meet a man she does not know, a prisoner now for thirteen years. She does not know this man and yet she has carried the memory of his hooded face, his youthful and powerful hands, since the night he shot her father, shot her also, left her for dead. And she has carried the memory all these years, like the still tender scar at the base of her skull.

Mel fancies herself a vagabond, and rightfully so. She is also a writer, but of this she must frequently remind herself, even though she has had numerous articles and even a book published, with another on the way. It is that travel has been her release and writing her anchor, and with her fears, somehow she has equated entrapment with success, freedom with travel. Although now, for the first time in thirteen years, she has settled into one place in one town for more than a month, and for the first time ever she is living with a man, someone she met while hitchhiking in Mexico — his name is Hank and he is as carefree as she is not; he is a wanderer also but not out of need; he is currently a ski instructor and a bartender at a resort near where they live, and he is in love with her. And this is why she is here — now that she has a home she is aware of a connection to this prison, to the man who possesses in his crime the greater part of her.

There is a solitary tower out front, a gate through a high fence and a walkway leading to a sixties-modern building fronting the stone wall. Mel enters the building via glass doors and stops at a desk where a uniformed officer hands her a form to read — visiting rules — and

another to fill out: Name, Address, Driver's license number, Name
and number of inmate, Relation to inmate. She does this quickly and
hands it along with her driver's license to the officer. She knows the
inmate's name — Alex Pitts — but because she does not know his
penitentiary number the officer must find it on a list. As to
"Relation," she has written: Friend.

Mel did not plan this visit. She is not sure what will happen. She
knows that Alex Pitts is here — her brother in Omaha has checked
every year for thirteen years to make certain — but she does not know
if he has a family now, a wife or a girlfriend who visits him. She knows
only that he was young when he arrived — eighteen, a year younger
than she — and that he was a drug addict, a homeless boy with a
record for burglary since he was ten.

She signs a waiver to be strip-searched, which a female officer
tells her is a formality and to which she will probably not have to submit. Mel wears no jewelry and has never carried a purse, so there is
nothing but her wallet to place in a nearby locker. She is dressed
according to the rules — no short skirt or dress (Mel has not worn a
dress in twenty years, since she was twelve and her father had to beg
her to attend an Easter party with him), no tight or see-through
blouses, no revealing sweaters — she wears what she usually wears:
sweatshirt and jeans and sneakers, a jacket with pockets for her note-
books and pens, empty now. The guard pats her down and assists her
through a metal detector, and suddenly she is on the other side of a
steel door and into a barred sally port — inside the prison now —
 through another door and into a wide, rectangular room with
cinder-block walls and a linoleum floor, square pillars supporting a
cement ceiling, thirty or forty metal tables surrounded by folding
chairs, a row of vending machines along one wall and an old wooden
desk in the corner, another uniformed guard behind it.

There are other people in the room — families, women alone —
but no inmates, although Mel is not sure what an inmate looks like,
what sort of outfit he wears. She finds an empty table against the wall,
eases herself onto the chair, and scans the room. It is curious — she
has never seen the races so thoroughly mixed — whites and blacks
and Hispanics not in groups but scattered here and there in the room
and even mingling at a row of tables that have been pushed
together — even the waiting areas of bus and train stations, all the air-
ports she has been in, are not like this.

A woman with yellow, strawlike hair and dreadfully thin arms,
sitting alone at the next table, smiles tentatively at Mel and lifts a
hand, wiggles her fingers in a halfhearted wave. "I haven't seen you

before," she says, her face the face of a sad clown, pouty red lips and chalky skin, dark circles like sinkholes around her languid brown eyes. "Did you bring quarters? You know, you can have quarters in here, for the machines." She opens her other hand and reveals a roll of coins. "I couldn't stand it here without a pop or a candy bar or something."

Mel nods and shrugs and can't think of anything to say. She has not brought quarters; nor does she drink pop or eat candy. Immediately the woman with straw hair is up and around her table and over to Mel's, where she sits across from her. "You here to see your father?" she says.

"My father?"

"Well, it can't be your husband or your brother, you're too young. Haven't you heard? This is Old Max. They moved the young-sters out to the new prisons and brought the old-timers here, all the cripples and sick people because this is where the hospital is. Isn't that the perfect name . . . Old Max?" She lifts an eyebrow. "You really are new here. You wanna Coke or something?"

Mel is about to reply but the woman jumps up again. "Be back," she sings, heading for the vending machines. Normally Mel would tell this woman who is probably younger than she is and who hasn't the courtesy to wait for an answer — that she wants to be alone, that no, she is not here to visit her father and for that matter it is none of her business, and anyway a Coke is about the last thing she needs right now — but the woman, as disheveled as she is in her shabby pink blouse and threadbare jeans and that crazy broom of yellow hair, has about her a toast-colored light, a pulsing aura of youthful warmth that follows her like a mist.

It is this that Mel sees. The year of recovery after the crime she had had a dream — that in removing herself from the pain she would sense what others could not, she would see differently; she would come to know and to trust people by their light. And slowly, over the years, with practice, the dream came true. So that what began as a nightmare has become for her not only a shield but a treasured advan-tage, a glimpse into the future, a head start.

It is a willful act, this seeing — she must allow her eyes to drift out of focus; it is more a sensing, although the qualities of vision are there: color, shape, density, the aspects of movement. And it is a tal-ent she dares not reveal — Hank is the only one who knows — for to tell someone, she is certain, is to bring the sort of attention she most wants to avoid.

The woman returns towing her blob of tawny light; she carries two cans of cola that appear as dark holes in her glowing hands. She sits and tells Mel her name is Angie and that, of course, she is here to visit her father . . . as she is every weekend, three years now, back and forth from Colorado Springs — God, the price of gas is killing her! and now this morning the car wouldn't start and she had to take a bus, a bus mind you, and how will she get back? there are no buses until tonight and she'll have to leave in an hour, probably have to hitchhike — "say, you wouldn't be heading that way, would you? I could wait if you are!" . . . abruptly she tilts the can to her mouth and gulps soda, eying Mel. When she finishes, she wipes her mouth and smiles.

"Why is he here?" Mel says. "Your father."

"Because I put him here."

Mel waits in the silence that follows. She knows what is coming next, although the words do not form in her head.

"He molested me," Angie says. "From the time I was five and until I was eighteen, when I got pregnant with his daughter. But when he touched my baby girl, I called the cops."

Mel hasn't liked canned soda since she can't remember when, her teens, she supposes, but now she pulls the tab and lifts it to her mouth. The taste is familiar still, the icy bubbles a curious relief. "And you've forgiven him?" she says.

"Never. I have three brothers who hate his guts — they even hate me for coming here. No, no, we'll never forgive him. Who would?"

Mel feels that she has pried, for no good reason. Or perhaps there is a reason, but it is not obvious. Why is this girl sharing her wound? As though they were friends, compatriots.

Somewhere a metal door clangs, and there is the sound of heavy footsteps on the stairs, laughter, a shuffling as of cattle let out of a pen. And now they enter the visiting room, one at a time through a door in the corner next to the desk. The first is a tall black man with a matted gray beard, hurrying to a table of women with enormous smiles. Two more inmates enter — dark green slacks, green pullover shirts with the all too obvious number on the pocket — then more, a middle-aged man on crutches, another who must be in his seventies, stooped and frail but with a full head of bristly white hair, part of it braided into a rat's tail at the back of his head. Then Angie stands as the next man enters — he, too, is bent forward, and carries a cane, a large man with bulging arms and a long, sagging face. He smiles at Angie and Angie places her Coke on the table and winks at Mel. "That's my dad," she says — proudly, Mel thinks. "That's my dad."

* * *

Fifteen, twenty men have entered the room, and Alex Pitts is not among them. Mel waits another ten minutes and then finally approaches the officer at the desk who in turn telephones a Control Center somewhere in the prison. "You know how it is, lady," he says with his hand over the receiver, "some of these guys never get a visit, so they ain't ready."

Mel returns to her table next to the wall. She sits and wishes she had something to read, some way to calm the churning in her stomach. The tabletop has been etched with overlapping layers of graffiti, probably years of work. And with what? she wonders. What sharp instruments? Some of it is tattoo flash — snakes and dragons and devils' heads, skeletons and motorcycles — but most is another message: love, loved ones, hearts and arrows and who loves who; and dates: parole dates, release dates, who was here when.

Still, inmates are arriving. Two more enter the visiting room, and five minutes later, another two. A half hour has passed and Mel is beginning to think she should have handled this differently — she should have called the prison first, she should have written to Alex Pitts and told him she was coming. But she did not want him prepared for her, no more than she, thirteen years ago, was prepared for him. No, she tells herself, this meeting will be what it is — even if he does not show, for her it will be what it is.

The room is noisy. Half a dozen children have taken to the floor in a game of hide-and-seek, and the officer at the desk is frowning at them. Angie and her father are eating sandwiches purchased from the vending machines. Most of the inmates and visitors are smiling and talking and holding hands; except for the bars on the sally port and the heavy metal doors, it is a church social in a church basement. And out the corner of her eye Mel sees the guard point his pencil at her — as she turns, another inmate enters the room.

He is younger than she expects, her age, but so much younger than the others. He is tall and powerfully built, with a narrow waist and wide shoulders — a build she does not remember — thick, sinewy arms filling the short sleeves of his green pullover. He is staring at her perplexed, now glancing self-consciously at the others in the room, then back at her, wondering. She does not recognize this man — the wide brow, the long and slightly crooked nose, the angular jaw — certainly not from the night long ago when he wore a mask, but not even from the news photos or the mug shots she saw months later at her brother's house, during the court proceedings. She had gone to the sentencing — a plea bargain to avoid the death penalty — in a wheelchair, still too weak to carry herself, but she had arrived late, nearly an hour after it was over and they had taken him back to his jail cell where she could not see him, could not look into his eyes and glimpse there the knowledge of his future, the suffering that would never be enough. Because it is the eyes she remembers — blue, with flecks of gray, the color of winter sky, but framed, made violent by the mask holes, huge and desperate.

The same eyes, only softer now, questioning. Mel stands. She must force herself to keep her hands apart, to keep from picking at herself like a bird. He looks back at the guard who has not moved, still with his elbows on the desk, hands folded, pencil dangling from his fingers, pointing at Mel. So he turns and walks up to her.

It was a foolish thing to say. She will think later, driving home, that it was dumb, silly. "I didn't bring quarters," she says. "I can't buy you anything from the machines" — Mel who is quick but who rarely speaks before thinking, who is ahead of possibilities.

He does not talk. She knows this, she has known it all along, since before the sentencing when her brother discovered that the man who shot his father and his sister could not talk, had not talked since childhood.

And now she wishes she had her notebook with her, a pen, although she supposes these items are not allowed in the visiting room. He is questioning her with his eyes, saying Who are you? What do you want? But then he tenses and she knows he has just now figured it out, has recognized her. He blinks and clenches his jaw in a controlled expression of pain and surprise, saying God! And Why?

Mel sits. She reminds herself that she is not here for revenge — she cannot erase the memory, or the fear, but she is not here to vent an anger she long ago buried. She has come to resolve something, to untie a knot in her head, although she is not sure how, or even if she is right to try.

His face is tanned, clean-shaven, and there is a faint odor of soap about him. Unlike the other inmates he has no tattoos she can see, no scars. His hair is dark and straight, combed back. His wrinkles are sun wrinkles; he has the leathery skin of a man who has labored out-doors for years. And those eyes — blue, and too easily read, studying her.

"You're Alex," she says. "You shot me. You killed my father and then tried to kill me."

He sits across from her, wary, on the edge of the chair. He does not seem to know what to do with his hands.

He had gotten in through a window in the basement, crept up the service stairs and into her bedroom, woke her by shoving a gun in her mouth. Then marched her to her father's room and forced them both to lie on the floor, tied their hands and feet. The safe — Mel will never forget — the note held to her face, the childish scribble on paper torn from a school notebook — Where was the safe and what was the combination? But there was no safe, there was never a safe in the house, and her father told him, pleaded with this man who would not believe them, who ransacked the house, tore the paintings off the walls and toppled the dressers, emptied the closets and returned in a rage, wild-eyed and shaking — and shot them. Killed her father with a bullet to the head, there, next to her on the rug, murdered him. Then aimed the gun at her hair as she turned, the final instant, the endless hollow roar . . .

" . . . Wait," Mel says. She stands and walks to the desk, asks the officer for a pencil and paper. The guard grunts and hands her his pencil and opens a drawer, finds a sheet from a notepad. She returns to the table where Alex Pitts sits with his shoulders hunched, arms on the table, perfectly still. "Here," she says, placing the paper and pencil before him.

But he does not write. He looks at her with his winter blue eyes, the long lashes beneath the thick, sunbathed brows. His jaw is square, his chin strong, and yet his mouth is small and moist, nearly heart-shaped, which lends a boyish and oddly vulnerable look to his face. His eyes are worried.

"You're in the labor gang, aren't you?" Mel says. "Is that why they keep you here, to do the jobs the old prisoners can't? Because they need you? You went to school, you took college courses and earned your degree, you've been here thirteen years and have only one report. That's pretty good, isn't it! . . ." She sits straight in her chair, feels an urge to clear her throat, but does not. " . . . Look, I know a lot about you from my brother. He calls here to check. You can understand that, can't you?"

But Alex Pitts does not answer. His body is as rigid as hers was the night he shot her. He is even beginning to tremble, ever so slightly, a nervous hand on the table.

The police had caught him in another house, a block away. A house with a safe. Melody had come to in a drying pool of blood, inched her way to the telephone and managed with her teeth to pull the old metal phone off her father's roll-top desk. The man with the ski mask — Alex Pitts — had fired the gun into her hair, her wild, curly hair, just as she had turned — and had wounded her, the bullet taking a piece of her skull but leaving her alive. And all because, as the police would tell her brother weeks later, a crazy kid, a drug addict named Alex Pitts, had mistaken her father's house for another. Had shot them because he was frightened and sick and maybe didn't know any better.

She sighs. "I didn't come here for this, to convict you again. But I have to tell you what it's like for me. You changed my life. I can't say you ruined it because that's up to me, but you hurt me beyond measure. Do you see that?" Mel catches herself staring at him, tapping her knuckles on the table. "Right now I'm not sure why I'm here. I don't know you. I don't know if you feel bad about what you've done, but by the look in your eyes I'd say you do . . . after all, you could have left, you could have walked out of the visiting room the moment you realized who I was."

Alex Pitts lowers his gaze. He exhales through his mouth. It is the first time Mel has noticed him breathe.

"Why did you shoot us? Were you frightened? Desperate? Did you care that little for life? Were we like dust to you, something you could brush off your sleeve? Am I still that to you?"

There it is again, a shiver, that nearly imperceptible trembling of the hand.

"I want to know why." Mel picks up the pencil and holds it out to him. "You owe this to me. Tell me why you shot us. I don't care if it's not enough. I want to know what you were thinking. I want to know why I'm the way I am today." She waits, holding the pencil . . . a second, five seconds . . . then finally withdraws it. "Don't you realize?" she says. "What you did happens to me every day, and in a sense, what I do, what becomes of me, happens to you now. Doesn't that mean anything to you? . . .

". . . Or is this your power? Was that why? Was it my loss and your gain? You shot me, so you own me, the rest of my life?"

She leans forward on the table, close to him now, as if to reveal a secret.

"Then let me tell you what you bought. Thirteen years, and I've had no home and no friends, because possessions and relationships can be merciless, when they're taken away. I have nightmares. I see things. Sometimes hooded faces with eyes like yours. I see all sorts of things, like auras and halos and even events before they happen. I'm afraid most of the time. I have this idea, as crazy as it sounds, that I'm worth shooting. That no matter what I do or who I become, I should be punished. So I compensate — sometimes I'm cruel, usually I'm blunt, unforgiving. Does any of that sound right to you? Is that what you wanted?"

But Alex Pitts does not respond. He sits there, looking at her, hardly breathing. He should leave, she thinks. Why doesn't he leave? A chorus of "Happy Birthday" begins at a table in the center of the room. The old prisoner with white hair flamboyantly opens a bag of popcorn and dumps it on the table, and everyone cheers and claps. The sound echoes off the walls and ceiling, reverberates in the sterile air above her head. Mel feels herself dwindling, folding into herself, losing her sense of time and space.

But then across the room she sees Angie and her father rise, hug for a second, and slowly head for the door. Suddenly Mel wants out; she is tired of feeling trapped, she knows in her heart she was wrong: that the power was never his, was hers all along. She feels ridiculous — for trying, for talking to this man, for even coming here. She also has an urge to cry, something she has not done since before the crime.

She stands, steadies herself for a moment — she is lightheaded, sweating now — and walks to the desk, asks the guard where the bathrooms are. On her way she stops and tells Angie to wait — not to hitchhike, please don't hitchhike, she'll be glad to drive her home — and then finds the women's room where at the sink she runs cold water on her wrists, cups her hands and splashes it on her cheeks, her neck. But this time she does not look at herself in the mirror, worried that she will see there the face from the past, unchanged, the face in the mirror at her father's house all those years ago. Still Melody.

In the visiting room again she walks directly to the table to tell Alex Pitts she is leaving, but as she arrives he stands and hands her the sheet of paper, folded. He lingers a second, blinks as though he wishes to say something, then starts across the room. At the desk he hands the pencil to the guard, and as he turns for the door Mel sees his light — a symbol of blue, clear and close to the body, but wispy, flickering, as though starved for fuel, a pale blue flame in the wind — and then he is gone, through the door and into the interior of the prison. Mel looks at the guard, who shrugs as if to say, "You know how it is, lady," and then she joins Angie who waits for her at the entrance to the sally port.

Outside, Mel and Angie are silent as they walk to the parking lot. The sky is cloudless, the sun high and unusually brilliant in the crisp air above the foothills to the west. It is a winter day, cold and fixed, and yet there is a hint of spring in this light, a fragile notion. At the car Mel fishes the keys from her pocket, but before she unlocks the door she unfolds the paper in her hand. "I'm sorry . . ." it begins.

1993 Colorado Territorial Correctional Facility
Cañon City, Colorado

Getting Out

In a conversation about this book's design, William Aberg suggested it include a section on release. At first I thought he meant the kind of escape, imaginative or physical, that inmates dream and lie about together in his poem "Reductions" (**Time and Its Terms**) and that shape Johnson's poem here, "Dream of Escape." Imagination is always escape, as M. A. Jones's poems pre- and postrelease testify. In "To Those Still Waiting," he is surprised by the ache of longing that accompanies recall of prison, then by the persistent habit of dreaming of better, even when life is splendid.

But what Aberg had in mind was the difficulty of effecting changes one had promised oneself in prison, the reunion instead with the reprobate self, and the ensuing pain. On the phone, he read me "Devotions,"* in which his striking a match to cook his drug reminds him of his mother lighting votive candles to pray "that I might find / healing, keep healthy, have enough / to eat. That I know how much / she loves me. But that I never come home again." In his poem "Stepping Away from My Father" here, Aberg takes on the grief he caused his father.

Writers wrestle to understand why getting out feels so little like release. In her poem "Stigma" (1996),* Allison Blake struggles to shake off the clinging monster the world imposes on the ex-convict. And with longer sentences and less training and education to prepare for release, it is harder than ever to counter the world's inhospitality.

In "After All Those Years," Ajamu C. B. Haki assesses the internal damage of institutionalization, showing how much easier it is to get out of prison than to get prison out of oneself. On the same theme, M. A. Jones writes in "Coming Out: The Man Who Fell to Earth"*: "To trust another man in prison was to risk my life. Outside it was different. Outside it was just as deadly not to trust, to remain apart. Because I didn't understand that, I stayed apart from other students and after a while I felt as if I were fine. I was free, but I acted like I was doing time." The responsibility of freedom so weighed on him that, unable to talk about his feelings, he returned to drugs — and prison. For others, after so many years, the social world of doing time has come to be the only one they understand.

For these and many other reasons, the exit from prison can be as menacing a portal as the entrance gate. In Robert Rutan's richly ironic story, the protagonist, a "penal commuter," exerts his will not to be taken back. Freedom for him is so bound up with disappointment, prison so identified with dreaming and story telling, that the final outcomes seems both surprising and inevitable.

Dream of Escape

Henry Johnson

The free side of the walls
Night, warmth, a parking lot.

But no keys.

You hear the sirens
shatter the fragile calm,

the yellow stench of fear,
thick and rolling in
like fog

filling every shadow.

The guards scurry out
in force
and they form a line,

their faces painted
beneath their SWAT caps,

brandishing imaginary guns
in the prison yard.

You decide to flee
through the dense woods,
where people line the trail

holding out cups of cold
vintage wine.

In front of you
a wood nymph

insinuates herself
between you and freedom,
promises pleasures

long denied.

You join her
for a few fierce seconds
of tenderness

in a clearing
hidden from all eyes

but the stars.

1987, Sing Sing Correctional Facility
Ossining, New York

After All Those Years

Ajamu C. B. Haki

After being punished
for 10, 15, 25, or more years,
do you think that you'll want to leave?
Can you imagine anything more terrifying
than walking through those gates
without looking back at that great square wall
that kept you in all those years?
Punishing you and comforting you!
Punishing you and comforting you!
Do you think that you will at least miss it?
That somehow, inside, you loved being here
under the tooth mother's wings?
You ain't got to worry about a damn thing!
You ain't got to worry about a damn thing!
You're Amerikkka's greatest son,
the tooth mother's greatest capture.
She has taught you how to bend your knees,
stand up curved back and mop her welcoming floors,
given you paint to embellish her halls of terror —
more terrifying!

And you've been smiling all those years at her morbid green,
her institutional colors, her slavery that fits you.
So do you think after all those years of being trained
that you can just un-train yourself and leave?
That you can enjoy the wonderful colors you've only enjoyed
as a crayoning child?
After all those years behind these gray walls —
the monotony!
The Sunday pancakes, refried french toast, and greasy chicken,
the Mondays you wish they had something edible,
the Tuesday Yakasorbi murder burgers,
the Wednesday killer liver,
the Thursday everything from the last four days mixed
together,
the Friday lumpy oatmeal and fluorescent Kool-Aid,
the Saturday cold cuts you go down to the mess hall just to
look at.
The cycle begins again on Sunday;
and you've gone to the mess hall for every meal,
didn't miss a single meal in all those years.
Now why do you think that you can get used to real food?
Home cooking, a gourmet restaurant,
after you've only had seven minutes to eat
and an ulcer bigger than your heart.
After all those years you still think that you can just leave?
Well, maybe, but remember — even though you leave the
    prison
the prison will never leave you.

    1996, Sing Sing Correctional Facility
    Ossining, New York

Stepping Away from My Father

William Aberg

My father leans toward the green, electric
dials of the transceiver, clicking the Morse key
between thumb and forefinger, talking in dashes and dots
with a man in Magadan, far
eastern Siberia, about how they put fire pots
all night beneath running truck engines to keep the gas
and oil from freezing. How the Sea of Okhotsk,
even now, in late March, is a plateau
passable only in the wake of icebreakers.
My father tells him how an early Maryland spring
has teased the flowers and trees into a bloom
that could still be murdered
by frost. This could be
the conversation of two men in a local
hardware store, arms folded across their chests
as they stand beside the snow shovels and salt shacks
and grouse about insurance, doctor's bills,
the motions of clouds and sun.
My father's face is warm, animate,
his lips silently forming the words
he taps out in code, the signals
flashing over the Atlantic, the skies of Europe,
over the snowy steppe and taiga of Holy Russia.
I, who have stood by the door
waiting to ask for a loan, back quietly
into the hall, not wanting to startle him
out of his easier intimacy with strangers, nor sense
the fear in his eyes when he sees his addict son.

1997, Federal Correctional Institute La Tuna
Anthony, Texas

To Those Still Waiting

M. A. Jones

In Boston, this first October Sunday
I've never felt so far
from where I started, yellow concrete room
looking out over barbed wire, Arizona desert
and out on the prison yard those men I called
brother still play handball, argue drug deals and
imagine a way out. How can I
explain to them this distance, how I've fled
to a city where people move casually
down streets lined with brownstones, maples
and in another week the leaves will flame orange, red.

To those still waiting
where there are no trees and the sunlight
touches reluctantly, how do I describe
the air that enters the window and blouses
the curtains, how in the next room
a woman makes coffee, and stepping
toward me her blue robe falls
open, the light catching a moment
on her breast. She sings a little as she
turns away and I don't think that she
understands much of this, how certain mornings
a part of me drifts back and wants
to sit all day in a yellow room and say
nothing, while believing in a world
that waits elegantly
just out of reach, some place I'd
invent for them if they asked and swear
were true, something more tangible
than the light that falls through the curtains
on an October morning, a woman's voice
that rises from another room,
these things around which my life settles.

1997, Recalling all the prisoners the author has known

The Break

Robert M. Rutan

Clutching the rope and hook in his worn and wizened hands, the old man crawled on his elbows and knees through the wet grass toward the wall. Craning his neck and looking up, up along the wall, up past the guard tower that sat upon it like a mythical monster, a multi-eyed sentinel whose cones of light pierced the darkened prison yard, he saw the gray clouds part and the moon emerge. The moonlight didn't bother him for, as long as he made it to the wall safely, it would make visibility poor within the steam when the time came.

The wet grass had surprised him, and that caused him some irritation: All the years he had watched the steam being blown off from the nearby prison powerhouse, it should have occurred to him that the condensation would dampen the grass. But it hadn't, and he considered his lack of foresight a bad omen. He tightened his grip around the rope and hook and crawled on, on to the base of the wall. Reaching it, leaning against it, he rested, for he was already tired.

The ground and the wall vibrated slightly, carrying the rumble of the huge boilers in the powerhouse. Off in the distance, a barge sounded on the river, its engines droning evenly as it slid through the night. The air was colder than he first thought; he zipped up his jacket and tugged the sleeves to his wrists. Lying on his back, he pulled the rope and hook to his chest and concentrated on the climb he'd have to make. Could he do it? He was an old man, but a determined one: He was going over and that was that. He had been a bull of a man once; now, wintered and weakened, he cursed his decrepitude and longed for his former strength. But he had two things in his favor — a good rope and a good hook.

And that was important. Years ago, when he was doing a ten-year bit in Menard — or was it Statesville? he wasn't sure — he and two others planned a break. He fished his memory for their names but caught nothing. The plan they had was simple, and they kept it to themselves, executing each step with cautious precision. Using an array of excuses, they manipulated the prison administration into housing them in the same cellblock. Once there, they acquired hacksaw blades from a retiring guard who charged them fifty dollars per blade. Each man sawed the bars of his cell almost but not completely through; then, caulking in the outcuts with putty, they repainted them. Next, in similar fashion, they sawed the window bars of the cellblock barber shop. The cooperation of the inmate barber cost another hundred dollars, but it was well worth it as the window led to the prison yard. They made a rope and a hook. From the hospital, they contrabanded skin-tone surgical gloves and three pairs of white pajamas.

Then they waited.

One January night, during a driving snowstorm, they made their move. Each man placed an ingenious dummy in his bed after the cellhouse guard finished the 2 A.M. count. The dummy heads, papier-mâché skulls pasted with human hair, were covered with blankets up to the hairline, while next to them, curled in repose on the pillows, the surgical gloves, filled with water and tied off like balloons, were left exposed, appearing remarkably lifelike. Pants and shirts, stuffed with rags and dirty laundry, lay bodylike under the covers from which feet, formed with toilet paper and covered with socks, extended. After first yanking out their bars with vice grips, they stole to the barber shop, slipped the doorlock, and yanked out the bars there. On the yard, unseen in the whirling snow, wearing the white pajamas over their prison denims, they dropped into a drainage ditch and crawled the fifty yards to the thirty-foot wall. One of the other men, a tall farmboy from Missouri with a glass eye (his name was on the tip of his tongue) tossed the hook up and over the wall; it bit into the opposite side and held true. They were on their way. The other man, the smallest of the three, started up. The rope stretched against his weight, but held. Using the footholds they had tied into the rope, he climbed up the wall; ten feet, twenty feet, almost to the top, when suddenly, irrevocably — the rope snapped.

The old man lay against the wall, shivering, trying to remember the names of the two men. Off in the night he heard another barge laboring against the current. He pressed himself to the wall, seeking warmth. Out of the murky waters of his subconscious two names washed up: Jerry Dayton and Roy Bollinger. That's who they were! He saw their faces clearly, but only for a moment as they slipped back into the dark waters of memory. They didn't make them like that anymore. Pieces of information bobbed up to him: Dayton was killed by the police during a robbery at Springfield; Bollinger died in the electric chair at the old Cook County Jail for the murder of a minor politician. Or was it Dayton who got the chair and Bollinger who was shot in the holdup? It didn't matter. The names were right. After so many prisons, so many jails and reformatories, it was hard to keep things straight, and if he got things screwed up now and then, what difference did it make? He knew hundreds of stories grounded on his long experience as a prisoner and a convict which he enjoyed telling despite his inability to keep facts straight, and the way he saw it, if he tacked on a little embellishment over the years, or if he had the wrong characters in the wrong story, or if he distorted the truth once in awhile so that he hardly knew the truth himself, what difference did it make? And who, now, would know? Or care?

He enjoyed telling his stories; they were his only wealth, and he had hoped to pass them to the boy. The cold night air caught him up, and he winked. Shifting closer against the wall, he listened to the increasing rumble of the boilers. The time was near.

He'd spent many years in this prison, and during his many stays had often watched the steam being blown off. Except for the newer additions, the prison was steam heated. The ancient, enormous boilers sat squat and Buddha-like on concrete slabs in the red-brick powerhouse close to the main wall. The three boilers, all alike and two stories high, rumbled violently, hissed enigmatically, and succeeded in giving the impression that explosion was imminent. At noon, when the convicts were eating in the prison industrial area, the boilers were blown off to let the excess steam escape. At night, the prisoners secured in their cells, the steam was bled every two hours.

From the dining room at noon, or from his cell at night, the old man had often watched the process. It fascinated him. On the black tar roof of the powerhouse, three openings were cut, from which the great steam stacks of the boilers piled seventy feet in the air. The three stacks, thick at their bases and starting flush in their openings, were made of sheeted steel that had been seamed together to rise cylindrically to the sky. When the steam blew, the hot jets rose like vaporous ejaculations whose high density lent them shape, substance, and color. The wail of the steam whistles was a perfect accompaniment, matching pitch with the velocity of the spewing steam. At first the steam rose in single pillars, then mushroomed into distinct caps and stalks. The caps sucked the stalks up, forming balls of steam that turned to clouds of steam that merged eventually to one single cloud that migrated toward the river. As the cloud drifted, gravity and the cooling air brought it down until it hung on the wall, enshrouding it. Only a few minutes passed from the time the whistles blew until the cloud dissipated completely.

Lying on his back, listening to the boilers, he shivered almost uncontrollably as the night cold crept into his bones. He remembered when he was a boy and had fled from an orphanage to take a job on a riverboat, an old sternwheeler that plied the Upper Mississippi between St. Louis and Davenport. Unless the weather was exceptionally cold for an extended period, the river stayed clear throughout the winter. The cold earth below him now triggered the memory of the bone-chilling winter river. He had told the boy about the riverboats and about the men and women who rode and worked them. He told the boy about the river itself, calling it his river and telling him how it wound in a childish scrawl, down through Iowa, Illinois, and Missouri, brown and milky and always contemptuous of its banks, to its confluence with the Missouri River at St. Charles and then down, all the way through the South to New Orleans and the Gulf of Mexico. The thought of the boy was depressing; he forced it from his mind and concentrated on the rumble of the boilers as best he could.

The boy, his daughter's only child, didn't like the old man. On one of his many paroles, he had lived with her and her son, Jimmy. He had been determined to make a friend out of the boy, not only for his daughter's sake and for the harmony of the household, but for his own sake too, as he knew he was old and close to death. Filled with the loneliness of the old that sprang from the inescapable self-alienation of one who wanted to live on despite the realization of approaching death, he saw his chance to do so through the boy. Jimmy, however, a hostile redheaded ten-year-old, resisted him from the start. The boy made it clear that he disbelieved the old man's stories, and the old man, much to his alarm, found himself disliking the youth, a realization that embarrassed him; yet, he persisted in his attempt to win the boy over, telling him wild stories of bank robberies, prohibition, prison riots, great escapes, gangsters, and shoot-outs until he exhausted his repertoire, while the boy, unimpressed, listened with undisguised boredom. He took the boy on walks, on trips to the zoo, to the movies, and to wherever else he thought a boy that age might want to go. Jimmy, an unwilling participant on these expeditions, went only under the admonishments of his mother, who was glad to have them both out of the house. Once, the old man succeeded in taking him fishing.

They fished in a small stream not far from home, and, sitting on the bank in the morning sun, the old man surveyed the stream: beer cans and bottles glinted from the creek bed, their reflections shimmering on the surface; old discarded tires and inner tubes lay filmed in silt, mouthing Os of protest against their abandonment; and no fish, fit to eat, lived there.

He shook his head, saying, "A goddamn shame." He baited his hook with a bloodfat nightcrawler and tried to show the boy how to do the same. But the boy, displaying an irritating squeamishness, refused to follow the old man's lead and lapsed into a sulk, so the old man fished alone. Eventually he caught a small bullhead; its white belly flashed with an oily iridescence as he pulled it from the muddy water. As he elevated his pole the fish swung crazily toward him, dancing on its tail; he reached for it with a slow uncoordinated hand and succeeded only in deflecting it. The fish spun away as he groped after it. The boy laughed at his effort — a deep howling, self-indulgent laughter. The old man turned and saw the boy's face, and the derision and mockery published there. The boy's dull-witted viciousness scared him; yet, at the same time it served to cancel his desire for rapport, and there was some solace in that. He turned from him, gathered the fish in, unhooked it, and tossed it back into the stream where it darted for safety in series of jerks, dissolving in the alluvial depth. Kicking over the can of worms, he tossed his pole and the boy's in some scrub and said, "Let's go." They walked home in silence.

One night, not long after that, he went to a neighborhood bar, got drunk, loud, and cantankerous. The management asked him to leave; he refused; they threatened to call the police, and he responded by throwing a full beer stein at an expensive mirror. The beer leapt in the air and hung momentarily as a droopy mustache of foam that fell with a slosh to the floor. The stein exploded into the mirror, and each burst to slivers and shards that tinkled musically to the countertop running below the mirror. The bartender called the police, who arrived in ten minutes with theatrical verve, having arrested the old man for similar misadventures. The old man, inimical to anything wearing a badge, stood ready to fight. When the first cop drew in range, the old man looped a left hook, but it flew like a hawk on the wing: swooping slowly, banking out and down, and the cop, fifty years younger, simply pulled his head back and let the hawk-hook glide by. The man fell flat on his face. The police dragged him from the bar, but only after he put up a resistance that belied his age, hollering over and over, "Oink, oink, oink."

They took him to jail and charged him with public drunkenness and destruction of private property. The next morning he went to court, his clothes soiled from jail and the fight. The young assistant prosecutor apprised the court of the charges pending, calling the court's attention to the fact that the defendant was a parolee on a life sentence, and though blind, Justice was attentive: With judicious economy the court dismissed the charges and revoked the parole.

That afternoon he was back in prison.

He had been paroled many times. When first convicted of armed robbery some forty years ago, he was tried as an habitual criminal, and as his record was already extensive then, his conviction netted him a mandatory life sentence. (The state's criminal code has since been revised. One of the revisions served to erase the mandatory life sentence clause of the robbery statute; however, the state's supreme court held that the revisions were not retroactive.) The parole board, on the other hand, was sympathetic toward him: his sentence was excessive; he was old, harmless; he had served more time than anyone in the prison system; his prison record was fairly good; and, probably more than anything else, he was a living anachronism, something left over from another age, and they simply felt sorry for him. Hence he was granted a lot of paroles, which, for one reason or another, he would violate and return to prison where he would stay until his next scheduled meeting with the parole board, which usually dispatched him on another pilgrimage to society. He became a veritable penal commuter, shuttling to and fro, from prison to society and back again, and he came to deeply resent the game, the pattern that society chose for him. He became determined to break the chains of conditioning that had held him for so long. But he was quite unable to do that, for the interminable years in prison had thoroughly institutionalized him. He had been polarized by prison steel, and no matter what he did or tried, it drew him like a magnet. Yet, the more it drew him, the more determined he was to exercise his will upon it, and now he had finally found a way. He doubted that there would be any more returns to prison or paroles from prison, for he knew his death was near. Whenever, in the last few years, he did make a parole, he stayed, not with his daughter and the boy, for he knew that they did not really want him, but at a rooming house near the prison and near the river. It was convenient.

He lay against the wall, opening and closing his hands, fighting the numbing cold. This time they would not take him back. He turned up his collar and wished he had a watch. The steam should have blown by now. Yet, despite his waiting, despite his preparation, when the steam whistles shrieked through the night with their deafening howl, he was caught off guard. His heart grew big in his chest and beat wildly. He tried to get up but found that he couldn't move, that he was frozen in the moment. Then it passed, and he scrambled to his feet. He was going over. That was that.

Letting the rope uncoil and fall to the ground, he held the loose end in one hand, with the hook poised in the other. The grappling hook had been wound with gauze and then rewound with electrical tape in the hope that it would hit the wall with a muted thud. He looked up the side of the wall, realized he was too close, stepped back, and locking his elbow and keeping his arm relaxed, he gave the hook a few imaginary practice pitches; then mightily, with every fiber of his being, he let it fly: It sailed into the night and arched magnificently over. The hook bounced on the other side and sent a tattoo of vibration to his hand. Slowly, he pulled it up. A few times it snagged on the rough contour of the wall, but jiggling his end a bit, he got it started again, until finally, two of the steel fangs bit resolutely into the slate lip that capped the wall. A good hold: This rope would not snap. But he had to hurry, for high above the gray, vaporous caps and stalks of the steam, mushrooms appeared against the darkened sky. The moon had vanished.

From the start he felt he wasn't going to make it. He had knotted the rope every eighteen inches which permitted him to stand on a knot, to reach up and to grab hold of the highest knot he could, and to pull himself up to stand on a higher knot. But the going was rough. He had only gone a few knots when the pain began to burn through his arms. His breathing came in shallow gasps, and he had to rest. He started up again: a knot; another. His feet slipped off a knot, and he hung from the rope, his arms stretching in their sockets. The pain raced up and down his shoulders, and his lungs ached to scream. His feet groped wildly for the knot. He turned on the rope, his back to the wall, and the rope came to him. He caught it with his knees, and his feet found the knot. Turning, he started up again. Up and up he climbed. The pain, like fire now, rolled over his back in waves, burned hot and sandy in his lungs, and surged through his legs and arms. It emanated from his chest where his heart pounded erratically, a chaotic drum to whose intense beat the pain quickstepped to every part of his body. Yet, up and up he climbed until, exhausted, he turned his back to the wall and rested, hanging squat and deadweighted, his feet quivering on a knot, sweat beading his forehead.

The whistles shrieked on, on into the night, but their shrillness was gone now, replaced by a tremulous wail that scaled down with the diminishing velocity of the steam. A film of moisture covered him as the steam settled on the wall, already dissipating.

He got off the wall and started climbing again. A knot, another, and another. The great pain, never gone but somewhat abated, returned instantly and fired him anew. But he climbed on. Now he saw the top, but he could hardly grasp the last knot as the angle of the rope and the wall was acute. He worked his hand behind the rope, burning his skin, and pulled himself up so that his eyes were level with the top. With a great final effort he threw his hand, arm, and elbow up and on the surfaced top and pulled himself onto it.

He lay on the wall, the pain pummeling his body, trying to breathe. The top of the wall was wet and slick with the rapidly condensing steam. A new wave of pain fired in his chest, and death edged closer. The cloud had become a thin mist. He had to get down before it vanished. Now. But he couldn't move; he had to rest.

Looking off, he saw the river. His river. At night it held a special appeal for him. It lay quiet and still, hushed in its banks, sliding slowly and silkenly, a lover's hand, sliding yet, ever gently, ever southward, winding down and down, tracing softly in its childish scrawl the way to the warmth of its design: its delta. The moon emerged and caught the river; out, out in its deepest channel, it quicksilvered and shuddered, and from high on the wall, the old man watched with an appreciative eye.

But the river was dying too. Once, running free and wild with a deep and fierce independence, it had had an autonomy that had not escaped his notice, but now, dammed and sluiced, polluted and spoiled, under the indifferent care of the Army Corps of Engineers, subjected daily to the flagrant abuse of industry and the apathy of a disinterested public, it was dying. In the hazy collage of his memory he saw the sickly bullhead and its oily iridescence. He dismissed the image, but the boy's face surfaced. He had left no mark on the kid. When the old man died, everything about him would die too. He had nothing to leave the boy who had rejected the legacy of the stories, and so, with a strange and comforting simplicity, known only to the very young and very old, he willed the boy his river and thought of him no more.

The mist had all but evaporated, but he remained lying on the wall, exhausted. He felt he could take one deep breath, and with its expiration, he could let his life escape from him. But he had known too many Jerry Daytons and Roy Bollingers, too many gangsters and colorful characters to go out like that — it was no way to end a story. What had once run deep in the river still ran deep in him.

He got up quickly. Pulling the rope up, he unhooked it, removed the grappling hook from one side of the slate top, and rehooked it on the lip of the other side. He dropped the rope down the opposite side of the wall and climbed down with a long forgotten sprightliness. When he got close to the ground, which was higher on this side, he dropped to his feet, almost falling. There was no grass on this side, only cinders, and they crunched and shifted familiarly beneath his feet.

Suddenly, in the nearest tower to him, the door flew open, banging against the guardrail that ran around its platform; instantly, all along the line of the wall, all the tower doors flew open, and before he could step from the shallow shadow of the wall, the spotlights had him — an ancient moth, caught in the cones of light. Just above him, to his right, from the near tower, a shotgun shell jacked into its chamber with a terrifying, metallic finality. The sound of the bolts going home to their chambers was repeated all along the line.

"Halt!" the guard in the tower above him yelled. The old man kept on walking. "Hallttt!!!" the tower guard screamed.

Unafraid, the man kept walking. The cones of light made a garish escort. He knew they wouldn't shoot. Not now. *Not going in this direction.* Reaching the harsh daytime glare of the inner prison yard, the cones left him as though he was no longer of interest. The inmates who worked nights in the powerhouse, alerted by the jacking shells, came outside and watched, stupefied. The old man continued to walk toward his old cellblock, wondering vaguely what old friends he might see, what stories he might tell, and selecting one of his favorites, he dusted it off a bit and added a twist here and there. A barge sounded on the river. The even hum of its engines told him it was going downstream.

1978, Iowa State Penitentiary
Fort Madison, Iowa

Death Row

Capital punishment has been at the center of controversy during the final decades of the century. In 1972, the United States Supreme Court struck down the death penalty laws on grounds that they were being applied in an "arbitrary and capricious" manner (*Furman v. Georgia*), violating the U.S. Constitution. The Court passed to the states the responsibility of drafting legislation that either abolished the penalty or reinstated it in a less discriminatory way. More than six hundred people had their lives spared. Thirty-eight states now have capital punishment. The exercise of the penalty continues to discriminate against the poor and people of color. It is our nation's highest-stakes lottery.

There are now more than thirty-five hundred people on death row, and nearly five hundred executions have taken place since the reinstatement of capital punishment in 1973, with a record-breaking seventy-four in 1997. Nevertheless, the abolitionist movement continues to grow. The case of Mumia Abu-Jamal and his writings have drawn many to it. Co-founder of Philadelphia's Black Panther Party and a popular radio journalist very critical of police brutality, he was convicted of murder and in 1982 sentenced to death. (Since Pennsylvania reintroduced the death penalty in 1978, Philadelphia authorities have sentenced to death more than eight times as many blacks as whites.) Then Sister Helen Prejean's account of her experiences as spiritual adviser to the condemned, *Dead Man Walking;* the movie based on her book; and her devoted activism helped to spur the formation of abolition committees across the country. Polls consistently show that support for the death penalty plunges in direct proportion to information about possible alternatives. Meanwhile, the restoration of death rows affects all prisoners, as Judith Clark's poem, closing this volume, shows.

Though from a certain vantage we all sit on death row, some of us know this better than others. The condemned struggle for physical, mental, emotional, and moral survival — and sometimes growth — like other convicts. But, like saints and existential philosophers, they also face the rigorous spiritual test of making annihilation their familiar while remaining human.

With executions multiplying across the land, prisoners awaiting release see the condemned as their doubles in extremis. Prompted by the restoration of the penalty to New York State, Kathy Boudin, in "For Mumia: I Wonder," seeks counsel from one more versed in resisting despair. What do you do with fear, how do you plant hope, she asks, and "how you grow your life / in a row they call death." Those who sit or have sat on the row offer a range of answers.

With remorse so deep and comprehensive it becomes visionary, Stephen Wayne Anderson's dreamlike meditation seems to say. Remorse for his crimes deepens with recall of early sorrow and expands with grief for the executed who have gone before him.

With a questioning sprit, Jackie Ruzas answers, in a haunting meditation written during his trial for a capital crime. The question he puts to the friendly priest drives him away. As Ruzas's whole life fills his empty cell, he poses riddles to himself and the condemning world that few would dare to raise themselves.

With bravado and gallows humor, Jarvis Masters would reply from San Quentin. The split consciousness of time and reality that prevails on death row gives form to his witty poem in which instructions on making prison hooch strictly alternate with the judge's intonation of his own grisly recipe for the poet's execution. Absorbing this ultimate prison toast, one wonders for whom the second cup of pruno is intended — the judge? the reader?

Death row writers are sometimes blessed with a capacity to see human experience whole, to break down imaginative barriers separating their readers from themselves, to engage us despite ourselves. Anthony Ross's story opens with the electrifying image of the condemned protagonist Walker in a coffin surrounded by mourners in dinner dress. As the centerpiece of a public feast, he reminds readers of our complicity in human sacrifice. Walker takes our imaginations hostage, enlisting each of us as his double, and craftily defers his own ultimate challenge to us when he writes: "Imagine seeing the end . . . your end — every day, until you die." Before being executed, Walker refuses the invitation to say any last words. But as the acidic gas seems to ignite his lungs, consuming his last chance to speak, he thinks, "Yeah, I do have something to say."

If, when we catch our breath, we wonder what it was that Walker had to say, we have only to consult ourselves. Ours, after all, is the last word.

For Mumia: I Wonder

Kathy Boudin

I wonder what you do with fear
  do you give it space to float
between the shadows of the bars that crisscross lines
  of mousegray cinder blocks
In the mustard yellow lights does it change
  into moving shapes of ghosts in pale green masks
I imagine
that you let fear flow
  like tears
to wash away the salt it brings.

I wonder how you plant your hope
  do you walk in fields of dreams
or find it in the magic of a spider's web
  in the ceiling corner of your cell,
    in the constancy of seasons,
      in the tenderness
        that somehow
          survives.

I wonder how you grow your life
  in a row they call death
Is it true
not enough hours in the day exist
  to write all the articles in your mind
that sleep takes you away
  from finding legal points to save the
lives of others on your tier
that life is full
when you are full of life.

I wonder what your lessons are
  for those of us who now await
  New York's first execution.

  1995, Bedford Hills Correctional Facility
  Bedford Hills, New York

Easy to Kill

Jackie Ruzas

The door,
I can see its molding if I scrunch in the
left corner of my cell
and peer through the bars to my right.
Each morning I awake
one day closer to death.

The prison priest, a sometime visitor,
his manner warm, asks
"How are you today? Anything I can do for you, son?"
"Is it just that I'm so easy to kill, Father?"
His face a blank, he walks away.

Play my life back on this death cell wall,
I wish to see my first wrong step.
To those who want to take my life,
show me where I first started to lose it.

> 1975, Madison County Jail
> Wampsville, New York

Recipe for Prison Pruno

Jarvis Masters

Take ten peeled oranges,
Jarvis Masters, it is the judgment and sentence of this court,
one 8 oz. bowl of fruit cocktail,
that the charged information was true,
squeeze the fruit into a small plastic bag,
and the jury having previously, on said date,
and put the juice along with the mash inside,

found that the penalty shall be death,
add 16 oz. of water and seal the bag tightly.
and this Court having, on August 20, 1991,
Place the bag into your sink,
denied your motion for a new trial,
and heat it with hot running water for 15 minutes.
it is the order of this Court that you suffer death,
Wrap towels around the bag to keep it warm for fermentation.
said penalty to be inflicted within the walls of San Quentin,
Stash the bag in your cell undisturbed for 48 hours.
at which place you shall be put to death,
When the time has elapsed,
in the manner prescribed by law,
add 40 to 60 cubes of white sugar,
the date later to be fixed by the Court in warrant of execution.
six teaspoons of ketchup,
You are remanded to the custody of the warden of San
    Quentin,
then heat again for 30 minutes,
to be held by him pending final
secure the bag as done before,
determination of your appeal.
then stash the bag undisturbed again for 72 hours.
It is so ordered.
Reheat daily for 15 minutes.
In witness whereof,
After 72 hours,
I have hereon set my hand as Judge of this Superior Court,
with a spoon, skim off the mash,
and I have caused the seal of this Court to be affixed thereto.
pour the remaining portion into two 18 oz. cups.
May God have mercy on your soul.

    1992, California State Prison–San Quentin
    San Quentin, California

Conversations with the Dead

Stephen Wayne Anderson

"These are the graves of the executed ones,"
he announced with a somber, indifferent
kind of respect . . .
and yet later, in quiet reflection,
I understood his tone came up out of
that secret reservoir of the soul which knows
"I, too, could end up as forgotten dust;
I, too, might die for nothing."

Often now I think back upon my journey
through that phantom land: a land caught
like evening haze at dusk, soon to perish
into the gathering darkness of night
but, for one brief moment, beyond time.

I recall its mute, mouthless people,
inhabitants of a dark land whose hopeless,
dying eyes gazed dully at my passage
from their skullish heads. They saw me
only as a traveler who wanted nothing
and took nothing from them. They knew only
that they were not harmed.

I remember the aura which lay like heavy
blankets over that tortured land, an aura
of scarred spirits vanquished by the
horrible vendetta of an angry god.

I remember the excited buzz of feasting flies
as they drank still-warm blood, ate the still-quivering
flesh, and lustfully gorged themselves
on all the disappointments man can devise.

I remember, as if it were now, the picture
of a burned statue of the Virgin Mary
and the image of a small child kneeling

in prayer before it, weeping for a murdered mother
whose name, also, was Mary.

I recall those I, too, have slain:
those by my wrath seized, stolen from life,
becoming but candles lit by children
who became adults before childhood lived.

I recall their dying, their sparks fading,
gone like that: out. Returned to the void.
Nothing.

"These are the executed ones," he said.
I recall standing there alone, filled
by the putrid odor of stinking jungles,
sunscorched deserts, savage streets,
knowing the drowning sensation of my own
awakening, pulling me down into the swirling
cauldron of enlightenment.

I recall how a warm wind brushed my face
and then was gone. I remember touching
a grim stone, experiencing how that dust
had lived: born of anguish to laugh,
make love, and perhaps do it again tomorrow
until at last death came,
speaking of one other place to be
consumed by life: that stopping place
where I, too, found these things.

"These are the executed ones," he stated, eyes
small sparks, and then was gone, dissolving
into the umbra arts of night,
leaving but those sparks which smolder in my soul,
like candles surrounding the powerless and
charred Virgin's image in a chapel.
"These are the executed ones," he announced,
studying a horizon of tombstones. "Pray for them . . .
and for those to come."

1990, California State Prison–San Quentin
San Quentin, California

Walker's Requiem

Anthony Ross

I could see myself in the dark mahogany coffin. How I had gotten there and why was something I couldn't remember. I could hear the hum of an organ playing softly in the background, as mourners began filling the pews of the small church. Most of the faces I didn't recognize, but there were a few mugs I was happy to see, homeboys from the old neighborhood — Big J.T., Lowdown, Spoony, and Spoony's little brother, Klepto, who, at the ripe old age of ten, was already a professional thief. I thought it was strange that they were wearing white dinner jackets and carrying serving plates. Then again, these were guys who'd wake up in the morning and smoke weed for breakfast. They probably thought there were going to be some eats after the funeral. I didn't blame them; these things can be pretty boring. I saw my family seated in the front row. My lawyer, with his secretary, Dora, was sitting behind them. My mother, who never dreamed she would outlive any of her children, looked on, stricken. I felt a pang of guilt.

The sound of the organ began to fade and the faint hush of whispers among the mourners slowly subsided.

Whack! "Now put that back!" I heard Spoony say, as he popped Klepto upside the head. Then they all began to stare hypnotically at the dark-robed figure standing ominously behind the wooden podium. His face was obscured by a large hood, and his hands were gloved. Man, this guy is straight outta the comic books, I thought.

When he spoke, his voice seemed to resonate off the walls of the church, sending icy chills through my skin like an arctic breeze.

"Let us all rejoice in the holy offering!" he bellowed.

Offering? What offering? I thought.

"Let us give thanks to the blessed one," he commanded, as everyone in the church began nodding their heads in unison and shouting, "Thank you, Lord! Thank you, Lord!"

Whooooaaaa! Back up, mister! What fucking offering? This is my goddamn funeral, not a —

"We shall partake of the sacrifice!" he thundered on, followed by another joyous chorus of "That's right, Lord. Thank you, Lord!"

Hey! What the hell is going on here? I tried to scream, but couldn't make a sound. He then beckoned to everyone to gather around the casket, and I could feel them pressing and pushing up against the sides, peering in at my lifeless body, lovingly . . . almost hungrily. Panic set in, and I tried to get up and run, but I couldn't move. *Aw, c'mon — let me outta here,* I pleaded. *I ain't no offering.*

I felt hands caressing and poking my body. Then I saw my little sister and Klepto licking their lips and my lawyer's secretary wiping off her silverware. The dark figure walked to the head of the casket and pulled back his hood. His face was hideous: there was no skin, just bone and pieces of rotting flesh. His mouth was twisted and mangled as he grinned, displaying rows of sharklike teeth, and his eyes were only gaping holes filled with maggots. I frantically looked around and saw everyone changing into grotesque and disfigured creatures. My mother was barely recognizable as she grabbed me by the throat with a clawed hand and began to lift me straight from the coffin. Filled with the horror of what was about to happen, I tried to close my mind to the gruesome scene. . . . I couldn't.

"Now! Let us all feast!" the robed thing said, as he snapped off one of my arms like a chicken wing.

Noooooo! I screamed in my mind, just as the thing that used to be my little sister dislodged one of my eyeballs from its socket with her easybake oven fork and greedily gobbled it down.

My eyes flew open and I quickly sat up in the bunk to survey the small cell. Everything was still. "Damn!" I whispered to myself. "You gotta get a grip, man." Dreaming is one thing, but this shit is ridiculous. Some would claim this was guilt eating away at my conscience . . . fuck them! I bet that prison shrink would have a field day analyzing my dream. *Fuck him, too.*

I looked out the small window directly in front of my cell. It was dark outside, making things seem almost peaceful. But that was an illusion. There was nothing peaceful about prison, nothing serene about death row, and at that very moment certain preparations were being carried out that placed me at the center of it all.

My name is Nathan Cole Walker; Nat Cole for short, a nickname my grandmother gave me on account of her fondness for the singer Nat King Cole. Personally, I can't hit a note and rap music is my thing. I must admit, I did have a smooth style that infatuated the young ladies. But that was eons ago and a helluva lot has changed since those days.

In less than twenty-four hours it will be my twenty-fifth

birthday, but there will be no celebrating, no party, no happy nothin'. Because I'm not gonna live to see it.

Six years ago, I was sentenced to death. The whys don't matter now, and the particulars aren't important. Today I have run out of time, destiny has come kicking at my door, and I am scheduled to be executed promptly at eleven thirty Wednesday night. It is now Wednesday morning . . . my last day on Earth.

I tried to shake the dream from my head, before beginning my routine of pacing the six-by-ten cell. It's a mode of controlling the rage of the half-man, half-animals we've become. A silent way of expressing our malediction at being caged. It is never escape — respite, maybe — but never escape.

"Anything wrong, Walker?" the guard who was posted outside my cell asked. He had been watching me from the moment I woke up, jotting down his observations on paper.

"Naw, nothin' I can't deal with," I shot back in disgust.

"What time is it?" I asked the guard. He glanced up from the *Playboy* he had stashed between the pages of a *National Geographic,* rubbed his eyes, and looked at his watch.

"It's almost six thirty." He yawned. "Just about time for me to be gettin' outta here," he added, with apparent relief. Six thirty was the shift change; another guard would be taking his place for second watch in a few minutes. I resumed my pacing.

Anyone put on death watch is provided with around-the-clock security and scrutiny, compliments of the Department of Corrections, just in case you decide to skip the scenic route to the gas chamber, in an attempt to cheat the state out of its judicial duty to personally kill you. The guard who would be coming on for second watch was named Ford. I had known Ford over the years; he was okay, as guards go. Sometimes we'd get in a game or two of chess, or shoot the breeze to break the monotony. When you're waiting to die, the boredom alone could kill you.

I could hear Ford locking the door.

"How's it going, Ford?" I said, still looking up at the ceiling.

"Not too bad, Walker. And you?"

"Same old tune." There was silence for a moment.

"You wanna get in a game of chess later?" he asked, trying to sound cheerful. We both knew we'd played our last game.

"I don't know — maybe."

"Well, if you do, just holler." He turned to his paperwork and I shut my eyes in a futile attempt to shield out reality. My mind was like a movie screen.

"Nigger, you got somethin' to say before I end you black ass life?" I didn't say a word as I watched the cop pull his pants leg and reach for the gun that was strapped to his ankle. I let the Glöck slide easily down my sleeve and into my hand. By the time the cop realized a gun was pointing at him, it was too late. The first bullet tore through the front of his neck and the second one entered his right eye. He died before hitting the ground. The scene repeated itself over and over. After all these years, that one event still seemed like it happened yesterday.

The ringing of the phone brought me back. "I'll ask him, hold on. Walker, it's Chaplain Graves," Ford said, with an ear-to-ear grin. "You wanna see him?"

"Fuck him!" I said. I sat up on the bunk and grabbed a book from the pile on the floor. It was Ralph Ellison's *Invisible Man*. I could relate to the main character, because all my life I've been invisible to folks. The only time they seemed to take notice was when I got into trouble. No one really knew me, not even my family — hell, I didn't even know myself. Everything I did brought me close to death, toward this very moment. I once read somewhere that desperate men are always running out of time. Well, right now, I must be truly desperate.

I must have read for almost an hour before putting the book down. I was just about to close my eyes when Ford asked, "Say, Walker? If you want, I can call the Muslim chaplain or something. I mean, in case you wanted to speak to someone."

"Thanks, but no thanks."

"Well, I just thought you might want to talk to somebody who can understand — well, who can relate to — you know what I mean?"

"I know what you mean, Ford."

"Say, Walker? Are you afraid of dying? I mean, I can't even imagine how I would feel in your place."

I thought about it for a moment, but I already knew my answer.

"Naw, I ain't afraid of dying. Dying is something I've been doing all my life. But when you know when and how it's gonna happen, all it takes is that one step over the edge inside your head — then bam! That's why most men are able to walk to their execution. They're already dead inside their heads."

"That's a helluva way of looking at it, Walker."

"I don't need to get nothing off my chest. And if there is a God out there, then he's gonna have a lot of fucking explaining to do when I reach the hereafter."

We both laughed; then there was a long pause. Empty of anything else to say, we both went back to what we were doing. I was tossed back to old times, and it wasn't long before I dozed off.

"Hey, Walker! Walker!" I heard my name being called from far away.

"Whaaat . . ." I mumbled, still half in the dream state.

"Walker. Someone here to see you," Ford said apologetically.

"Who?" I demanded, fully awake now.

"Doctor Cohen."

"Doctor Cohen?" I tried to place the name. Cohen was the prison shrink. This was his third visit; the first two times I simply ignored his ass.

He pulled the extra chair from the desk and planted it in front of the cell. We were face to face with the cell bars between us.

"What's up, Doc?" I smiled.

"How are you feeling today, Walker?" He always started off with the same stupid ass question, trying to sound as sincere as possible.

"Well, you caught me in a good mood today, Doc. I was just about to start playing with my dick . . . but what can I do for you?"

"I came by to see how you are doing."

"For cryin' out loud, all of a sudden everyone is concerned about my fucking welfare. What gives?"

"I'm just doing my job, Walker," he stated matter-of-factly.

"And what is that, Doc?" He looked at me, puzzled.

"Well, to talk, mainly."

"About what?"

"About emotions you're feeling, about things that may be going through your mind, or dreams you may be having." His mention of dreams caught me off guard, and I wondered if I had talked in my sleep.

"Dreamt I walked on water, Doc," I said sarcastically.

"Walker, I understand that under the circumstances it's normal to feel anger, but you don't have to be confrontational."

"Wrong! That's my style, man, plus I like testing seersuckah-suit mothafuckahs like you, just to see that geek look you get on your face." I burst out laughing; he just sat there, turning beet red. His mouth opened and closed, as if he were trying to find something to say.

"Okay, Walker, you crazy bastard!" he whispered through clenched teeth, trying vainly to maintain his clinical composure. "If you want to play fucking games —"

I immediately stopped laughing and sprang to my feet, cutting him off. I had him and he knew it.

"Game! Naw, this is far from a fucking game, Doctor. Here the stakes are much higher."

"Well, then, what would you call it?"

"I call it . . . my personal responsibility to upset bullshit mental tacticians like yourself. You waltz in here doing your friend routine, thinking you'll become famous at my expense by getting me to expose the juicer morsels of my brain — so you can jump in front of the camera seconds after I'm dead, claiming you were the only one I would talk to, the only one I trusted."

"Walker, that's not true," he said, nervously shaking his head. "I would never do anything like that."

"Tell me, Doc, when were you planning on cutting a book deal — while the dirt was still moist on my grave, or after it dried?"

"I'm telling you, Walker, no such thing has ever crossed my mind. Nothing that's mentioned here will go beyond these walls. I'm a professional doctor, for Christ's sake!"

"When you look at me, all you see is an experiment . . . some data that might make you famous. But you sit there confident, grinning inside, never realizing that by trying to look into my head, you incriminate yourself, just like all the others who will watch me suffocate, watch me slowly, painfully, pass into nonexistence. My death will render me not guilty, but it illuminates your guilt, your savage necrophilia. I'm every bit as human as those who seek to strip me of my humanity."

He sat there looking like a kid who just got busted bang with his hand in the cookie jar. If I had been in doubt, his eyes convinced me that my words had hit their mark.

He stood abruptly, began to walk toward the door, hesitated, and then left. I lay back on the bunk with my hands behind my head, staring at the ceiling.

"What time is it, Ford?" I called out.

"Ten twenty," he called back.

My lawyer, Duncan Brock, would be coming around noon, as he did every day. He was the only person I still cared to talk to. "Ten twenty, "I said to myself. *You're gonna be a statistic, Nat Cole, in less than fifteen hours.*

I lay there for about thirty minutes. I had already resigned myself to the fact that the courts weren't going to give me any action. All this waiting around was starting to make me edgy.

The phone rang. Ford answered it.

"Walker, your attorney is here. They're on their way to pick you up."

"All right, thanks."

Two guards escorted me to the small room where they allowed me to visit. When I walked in, Duncan Brock stood up to greet me. We shook hands warmly, then sat at the small table. He looked tired, and I knew he had probably slept only a few hours in the last four days. His otherwise immaculate suit was rumpled, his hair halfheartedly combed, and there were noticeable dark spots beneath his eyes.

"How are you holding up, Nat?"

"So-so, but you look like you been mugged." We both smiled. Duncan was one of the few people left in the world I truly respected. Over the years we'd had our share of differences but always managed to work them out. It made us respect each other as persons, as friends. I felt sorry for him. He had done his best, yet I thought he was always going to feel that there was something more he could have done. Even in these final hours, Duncan was optimistic.

We talked about how my family was doing, and about the people outside the prison protesting my execution. Then he began to tell me about the legal strategies he was trying.

"Listen, Nat, I filed a new writ with the Ninth Circuit Court challenging —"

My thoughts began to drift, and images floated through my mind. "Son, where are you going?" "To basketball practice, Momma —"

"I talked to one of my law professors and he thinks —"

"Momma, Nat hit me —"

"— also the Supreme Court could —"

"Homeboy! Nat Cole is straight crazy —"

"— other options that legally —"

"Mrs. Walker, we've arrested your son for —"

"— the main thing is the constitutionality of —"

"You are hereby sentenced to be put to death in the —"

Like a motion picture the scenes came and went, until one thing remained; the words *The End*.

We sat there exchanging small talk until a guard showed up at the gate, announcing it was time for me to go back. We stood and embraced each other.

Then the guard motioned me to him. I walked over, turned around, and he put the cuffs on and opened the gate to escort me back upstairs.

"Take care, Duncan," I said.

"I'm not going to give up, Nat!" he said strongly. I didn't answer. I knew this was the last time we would see each other.

Back at my cell, it was a little after four o'clock. The phone had been installed right outside, a direct link to my lawyer for good news . . . or bad.

It was almost six o'clock when Ford called to me. At first my mind couldn't compute the reality of his question. I was stunned by its finality, even though I knew they would ask me.

"Walker, the warden wants to know what you'd like for your last meal."

I didn't say anything. My mind locked on the question. The concept loomed like a giant neon sign, pushing all other thoughts to the side, until it alone remained. *Last meal!* Hell, how in the fuck was I supposed to enjoy something like that? My stomach did some gymnastics and I knew there was no way I was going to be able to eat anything. The very thought of crapping on myself while choking to death was enough to deter me from eating. When they pulled me out of the chamber, my drawers were going to be clean.

"Fuck that, man. I don't want nothin'!" I told Ford.

"Sure?"

"Absolutely. I don't want shit!" I could imagine the warden's expression. He'll probably try to send that shrink over here. But I doubt he wanted to see me again. I got off the bunk and began pacing again. I also started singing every song I knew in my mind, but after a while, I would sing the first verse, then nothing . . . hum a few notes, then nothing. It was like the words were just vanishing from my memory. Verses got mixed up, songs became intertwined. I finally gave up.

"What time you got, Ford?"

"Seven thirty-five."

"I need to use a pencil and paper."

"No problem." He went in his desk and got out some sheets of paper and a small pencil that had been broken in half, for my supposed safety.

I rolled my mattress back so I could use the flat steel bunk as a table. I was going to write one last letter, but instead found myself just sitting there, staring at the paper. After about an hour of scribbling on several sheets of paper and tossing them into the toilet, I finally wrote something. I titled it *A Seminar in Dying*. It was a poem, the kind only a desperate man could write.

> Imagine seeing the flash of a camera, and in that same instant you
> witness the most violent and brutal scene of your life.
> Imagine seeing a contorted face, broken limbs, blood flowing.
> Imagine the terrified screams, the unbearable pain, the pleas for help,
> the tears.
> Imagine death, as you fall to your knees, embracing a dying body . . .
> your body.
> Imagine that last look, that last word, that last touch . . . that last
> breath.
> Imagine life the day after, the week after, the year after . . . the hereafter.
> Imagine seeing that camera flash in your sleep and your waking
> moments
> . . . over and over, every second, every minute, every hour, in
> your mind.
> Imagine seeing the end . . . your end, every day, until you die . . . imag-
> ine.

It was all I had left in me. I folded the paper, got an envelope from Ford, and addressed it to my lawyer.

"Make sure he gets this after — you know, when things are over."

"He'll get it, don't worry."

Sometime later, the phone in front of my cell rang. I just stared at it, uncertain of what to do.

"Answer it," Ford said, enthusiastically. I reached gingerly through the bars and picked it up.

"Yeah?" I whispered.

"Nat?" It was Duncan. He sounded exhausted.

"Yeah?" I whispered again.

"Nat, the courts turned us down, but —"

I put the phone down, not hanging it up, just laying it on its side. I could hear Duncan still calling my name, but there was nothing else to say, nothing else to hear.

"What time you got, Ford?"

"Eleven-o-five." Just then, the phone on his desk rang. The sudden change of his expression told me everything.

"Walker," he said solemnly, as he hung up the phone.

"Yeah, I know." They were on their way to get me. This was it — time to face the matador.

"You want some more orange juice or something, Walker?"

I just looked at him. I knew he was trying the break the overwhelming sense of dread that had started to condense like storm clouds around us. I looked down at my feet. I didn't recognize them. They seemed like independent machines separate from my body, and they would of their own volition lead me right to the gas chamber. Looking away, I thought, *I would hate to have to whack you guys off.* I put my shoes on and splashed some cold water on my face. I took a piss, washed my hands, and combed my hair — but as I was combing it, I was struck by the realization that everything I was now doing would be my last time doing it. I suddenly felt completely alone; my heart started to thump somewhere in my throat.

"Walker, it's time to go." The warden and two guards were waiting like stone sentinels. I walked over to the bars, consciously controlling each step. One guard put the cuffs on through the tray-slot. Ford opened the gate and, as I stepped out, I nodded to him slightly. He nodded back. I walked slowly, my breath hard. The sound of it echoed in my head like giant waves. I turned to the warden.

"Do me a favor, Warden?"

"What is it?" he asked, bewildered.

"Well, do you think we could make this long walk short?"

"How?" He looked even more confused.

"By running!" I said and burst out laughing.

They all looked at me like I had just snapped, Ford included. They stood there, uncertain of what to do next.

"Aw, c'mon guys, it's a joke," I said. "I'm just trying to ease the gloom. Hell, the way you dudes look, a person would think you're the ones about to get x'ed out."

"Walker, how can you joke at a time like this?"

"Yeah, you're right, Warden. So when do you think would be a good time for me to joke?"

Then, looking him straight in the eye, I asked him seriously, "Warden? When was the last time you been to a circus?" But I didn't give him time to answer. "Let's go," I said. "There's one waiting for us."

We walked out into a long, narrow hallway.

The warden stuck a key into a slot where the buttons should have been and turned it. It took a few seconds for the door to open and I could hear the elevator lumbering toward the top. The door opened suddenly with a whoosh, and we all stepped in. The guards positioned themselves behind me, while the warden remained at my side. It had all been rehearsed, their roles, the parts they would play. I imagined them practicing it. I wondered who they got to play me.

The elevator stopped and the door whooshed open. We stepped into a smaller hallway, made a right, and walked toward a large green steel door. I thought I could hear a murmur of voices on the other side and I imagined rows of people drinking soda, eating popcorn, and chanting, "Kill him, kill him, kill him!"

The warden pressed a button this time, and a few seconds later the door popped open. As we walked in, my entire body grew hot and the palms of my hands started to sweat. The first thing I saw was the gas chamber.

Everything became dreamlike and every second was an eternity. My mind went numb, my throat bone dry. This was my first real look at the chamber — I stood there, my eyes transfixed on the cylindrical shape and the chair sitting directly in the middle. The feeling of déjà vu hit me again, this time much stronger. Now don't get the wrong impression — I didn't all of a sudden get religion. But when dying is the central theme of your life, your perspective on things can change. I don't think it's an issue of whether or not we're afraid of dying — it's more like being afraid of not having existed, you know what I mean? I guess that's why people tend to believe in things like reincarnation, heaven, and transmigration, because those things offer a sense of continuity or immortality. Hey, life after death sure beats ashes to ashes.

"Let's go, Walker," the warden said, taking hold of my arm. We walked to the door of the chamber. One of the guards pulled open the door and, as I stepped in, the air was stale and oppressive. I swear I could sense the men who had gone before me — that somehow I could feel them still in that room. If my mind was playing a trick on me, it was a damn good one.

I sat down hypnotically. The chair was hard and cold. The two guards began immediately to strap me in, wrists first, then my waist and legs. My eyes were wide, alert, as if trying to suck in the last images of life. They darted around the chamber seeking anything . . . everything. The cubicle was spotless, almost as if all trace of reality itself had been vacuumed out. It was the only place I had ever been inside prison where there was absolutely no graffiti . . . no "Kilroy was here," no "Jesus loves you," no gang writing, not so much as a scratch. I guess anyone coming in here ain't in a position to do nothing but die — and the only thing that will ever deface these walls will be the souls of dead men. The warden double-checked the straps after the guards had finished. Then in a well-practiced monotone, he asked, "Do you have any last words, Walker?"

Ignoring his question, I swallowed the large lump that had formed in my throat and stared straight ahead at the dark glass window in front of me. I knew there would be people sitting on the other side, waiting to watch my death. Well, enjoy the show, folks, I said to myself. The warden asked me again if I had any last words. I said nothing, still staring at the window. He then proceeded to tell me in the same flat voice how the sentence of death was being carried out by order of the court. When he had finished, he and the two guards left without looking back. I heard the latch locking the door, and except for my breathing, there was absolute silence. I pulled against the strap — nothing. I knew it was useless at this point, but still . . .

I could feel my muscles tightening, as my pulse vibrated throughout my entire body. An eternity seemed to pass as I sat there, waiting for something to happen. I kept thinking that they were going to come through the door at any second. My eyes were frantically searching the window for any movement. Finally, I closed them and let my head fall back. I felt some sweat or a tear rolling off my cheek. I opened my eyes just in time to catch it falling from my face, and as I watched it fall in slow motion, I suddenly tasted something bitter and acidic in my mouth, and my lungs seemed to ignite into flames. Without even thinking about it, I quickly held my breath and, at that very moment, I knew that once I let it go, it would all be over.

With each second, the pain in my chest grew more unbearable — inside I was on fire. I began spinning and tumbling, my head falling backward and forward. I could feel the explosion in my chest heaving upward, as the pain began to burst into a billion pieces of light . . . and then I was falling, falling toward the sky, higher and higher, until I could no longer see beneath the clouds, until darkness began to engulf me. It was almost over. "C'mon, Nat, warp speed, man." *Yeah,* I thought, *I do have something to say* . . . then I felt the rush of warm wind, and I breathed out.

1995, California State Prison–San Quentin
San Quentin, California

"Write a poem that makes no sense"[†]

Judith Clark

Marlene squatted on the hospital rooftop
agitated, wary
her frayed bonds with life
ready to snap, while

below, a rush of blue and gray uniforms
pleading voices, as her
sister convicts
piled mattresses on the ground
that saved her
   when she leapt
       over the precipice

Today, guards tramp on that roof
and under it,
workmen erect walls within walls
seal openings
to air and light
tear apart the old balcony to
build a steel mesh and iron cage

Death row
they are building
death row

here,
at Bedford Hills
on the third floor of the hospital
next to the nursery

a shadow
over the wide-eyed infants,
   robust toddlers,

[†] An exercise given by Hettie Jones at the Bedford Hills Writing Workshop.

a curse upon their mothers,
   all of us

Marlene rests quietly
her wounds heal
but the mad fury that drove her
is loose

sweeping over the prison
   through this land
waiting to taste first blood

no mattresses next time
no mercy

     1995, Bedford Hills Correctional Facility
     Bedford Hills, New York

Notes

Introduction

p. xiv   Like slave ... Auburn prison. Scott Christianson, *With Liberty for Some: 500 Years of Imprisonment in America* (Boston: Northeastern University Press, 1998), pp. 265–69.

p. xiv   In July ... hunger strike. Tom Wicker, *A Time to Die* (New York: Quadrangle, 1975), pp. 6–8.

p. xv   Penologists Andrew ... United States. Andrew von Hirsch, *Doing Justice* (New York: Hill and Wang, 1976); Robert Martinson, "What Works? — Questions and Answers about Prison Reform," *Public Interest* 35: 22–54; cited by Christianson, pp. 277–78.

p. xv   People of ... drug crimes. A. Blumstein, "Racial Disproportion of U.S. Prison Populations Revisited," *University of Colorado Law Review* 64: 759.

p. xvi   As former ... ever seen." *Prison Life* (January–February 1996): 38.

p. xvi   In 1980 ... their keepers. Joycelyn M. Pollock, *Prisons: Today and Tomorrow* (Gaithersburg, Md.: Aspen Publishers, 1997), pp. 255–56.

p. xvi   "a predatory ... more overtime." Victor Hassine, *Life Without Parole: Living In Prison Today* (Los Angeles: Roxbury Publishing Company, 1996), pp. 31, 37, 65.

p. xvi   But physical violence ... brutal treatment. Interview with Ellen Barry, October 22, 1998.

p. xvii   The incidence ... rights protests. *All Too Familiar: Sexual Abuse of Women in U.S. State Prisons,* Human Rights' Watch, Women's Rights Project (New York: Human Rights Watch, 1996).

p. xviii   Yet, as ... whole communities. Elliot Currie, *Crime and Punishment in America* (New York: Metropolitan Books, 1998), pp. 5–10.

p. xix   "To be ... be listening." Kathrin Perutz, "P.E.N. and Prisons," *Witness: Special Issue: Writing from Prison* (Fall 1987): 149.

p. xx   The bibliography ... through 1981. H. Bruce Franklin, "An Annotated Bibliography of Published Works by American Prisoners and Ex-Prisoners," *Prison Literature in America: The Victim As Criminal and Artist.* (New York and Oxford: Oxford University Press, 1989), pp. 291–341.

p. xx   Under Reagan ... gone under. Joseph Bruchac, "The Decline and Fall of Prison Literature," *Small Press* (Jan./Feb. 1987): 28–32.

p. xx   Now, with ... been suppressed. McGrath Morris, *Jailhouse Jounalism: The Fourth Estate Behind Bars* (Jefferson, N.C.: McFarland and Company, 1998). See *Life Sentences: Rage and Survival Behind Bars,* eds. Wilbert Rideau and Ron Wikberg of *The Angolite,* New York: Times Books, 1992, and *The Ceiling of*

America: An Inside Look at the U.S. Prison Industry, eds. Daniel Burton-Rose, Dan Pens, and Paul Wright of *Prison Legal News,* Monroe, Maine: Common Courage Press, 1998.

Routines and Ruptures

p. 48   The beat . . . Fernandez. A 1970s study group in Greenhaven Prison found that over 75 percent of the New York State prison population came from just seven New York City neighborhoods. *Prison Life* (October 1996): 50.

Work

p. 71   *You ought . . . the men.* "Ain't No More Cane on This Brazis." Sung by Ernest Williams and group, Sugarland, Texas, 1933. Recorded by John A. and Alan Lomax. Library of Congress Music Division, Archive of American Folk Music.

p. 71   Some historians . . . in 1796. See Christianson, pp. 94–106. Christianson argues that the replacement of penal slavery with racial slavery was legitimized through the Thirteenth Amendment. See also H. Bruce Franklin, "Introduction," *Prison Writing in 20th-Century America* (New York: Penguin, 1998), pp. 1–20.

p. 72   Founded in . . . goods annually. Pollock, 124.

p. 72   Since 1990 . . . private companies. Florida Corrections Commision, 1997 Annual Report, p. 1.

Reading and Writing

p. 97   In prison . . . high school. The Center on Crime, Communities, and Culture, "Research Brief: Education As Crime Prevention" (September 1997): 4–5.

p. 98   Women in prison . . . the results. For example, the women at Bedford Hills Correctional Facility have published *Breaking the Walls of Silence: AIDS and Women in a New York State Maximum Security Prison* (New York: Overlook, 1998).

p. 98   "A lack . . . to empathize." *Small Press* (Jan./Feb. 1987): 87.

p. 98   In "Colorado . . . of react." *Prison Life* (June 1994): 46.

Race, Chance, Change

p. 175   In the . . . white person. Comprising 9 percent of the general population but 16 percent of prisoners, Hispanics are the fastest-growing race behind bars. Marc Mauer, *Responding to Racial Disparities in Prison and Jail Populations* (The Sentencing Project: Washington, D.C., 1998), pp. 1–2.

p. 175   "I've heard . . . old biases." Richard Stratton, "Common Ground," *Prison Life* (October 1994): 3.

Family

p. 218   Even if . . . but failed." Bruchac, *The Light from Another Country: Poetry from American Prisons* (Greenfield Center, New York: Greenfield Review Press, 1984): p. 151.

Getting Out

p. 285   On the . . . home again. *The Listening Chamber* (Fayetteville: University of Arkansas Press, 1997).

Death Row

p. 301   (Since Pennsylvania . . . as whites.) *United States of America: Rights for All* (New York: Amnesty International Publications, 1998), p. 109.

Text Credits

Aberg, William: "Stepping Away from My Father," "Siempre," and "Reductions" from *The Listening Chamber* by William Aberg. Copyright © 1997 by William Aberg. Reprinted by permission of the University of Arkansas Press.

Amberchele, J. C.: "Mel" and "Melody" copyright © 1999 by J. C. Amberchele. "Melody" first appeared in *Oasis* 2 (1993).

Anderson, Stephen W.: "Conversations with the Dead" copyright © 1999 by Stephen W. Anderson.

Antworth, Scott A.: "The Tower Pig" copyright © 1999 by Scott A. Antworth.

Baca, Jimmy Santiago: "Coming into Language" from *Working in the Dark: Reflections of a Poet of the Barrio* by Jimmy Santiago Baca. Copyright © 1992 by Jimmy Santiago Baca. Reprinted by permission of Red Crane Books. "Ancestor" from *Immigrants in Our Own Land* by Jimmy Santiago Baca (Louisiana State University Press, 1979). Copyright © 1999 by Jimmy Santiago Baca. "Letters Come to Prison" copyright © 1999 by Jimmy Santiago Baca.

Blake, Allison: "Prisons of Our World" copyright © 1999 by Allison Blake. First appeared in *Concrete Garden* 4 (1996).

Boudin, Kathy: "For Mumia: I Wonder" copyright © 1999 by Kathy Boudin. First appeared in *Concrete Garden* 4 (1996). "Our Skirt" copyright © 1999 by Kathy Boudin. First appeared in *Aliens at the Border* (Segue Books, 1997). "A Trilogy of Journeys" copyright © 1999 by Kathy Boudin.

Bratt, Larry: "Giving Me a Second Chance" copyright © 1999 by Larry Bratt. First appeared in the *Washington Post*, May 19, 1996.

Buck, Marilyn: "Clandestine Kisses" copyright © 1999 by Marilyn Buck. First appeared in *Concrete Garden* 4 (1996).

Clark, Judith: "To Vladimir Mayakovsky" copyright © 1999 by Judith Clark. First appeared in *Aliens at the Border* (Segue Books, 1997). "'Write a poem that makes no sense'" copyright © 1999 by Judith Clark. First appeared in *Prison Life*, February 1997. "After My Arrest" copyright © 1999 by Judith Clark. First appeared in *Prison Life*, August 1996.

Culhane, Chuck: "Autumn Yard" copyright © 1999 by Chuck Culhane. First appeared in *Witness*, fall 1987. "There Isn't Enough Bread" copyright © 1999 by Chuck Culhane. First appeared in *The Light from Another Country: Poetry from American Prisons* (Greenfield Review Press, 1984). "After Almost Twenty Years" copyright © 1999 by Chuck Culhane. First appeared in *Candles Burn in Memory Town* (Segue Books, 1988).

Falcone, Anthony La Barca: "A Stranger" copyright © 1999 by Anthony La Barca Falcone.

Fernandez, Raymond Ringo: "poem for the conguero in D yard" copyright © 1999 by Raymond Ringo Fernandez. First appeared in *The Light from Another Country: Poetry from American Prisons* (Greenfield Review Press, 1984).

Grindlay, J. R.: "Myths of Darkness: The Toledo Madman and the Ultimate Freedom" copyright © 1999 by John R. Grindlay. First appeared in *Confrontation*, no. 15 (fall 1977/winter 1978). Courtesy of Genevieve Grindlay.

Haki, Ajamu C. B.: "After All Those Years" copyright © 1999 by Ajamu C. B. Haki. First appeared in *Candles Burn in Memory Town* (Segue Books, 1988).

Hassine, Victor: "How I Became a Convict" from *Life without Parole: Living in Prison Today* by Victor Hassine. Copyright © 1996 by Victor Hassine. Excerpted by permission of Roxbury Publishing Co., Los Angeles.

Hogan, Michael: "Spring" copyright © 1999 by Michael Hogan. First appeared in *Letters for My Son* (Unicorn Press, 1975).

Hunter, Michael Wayne: "Sam" copyright © 1999 by Michael Wayne Hunter. First appeared in *Columbia*, no. 28 (1997).

Jaco, Roger: "Killing Time" copyright © 1999 by Roger Jaco. First appeared in *Creative Righters Anthology, 1978–1980* (1981). Courtesy of Gladys Jaco.

Johnson, Henry: "The Ball Park," "The 5-Spot Cafe," and "First Day on the Job" copyright © 1999 by Henry Johnson. First appeared in *The 5-Spot Cafe* (Castillo Cultural Center, 1990). "Dream of Escape" copyright © 1999 by Henry Johnson. First appeared in *Candles Burn in Memory Town* (Segue Books, 1988). All works courtesy of Mary Johnson.

About the Authors

(Unless otherwise indicated, prizes mentioned below were awarded in the PEN Prison Writing Contest.)

William Aberg (1957) grew up in Maryland, from which, he reports, he fled to the Southwest to escape arrest for a series of drug-acquiring crimes. Caught and imprisoned in Arizona, he entered Richard Shelton's writer's workshop which, he says, transformed his life. "Many of my poems are extreme icons of emotional exile: separation, hopelessness, needle and spoon. Others arise from humor or reverie, or a combination of the two. Ultimately, they arrive out of necessity." He earned an A.A. degree from Pima College in Tucson. His first sentence, from 1978 to 1984, in an era of revitalization in prison programming, contrasts sharply, he says, with a second (for possession of World War I rifles) from 1994 to 1997. "The deadness in the eyes, the psychic numbness, of prisoners and staff was appalling."

"Reductions" won first prize for poetry in 1982. *The Listening Chamber,* published in 1997 by the University of Arkansas Press, won the University of Arkansas Poetry Award. Living in the Washington, D.C., area, Aberg now plays bass in local bands and is working on one book of short stories and another of verse. He is an amateur photographer and Russophile.

J. C. Amberchele was born in Philadelphia (1940) and attended a Quaker school, then colleges in Pennsylvania and New York, earning a B.A. in psychology. "A drug trafficker for fifteen years," by his own account, he has served time in a Mexican federal prison as well as in Colorado and Minnesota. He began writing early in his sentence, borrowing instruction books from the prison library. "Writing began for me as a desire to be heard, to be accepted, but soon moved into a form of self-discovery that eventually became mind-opening." After a long fallow period, "it appears about to begin again. I don't know where it will take me. My passion now is Buddhism and Christian mysticism, and perhaps this will play a part." With other prisoners in Colorado Territorial Correctional Facility, he helped to start a literary magazine and a writer's workshop, which along with other programs, were canceled in 1992.

Published in *Quarterly West, Writer's Forum, Blue Mesa Review, Portland Review,* and *Oasis,* Amberchele has also won three fiction prizes — first prize for "The Ride" (1990), second for "Melody" (1992), first for "Mel" (1993). He is searching for a publisher for a collection of short stories.

"Born in St. Louis (1953) and raised in New Mexico, I was passing through California when I shot someone during an eighty-dollar bungled burglary and found myself a permanent resident," **Stephen Wayne Anderson** writes from San Quentin's death row, where he has been since 1981. "That residency grows short; my lease is coming due." Having ignored education as a youth, he is making up for it now. He reads and enjoys Emerson and Dickinson, Tolstoy and Dostoyevsky, Coleridge and Stephen King. "I received a book whose footnotes were *all* in Latin and became thoroughly pissed off. I invested in a Latin course so as to read them. By the time I taught myself enough of the basics I no longer had the book which had caused my original motivation."

"Conversations with the Dead" won first prize in poetry in 1990; "Friday Crabs" won second prize for poetry in 1991; he published a third poem in *Sojourner* in September/October 1989. "A sentence of death made me realize the value of life, and of living."

Scott A. Antworth (1965) was born and raised in Augusta, Maine. After serving four years in the army, he was arrested in 1987 and has been incarcerated ever since. In prison he earned a B.A. in social sciences from the University of Maine. He plans to study for a master's in social work after his release.

Antworth's *Lawn Sale of Truth* tied for third prize for fiction in 1997. "I've been writing for as long as I can remember," he says, "but only started getting serious at it a few years ago, when some wonderful guidance transformed what would otherwise have been empty time." He names Hemingway, Paul Theroux, and Jaimee Wriston Colbert as having had the greatest impact on him. His work has appeared regularly in *Flying Horse* and in two collections — *Trapped Under Ice* (1995) and *Frontiers of Justice, Vol. 2* (1998) — published by Biddle Publishing Company.

Jimmy Santiago Baca (1952) was born in Santa Fe of Chicano and "detribalized Apache" parents. In "Coming into Language," he describes how he learned to read and write in prison at twenty years of age. Even while he was in the hole, he read everything he could. Pablo Neruda and Emily Dickinson, he says, are the writers most important to him. In 1976, he won an honorable mention for "Letters Come to Prison," and a few years later, with Denise Levertov's encouragement, he published *Immigrants in Our Own Land*. Writing "has enabled me to rise from a victim of a barbarous colonization to a man in control of his life," he says. "All of us who went to prison were lied to, and poetry is the only thing that didn't lie. Everything that is not a lie is poetry. In order to bring order to our world, we were forced to write.

Writing was the only thing that could relieve the pain of betrayal, the only thing that filled the void of abandonment."

For twenty years, Baca has made his living by writing. In 1988, he won the American Book Award for *Martín and Meditations on the South Valley.* His film career was launched with *Blood In, Blood Out,* a movie about Chicano life, partly filmed in San Quentin. Now he volunteers teaching English in poor neighborhoods around Albuquerque. Forthcoming are a novel, two books of poems, and three films.

Allison Blake (1947) was born and raised in Manhattan. Incarcerated for a white-collar crime, she began to write creatively for the first time in Hettie Jones's writing workshop at Bedford Hills. Her poem "Prisons of Our World" was published in *Aliens at the Border.* She also received her state legal research certificate, and later, at Albion Correctional Facility, became the first inmate to teach the state legal research course; 90 percent of her students passed the state exam as compared with 33 percent previously.

Her play *Jailhouse Lawyers,* born out of her own experiences, won third prize for drama in 1996. She published other poems in *Concrete Garden* and *A Muse to Follow* (National Library of Poetry, 1996). She now works for a lawyer as a paralegal. Her impulse to write seeming to have expired with her sentence, she is studying digital art. Allison Blake is a pen name.

Kathy Boudin (1943), born and raised in New York, her mother a poet, her father a civil liberties lawyer, is a Bryn Mawr graduate. Incarcerated at Bedford Hills Correctional Facility, she has earned a master's degree in education from Norwich University in Vermont. She has also been involved in a range of activities involving mother-child relationships, parenting from a distance, AIDS and women's health, and higher-education programs. In writing, she finds "enrichment and survival of current experience, a path toward facing past tragedies and anchoring onto her inner self while in a whirlwind of activity."

"A Trilogy of Journeys" shared first prize for poetry in 1998. Other writings have appeared in two volumes from the BHCF Writing Workshop: *More In Than Out* and *Aliens at the Border* and in *Prison Writing in 20th-Century America.* "Participatory Literacy Education Behind Bars: AIDS Opens the Door" appeared in the *Harvard Educational Review* (Summer 1993) and she is editor and one of the primary authors of *Breaking the Walls of Silence: AIDS and the Women in a New York State Maximum Security Prison* (Overlook, 1998). Her essay "Lessons from a Mothers Program in Prison" appeared in *Women and Therapy* (1998), and with

Rozann Greco, she edited *Parenting from Inside/Out: Voices of Mothers in Prison.*

Baltimore-born (1942) **Larry Bratt** writes, "I started conscious life as a student and progressed to soldier to criminal to writer." While serving a life sentence in Maryland, he works as a literacy tutor and a facilitator for the Touchstones Discussion Project, a program that teaches prisoners critical thinking. He attributes the beginning of his self-rehabilitation to the discovery of yoga; he became a Buddhist, but now is converting to Judaism. He admires the work of Kahlil Gibran.

For "Prisoners: The Forgotten Illiterates," Bratt won second prize for nonfiction in 1997; in 1995 he received an honorable mention for nonfiction. *Prison Life* awarded him a second prize for nonfiction in 1995. In 1997 he was a semifinalist in the Faulkner Society personal essay competition. He has published extensively in *Yoga Journal* and the *Washington Post,* and more recently in *Nyt Aspekt,* a Danish self-help magazine.

Texan **Marilyn Buck** (1947) became politically active when she was eighteen, awakened by struggles to end the war in Vietnam and fight oppression of black people in the U.S. Convicted of several politically motivated conspiracies and acts — including the freeing of Assata Shakur, who lives in Cuba under political asylum — and of attacks on the U.S. military establishment, her sentences add up to eighty years. She has been incarcerated for more than seventeen years.

"Because prison is a mechanism to repress and control people, I write to retain my voice and to encourage others to lay claim, or hold on, to their own voices — to scream, if necessary. For women in particular, the silence of self-censorship is suicidal. I believe that women must continue to demand our full equal participation in reconstructing the world's societies to be safe for ourselves, our children, and our communities. Only then can justice, equality, and human dignity be achieved. I look to writers like June Jordan, Audre Lorde, Mitsuye Yamada, Nawal El Sadawi, Margaret Randall, among others, who with their words reflect both the realities of oppression and the possibilities of liberation."

Buck's essay "Censored Women Speak" tied for third prize in nonfiction (1992) and was published in *Phoebe.* "Clandestine Kisses" appeared with other work of hers in a special issue of *Concrete Garden,* devoted to women. In 1998, she won an honorable mention for poetry.

Judith Clark (1949) grew up in Brooklyn, New York. By her early teens, she was deeply involved in social protest movements. "Unwilling to heed the moderating influences of aging, changing conditions, or even motherhood," she says, she was arrested in October 1981, for participating in an attempted robbery of a Brinks truck, in which three people were killed. She is serving a sentence of seventy-five years to life in Bedford Hills Correctional Facility.

"In prison, faced with the deadly and destructive consequences of violence and group-think, and groping for a way to reclaim my humanity and sustain a relationship with my child, I discovered the power of the word, first through reading and then through writing."

"To Vladimir Mayakovsky" won second prize in poetry in 1993. " 'Write a poem that makes no sense' " won first prize in 1995 and was published in *Prison Life*. "After My Arrest" was published in *The New Yorker*. *IKON, Global City Review*, and *Aliens at the Border* have also included her poems. Clark earned a B.A. and an M.A. in psychology while in prison. She teaches prenatal and parenting classes to pregnant women and new mothers who live with their babies in the prison's nursery program. Her articles on mothers in prison have appeared in the *Prison Journal* and *From Zero to Three*. She helped write *Breaking the Walls of Silence* (Overlook Press), about the AIDS Counseling and Education Program at Bedford.

When Bronx-born (1944) **Chuck Culhane** and two other prisoners were being transported from Auburn Prison to court in 1968, one prisoner killed a deputy and lost his own life. Culhane and the other prisoner, Gary McGivern, were convicted of felony murder and sentenced to death. After the Supreme Court temporarily abolished capital punishment laws in 1972, Culhane and McGivern refused a plea to manslaughter and were sentenced to twenty-five years to life. Released in 1992 with a B.A. and most of his M.A., Culhane teaches a college course in criminal justice. Vice president of Western New York Peace Center's Prison Action Committee, he is working on "abolition of the death penalty and the liberation of the innocent, the not-so-innocent, and the downright guilty who've paid their price.

"Initially writing was a defense against the crushing isolation and pain I felt when I started doing time at nineteen. I was partly inspired by a fictional biography of Arthur Rimbaud, who ironically *stopped* writing at nineteen. I was in the 'hole' at Elmira in 1964; prisoners were allowed to write one letter a week. I was given a pencil for one hour to write my letter. Afterward, I'd scribble rhymey stuff on the backs of envelopes — self-pitying, syrupy crap." Reading "the masters, like Whitman, Neruda," taught him his craft.

Culhane won first prize in poetry for "Of Cold Places" (1987) and second prize for "After Almost Twenty Years" (1986). He also received prizes for drama (1990, 1988), fiction (1989), and nonfiction (1988). His work has appeared in *Prison Writing in 20th-Century America, The Light from Another Country,* and *Candles Burn in Memory Town.*

Anthony La Barca Falcone (1961) grew up in Gravesend, Brooklyn, and attended Kingsborough College. What pushed him along as a writer? Sylvia Plath, William Blake, and Coleridge, "and my sister told me my written thoughts sounded like nothing I'd ever said, it sounded like poetry." Now serving time at Coxsackie Correctional Facility in New York, he says, "I write for myself, to try to understand why I am so sad and lonely, why I can't seem to get out of my own way, why I chase away anyone who seems to get too close — and because I love words."

His poem "A Stranger" won an honorable mention for poetry in 1996.

Born in Puerto Rico, **Raymond Ringo Fernandez** (1949) says, "I grew up in Brooklyn and kind of died in Vietnam 1968–69. I've always wanted to write, sing, entertain, but growing up Rican, not to mention being the oldest son, wasn't exactly conducive to the arts. For many years I was macho just to please my father. I was a bad ass Brooklyn bum with a rep that led me to jail time and time again. Half my life has been spent behind bars." But most of what he learned, he says, came from taking advantage of his incarceration. "Prison is a hard-edged life, authority is capricious, thoughts are contraband, and writing is a serious, deadly business which I love. Never mind all the time in the hole that prison writers get. To me it meant that my voice was a voice to be reckoned with."

Fernandez won first prize for drama in 1988 for *If This Is Serious, Why Am I Laughing,* based on the exchange of prison "toasts" between Whitey, Indio, and Black. His play *Looking for Tomorrow* won an award from the New England Theater Festival. He has offered readings and promoted AIDS awareness in the Save Our Youth program. "PEN takes the cake," he says, "because it encourages an involvement between the prison, the writer, and the subject, perhaps because the folks at PEN realize that prison life does indeed force involvement and that that involvement is life-saving."

J. R. Grindlay (1949–93), born in Elizabeth, New Jersey, was educated in Westfield and Scotch Plains; "He was so bright," his mother, Genevieve Grindlay, recalls, "that teachers let him take over the class in grammar school." Honorably discharged after serving in Vietnam, he was attending Livingston College of Rutgers when he was convicted of manslaughter.

"Myths of Darkness: The Toledo Madman and the Ultimate Freedom" won first prize in fiction in 1976 and was published in *Confrontation.* "In a bleak, unchallenging existence it's all too easy for the mind and will to atrophy. A man needs to create his own goals and to consciously force himself to work toward them," he wrote to PEN about the effect of the contest on prisoners. "For many men, writing serves to fill that need, and to provide a means of expression unlike any many of them have ever known." The contest "gave me a focal point to direct my energies toward. I felt less isolated; more a part of the real world." Upon release, he completed his B.A. in English. His poem "Steal the Dawn" was published in the *Hudson Review* in autumn 1977.

The mother of **Ajamu C. B. Haki** (1969) died giving birth to him on the Caribbean island of St. Vincent. He was raised by great-grandparents until the age of ten when he came to the United States. He grew up in Brooklyn. "That's where my education began," he writes, "in school and in noticing the perils of urban lives." He had finished high school and started college and was a boxer training for the '92 Olympics when he was arrested. "All I had to keep me sane in prison was my typewriter and my mind," he writes. "Writing had to become my lover and friend, my guide and adviser." Edgar Allan Poe's work inspired him to emulation, until he found his own voice. His poem "Turned Out on 42nd Street" won first prize for poetry in 1996.

"My life has been marked by great sweeps of changing fortune," writes **Victor Hassine** (1955). Exiled as Jews from Egypt in 1956, his family relocated as refugees in France, then in 1961 in Trenton, New Jersey. Hassine earned a B.A. from Dickenson College in Pennsylvania, and a J.D. from New York School of Law. His American dream ended with a murder charge and a sentence in 1981 to life without parole. At Graterford, he says, "My first efforts at self-expression consisted of an almost death-defying activism" that challenged "longstanding inmate leaderships and practices as well as the might of the prison administration." Hassine founded the first accredited synagogue in an American prison. With others, he filed a conditions of confinement lawsuit, which resulted in $50 million in improvements to Graterford. Transferred to Western Penitentiary just after a brutal prison riot there, he joined another lawsuit, resulting in $75 million in improvements to Western. He also headed the prison's chapter of the NAACP.

Hassine was "too angry, frightened, insecure, and ashamed" to think of becoming a writer until his first poem — provoked by a young convict's suicide attempt — won an honorable mention in 1987. Two first prizes in nonfiction and two honorable mentions each in nonfiction and drama followed. The nonfiction led to his writing *Life Without Parole: Living in Prison Today*. His play *Circles of Nod* challenges the purpose of the death penalty; an all-inmate cast performed it in Rockview Prison within two hundred feet of the death chamber. Most influential writers: Viktor Frankl, Jerzy Kosinski, and Michael Ondaatje.

New Englander **Michael Hogan** (1943) moved to Arizona in his early twenties where he was later convicted of forgery of state supreme court documents and sentenced to fourteen years in prison. In 1975, while in a writing workshop with poet Richard Shelton, Hogan received first prize in poetry for "Spring." The following year he became the first prisoner to win an NEA Creative Writing Fellowship. In 1977 his sentence was reversed and he was released.

From the University of Arizona Hogan received a B.A. in literature and an M.F.A. in creative writing. For several years he was Poet in the School in Arizona, California, New Mexico, Utah, and Montana and conducted creative writing workshops in prisons in Washington and Colorado. In 1993 he earned a Ph.D. in international relations and Latin American studies. He currently teaches and lectures in Costa Rica, Colombia, and Mexico, where he makes his home. His twelve books include a history of the Irish Battalion in Mexico, a book of short stories, and several collections of poetry.

"I believe that words are like snakes we sleep with," Hogan writes. "If we honor them and respect them, they will protect us from the darkness which surrounds us. If we do not, then we are in real danger both as individuals and collectively as a society. As a reader I know that poetry gave me sustenance in the dark night of the soul. As a writer I hope to give some of that vital energy back."

Michael Wayne Hunter (1958) was born and raised in Sunnyvale, California, joined the navy, and spent four years operating computer systems on a carrier-based S-3A jet aircraft. Honorably discharged, he worked as an electronics technician in San Francisco until 1982, when he was arrested for murder. Five days before being sentenced to death row, he married a coworker from the computer company. Writing to his wife every night until they divorced five years later acquainted him with writing, he says. Then a legal secretary who had been reading his letters to lawyers urged him to write professionally.

"So like many misadventures of men, this one started with an attractive woman telling me she thought I could do something. No one was more surprised than I when my first story, 'Mother Teresa on Death Row,' was published by *Catholic Digest*." When another story was published in *Prison Life* along with Susan Rosenberg's "Lee's Time," which had won a PEN award, "I was struck by her courage in addressing the virulent racism behind bars. "Without 'Lee's Time,' there would have been no 'Sam,' so Susan has in a way contributed twice to your anthology. The PEN awards allowed me to set aside commercial ventures and try to do my best writing." "Sam" tied for first prize in fiction (1995).

For the past two years, Hunter has been working on two book-length manuscripts, one of which has been optioned for a movie.

Roger Jaco (1944) was born in McMinnville, Tennessee, one of nine children — all the boys given names beginning with R. At a young age they lost both their parents in an automobile accident. The children were scattered, Roger placed in a home in Kentucky. His sister Gladys, always impressed with his high intelligence and his artistic bent, remained in contact with him. After Jaco had completed his military service, he joined Gladys in Virginia. When he was imprisoned for armed robbery, Gladys bought him a typewriter to encourage him.

With that typewriter, he wrote a story that won first prize for fiction in 1979; Jaco wrote, "In a world where I am reminded of only my faults while being expected to give my best, hopes are not easily grasped. Until I began writing, I never met myself . . . Now that I can see myself more clearly, I have discovered that the world contains other humans, all with feelings, trucking toward visions of something more meaningful." His poem "Killing Time" took an honorable mention in 1980 and was published by Janet Lembke in *Creative Righters Anthology, 1978–1980*. When his writing about prison officials falsifying records led to his manuscripts being confiscated, PEN protested, and the prison backed down, Lembke recalls. "Through my writings," Jaco wrote in 1981, "I began to discover how great and ornery I really am."

Jaco's current whereabouts are unknown. His sister attributes his love of roaming to his artistic nature.

Saxophonist **Henry Johnson** (1949–1996) of Brooklyn wrote that workshops with Joe Bruchac, Paul Corrigan, and Judith McDaniel stimulated his interest in writing: "I believe that the good in man will ultimately overcome the shadier side. In the meanwhile, I'll keep composing lullabies for the sun." In Sing Sing, Johnson earned a B.A. in sociology from Skidmore College, a master's of professional studies in ministry and pastoral counseling, cum laude, from New York Theological Seminary, and an M.F.A. in poetry from Vermont College. Chaplain's assistant and leader in the Alternatives to Violence Project, he also taught literacy and led poetry workshops in Sing Sing.

Johnson won second prize for poetry (1982), honorable mention for nonfiction (1988), and the Madeline Sadin Award in 1985. He published in the *New York Quarterly, Light from Another Country, Candles Burn in Memory Town,* and two chapbooks: *The Problem* and *The 5-Spot Cafe* (1990, Castillo Cultural Center). Upon release, he worked briefly for the Fortune Society. Janine Pommy Vega, Johnson's prison workshop teacher, recalls his visit to Woodstock in 1990. "It had begun to snow, he didn't have proper boots. We stopped in a secondhand bookstore. He spotted a book by Browning. 'I love this guy!' he said, and bought the book. As we walked out in the snow, I had to laugh. There he was, huge and very dark, in thin shoes in the snow, grinning and clutching that book to his heart. 'Hank!' I said, 'look at you! This is the story of your life!'"

Writing and drugs overlap for **M. A. Jones**, who writes: "Addiction facilitated my incarceration; writing helped to free me. I felt (and still feel) a particular sensitivity or openness to emotional pain. Narcotics, for me, served as 'medicine.' When they were unavailable, I discovered language. In James Baldwin's story 'Sonny's Blues,' his brother asks Sonny, a heroin addict and jazz musician, whether he needs dope to play music. Sonny replies 'It's not so much to play. It's to *stand it,* to be able *to make it* at all.' Listening to Sonny play with his band, the brother discovers how music affords Sonny a means to transform his personal anguish into art.

"Today I am clean. I have finished graduate school and I am working toward a doctorate. As an English instructor in a Boston-area university I teach the Baldwin story to my students, who at first 'don't get it.' Like Sonny's brother, they resist understanding; if they struggle with the story, however, they learn something about human pain and art and how art — making it, responding to it — affords insight into our own suffering and joy, these things that make us human."

M. A. Jones won second prize in fiction (1978–79), first in poetry for "Overture" (1980), and third in poetry for "Prison Letter" (1981).

Robert Kelsey (1953) was born in New York, raised in northern California, and educated at the Putney School in Vermont. He worked as a carpenter and had his own sawmill, until a drunken driving accident landed him in a New York prison for second-degree manslaughter. Paroled to California, he took Amtrak, "a wonderful contemplative experience after seven years locked up." He is completing a B.A. at the University of San Francisco. Only in prison, with the encouragement of a community college teacher, did he take writing seriously, confessing in a class paper, "Writing is the therapist I never leveled with, the woman who never understood me, the father who never paid much attention to me."

"Suicide!" won first prize in fiction in 1994. Kelsey has also published in *Virginia Quarterly Review,* the *Sun,* and *Massachusetts Review,* among others. His "Mother and Child Re-Union" was listed in "Notable Essays of 1993" in *Best American Essays, 1994.*

After the murder of Martin Luther King in 1968, the family of **Reginald S. Lewis** (1954) moved from riot-torn Richmond, Virginia, to Philadelphia. There Lewis joined a gang called Twelfth and Oxford Street, "one of largest and fiercest in Philly," says Lewis. Later he would join the Nation of Islam. A high-school dropout, he got his G.E.D. in Rahway State Prison in New Jersey, where he was the Rahway State welterweight champion. Paroled in 1981, he attended Temple University for one year, then was convicted again in 1983 and sentenced to death.

"Reading has always been my greatest passion." He admires James Baldwin, Sidney Sheldon, Toni Morrison, Richard Wright, and Langston Hughes. "When I received the death penalty, the pain and humiliation spurred an emotional torrent of words. Writing is my life, my spiritual connection to God. Like all writers, I yearn to write the literary masterpiece that would hurl me into immortality, in the company of the literary legends."

Lewis won first prize in poetry for "In the Big Yard" (1988), third prize in nonfiction (1987) and tied for third place in drama (1998). From death row, he has published articles, poems, plays, in the *Philadelphia Daily News, Bitterroot International, North Coast Xpress,* the *Other Side,* and *Maine in Print,* among others. He has a still-unpublished collection of poems called *Leaving Death Row.*

Lori Lynn McLuckie (1961) was born and raised in suburban New Jersey "with the rich cultural influence of Manhattan only a short drive away." She attended Antioch University in Yellow Springs, Ohio, earning a B.A. in literature in 1984. In 1988, she began serving a sentence of forty years to life for first-degree murder. "Although I can see the majestically awesome Rocky Mountains from my cell window, I desperately miss the East Coast."

"Trina Marie" won first prize for poetry in 1992. Writers McLuckie admires are "Charles Dickens, for his wit; Ernest Hemingway for his style and imagery and for showing me how I would like to sound; Ayn Rand for her brazen ideas; Bob Dylan for his magical poetry; Stephen King for his insight into the human psyche; Oliver Sachs for his faith in human nature." She is currently at work on a novel.

Jarvis Masters (1962) was born in Torrance, California, and raised in a series of foster homes in southern California. In and out of institutions from the age of twelve, a series of holdups led him to San Quentin in 1981. There he was convicted of conspiracy in the 1985 killing of a correctional officer. During his death penalty trial, he happened on the writings of Tibetan Buddhist lama Chagdud Tulku Rinpoche. "For a long time I was my own stranger," Masters writes, "but everything I went through in learning how to accept myself brought me to the doorsteps of dharma, the Buddhist path." In *Finding Freedom: Writings from Death Row,* he describes Rinpoche's visits, his own meditation, and becoming a "peace activist" among the condemned.

"Recipe for Prison Pruno" tied for third prize for poetry in 1992. Masters finds writing to be "a way of expressing my human worth and a means for helping others both inside and out of the nation's prison system." Masters's work has appeared in *Brotherman: The Odyssey of Black Men in America; Where the Heart Is; The Awakened Warrior: Living with Courage, Compassion, and Discipline; Utne Reader;* and the *San Francisco Chronicle.*

After **Diane Hamill Metzger** (1949) finished high school near her native Philadelphia, she postponed college, intending to go on in a few years. "But then life blinked," she says. She married a man who then killed his ex-wife during a custody fight, while Metzger and her then-infant son were outside in the car. Although she had done no violence, she says she did aid her husband in the coverup and was a fugitive with him and their baby for over a year before being arrested in Boise, Idaho. For accomplice liability, she received a life sentence. In Pennsylvania, there is no parole for lifers, and, Metzger says, only thirty out of three thousand lifers have had their sentences commuted in the past twenty years.

Among other awards, Metzger has won citations from Pennsylvania's House of Representatives and Senate for being the first female to earn a baccalaureate degree (in political science) while incarcerated. She also holds an A.A. in business administration, certification as a paralegal, and a master's in humanities/history. She won honorable mentions in poetry (1978, 1988), third prize in fiction (1981), and first in poetry (1985) for "Uncle Adam." First published at age twelve, she has work in *Pearl, Anima,* and *Collages and Bricolages,* as well as her own chapbook, *Coralline Ornaments.*

Vera Montgomery (1936–1992) was born, raised, and died in Newark, New Jersey. Beginning in her teens, she spent much of her life in Edna Mahan Correctional Institution for Women in Clinton. "No one could forget Vera," Lois Morris, former assistant superintendent says. "She was very bright and had a delightful sense of humor, though from the administrative point of view, she was a management problem. Her philosophy was that rules were made to be broken." When the Supreme Court mandated that prisons have law libraries, Montgomery became a full-time jailhouse lawyer, helping other women with appeals and representing them in disciplinary hearings.

Montgomery had "absolute integrity and fought like a fiend for what she thought right," according to her attorney, Raymond A. Brown, who represented her successfully in a case involving escape and assault. Montgomery became director of the Inmate Legal Association. Jennie Brown, then a member of the State Advisory Board of Control, knew Montgomery well. "She developed herself in prison, she became a talented tailor and a leader. Being fearless, Vera was always prepared to help staff with an inmate in crisis."

"solidarity with cataracts" won first prize for poetry in 1976. Albert Montgomery remembers his favorite aunt as "no follower, but a good-hearted person and a loyal friend. And she was always creative." Near the end she told him she wanted to write a book.

Writer **Robert J. Moriarty** (1946) was born in Schenectady and raised in the West. His military records show that as a U.S. Marine fighter pilot, he won forty-one air medals from July 1968 to March 1970 in Vietnam and three Distinguished Flying Crosses in addition to several honors from South Vietnam. He was also distinguished for having started flying combat as a twenty-year-old second lieutenant and becoming a captain at the age of twenty-two. Five years after leaving the service, Moriarty became a transoceanic ferry pilot and a part-time long-distance racer. His logbooks show twelve thousand hours total time, more than two hundred forty transoceanic crossings, and first place in two New York-to-Paris air races flying his favorite Bonanza V-35. On a lark, he became the first man to fly between the arches of the Eiffel Tower on March 31, 1984; *Air-Space* published his account in October 1996.

"Pilots in the War on Drugs" took first prize in nonfiction in 1989 and "Against the Prohibition of Drugs" won second prize in 1990. How did he become a writer? "I just sat down and started writing." He has also published in aviation magazines and currently runs a successful Internet business.

Paul Mulryan (1954) born in Fort Sam Houston, Texas, and raised in Savannah, Georgia, was arrested in Batavia, Ohio, for aggravated robbery and gun charges in 1983 and has been in prison ever since. At Lucasville, he studied printing and industrial electricity and took three years of college with an emphasis on art, writing, and music theory as well as liberal arts prerequisites. Now working and apprenticing at Mansfield Prison in the electric shop, he also paints and teaches music theory for guitar.

"Eleven Days Under Siege: An Insider's Account of the Lucasville Riot" won first prize in nonfiction in 1995. It was first published in *Prison Life,* as did one of his paintings. Mulryan says he has no favorite writers, though he has always been moved by Sylvia Plath's poetry.

Patrick Nolan (1963) of "Cabbagetown," an Irish neighborhood in Toronto, grew up in boys' homes and on the street, and went to prison for three years at age sixteen. After two years of freedom, he says, "I gave up on life. Instead of ending what I commonly refer to as my wretched exist-ence I took the coward's way out, taking the life of another." At Folsom Prison, he spent two years in the hole, reading and writing essays about what he felt. "The person who changed my life was Viktor Frankl — his book, *Man's Search for Meaning.* I also fell in love with the writings of Martin Luther King Jr. and Henry David Thoreau. When I was finally released from the hole I had only one purpose — to transform my life." There was no arts program, but Nolan and others started a poetry workshop, with poet Dianna Henning as instructor. "In poetry I have found a process to look inward and find meaning to what I considered an otherwise meaningless life." Among influences, he cites Robert Bly, Robert Hayden, Etheridge Knight, and Jimmy Santiago Baca.

"The Family Outing" tied for third place for poetry in 1997. Nolan has also taken prizes for poetry in the William James writing competition, and for drama in *Prison Life.* He has published in *Psychological Perspectives, Poetry Flash, Tule Review,* and *Rattle.* For the past year he has facilitated his own poetry workshop.

Charles P. Norman (1949) attributes his storytelling ability to his grand-mother, who told him tales of pioneer life in Texas, where he was raised. At the University of South Florida, he studied finance, writing, and romance languages. After his marriage fell apart, he got involved in bank fraud and was arrested and was convicted of a murder that occurred three years pre-viously. Serving a life sentence in prison, he won a MENSA scholarship, which enabled him to continue his college education. He also studied busi-ness, graphic arts, the printing business, and horticulture, and puts these skills to work in prison. He has taught computer classes and writing and worked as a teacher and counselor for four years in a prisoner self-help pro-gram and two more in a bootcamp for first offenders.

"Pearl Got Stabbed!" won an honorable mention for nonfiction in 1992; Norman has also won prizes for other nonfiction and for his plays *Why Me?, Hang, Man,* and *Tattoo Blues.* The last won first prize from *Prison Life.* His plays have been read and produced at PEN award ceremonies and in Florida prisons.

When **Judee Norton** was born in 1949 in an Arizona farm town, her father was a twenty-two-year-old farmboy, one of ten children, her mother "a fifteen-year-old beauty with the look of gypsies about her," one of thirteen children of itinerant fruit-and-cotton pickers. Norton and her four siblings battled a legacy of "addiction, poverty, low self-esteem, and a general sense of bewilderment about the business of living." Her own battles led her to Arizona State Prison, Perryville, to confront her demons. Instead of a demon, she writes, she found "a little girl cowering under the covers waiting for the next blow to fall. All I had to figure out was how to get her out of prison in one piece and I did that by writing."

She has won two first prizes in fiction, for "Summer, 1964" (1988) and for "Norton #59900" (1991). The two pieces are part of a larger work, *Slick,* "fictional reflections on how and why I made bad choices."

William Orlando (1953), a war baby, half Korean, half black, was adopted but ran away from a strict home in Los Angeles. "I had a criminal record before a mustache," he writes. "At seventeen, I strolled into the army. Saw Germany and next met heroin in Vietnam. Came back a dope-shootin' bank-robbn' fool. I've spent the shank of my life in prison. Those are the bare bones. The rest is apologia."

"Dog Star Desperado," an excerpt from a novel, tied for second prize in fiction in 1997. Part of Orlando's second novel, *Chino,* was published in the *North American Review* in November/December 1997. "As a square peg kind of kid, I read for transport" — works like Beowulf and novels by London, Stevenson, and Twain — "until I learned to smoke and drink and cuss and fight and swagger in leather to a raucous dice game, and street life claimed me from the books." In prison, he earned a B.A. in sociology, studied Spanish and German, and reads omnivorously, finding "gems among the rhinestones" of prison libraries. "Reading made the writer. That, and the crucible of experience. Writing is all I have, a lament and a boast."

Alejo Dao'ud Rodriguez (1962) was raised first in the Bronx, New York, then in East Los Angeles and Pomona, California. He is serving eighteen years to life for murder. While incarcerated, he received a B.A. from Syracuse University and a master's in professional studies from New York Theological Seminary. "I daydream a lot so I guess I've always written poetry in my head," he writes. "Daydreams are hard to explain to people, sometimes hard to explain to myself. Writing them out is sort of like giving daydreams a life longer than a fleeting thought. Yet writing is a double-edged sword for me. I love to write, but I hate the rules of grammar — too restricting. That's why poetry likes me. She encourages me to take liberties and sometimes they even turn out to be a poem."

"Ignorance Is No Excuse for the Law" won an honorable mention in 1997.

When he was sixteen, **Daniel Roseboom** (1972) put his rural hometown near Cooperstown, New York, behind him to travel alone. After several arrests for petty crimes ("nonviolent and non-drug-related — freedom was my high"), he was sent to a shock incarceration camp at seventeen. Escaping, he fled west, until caught in Missouri and extradited to New York. Months in solitary and keep-lock confinement to his cell for the escape introduced him to books and to writing. While in Auburn, he took Syracuse University courses. Compared to the "intense atmosphere" of those classes, his courses in the world seem "a shame." Since release, he has become a self-employed building contractor.

His first experiment in writing, "The Night the Owl Interrupted," based on a real experience, won third prize for fiction in 1993.

An activist in the student, antiwar, and women's movements in the 1970s, New Yorker **Susan Rosenberg** (1955) studied at City College of New York and Montreal Institute of Chinese Medicine, becoming a doctor of acupuncture and traditional Chinese medicine. Targeted by the FBI for her support of the Black Liberation Army, she went underground in the 1980s. In 1984, she was convicted of possession of weapons and explosives and sentenced to fifty-eight years. Spending almost eleven years in isolation and semi-isolation, she says, "I write in order to live in the most creative, productive, and challenging way available to me. Prison life is stripped to the bone, and all the good and bad is held up in the sharpest light. I watch and listen and struggle with what I see in order to write about it. This forces me to remain conscious of the suffering around me and to resist getting numb to it."

Winner of first prizes in poetry (1991), fiction (1992), and memoir (1994) as well as two honorable mentions, Rosenberg has published in many anthologies and has two poems in *Rattle* (Winter 1998). She has written about women casualties of the drug war and has adapted "Lee's Time" for film. She is studying for an M.A. in creative writing with the McGregor School of Antioch University.

As a child, **Anthony Ross** (1959) wrote "butchered versions of 'Little Red Riding Hood,' 'Hansel and Gretel,'" but his ambition was to be a cartoonist. At twelve his life became entangled with the gang life of his native L.A. and "whatever could go wrong, did go wrong." In 1981, at the age of twenty-two, he was arrested and subsequently received the death penalty. He is currently in San Quentin Prison.

A high-school dropout, he took advantage of academic courses until the education programs were eliminated for death row prisoners. With his codefendant, "we studied on our own, writing every university, organization, church, bookstore, and small mom-and-pop press we can find asking for free literature," eventually amassing "a formidable library." At times, they have been forced to write with stubs of pencils and the flexible ink-cores of pens. "To me, writing is dyadic — cathartic at one end, obsessive at the other," Ross says. He continues to write on a daily basis.

"Walker's Requiem" tied for first prize for fiction in 1995. Ross is now trying to publish a collection of his own fiction and an anthology of death row writings.

Robert M. Rutan (1944) attended Catholic schools in his native Philadelphia. In prison from the age of twenty-four on, he garnered another sentence for manslaughter and was not released until he was forty-three. He took courses at the University of Iowa, dreaming of its famous Writers' Workshop. That dream was deferred by a conviction for unarmed robbery and escape.

In 1978, "The Break" won first prize in fiction; it was published in *Time Capsule*. "Partners" won third prize in fiction in 1982. Now Rutan writes only poetry. "Love of language and literature drove my desire to write. I admire the nineteenth-century novel in the hands of Eliot and Hardy, and I like the poetry that came out of Spain during the thirties. But my real passion is Shakespeare." As to why he writes, "The way out is the way in," he says. "Writing provides the release that comes with disclosure."

Of Irish and Lithuanian stock, **Jackie Ruzas** (1943) grew up in Queens. At parochial school, "I received both an education and bruises from the Grey Nuns." Turning sixteen at Aviation Trades High School, he was invited to quit or be expelled. He joined the ranks of construction workers. "When the sixties brought protest, alienation, and drugs, I joined those ranks as well. It all led to a final curtain on a sunny autumn day in October 1974, when a confrontation between a state trooper and myself resulted in his tragic death."

Though charged with a capital crime, a jury spared him a death sentence; he is serving "an exile of twenty-five years to life." He earned a G.E.D., but says he is mostly self-taught, "with a twenty-four-year addiction to the *New York Times*."

"I realized many years ago that writing provided me with a sense of flight to anywhere I chose to travel. I could leave my cell without sirens in my ears and dogs on my heels. Over the years I have tutored in class-rooms in every maximum security prison in this state, and nothing gives me greater satisfaction than being part of an inmate's journey from illiterate to literate." He is organizing to restore college programming to Shawangunk Correctional Facility.

"The Day the Kept Lost Their Keeper" won first prize in fiction (1982) and "Ryan's Ruse" an honorable mention (1994). His poems have appeared in *Candles Burn in Memory Town* and *Prison Writing in 20th-Century America*.

Paul St. John (1956) grew up in Long Island and holds an M.A. in sociology. "I went down in the war on drugs" he says, "but decided that my life wasn't over. I started writing fiction as a means of experiencing what I could not otherwise." He won third prizes for fiction in 1992 for "Peeks by the Gnome of the Slums on the Bad Hardened to the Absolute" and in 1994 for "Behind the Mirror's Face." He has received other honorable mentions in PEN contests. He has published fiction in *Midnight Zoo* and is working on his third novel. He plays jazz piano and trumpet and writes music as well.

The son of a cardplayer, **Michael E. Saucier** (1948) hails from a small Cajun town in Louisiana. He graduated from Mamou High in 1966, hitchhiked to Haight-Ashbury with his guitar, and protested the war instead of going to Vietnam. "I drifted across the USA and Mexico living a vagabond's life until I finally and mercifully got busted for drug dealing in 1990." His prison job, literacy tutor, gave him access to a decent library and a grammar book that he devoured, testing himself until he could write clearly. With time and money enough for writing supplies, "I had no more excuses. I told myself that if I wasn't willing *and* enthusiastic about writing a novel then I had to shut up and never talk about writing again. That scared the hell out of me." He wrote his first novel twelve times, then another, *Saga of an American Hippie,* and a screenplay. Currently he is concentrating on songwriting and performing Cajun music.

Saucier won an honorable mention in drama for *Thinking Twice* (1991), third prize in poetry for "Cut Partner" (1992), and first prize in poetry for "Black Flag to the Rescue."

"A child of the oil fields," **Barbara Saunders** was born (1944) in Lubbock, Texas. Her father was an independent driller. The family followed the "boomtowns" of Texas, Oklahoma, Kansas, Colorado, New Mexico, and

Louisiana, and, at five years of age, she began writing to entertain herself. Saunders was a U.S. Navy nurse. In the late sixties, she earned master's degrees in art education and in counseling psychology.

"I write because I have to," she says. "I sculpt my life through writing." She cites her poem "The Poet's Plight": "words slide behind my eyelids / go crashing through my brain / crying ancient sorrows / speaking ancient pain."

"The Red Dress," won second prize for poetry in 1996, "Wolf" won second prize for poetry in 1998. Her work has been published in *Rattle*.

Oklahoma native **Jon Schillaci** (1971) was raised in Dallas, Texas. "When I was four years old, my parents gave me an enormous Underwood manual typewriter — the thing weighs as much as I did — and I promptly wrote my first story." He says he does not recall ever wanting to be anything but a writer.

"The writers who matter the most to me are the ones who stretched my view of what was possible in the art" — Dylan Thomas for poetry, James Joyce for the novel. "Writing is a way to capture an experience — not merely a thought or story but an entire experience with thoughts, emotions, values all wrapped together — and present it in a way technically designed to make it happen again. If you read my writing, and feel something like what I felt, then I have succeeded."

Schillaci has an M.A. in humanities from the University of Houston at Clear Lake and is working toward a second master's degree in literature. He is a member of the National Honor Society of Phi Kappa Phi. His poem "The Danger in Crowds" won an honorable mention in poetry in 1997; and "Americans" tied for first place in poetry in 1998. His poems have been published in *Rattle, RE:AL,* and *Heliotrope.*

Joseph E. Sissler (1949) was born in Washington, D.C., attended the naval prep school Admiral Farragut Academy, enlisted in the navy, received a B.A. in English from the University of Maryland, and served forty-eight months at FCI Morgantown for "the all-American charge of conspiring to possess." There his appeal was opposed, he is pleased to report, by Solicitor General Kenneth Starr. From Morgantown, "a thick sandwich of boredom and despair," he writes, "I was shipped to a Virginia county jail — my halfway house — and soon farmed out to the local stockyard for employment." Free of the system, he acquired some cattle of his own for Gobbler Holler Farm, and now returns to the stockyard for hay "in exchange for running with the bulls on sale days."

"I See Your Work" tied for third prize in fiction in 1995; it is adapted from an unpublished novel, *House of Sympathy*. Sissler has published in *Harper's*. "I read a great deal and writing seems to be a responsibility flowing from it. I suppose that writing is a way to get things right even if I never quite seem to grasp that goal," he says. His favorite writer, "the one that seemed to most persistently pursue and pin down America's nightmare shadow," is Robert Stone, and he admires Thomas Pynchon.

Richard Stratton (1946) grew up in Wellesley, Massachusetts, and was a writing fellow at the Fine Arts Work Center in Provincetown, Massachusetts, in 1970. Convicted of conspiracy to import marijuana and hashish in 1982, he was sentenced to twenty-five years in prison. While incarcerated, he wrote a novel, *Smack Goddess* (1990), and "A Skyline Turkey," which won first prize for fiction (1989). He also became a jailhouse lawyer, wrote his own appeal, and had his sentence vacated. He was released in 1990 and read at the PEN Awards ceremony in 1991. There he met Kim Wozencraft, ex-convict author of *Rush;* they married and for two years collaborated in producing *Prison Life*.

Earlier Stratton had edited *Fortune News,* the journal of the Fortune Society. His writing has appeared in journals such as *Rolling Stone, High Times, Spin, Penthouse,* and *Newsweek.* He is co-author and producer of the dramatic film *Slam,* about the prison experience of a performance poet; it won the 1998 Sundance Grand Jury award and the Cannes Film Festival's Camera d'Or. Stratton has several other film and TV credits. An activist in criminal justice reform, he testifies as an expert witness on prison culture and violence.

As the son of a navy man, **David Taber** (1950) moved from his native Philadelphia to Hawaii, Tennessee, Morocco, Virginia, Massachusetts, and Maine. With a B.A. in classical languages and German from the University of Colorado, he later studied for two years at the University of Tübingen, and earned an M.A. in English from the University of Massachusetts in Boston. He most admires German Expressionist poetry; his models for poetry are Sylvia Plath and George Trakl.

"Diner at Midnight" won first prize in poetry in 1997. He has published three poems in *Inner Voices* and an abridged version of a collection of poems, *Luna Moth.* He organizes poetry recitals at Massachusetts Correctional Institution at Norfolk; Derek Walcott, Robert Pinsky, and Rosanna Warren are among those who have read there.

Jon Marc Taylor (1961) was born in Topeka, Kansas, finished high school in Indianapolis in 1979, and in 1980 was incarcerated in Indiana. After more than thirteen years, his sentence was reduced to time served, with the original sentencing judge observing that this was "the most remarkable case of self-rehabilitation" he had ever seen. Taylor was remanded to Missouri to commence another sentence. He has earned four college certificates and degrees. He received the American Red Cross Certificate of Merit for administering CPR to a heart-attack victim. He has worked as a literacy tutor, first aid and CPR instructor, and narrator for and director of the Missouri State Prison's Center for Braille and Narration Production.

In 1989 Taylor became a crusading journalist on behalf of what he believes to be the best hope for successful rehabilitation in U.S. prisons: post-secondary correctional education. His essay "Pell Grants for Prisoners" won the Nation/I.F. Stone and Robert F. Kennedy Student Journalism Awards in 1992–93. Since then, his endeavors have centered on efforts with Missouri legislators to create prisoner-generated alternative funding to reinstate post-secondary programs in the state's prisons.

Taylor has won a second prize and three honorable mentions for fiction and nonfiction. His research in corrections and educational policy has appeared in journals such as *Criminal Justice, Educational Policy,* and *Federal Probation.* His op-ed pieces have appeared in the *St. Louis Post-Dispatch, Indianapolis Star,* and the *New York Times;* the *Times* piece was read into the Congressional Record during the debates on Pell Grants to prisoners.

Easy Waters (1960) of Brooklyn, New York, was convicted in 1976 for felony murder as a nonkilling accomplice. While imprisoned, he earned a master's degree in theology from New York Theological Seminary after earning two bachelor's degrees in sociology and in history/English. "I started writing," he says, "because I learned that if one doesn't tell his or her story, others will. I agree with Isak Dinesen that 'all sorrows can be borne if you put them into a story or tell a story about them.' That is how I have done twenty-two years in prison."

Waters has won six prizes as well as four honorable mentions in poetry, drama, and nonfiction. In his prizewinning 1997 poem "My Hero Was a Street-Corner Philosopher," he describes learning to raise questions about history from old-timers in the ghetto. His writing has appeared in the *New York Times* and *Newsday,* the *Defender,* the *Other Side,* and *AIM* and in several poetry anthologies. He plays Scrabble.

J. L. Wise Jr. (1954) of St. Louis, Missouri, was raised mostly by his grandmother; after her death, he went to a boys' home and then to prison. Now he is on death row at Potosi Correctional Center. He has earned a general education degree and taught himself to read and write music: "I just gathered all the books I could, made drumsticks out of pencils and fretboards and keyboards out of cardboard, and went to work." He went on to teach music fundamentals and instrumentation and to lead prison bands. When fellow musician Robert Anthony Murray was executed, "his creativity and musicianship were stripped from the world," Wise writes; "people do change while incarcerated," regardless of their crimes, "but no one takes notice of that fact." So Wise composed "Lament for Tony M."

In "No Brownstones, Just Alleyways & Corner Pockets Full" (second prize for poetry in 1994), Wise experimented with narrative that is "not rap or standard verse." Admiring works by Toni Morrison, Audre Lorde, Alice Walker, and Stephen King, he became a writer in prison "through pure self-determination." He sold a teleplay for the sitcom *The Jeffersons* to CBS in 1984 and has completed one screenplay and has others in progress. "I want to write my books so bad," Wise says. "When they come to get me, I just want to tell them that I'm not through with this life, that I have so much to say, and ask them if they can wait awhile. Crazy, isn't it?"

Born in Manassas, Virginia (1957), **David Wood** was raised in Pennsylvania and in Florida, and earned a B.A. degree. Although he began writing at twelve and had published fiction and poetry before he did time, he has now published fifteen more stories and one hundred poems. "Although I'm sure that after ten years I am institutionalized to some degree, writing has been most responsible for helping me keep what lucidity, reasoning, and sanity I still have." In prison he has become a Buddhist.

"Feathers on the Solar Wind" won first prize for fiction in 1997; *Listen to the River* won first prize for drama in 1994. Wood has won several other prizes and honorable mentions in fiction, drama, nonfiction, and poetry. He has published in the Jacksonville *Florida Times-Union, Sun Dog, State Street Review,* and *Black Ice.* "Whenever I get published outside these walls," he writes, "it is as though a piece of me gets out."

Born in Chicago, raised in Miami, **Dax Xenos** (1949) took a degree at the University of Texas. After traveling in Europe, he settled in Los Angeles where he began writing and painting. He painted a sixty-by-twelve-foot mural on Westwood Boulevard and, for twelve duck dinners, a Chinese restaurant. He worked as a lifeguard, carpenter, painter, model, contractor, magazine editor, fisherman, and as a taxi driver in Watts after the riots. Arrested for possession of cocaine in Texas in 1981, he spent thirty-four months in maximum security. He resurrected the award-winning prison newspaper the *Echo,* wrote several screenplays (unproduced), a novel, *Twist* *of Faith,* and many stories, including "Death of a Duke," which tied for first prize in fiction (1984). "Duke" was later published in *Witness* and in the 1989 O. Henry Awards volume. Xenos is happily married and is writing, painting, and producing videos. He publishes widely (using pseudonyms). He values his family life above all else.

DATE			